CW01394482

Deterrence and Escalation in Competition with Russia

The Role of Ground Forces in Preventing Hostile Measures Below Armed Conflict in Europe

STEPHEN WATTS, BRYAN ROONEY, GENE GERMANOVICH,
BRUCE McCLINTOCK, STEPHANIE PEZARD, CLINT REACH,
MELISSA SHOSTAK

Prepared for United States Army
Approved for public release; distribution unlimited

RAND | ARROYO CENTER

For more information on this publication, visit **www.rand.org/t/RRA720-1**.

About RAND

The RAND Corporation is a research organization that develops solutions to public policy challenges to help make communities throughout the world safer and more secure, healthier and more prosperous. RAND is nonprofit, nonpartisan, and committed to the public interest. To learn more about RAND, visit www.rand.org.

Research Integrity

Our mission to help improve policy and decisionmaking through research and analysis is enabled through our core values of quality and objectivity and our unwavering commitment to the highest level of integrity and ethical behavior. To help ensure our research and analysis are rigorous, objective, and nonpartisan, we subject our research publications to a robust and exacting quality-assurance process; avoid both the appearance and reality of financial and other conflicts of interest through staff training, project screening, and a policy of mandatory disclosure; and pursue transparency in our research engagements through our commitment to the open publication of our research findings and recommendations, disclosure of the source of funding of published research, and policies to ensure intellectual independence. For more information, visit www.rand.org/about/principles.

RAND's publications do not necessarily reflect the opinions of its research clients and sponsors.

Published by the RAND Corporation, Santa Monica, Calif.
© 2022 RAND Corporation
RAND® is a registered trademark.

Library of Congress Cataloging-in-Publication Data is available for this publication.
ISBN: 978-1-9774-0778-8

Cover: Maj. Joe Bush/U.S. Army.

Limited Print and Electronic Distribution Rights

About This Report

This report documents research and analysis conducted as part of a project entitled *Avoiding Escalation in Competition with Russia and China*, sponsored by U.S. Army Europe. The purpose of the project was to provide insights and actionable recommendations on how to protect and advance U.S. interests in great power competition while mitigating the risk of inadvertent escalation to the level of direct armed conflict.

RAND Arroyo Center

This research was conducted within RAND Arroyo Center's Strategy, Doctrine, and Resources Program. RAND Arroyo Center, part of the RAND Corporation, is a federally funded research and development center (FFRDC) sponsored by the United States Army.

RAND operates under a "Federal-Wide Assurance" (FWA00003425) and complies with the *Code of Federal Regulations for the Protection of Human Subjects Under United States Law* (45 CFR 46), also known as "the Common Rule," as well as with the implementation guidance set forth in DoD Instruction 3216.02. As applicable, this compliance includes reviews and approvals by RAND's Institutional Review Board (the Human Subjects Protection Committee) and by the U.S. Army. The views of sources utilized in this study are solely their own and do not represent the official policy or position of DoD or the U.S. Government.

Acknowledgments

We are grateful to GEN Christopher Cavoli (Commanding General) of U.S. Army Europe for leading the sponsorship of this project. We also thank LTC Kurt McDowell, LTC Joseph Merrell, and COL Jon Parvin for monitoring the project and providing constructive feedback during the course of research.

Nearly all of our interviews were conducted on a strictly not-for-attribution basis. Although we cannot thank all of our interview subjects by name given the conditions under which they spoke to us, our research benefited tremendously from the time and insights they shared with us, and we owe them all a debt of gratitude.

We would like to thank our two reviewers, Hal Brands (Johns Hopkins University School of Advanced International Studies) and Angel O'Mahony (RAND) for their excellent reviews. We would also like to recognize the contributions of our colleagues at RAND who participated in workshops and numerous informal discussions in which we explored various scenarios and tested some of our emerging insights. Dara Massicot offered helpful insights and feedback throughout our research, and Caitlin McCulloch offered her insights and research support for our analysis of Georgia. We thank Natalie Ziegler for her indefatigable efforts to format this report. We also thank Jennifer Kavanagh for her very helpful review of the draft report and management oversight. Any remaining mistakes in the report are solely the fault of the authors.

Summary

The deterrence of armed conflict has been studied intensively for decades, as have escalation dynamics along the path to such conflicts. The deterrence of forms of aggression below the level of armed conflict—such hostile measures as economic coercion, political subversion, and military intimidation—has received much less attention. Such forms of strategic competition, however, lie at the heart of the United States' current National Defense Strategy.

In this report, we seek to understand how the United States might use its military posture in Europe—particularly focusing on ground forces—as part of a strategy to deter Russian malign activities in the competition space. At a broad level, we seek to understand:

- Under what conditions has U.S. forward military posture historically deterred competitors from undertaking hostile measures below the level of armed conflict?
- When has the U.S. forward military posture provoked competitors to undertake even greater hostile measures?
- When changes in U.S. forward military posture have provoked competitors, what forms have their hostile measures taken?

More narrowly, we explore how these dynamics should inform U.S. posture decisions for Europe, asking:

- How might the United States' forward military posture be used to deter Russia from additional aggressive actions in the competition space?
- What U.S. military posture might provoke Russia to escalate?
- What are Russia's escalation options and their implications?
- What preventive or mitigating measures can the United States take to reduce the likelihood of escalation?

The Logic of Deterrence and Escalation in Competition

U.S. forward military posture can both deter and provoke armed conflict. On the one hand, it can deter opportunistic powers bent on aggression by providing a strong signal of U.S. commitment to its allies and partners and in-theater capabilities to defend them. On the other hand, building up U.S. military capabilities overseas can make other powers feel threatened and thus more likely to take aggressive measures to warn the United States against further strengthening its regional presence or to impose costs on the United States or its allies and partners.

A similar logic pertains below the level of armed conflict, although this area has received considerably less attention. In this report, we identify how forward posture could deter hostile measures in the competition space through the following mechanisms:

- It can serve as a signal of the United States' commitment to its allies and partners.
- It can provide "irregular" capabilities (such as for foreign internal defense) for allies and partners threatened with political subversion or similar hostile measures.
- It can provide conventional capabilities to neutralize hostile powers' attempts at military intimidation and coercion.
- It can provide support for other instruments of U.S. national power, such as economic sanctions.

Despite these potential advantages of U.S. forward posture in competition, there are also reasons to believe that it could lead to an escalation in competitor activities:

- It could increase competitors' sense of threat, leading them to take aggressive actions to respond to U.S. measures that the United States perceives to be defensive (the so-called security dilemma).
- The United States' success at deterring armed conflict could enable or even incentivize partners to undertake aggression at levels below armed conflict (related to the so-called stability-instability paradox that was a recurring feature of the Cold War).
- U.S. forward posture could provide incentives for third parties to act in ways that increase the likelihood of confrontation (for instance, by creating *moral hazard* dynamics in which U.S. allies and partners believe that the United States will shield them from the consequences of even reckless actions).

The United States' historical experience is filled with examples in which U.S. forward posture has both deterred and provoked adversaries. Moreover, as the archival sources referenced in the research for this report make clear, U.S. decisionmakers often disagreed sharply about whether deterrent or escalatory effects were likely to predominate when considering posture changes. The objective of this report is to help illuminate the ways in which U.S. forward posture can be structured to maximize its deterrent value while reducing its escalatory risks.

Research Approach

To determine the likely effects of U.S. posture choices on competitors' use of hostile measures, we distinguish among six types of hostile measures to be deterred, four types of U.S. forward posture, and three intervening factors that condition the effects of U.S. posture. These building blocks are summarized in Table S.1.

The analysis of the ways in which U.S. forward posture deters or provokes hostile measures was conducted in three steps. First, we examined broad patterns of interactions between the United States and its competitors over the course of several decades using statistical analysis. This quantitative analysis is useful for detecting general trends and subtle effects, such as a minor increase in the risk of escalation that might be missed in individual case studies. Second, we analyzed five case studies of U.S.-Russian (or U.S.-Soviet) competition, selected

TABLE S.1

Key Elements of the Analytic Framework

Forms of U.S. Forward Posture	Factors Conditioning the Effects of U.S. Forward Posture	Hostile Measures to Be Deterred
• Military forces • Military activities (including multilateral military exercises, training, and materiel transfers) • Footprint (infrastructure and prepositioned equipment)* • Agreements (such as alliance treaties and status-of-forces agreements)	• Continuity (or discontinuity) of U.S. forward posture • Proximity of U.S. forward posture to competitors • Specific capabilities possessed by forward-positioned U.S. forces	• Use of force • Military intimidation • Proxy warfare • Economic coercion (threatened and imposed economic sanctions) • Competitive arms transfers • Influence operations, misinformation, and electoral interference*

* Although *footprint* is an important element of U.S. forward posture, it was dropped from the analysis because of insufficient historical data. Similarly, *influence operations* were dropped from the statistical analysis because of a lack of appropriate data, although the case studies provide some insights into this type of malign activity.

to encompass a variety of cases—ones in the center of Europe and others along the European periphery, ones from lower periods of geopolitical tensions and others from heightened periods of tension, and ones that include every type of forward posture examined in this report. The case studies help to determine whether the patterns observed in the statistical analysis occur for the reasons suggested by the deterrence literature—that is, that U.S. forward posture is actually the cause of the observed trends rather than merely a correlate. Finally, we convened two workshops and conducted interviews with practitioners and policy experts to explore several scenarios related to possible future changes in U.S. forward posture in Europe. This scenario analysis helped to refine the historical analysis and determine the ways in which it might relate to future decisions.

Research Findings

The central findings can be understood in two steps: (1) the baseline likelihood that a particular type of U.S. forward posture will deter or provoke and (2) the ways in which the intervening factors of continuity, proximity, and capability can mitigate—or potentially exacerbate—the baseline risk of escalation.

Baseline Findings on Types of U.S. Forward Posture

Existing work on deterrence suggests that different types of U.S. forward posture are likely to have variable effects on the likelihood of armed conflict. This same work can be applied to forms of aggression below the level of armed conflict.

The forward deployment of U.S. forces represents a particularly strong form of deterrence. By positioning U.S. forces overseas, the United States sends a strong signal of its commitment, and it provides important capabilities to defend its allies and partners.

Military activities, such as multilateral military exercises, training events, and materiel transfers, also signal some degree of U.S. commitment, and they could build capabilities over the long term. But they do not precommit the United States to defend its allies or partners in the same way as forward-positioned forces. Moreover, by interjecting greater uncertainty about U.S. and other states' intentions and local capabilities, these activities can cause competitors or potential adversaries to miscalculate (for instance, by interpreting a large-scale military exercise as a precursor to aggression).

Finally, military agreements may also deter malign activities. By entering into an alliance, the United States places its international prestige at stake if it fails to come to the defense of an ally and thus represents a strong form of commitment. Lesser military agreements—such as status of forces agreements (SOFAs) or logistics and sustainment activities—may also signal some degree of commitment, but they are less visible and thus represent a less powerful form of deterrence.

Table S.2 summarizes the results of our analysis. Different forms of U.S. forward posture could deter in some circumstances and provoke in others. Our findings suggest that the logic of deterrence applicable to armed conflict largely holds true for deterring hostile measures below the level of armed conflict as well.

TABLE S.2

Baseline Relationships Between Types of U.S. Forward Posture and the Incidence of Hostile Measures

Element of Forward Posture	Deterrent and Escalatory Effects in Competition
Forces	• U.S. military forces positioned in a vulnerable country appear to have mixed effects, associated with both increases and decreases of some hostile measures. • U.S. military forces stationed near vulnerable states, however, are associated with apparent deterrence of a variety of hostile measures throughout the region. • These relationships are roughly linear, suggesting that small, tripwire forces positioned in vulnerable states are unlikely to provoke severe reactions.
Activities	• U.S. military activities, such as multilateral military exercises, training events, and materiel transfers, typically seem to be associated with increases in hostile measures more often than they deter them. • These relationships are muted in more–politically stable states.
Agreements	• Alliances are associated with a decrease in the likelihood of the partner being targeted with the use of force; SOFAs might be as well, although the evidence is less clear. • SOFAs, however, are associated with an increase in the probability that competitors will respond with some hostile measures below the level of armed conflict, including military intimidation and competitive arms transfers.

Intervening Factors and Opportunities to Mitigate Risk

For U.S. decisionmakers and military planners, it is important to understand not only the general patterns associated with different types of U.S. forward posture but also the ways in which context conditions those general patterns. Where contextual factors blunt the escalatory risks associated with U.S. forward posture, they might help decisionmakers and planners to calibrate posture in such a way as to mitigate escalatory risk while enhancing deterrence. The three intervening factors examined in this report are continuity, proximity, and capability.

Deterrence theory that is focused on armed conflict can again be applied to hostile measures below the level of armed conflict. This theory suggests that continuous presence is likely to enhance deterrence while sharp discontinuities in U.S. forward posture undermine it. Such discontinuities increase the opportunities for misperception or miscalculation on the part of U.S. competitors or potential adversaries.

The proximity of U.S. forward posture to competitors or potential adversaries is also likely to influence the extent to which U.S. presence is escalatory. Although positioning forces close to a competitor or adversary could help to deter short-notice forms of conventional aggression, they also are likely to be viewed as threatening by other powers. These powers may respond by targeting the host countries with hostile measures to signal their opposition to the U.S. presence, impose costs on the host countries, or do both.

Finally, the military capabilities involved in U.S. forward presence are likely to influence outcomes. Any capabilities that pose a direct threat to a potential adversary's state security, leadership, or regime stability are likely to be particularly sensitive. These capabilities include long-range precision fires (LRPF) that might be used in a "decapitating" strike against adversary command and control or cyber or information capabilities that might be used to destabilize a regime.

In general, our findings suggest that the same expectations that are described by the literature on deterring armed conflict also apply to hostile measures below armed conflict. Table S.3 summarizes these findings.

Taken together, the following three conditioning factors offer additional levers that decisionmakers and military planners can use to mitigate the escalatory risks associated with U.S. forward posture and maximize its deterrent value:

- A persistent, predictable U.S. forward posture is associated with lower levels of malign activity in the competition space, while sharp, unpredictable discontinuities are associated with much more escalatory outcomes.
- Forward posture that is positioned in the general region to be defended—but not too proximate to the U.S. competitor—appears to deter a variety of hostile measures. Forces that are positioned close to the U.S. competitor—especially if they are positioned in a host country that is vulnerable to hostile measures—are much more likely to be associated with an increase in malign activities, at least if they are sizeable.
- Finally, sensitive military capabilities that pose a direct threat to a potential adversary's state security, leadership, or regime stability represent a particular escalatory risk. Such

TABLE S.3
Role of Intervening Factors in Mitigating or Exacerbating Escalatory Risk

Intervening Factor	Apparent Deterrent and Escalatory Effects in Competition
Continuity	• Continuously present U.S. forces (both in-country and in-region) are associated with a strong deterrent effect on many forms of malign activities, while sharp discontinuities are associated with an increase in the likelihood of malign activities. • Sharp changes in U.S. activities are associated with an escalatory effect; persistent, predictable activities are not associated with deterrence, but they appear to reduce the most-dangerous forms of escalatory risk.
Proximity	• Close proximity to a competitor is associated with reduction in the deterrent value of U.S. agreements,[a] while greater distance appears to be associated with an increase. There is also evidence (although somewhat weaker) of a similar pattern with U.S. forces, while the evidence for activities is somewhat more mixed. • Close proximity is especially threatening for Russia (and previously the Soviet Union).
Capability	• Sensitive capabilities (such as LRPF) appear to be perceived as highly threatening by Russia and have provoked hostile measures in the past.

[a] Agreements with greater proximity are those between the United States and countries closer to the adversary or rival. Proximity of agreements would be lower when the U.S. partner is farther from the rival or adversary.

capabilities could be important for deterring armed conflict, but they are likely to trigger hostile measures directed at the host countries unless substantial mitigation measures (such as positioning them well out of range of sensitive sites in the potential adversary) are undertaken.

To understand the role of proximity and sensitive capabilities in escalation and deterrence dynamics in more-concrete terms, it can be helpful to examine a map of Europe. Figure S.1 depicts several subregions of Europe and hypothetical ranges for missile systems capable of striking Russian critical infrastructure and leadership, an area of particular concern for Russia.

The subregions in this figure provide a rough indication of proximity. As many previous studies have documented, Russia is most concerned about U.S. and North Atlantic Treaty Organization (NATO) military encroachment within the former Soviet space (excepting the Baltic states). The next most sensitive region includes those countries that are contiguous with Russia (including the exclave of Kaliningrad)—as depicted in Figure S.1, the states of Northeastern Europe.[1] Most of Southeastern Europe and the European periphery represent less-sensitive regions for Russia, although the lower levels of political stability in many countries in these regions provide Russia with many opportunities to conduct hostile measures. Finally, Western Europe represents the region of least sensitivity and opportunity.

---

[1] Sweden is depicted as belonging in the region of Northeastern Europe despite not sharing a border with Russia. The importance of Swedish territory, including Swedish islands in the Baltic Sea, in contingencies involving armed aggression against the Baltic states suggests that it is appropriate to include Sweden as an exception in this region.

FIGURE S.1

Subregions of Europe and Ranges for Long-Range Precision Fires

Overlaid on top of these subregions are circles indicating the range of LRPF systems that the U.S. Army is developing. These range-rings for potential U.S. missile systems illustrate how one particularly sensitive capability (LRPF) could range critical sites in Russia, a metric that almost certainly has implications for Russian response to U.S. presence in the region. The circles extend concentrically from Grafenwoehr, Germany, the U.S. Army's training hub in Europe and currently home to the 41st Field Artillery Brigade (FAB), which was activated in 2018 and now includes three M270A1 Multiple Launch Rocket System (MLRS) battalions in Europe. The rings illustrate 500-km, 1,500-km, and 2,500-km ranges, corresponding to systems that the U.S. Army currently has under development or is actively considering.

In general, our findings suggest that U.S. posture enhancements (such as military exercises or training events) are likely to run a high risk of provoking Russian malign activities when conducted in the former Soviet space, a moderate to high risk in Northeastern

Europe, and low risk in Western Europe, where they are much more likely to have net deterrent effects. Posture enhancements involving LRPF might not be particularly provocative to Russia when positioned in Germany, especially for the shorter end of the possible ranges of these systems. Longer ranges, however, could well provoke hostile measures, as might positioning these systems closer to Russia.

Application of the Analysis to Specific Posture Options

To indicate how the analysis might be applied to future posture decisions, we developed a list of illustrative U.S. posture options throughout Europe and its periphery. The expected outcomes of each posture option were formulated using the findings from the statistical, case study, and scenario analyses.

Table S.4 summarizes these posture options, their values on the key factors in the analytic framework, and the projected outcomes for each decision. Throughout the table, color-coded arrows summarize what the findings of the research in this report suggest about the likely effects of a given force posture decision. The projected outcomes in the table represent the direct consequences of a given U.S. posture decision on Russian hostile measures in the competition space using the analysis in this report. A green, downward arrow indicates lower risk of Russian hostile measures (greater deterrent value); a red, upward arrow indicates greater risk of Russian hostile measures (greater escalatory risk); and a gray, horizontal arrow indicates neutral, ambiguous, or mixed implications. The projected outcomes are based on the interaction of the *type of force posture* (forces, activities, agreements) with the *intervening factors* in the framework (proximity, continuity, and capability). For each posture option, each of the intervening factors is described as being more prone to enhance deterrence (distant, continuous, and/or nonsensitive posture) or more prone to escalatory risk (proximate, discontinuous, and/or sensitive). As with the outcomes, these descriptors are color-coded, with more-escalatory values depicted in red and more-deterrent values depicted in green.

The outcomes discussed here are relative; that is, they indicate a somewhat higher or somewhat lower degree of risk or reward. U.S. forward posture is only one factor that influences outcomes; typically, it will be a contributing factor but not decisive. Because U.S. posture changes often carry only a small escalatory risk, in many cases any single change might not be provocative enough to produce an observable reaction. If the United States repeatedly accepts risk in its force posture choices, however, the opportunities for escalation will accumulate. Although consequences might be imperceptible in the short term, over the course of the 15-year time horizon used in this report, such decisions could ultimately trigger Russian hostile measures in the competition space or even major crises that threaten outright war.

TABLE S.4

Illustrative Posture Options and Projected Implications for Likelihood of Russian Malign Activities in Competition

Option	Proximity	Continuity	Capability	Projected Direct Outcome	Rationale
Forces (Augment)					
Maintain or modestly increase U.S. forces in Western Europe	Distant	Continuous	Nonsensitive	(green arrow)	Existing U.S. forces in Western Europe deter malign activity and conflict with little escalatory risk.
Augment U.S. forces in Western Europe with precision strike munitions	Distant	Discontinuous	Sensitive	(gray arrow)	Precision strike munitions could help to deter conflict, and escalation risk could be mitigated by stationing to the west, but also could invite hostile influence operations or worse.
Augment U.S. forces in Northeast Europe (e.g., Poland) to division-level or higher	Proximate	Discontinuous	Neutral	(red arrow)	Ground forces generally possess fewer sensitive capabilities than air forces, although large numbers might result in outsized Russian reactions.
Deploy LRPF to Northeastern Europe	Proximate	Discontinuous	Sensitive	(red arrow)	Deployment of such sensitive capabilities close to Russia would be highly likely to make host countries targets of Russian hostile measures.
Forces (Reduce)					
Modest reductions in U.S. force levels in Western Europe	Distant	Discontinuous	Nonsensitive	(red arrow)	Reductions in U.S. forces would, at a minimum, signal decreasing U.S. commitment to Europe.
Withdraw U.S. forces from Kosovo	Distant	Discontinuous	Nonsensitive	(red arrow)	Withdrawal of U.S. forces would signal U.S. disengagement and invite potential crises that Russia could exploit.
Downsize Operation Atlantic Resolve	Proximate	Discontinuous	Nonsensitive	(red arrow)	After years of bolstering defenses, a change in U.S. direction without reciprocal change from Russia could be seen as weakening commitment.

Table S.4—Continued

Option	Proximity	Continuity	Capability	Projected Direct Outcome	Rationale
Activities					
Routine materiel transfers and training in Western Europe	Distant	Continuous	Nonsensitive	(green arrow)	Such routine behavior is highly unlikely to provoke Russia and could signal continued U.S. commitment.
Materiel transfers to make Northeastern Europe "hedgehogs" or "poison pills"	Proximate	Continuous	Nonsensitive	(gray arrow)	Activities to make Northeastern Europe states more "costly" targets of conventional aggression are unlikely to deter malign activities but also unlikely to provoke it.
Transfer of LRPF and training for Western Europe	Distant	Neutral	Neutral	(gray arrow)	Many Western European states have air- and/or naval-launched LRPF; such transfers are less likely to be problematic unless they are long range (1,000 km+).
Increase materiel transfers and partnership activity in Southeastern Europe	Distant	Continuous	Neutral	(gray arrow)	Many such activities would likely have some positive effects, although others (e.g., offensive capabilities for Serbia) could be escalatory.
Routine military exercises in Northeastern Europe	Proximate	Continuous	Nonsensitive	(gray arrow)	Routine exercises could provoke low-level hostile measures, but risks are low if the United States communicates intent and forces involved and coordinates with allies.
Repeated exercises in Northeastern Europe, such as Trident Juncture-18 or larger	Proximate	Discontinuous	Neutral	(red arrow)	Large-scale exercises in Northeastern Europe run risks of escalation in competition and inadvertent conflict.
Transfer of substantial LRPF and training for Northeastern Europe	Proximate	Discontinuous	Sensitive	(red arrow)	Small-scale transfers (e.g., Joint Air-to-Surface Standoff Missile sales to Poland) might not be escalatory, but large transfers would likely provoke hostile measures.
Agreements					
Agreements to enhance border transit, military contracting in Western Europe	Distant	Continuous	Nonsensitive	(green arrow)	Although predominantly targeted at conventional conflict, such measures can demonstrate U.S. commitment and reduce likelihood of intimidation.
Agreements to enhance border transit, military contracting in Northeastern Europe	Proximate	Neutral	Neutral	(gray arrow)	Such agreements represent only incremental change with NATO allies; with Finland or Sweden, there is a higher risk of hostile measures.

Table S.4—Continued

Projected Direct Outcome: The outcome that the research in this report suggests is most likely to result from a given change in U.S. posture. These outcomes represent only the direct results of U.S. posture changes; indirect effects (such as assuring allies and partners or increasing their capabilities) are not evaluated.

➡ A given U.S. posture decision is projected to result in a decrease in the incidence of a given type of hostile measure (a deterrent relationship).

⬅ A given U.S. posture decision is projected to result in an increase in the incidence of a given type of hostile measure (an escalatory relationship).

Proximity: The distance between a given U.S. posture change and Russia.

Distant — U.S. forward posture not located in Russia's immediate environs, including the states of the former Soviet Union and states in Northern and Eastern Europe contiguous or nearly contiguous to Russia; the green shading of the word indicates a reduced likelihood of aggressive Russian response.

Proximate — U.S. forward posture located in Russia's immediate environs, including the states of the former Soviet Union and states in Northern and Eastern Europe contiguous or nearly contiguous to Russia; the red shading of the word indicates an increased likelihood of aggressive Russian response.

Continuity: The extent and rapidity of change in U.S. forward posture.

Continuous — U.S. forward posture that remains the same or changes only gradually, thus increasing its predictability; the green shading of the word indicates a reduced likelihood of aggressive Russian response.

Discontinuous — U.S. forward posture that changes rapidly (either qualitatively or quantitatively), thus increasing its unpredictability; the red shading of the word indicates an increased likelihood of aggressive Russian response.

Capability: The sensitivity of capabilities possessed by forward-positioned U.S. forces or military activities, with sensitive capabilities understood as those that Russia perceives as posing a severe threat to state or regime security (especially weapon systems that could theoretically give the United States a debilitating first-strike capability or a large-scale build-up of more traditional capabilities).

Nonsensitive — U.S. forward posture that does not pose a severe threat to Russian state or regime capability.

Sensitive — U.S. forward posture that Russia perceives as posing a severe threat to Russian state or regime capability.

Policy Recommendations

Adopt Specific and Appropriately Scoped Goals for U.S. Forward Posture

In this report, we suggest that U.S. military posture has a variety of effects in competition. For the most part, however, these effects tend to be subtle. Each posture decision may only incrementally increase or decrease the risk of Russian aggression across the competition continuum. Over the course of the 15-year time horizon adopted for this report, however, these incremental changes can have important effects, both positive and negative.

These outcomes suggest that U.S. decisionmakers should think of U.S. posture primarily as an enabler of a much broader strategy that incorporates the full range of the instruments of national power. Understood in these terms, military posture can be one important contributor to a competition strategy, especially when focused on countering hostile measures for which the military has inherent advantages (such as military intimidation or proxy warfare). But a competition strategy that weights military instruments heavily is almost certain to disappoint.

These outcomes also suggest that U.S. decisionmakers should base U.S. forward posture changes on specific objectives. It is not enough to attempt to complicate competitor decision-making, impose costs, expand the competition space, or any other vague goals that some observers suggest. On balance, a great many posture changes have more escalatory consequences than deterrent ones. Without clear goals, it is difficult to weigh whether the escalation risks can be justified.

Despite these cautions, escalation is not something to be avoided at all costs. Decisionmakers may decide that the risk of escalation is warranted in some cases. The analysis in this report cannot determine when precisely leaders should accept risk. It does, however, provide a tool with which to assess the likelihood that Russia will respond to posture changes with malign activities—information that decisionmakers can use to craft changes to posture in a way that mitigates these risks.

Retain U.S. Forces Currently Positioned in Europe

U.S. forces currently positioned in Europe play an important role in deterrence—not just deterrence of armed conflict, but also, more subtly, numerous forms of malign activity. The relationship between U.S. forces and the maintenance of stability is perhaps most obvious in the case of Operation Atlantic Resolve and NATO's Kosovo Force, forces that are directly tied to deterring armed conflict but also subtler forms of destabilization. However, our research suggests that U.S. forces near but not in the most vulnerable countries (e.g., in Germany) play an important deterrent role through what is, in effect, an implicit threat to respond to acts of aggression. In fact, such a placement might be *more* effective than stationing more troops (beyond the current tripwire forces) closer to the "front lines." Forces stationed in vulnerable states can make the host countries targets for a variety of hostile measures, from military intimidation (with the ever-present risk of inadvertent escalation) to subtler forms of aggression intended to impose costs on or weaken the will of host nations. Forces positioned in less-vulnerable countries pose fewer threats to the host country but still could be repositioned quickly as needed.

Limit Reliance on Dynamic Force Employment

The 2018 National Defense Strategy introduced the concept of Dynamic Force Employment (DFE). Although still an evolving concept, DFE appears to emphasize short-term deployments and unpredictable military activities over committing to permanent (or at least long-term) forward-stationing of U.S. forces in an effort to realize the potential deterrent value of forward posture without the commitment of full-time overseas basing. There are many reasons why the concept is attractive in theory and from a fiscal perspective, and such tools might be useful for signaling in crises. But under steady-state conditions, it is not clear how much deterrent value there is in being unpredictable. Our research suggests that there are inherent escalatory risks in relying on military exercises and similar activities to establish deterrence. Some of these risks can be mitigated through manipulation of such factors as proximity, but operational unpredictability implies discontinuity—a factor frequently associated with escalation in our analysis. DFE is best used as a supplement to persistent presence, not a substitute, and only if appropriate measures are taken to mitigate the associated risks.

Place More Emphasis on Rigorous Risk Assessment and Evaluation

There was often little agreement among the experts and practitioners whom we consulted about what "worked" in competition—a lack of consensus that was also reflected in the scholarly and policy literature in this field. Some of these practitioners recognized this fact and emphasized the need for more-rigorous efforts to assess the consequences of U.S. posture decisions.

These consequences can be assessed prospectively through risk assessments and retroactively through evaluations. Both are needed to improve U.S. performance in competition. Particularly for those options shown to be high-risk in this report, the United States should adopt rigorous interagency risk assessment processes. When evaluating the consequences of U.S. posture decisions after the fact, the United States should not only look for immediate Russian reactions but should also explore longer-term and indirect dynamics.

Contents

Figures and Tables

Figures

Tables

CHAPTER ONE

Introduction

Research Objectives and Questions

The U.S. National Security Strategy and National Defense Strategy (NDS) emphasize that the United States is locked in competition with other powers, a competition in which hostile powers seek advantage, often through coercive measures, without escalating to the level of armed conflict.[1] Despite the clearly articulated threat to U.S. national interests, U.S. guidance is much less clear about how to deter such malign activities.

Historically, the United States has relied on its *forward military posture* (U.S. overseas forces, the activities they conduct, and the agreements and logistical footprint they require) as a core pillar of deterrence. How relevant is such forward military posture, however, in a competition that is waged frequently (if not primarily) through nonmilitary tools? In this report, we offer insight into these dynamics of deterrence and offer corresponding recommendations for U.S. defense policy. We have two objectives: First, we seek to illuminate past patterns of deterrence and escalation in competition below the level of armed conflict in hopes of refining concepts for deterrence in the competition space. Second, we apply insights from this analysis to understand which future U.S. forward military posture decisions might deter Russian hostile measures below the level of armed conflict without escalating competition to more-dangerous levels.

More specifically, we seek answers to two sets of questions. The first set of questions concerns the broad patterns of deterrence and escalation in the competition space:

- Under what conditions has U.S. forward military posture historically deterred competitors from undertaking hostile measures below the level of armed conflict?
- When has U.S. posture provoked competitors to undertake even greater hostile measures?

---

[1] Donald J. Trump, *National Security Strategy of the United States of America*, Washington, D.C.: White House, December 2017; and Jim Mattis, *Summary of the National Defense Strategy of the United States of America: Sharpening the American Military's Competitive Edge*, Washington, D.C.: U.S. Department of Defense, 2018.

- When changes in U.S. forward military posture have provoked competitors, what forms have their hostile measures taken?
  - Do they tend to respond symmetrically (with a proportionate response proximate in both space and time to the change in U.S. posture)?
  - Do they respond often in unexpected ways, far removed in space or time from the initial U.S. action?

The second set of questions are specific to contemporary U.S. competition with Russia:

- How might the United States' forward military posture be used to deter Russia from additional aggressive actions in the competition space?
- Which U.S. military postures might provoke Russia to escalate?
- What are Russia's escalation options and their implications?
- What preventive or mitigating measures can the United States take to reduce the likelihood of escalation?

An Example

Before plunging into the analysis, it might be helpful to review an historical example of deterrence and escalation in the competition space to make more concrete some of the complexities currently faced by U.S. decisionmakers and defense planners. The deployment of U.S. ground-based, intermediate-range nuclear missiles to Europe in the 1980s illustrates many of the dynamics of concern to the United States and its European allies and partners today.

In 1976, the Soviet Union deployed a new generation of nuclear missile—the SS-20—that posed a new threat to the United States' European allies. U.S. decisionmakers feared that these new missiles could be used to intimidate the Europeans and thereby influence their foreign and security policy. If the Western Europeans could not be assured that the United States would protect them from the Soviets, then they would need to hedge against the risk—however remote—of a Soviet attack. Such hedging strategies could include adopting foreign policies that showed a greater level of deference to Soviet preferences. Such concerns were not simply theoretical; the Chancellor of the Federal Republic of Germany publicly warned about these potential consequences of the strategic imbalance, and then–U.S. National Security Advisor Zbigniew Brzezinski admitted that the White House shared these concerns.[2]

In response to this threat, the United States developed its own theater nuclear delivery vehicles, the so-called Euromissiles, and deployed them to Western Europe. These deploy-

---

[2] See Thomas L. McNaugher and Theodore M. Parker, *Modernizing NATO's Long-Range Theater Nuclear Forces: An Assessment*, Santa Monica, Calif.: RAND Corporation, P-6486, October 1980, p. 2; and William Leonard, *"Closing the Gap": The Euromissiles and President Carter's Nuclear Weapons Strategy for Western Europe (1977–1979)*, Washington, D.C.: Center for Strategic and International Studies, 2010.

ments created enormous strains within the transatlantic alliance between those who favored the deployments and those who opposed them. But U.S. policymakers also had to contend with the risk that the Soviet Union might escalate tensions with the United States, potentially in theaters far removed from Europe. In a memorandum for the Secretary of State, the Director of the Office of Policy Planning warned,

> we do not believe that the Soviets will go still further to initiate specific challenges to the West in the Third World, merely as extra retaliation on INF [Intermediate-Range Nuclear Forces]. For such Soviet opportunities are defined above all by local circumstances. Yet Soviet assessments of their opportunities could conceivably be affected at the margin. On any occasion where they face a choice between being more or less constructive, the Soviet leadership may lean toward even less cooperation with us. Central America, southern Africa, and the Middle East are the regions where such choices are most likely to arise.[3]

This example illustrates the complex interrelationship between the potential conduct of armed conflict and the repercussions for strategic competition below armed conflict. In this case, Western leaders feared that Soviet capabilities for armed conflict could be used to influence U.S. allies' conduct of diplomacy in peacetime. But in seeking to reestablish parity in theater-level capabilities, the United States risked escalation—not necessarily to direct armed conflict with the Soviet Union (although that was a risk), but also, and perhaps more likely, to higher levels of confrontation below the level of armed conflict, potentially in theaters and at times far removed from the proximate cause of tensions. The relationship between U.S. forward military posture and deterrence (or escalation) below the level of armed conflict was hotly debated in the 1980s.[4] Nearly 40 years later, very similar debates are again engaging policymakers.

Definitions and Scope

To clarify our core concepts and research focus, we define key terms here and specify the geographical and temporal scope of our research. Other concepts will be defined throughout the report as they arise in the discussion.

Competition and Conflict

The 2017 U.S. National Security Strategy and 2018 NDS emphasize that the United States is in a new era of great power competition, but what exactly this competition comprises and how it is to be conducted remain unclear. As defined in U.S. Department of Defense (DoD) docu-

---

[3] Stephen Bosworth, "Soviet Responses to INF Deployment," memorandum to the Secretary of State, June 16, 1983.

[4] In the case of the memorandum quoted previously, for instance, the Bureau of European Affairs did not concur with the judgments of the Office of Policy Planning.

ments, the competition space is extremely broad, covering nearly all activities short of direct military conflict in which any element of coercion is present.[5] We borrow from a prior RAND Corporation report to define *competition* in the international realm as "the attempt to gain advantage, often relative to others believed to pose a challenge or threat, through the self-interested pursuit of contested goods such as power, security, wealth, influence, and status."[6] Under this understanding, crisis bargaining under the shadow of imminent war could be included, but so could such minor confrontations as competitive offers of aid to a potential partner state that two competitors seek to influence. Our primary concerns are with dynamics between these two extremes, including the use of economic coercion, military intimidation (such as large-scale military exercises on the borders of competitor states or harassing of air patrols or freedom-of-navigation activities), the large-scale sale of arms to competitor countries, support to proxies or surrogates engaged in military conflict with partner regimes, and so on.

Forward Military Posture

In this report, we focus on the consequences of U.S. overseas military capabilities, typically referred to as *forward military posture* (or, as we will often refer to it in this report, simply *forward posture*). Unfortunately, no doctrinal definition of this or closely related terms exists, which frequently creates confusion about what the concept encompasses.[7] In this report, we define forward military posture broadly as the combination of U.S. overseas forces, footprint, activities, and agreements used to project military power.[8] Each of these four elements, in turn, requires definition:

---

[5] Joint Doctrine Note 1-19, *Competition Continuum*, Washington, D.C.: Joint Chiefs of Staff, June 3, 2019.

[6] Michael J. Mazarr, Jonathan S. Blake, Abigail Casey, Tim McDonald, Stephanie Pezard, and Michael Spirtas, *Understanding the Emerging Era of International Competition: Theoretical and Historical Perspectives*, Santa Monica, Calif.: RAND Corporation, RR-2726-AF, 2018, p. 5.

[7] The most recent version of DoD's official dictionary of military terms does not include a definition for the terms "posture," "force posture," "military posture," or "forward posture" (although the term "posture" does appear as a word in several narrower concepts in the dictionary). See Joint Chiefs of Staff, *DOD Dictionary of Military and Associated Terms*, Washington, D.C.: Department of Defense, January 2021.

[8] This definition is consistent with broad DoD usage of the term. In the most recent DoD Instruction (DoDI) on global defense posture, the term *global defense posture* referred to "DoD's forces, footprints, and agreements that support joint and combined global operations and plans in foreign countries and U.S. territories and in defense of the homeland." See DoDI 3000.12, *Management of U.S. Global Defense Posture*, Washington, D.C.: U.S. Department of Defense, incorporating Change 1, May 8, 2017, p. 2. In one of DoD's posture reports to Congress, *posture* was defined as "a network of forces, footprint, and agreements that maintains U.S. global reach, projects and sustains power abroad, promotes the security interests of the U.S., its allies, and partners, and supports other foreign policy objectives" (DoD, *2012 U.S. Global Defense Posture Report to Congress*, Washington, D.C., May 2012). The "forces" component of these definitions often was taken to imply not only the size and capabilities of those forces but also their activities. In this report, we break out activities as a separate element.

- *Forces* refers to all U.S. military forces overseas, both those permanently stationed and those on rotational or other deployments. Following previous RAND research, we focus primarily on the role of ground forces, although air and naval forces receive some attention.[9]
- *Footprint* refers to all U.S. overseas military facilities and prepositioned equipment and other stocks.
- *Activities* can include all official actions of U.S. overseas forces, but in practice it principally refers to (1) security cooperation activities with U.S. allies and partners, such as multilateral military exercises and military training or exchanges, and (2) intelligence, surveillance, and reconnaissance (ISR) activities.[10]
- *Agreements* include all formal military agreements between the United States and its allies and partners that establish the formal obligations of both parties. They could range from alliance treaties to status-of-forces agreements (SOFAs) to agreements related to military movement and the availability of fuel, contracted support, and other military support requirements.

Deterrence and Escalation

U.S. forward posture can have a variety of consequences, including assuring allies of U.S. commitment to their security, improving U.S. military mobility and sustainment for ongoing operations or future contingencies, improving U.S. military personnel's understanding of specific operational environments, and providing platforms for the collection of intelligence. In this report, we are interested in the effects of U.S. forward posture on the likelihood of confrontation with competitors or adversaries.

Following others, we define *deterrence* as "the persuasion of one's opponent that the costs and/or risks of a given course of action he might take outweigh its benefits."[11] We primarily focus on deterrence as a form of "dissuasion by means of threat"[12]—that is, we focus on the ability of military instruments to impose costs on and deny benefits to a potential aggressor

---

[9] Prior RAND research suggests forward-positioned ground forces play a particularly important role in deterrence. See Bryan Frederick, Stephen Watts, Matthew Lane, Abby Doll, Ashley L. Rhoades, and Meagan L. Smith, *Understanding the Deterrent Impact of U.S. Overseas Forces*, Santa Monica, Calif.: RAND Corporation, RR-2533-A, 2020.

[10] In practice, we focus on relatively sizeable commitments. The precise definition of *sizeable* varies depending on the research approach and will be discussed in more detail in later sections of this report. In general terms, such activities as senior leader engagements and technical exchanges between a handful of officers would not be included, while a military exercise involving thousands of soldiers would be.

[11] Alexander L. George and Richard Smoke, *Deterrence in American Foreign Policy*, New York.: Columbia University Press, 1974, p. 11.

[12] Paul Huth and Bruce Russett, "Deterrence Failure and Crisis Escalation," *International Studies Quarterly*, Vol. 32, No. 1, March 1988, p. 30.

rather than on potential inducements. Although inducements are outside the scope of this particular study, they also play a critical role in a broader foreign policy designed to influence competitors or adversaries.[13]

We are specifically concerned with what is known as *extended deterrence*, preventing an act of aggression against an ally or partner rather than an act of aggression targeted directly at the United States homeland itself. We also focus principally on steady-state conditions in competition rather than on specific crises that have already escalated to the threshold of armed conflict (although forward posture can offer many tools for crisis response as well). Deterrence under steady-state conditions is typically referred to as *general deterrence* in contrast to deterrence under crisis conditions, which is termed *immediate deterrence*. Thus, the primary focus of this report is on extended general deterrence.[14] These concepts are depicted in Figure 1.1.

FIGURE 1.1
Competition and Conflict Spectrum

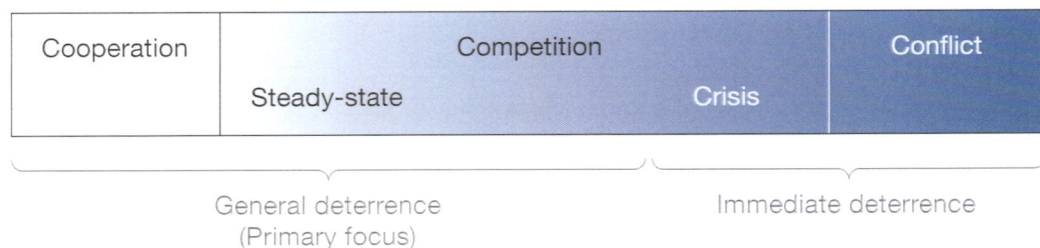

Cooperation	Competition		Conflict
	Steady-state	Crisis	

General deterrence
(Primary focus)

Immediate deterrence

SOURCE: Stephen Watts, Sean M. Zeigler, Kimberly Jackson, Caitlin McCulloch, Joseph Cheravitch, and Marta Kepe, *Countering Russia: The Role of Special Operations Forces in Strategic Competition*, Santa Monica, Calif.: RAND Corporation, RR-A412-1, 2021.

---

[13] Although it is necessary to limit our focus in this report, there are risks to focusing only on negative sanctions (threats) rather than positive ones (inducements). Columbia University professor Robert Jervis warns that focusing on negative sanctions and military threats only "may be ruling out consideration of an important tool of influence. Unless scholars know the conditions under which these tools cannot be used, they will sometimes apply deterrence theory to cases which it cannot explain. And decision makers who are guided by the theory and do not heed the qualification that the use of rewards lies outside its scope will rely too heavily on threats and force" (Robert Jervis, "Deterrence Theory Revisited," *World Politics*, Vol. 31, No. 2, January 1979, p. 295).

[14] See Paul K. Huth, *Extended Deterrence and the Prevention of War*, New Haven, Conn.: Yale University Press, 1988; and Paul K. Huth, "Deterrence and International Conflict: Empirical Findings and Theoretical Debates," *Annual Review of Political Science*, Vol. 2, June 1999, p. 27. For a primer on central concepts of coercion, deterrence, and compellence, see Robert J. Art and Kelly M. Greenhill, "Coercion: An Analytical Overview," in Kelly M. Greenhill and Peter Krause, eds., *Coercion: The Power to Hurt in International Politics*, New York: Oxford University Press, 2018.

Traditionally, in strategic studies, *escalation* is defined as "an increase in the intensity or scope of conflict."[15] We broaden this definition to include an increase in the intensity or scope of hostile measures below the level of armed conflict, such as proxy warfare or military intimidation. Particularly sensitive changes in U.S. posture (such as those that threaten competitors' nuclear deterrent) might escalate directly into a crisis with the potential to cross the threshold into armed conflict. More commonly, however, changes in U.S. forward posture trigger a series of reactions from U.S. competitors that include efforts to signal their opposition to those or future similar changes or to impose costs on the United States and its allies and partners in hopes of pressuring the United States to change course. Most of these reactions are likely to be symbolic measures, such as diplomatic protests. But some might cross into what are frequently known as *hostile* or *malign activities*, directed at the countries hosting U.S. forces or other forms of forward posture. These activities might include military intimidation (such as large "snap" exercises on the borders with these host countries), funding or arming surrogates in a civil war in the host country, providing arms and other military support to the adversaries of host countries, using economic sanctions or other forms of coercion, or engaging in influence activities such as misinformation or electoral interference. These malign activities, in turn, might provoke further measures by the United States, potentially leading to a spiral of confrontation in the competition space that threatens to escalate into direct armed conflict. In this report, we are attentive to both escalation pathways, but our focus is on escalating spirals in the competition space and how they might be defused while still protecting U.S. interests.

Scope

The primary concern of our report is understanding potential Russian responses to U.S. forward posture through approximately the year 2035. Current U.S. Army planning guidance uses the year 2035 as its horizon for longer-term planning and 2028 for nearer-term planning.[16]

The geographic focus of our research is on dynamics of confrontation between the United States and Russia in the U.S. European Command (EUCOM) area of responsibility. This geographic area spans all of the North Atlantic Treaty Organization (NATO) and non-NATO countries of Europe, including Russia, Turkey, and the Caucasus, as well as Israel, although it excludes Central Asia. Our historical analysis draws on cases outside this region to help illustrate broader patterns. Our contemporary and forward-looking analysis, on the other hand,

---

[15] Forrest E. Morgan, Karl P. Mueller, Evan S. Medeiros, Kevin L. Pollpeter, and Roger Cliff, *Dangerous Thresholds: Managing Escalation in the 21st Century*, Santa Monica, Calif.: RAND Corporation, MG-614, 2008, p. 1.

[16] U.S. Army Training and Doctrine Command, *The U.S. Army in Multi-Domain Operations 2028*, TRADOC Pamphlet 525-3-1, Fort Eustis, Va., December 6, 2018.

is largely restricted to this region, although we briefly discuss the implications of our analysis for the immediate periphery of this area of responsibility.

The Policy Stakes

Studies of deterrence and escalation typically have focused on the risk of armed conflict. There are, however, important reasons to examine how forward posture influences competition below the level of armed conflict.

Forward posture might deter both conflict and hostile measures below the level of armed conflict. In this case, the key policy question is how to maximize forward posture's benefits in the competition space while still deterring armed conflict. However, forward posture might deter armed conflict but increase hostile measures below armed conflict as competitors seek to signal their opposition to "provocative" U.S. posture decisions or impose costs on the U.S. allies and partners who host U.S. forces or security cooperation activities. In such cases, U.S. posture decisions might place vulnerable allies and partners at risk. The critical policy questions in such circumstances concern how to avoid exposing vulnerable allies and partners to retaliation or how to minimize the risks to those who are targeted. Alternatively, U.S. forward posture might increase the risk of malign activities below the level of armed conflict and, ultimately, armed conflict itself. If such competitors as Russia seek to signal their opposition to U.S. military presence through malign activities, it could touch off an escalatory spiral of increasingly dangerous tit-for-tat measures designed to force the other power to back down. In these cases, the critical issue for U.S. policymakers is to better understand the escalatory chain between hostile measures and armed conflict.[17]

This report does not assume that deterring hostile measures below armed conflict is an end in and of itself. It could be that U.S. forward posture successfully deters armed aggression, but, in doing so, pushes an adversary toward aggression below the level of armed conflict. Such an outcome could be considered at least a partial success, even though the scope or intensity of hostile measures increased.[18] And hostile measures in the competition space ultimately might be self-defeating, rallying states in opposition to U.S. competitors who are seen as aggressors.[19] Without a better understanding of the relationship between forward military

---

[17] A number of studies have recently warned of the risks posed by the poorly understood escalation chain between nonmilitary and military measures. See, for instance, Elizabeth Rosenberg and Jordan Tama, *Strengthening the Economic Arsenal: Bolstering the Deterrent and Signaling Effects of Sanctions*, Washington, D.C.: Center for a New American Security, December 16, 2019.

[18] Joint Chiefs of Staff, *Joint Concept for Integrated Campaigning*, Washington, D.C.: U.S. Department of Defense, March 16, 2018; and Joint Doctrine Note 1-19, 2019, p. 11. This is essentially an alternative framing of the well-known stability-instability paradox.

[19] See, for instance, Sean M. Zeigler, Dara Massicot, Elina Treyger, Naoko Aoki, Chandler Sachs, and Stephen Watts, *Analysis of Russian Irregular Threats*, Santa Monica, Calif.: RAND Corporation, RR-A412-3, 2021; and Laurynas Jonavicius, Laure Delcour, Rilka Dragneva, and Kataryna Wolczuk, *Russian Interests,*

posture and hostile measures below the level of armed conflict, however, U.S. policymakers risk, at a minimum, aggravating the challenges faced by U.S. allies and partners—and potentially risk much more dangerous escalation.

Research Approach

If the general relationship between U.S. forward posture and competitors' use of malign activities were well-understood, then developing prescriptions for the European theater would be a relatively straightforward matter of applying those principles to current conditions. Unfortunately, there is little agreement on those principles, not within the theoretical literature on deterrence, in U.S. defense concepts and guidance, or among the many practitioners whom we interviewed in the course of our research. Complicating matters further, policy decisions about posture frequently must be made years in advance. If the United States closes bases in Europe, it is a difficult and slow process to reintroduce permanently stationed forces in the theater. If the United States premises its deterrence policies for Europe on particular weapons systems, it will take years to reorient its approach toward different capabilities. Thus, the key questions addressed in this report concern not how Russia is likely to react to U.S. posture in the coming decade, but how it is likely to react years from then.

The policy questions at stake in this report are complex, and answering them calls for a similarly complex research approach. If we were interested solely in the broad question of whether and how U.S. forward posture deters malign activities in strategic competition, we could simply examine historical patterns. But such an approach would partially illuminate only how the Russia of 2020 or 2035 would be likely to respond to changes in U.S. posture. If we were interested only in contemporary Russian behavior, we could analyze recent Russian reactions to U.S. initiatives—but without access to Russian archives, such an analysis would be limited in its ability to help us understand why Russia has undertaken the actions it has, and it would be limited in its ability to help us see how recent actions might shape Russian behavior in the next several years. Finally, we could conduct a scenario analysis of likely Russian reactions to U.S. forward posture at future points in time, but without a deep understanding of past patterns of behavior, such scenarios would be lacking a rigorous empirical foundation. Our report combines all of these approaches so that the weaknesses of any one approach are offset by the strengths of others.

Details of each research method are provided in the chapters to follow and in supporting technical appendixes. To orient the reader to our overall approach, however, we provide a brief overview here.

We begin our analysis with a review of the relevant literature in this field. Chapter Two provides an overview of U.S. military doctrine on strategic competition and deterrence, the

Strategies, and Instruments in the Common Neighbourhood, Berlin: EU-STRAT, EU-STRAT Working Paper No. 16, March 2019.

broader policy debates about these topics, and central academic theories and findings in this field. Chapter Three compares these Western perspectives on deterrence with the record of how Russian policy circles themselves currently talk and write about their perceptions of Western threats and their possible responses below the level of conventional armed conflict. It concludes by introducing a framework for understanding the likely consequences of U.S. posture enhancements and potential trade-offs between different types of risk.

Chapters Four and Five turn to a historical analysis of the relationship between U.S. forward posture and deterrence and escalation outcomes. Chapter Four provides a statistical analysis of the relationship between changes in U.S. forward posture and a variety of competitor responses. The focus of this analysis is on malign activities below the level armed conflict, although it also incorporates the potential for escalation to the level of armed conflict. Chapter Five complements the statistical analysis with a qualitative analysis of specific cases of U.S.-Russian (and U.S.-Soviet) strategic competition, making use of declassified archival material when possible.

Chapter Six turns to the future. It uses scenario analysis to anticipate Russian responses to potential U.S. posture changes in Europe. These possible Russian reactions are derived first from patterns emerging from the empirical analysis in the prior three chapters. We then compare these estimates of likely Russian responses with the judgments of experts in the field to whom we provided details of the scenarios.

Finally, Chapter Seven concludes with a summary of our findings and recommendations for future U.S. forward posture in the European theater. Technical appendixes describing our methodology follow.

CHAPTER TWO

Contending Perspectives on Competition

Before evaluating the relationship between U.S. forward posture and the outcomes of strategic competition, it is helpful to first understand contemporary debates about this relationship. What, exactly, does the United States hope to achieve in competition? To what extent do Russia's goals conflict with those of the United States? Where there are fundamental incompatibilities between the two countries, how does each side attempt to realize its goals and minimize the threats posed by the other without risking escalation to armed conflict? Only when we have some understanding of the answers to these fundamental questions can we begin to understand how U.S. forward posture might influence the conduct and outcomes of competition.

This chapter is divided into two main sections. The first is devoted to U.S. perspectives on competition. We briefly review U.S. goals in competition with Russia, its perception of the threats that Russia poses, its concepts for the conduct of strategic competition, and its concepts of how U.S. forward posture may help secure advantage in competition with Russia. In the second section, we examine Russian perspectives on the same issues. In both cases, the analysis draws on official policy statements, military concepts and doctrine, and broader discussions in the policy communities of the two states.

U.S. Perspectives on Competition

Great power competition was the centerpiece of the 2018 NDS,[1] but the U.S. government's concern with competition generally and Russia specifically predates that document.[2] Although tensions in the U.S.-Russian relationship had been growing for several years, the Russian invasion of Ukraine in 2014 marked a turning point in the relationship. Despite several years of senior U.S. decisionmaker focus on this topic, however, there is still no consensus on how exactly Russia is to be countered.

---

[1] Mattis, 2018.

[2] In 2015, the United States' National Military Strategy began, "This 2015 National Military Strategy addresses the need to counter revisionist states that are challenging international norms. . . ." Joint Chiefs of Staff, *The National Military Strategy of the United States of America, 2015: The United States Military's Contribution to National Security*, Washington, D.C.: Department of Defense, 2015, p. 1.

U.S. Goals and Threat Perceptions in Europe

The most recent U.S. National Security Strategy, published in 2017, states that a "strong and free Europe is of vital importance to the United States."[3] It suggests that the transatlantic relationship benefits the United States in several ways, including through strong trade ties, the diplomatic weight of the transatlantic community, military access, and burden-sharing. And the document makes clear that Russia poses a threat to these interests by weakening and intimidating U.S. allies and partners in Europe and undermining transatlantic ties.

As the overarching guidance for U.S. security strategy, the National Security Strategy's discussion of Russia is necessarily brief. But other U.S. government documents are much more explicit about the threat Russia poses. Every year, each geographic combatant command reports to Congress on the threats that it faces in its respective theater and the capabilities and activities that it uses to counter those threats. EUCOM's 2019 posture statement offers an assessment of the Russian threat that is worth quoting at some length:

> Russia is a long-term, strategic competitor that wants to advance its own objectives at the expense of U.S. prosperity and security and that sees the United States and the NATO Alliance as the principal threat to its geopolitical ambitions. In pursuit of its objectives, Moscow seeks to assert its influence over nations along its periphery, undermine NATO solidarity, and fracture the rules-based international order. Russia actively pursues an aggressive foreign policy in violation of other nations' sovereignty, carrying out subversive and destabilizing activities in Europe and the U.S. and exploiting opportunities to increase its influence and expand its presence in Afghanistan, Syria, and Asia.[4]

Three things are notable in this threat assessment. First, the competition is described in zero-sum terms: Russia can advance its interests only "at the expense of U.S. prosperity and security." Second, Russia's purported goals are both broad and ambitious; Moscow does not simply seek to protect itself from a NATO that has advanced to its borders or to reallocate decision rights within the current international system, but instead to "undermine NATO solidarity" and "fracture the rules-based international order." Finally, in EUCOM's assessment, none of Russia's goals are principally military ones; they all involve influencing others, weakening solidarity, or undermining norms.

If none of Russia's goals are principally military, what role do Russian military forces play? Again, the EUCOM posture statement provides an answer:

> Russia employs a whole-of-society approach through a wide array of tools to include political provocateurs, information operations, economic intimidation, cyber operations, religious leverage, proxies, special operations, conventional military forces, and nuclear

---

[3] Trump, 2017, p. 47.

[4] Curtis M. Scaparrotti, "Statement of General Curtis M. Scaparrotti, United States Army, Command, United States European Command," testimony to the United States House of Representatives Committee on Armed Services, Washington, D.C., March 13, 2019, p. 3.

forces. Russia pursues its strategic objectives in Europe, while avoiding direct military conflict with the U.S. and NATO, by targeting countries through indirect action—backed up by the coercive threat of its conventional and nuclear forces. Such actions include questioning a government's legitimacy, threatening a country's economic interests, mobilizing fringe opposition groups, and utilizing proxies or armed civilians, such as private military contracting companies with opaque ties to the state.[5]

In this conception of the Russian threat, military forces primarily provide a backstop to nonmilitary instruments, a threat to escalate depending on how Russia's adversaries respond to its indirect actions.

U.S. Concepts of Competition and the Role of Military Force

This description of the Russian threat suggests that there is potentially an important role for U.S. military forces, but it is primarily an indirect one. For quite some time, however, DoD has struggled to articulate exactly how U.S. military capabilities can influence the course of a strategic competition conducted primarily through non-military instruments. Recognizing that the NDS guidance on strategic competition was vague, just one year after its release, DoD published a Joint Concept for Integrated Campaigning, followed by a Joint Doctrine Note on the Competition Continuum.[6] Conceptual progress on the appropriate role of the military in competition, however, was incremental in both documents. As one observer noted, "Despite clarifying the language of competition below armed conflict, the [Joint Doctrine Note] fails to provide concrete examples of the concept's implementation, to include the Joint Force's role in deterrence."[7]

The Army's multi-domain operations concept was an important step toward defining what the military's role in competition might be. The concept sets out competition as a phase of equal importance to armed conflict. It proposes three primary roles for the Army in the competition phase: (1) enabling defeat of information warfare and unconventional warfare methods, (2) conducting intelligence and counter-reconnaissance, and (3) demonstrating a credible deterrent. Despite these advances, the concept primarily remains focused on armed conflict, the phase that occupies roughly two-thirds of the pages in the document. Even when it focuses on competition, there is a tendency to concentrate on tasks related to "setting the theater" for armed conflict rather than articulating how military forces can be used to deter hostile activities in competition or potentially compel a competitor to cease such activities.[8] As will be seen in the section that follows, on Russian perspectives, this focus on "setting

---

[5] Scaparrotti, 2019, p. 4.

[6] Joint Chiefs of Staff, 2018; and Joint Doctrine Note 1-19, 2019.

[7] James P. Micciche, "Options for Deterrence Below Armed Conflict," *RealClearDefense*, December 23, 2019.

[8] U.S. Army Training and Doctrine Command, 2018.

the theater" for conventional warfare stands in marked contrast to the Russian approach to competition.

The broader U.S. policy community has helped to articulate ways in which military capabilities can be used to gain advantage in strategic competition. The military's contribution to irregular warfare, operations in the information environment, and intelligence and counter-reconnaissance have been described in multiple publications.[9] Others have detailed how the U.S. military might help to prevent military intimidation below the level of armed conflict.[10] Yet others have seized on the NDS' injunction to "expand the competitive space," suggesting that the United States "'weaponize' the greatest number of alternative competitive instruments" (including the military) and "force our adversaries to recalculate their position."[11]

But there is nothing like consensus within the U.S. policy community about *whether* military instruments provide an important tool of competition, much less the ways in which they do. One recent think-tank brief, for instance, argued that "Relying on the military tool is too slow and often creates unnecessary crisis points."[12] Even studies that detail relevant military capabilities and activities or propose options for countering U.S. competitors seldom evaluate their effects.[13] The end result is a lack of consensus on the value of military capabilities and activities as part of a broader strategy of competition.

U.S. Understanding of How Force Posture in Europe Yields Advantage in Competition

This lack of consensus about the role of the military in competition generally is reflected in contemporary debates about the potential role of U.S. posture in Europe specifically.

The 2019 EUCOM posture statement provides some details about how U.S. military posture could influence strategic competition with Russia in Europe. In the statement, the commander of EUCOM stated that "We are particularly focused on expanding the competitive

---

[9] See, for instance, Ben Connable, Stephanie Young, Stephanie Pezard, Andrew Radin, Raphael S. Cohen, Katya Migacheva, and James Sladden, *Russia's Hostile Measures: Combating Russian Gray Zone Aggression Against NATO in the Contact, Blunt, and Surge Layers of Competition*, Santa Monica, Calif.: RAND Corporation, RR-2539-A, 2020; and Joseph D. Becker, "Building Strategic Influence: The SOF Role in Political Warfare," *Special Warfare*, Vol. 31, No. 1, January–March 2018.

[10] See, for instance, Lyle J. Morris, Michael J. Mazarr, Jeffrey W. Hornung, Stephanie Pezard, Anika Binnendijk, and Marta Kepe, *Gaining Competitive Advantage in the Gray Zone: Response Options for Coercive Aggression Below the Threshold of Major War*, Santa Monica, Calif.: RAND Corporation, RR-2942-OSD, 2019.

[11] Mattis, 2018, p. 4; Michael E. O'Hanlon and Eric Wesley, "How Is the Army Modernizing?" transcript from event at the Brookings Institution, Washington, D.C., September 24, 2019; and Nate Freier, "Game On or Game Over: Hypercompetition and Military Advantage," blog post, *War Room*, May 22, 2018.

[12] John Schaus, Michael Matlaga, Kathleen H. Hicks, Heather A. Conley, and Jeff Rathke, "What Works: Countering Gray Zone Coercion," Center for Strategic and International Studies, July 2018, p. 1.

[13] In fairness, such evaluations are extremely challenging—a point to which we will return in our discussion of deterrence theory and research design in the following chapter.

space with Russia by increasing the lethality of our forces and strengthening alliances and partnerships."[14] Left unstated is how, exactly, lethality in combat affects competition outside combat and how U.S. military presence strengthens relations with countries in the theater. In the statement, the commander also states that the command "is working with the interagency to effectively compete below the level of armed conflict," although the only details mentioned are that EUCOM and other entities within the U.S. government "share information and collaborate."[15] Finally, the statement notes that special operations forces help allies and partners strengthen their institutions, develop capabilities for border security, and build "resilience to Russian malign influence."[16] All of these pieces could potentially fit together to provide the United States with competitive advantage in the theater. The vagueness about the ways in which U.S. force posture achieves those advantages, however, leaves open important questions about what types of forces and how many are required, where they should be present, and what activities they should conduct and on what scale.

In part this ambiguity is intentional. The NDS introduces the concept of DFE, which is intended to replace—at least in part—long-standing commitments of forward-deployed or -stationed forces with more-flexible and unpredictable uses of U.S. forces. In line with this vision, the EUCOM posture statement contends that "our execution of the DFE concept, along with our operations and exercises, introduce operational unpredictability to our adversaries."[17]

But this ambiguity could have unintended consequences as well. First, the DFE concept fails to articulate a clear logic behind specific U.S. military commitments to U.S. domestic audiences, which makes it easier for skeptics of forward posture to criticize U.S. posture choices and the costs they entail. Second, it could introduce more strategic-level uncertainty into potential adversaries' calculus. Large numbers of U.S. forces permanently stationed overseas provide relatively little uncertainty about U.S. commitments to deter aggression overseas or the forces' capabilities to do so.[18] In contrast, an overseas presence that is generally smaller but is always changing could invite miscalculation—either of a lack of commitment when U.S. military presence is low, or of aggressive intent when the United States moves large numbers of forces forward for exercises or other activities.

The utility of U.S. forward posture in contemporary Europe has been questioned repeatedly in recent years. Some have argued for extensive forward posture in Eastern Europe, while others have warned that such posture could be sharply escalatory.[19] The intention of the

---

[14] Scaparrotti, 2019, p. 10.

[15] Scaparrotti, 2019, p. 17.

[16] Scaparrotti, 2019, p. 18.

[17] Scaparrotti, 2019, p. 10.

[18] John J. Mearsheimer, *Conventional Deterrence*, Ithaca, N.Y.: Cornell University Press, 1983.

[19] David A. Shlapak and Michael W. Johnson, *Reinforcing Deterrence on NATO's Eastern Flank: Wargaming the Defense of the Baltics*, Santa Monica, Calif.: RAND Corporation, RR-1253-A, 2016; Elbridge Colby

Trump administration to withdraw U.S. forces from Germany similarly produced a variety of responses; some strongly objected, while others stated that a reduction in forces itself was not a problem but a failure to consult with allies in advance was.[20] For the most part, however, these debates have focused around conventional deterrence; far less attention has been paid to the potential utility of U.S. military forces for strategic competition.

Conclusion

Official U.S. policy documents are clear in depicting the threat that Russia poses in competition below the level of armed conflict. The logic by which U.S. forward posture can deter malign activities in the competition space is less clear. From policy documents, military concepts, and strategic debates more generally, at least four contributions can be discerned. Military posture can provide:

- a symbol of U.S. commitment to stand by its allies and partners and help them resist Russian malign activities or armed aggression
- capabilities for irregular warfare, unconventional warfare, or both, including intelligence collection and surveillance, operations in the information environment, and building the capacity of allies and partners to resist malign activities
- capabilities to neutralize an adversary's efforts at military intimidation
- capabilities to serve as a "backstop" to nonmilitary instruments of national power (such as economic sanctions), enabling U.S. decisionmakers to use these other instruments with less fear of escalation to an armed conflict for which U.S. decisionmakers are ill-prepared.[21]

The extent to which military forces are effective in any of these respects, however, remains highly uncertain, as is their potential to contribute to escalation of the strategic competition with Russia.

---

and Jonathan Solomon, "Facing Russia: Conventional Defence and Deterrence in Europe," *Survival*, Vol. 57, No. 6, 2015; Elbridge Colby and Jonathan F. Solomon, "Avoiding Becoming a Paper Tiger: Presence in a Warfighting Defense Strategy," *Joint Force Quarterly*, Vol. 82, 2016; and Michael Kofman, "Permanently Stationing U.S. Forces in Poland Is a Bad Idea, but One Worth Debating," *War on the Rocks*, October 12, 2018.

[20] Mac Thornberry, Don Bacon, Jim Banks, Jack Bergman, Rob Bishop, Bradley Byrne, Liz Cheney, Michael Conaway, Paul Cook, Mike Gallagher, Sam Graves, Vicky Hartzler, Trent Kelly, Doug Lamborn, Paul Mitchell, Mike Rogers, Austin Scott, Elise Stefanik, Mike Turner, Michael Waltz, Joe Wilson, and Robert Wittman, "Letter to the President of the United States," Washington, D.C.: Congress of the United States, June 9, 2020; and Philip H. Gordon, "Trump's Sudden and Dangerous Troop Withdrawal from Germany," blog post, Council on Foreign Relations, June 8, 2020.

[21] Military forces can also potentially strengthen allies' and partners' resolve and enhance their capabilities. Although these forces are important, these effects are related to how U.S. actions affect allies and partners rather than how they deter or provoke U.S. adversaries and thus are outside the scope of this report.

Russian Perspectives on Competition

Russia believes there is an ongoing intensification of competition (*konkurentsiia*) among great powers. The nature of this competition centers on the alleged shift of power from the West to other regions and the resultant struggle for influence to achieve national security and prosperity. One of the key fault lines in great power competition lies between divergent development models, which each side uses as a tool to expand its influence. Russia views the promotion by the United States and its allies of political and military integration mechanisms that prioritize democratic governance and universal human rights—particularly along Russia's periphery—as a way to strengthen the United States' global position at the expense of Russia. Alternatively, Russia, as a reemerging power center, has promoted a nascent model that is based on regional spheres of influence, so-called traditional values, and proclaimed policy of noninterference in the internal affairs of others (even as it meddles in others' internal affairs). The friction between the Russian model and that of the United States and the European Union forms a foundational part of state competition in Europe and informs Russia's strategy to alter Western views and behavior below the threshold of war.

Russian Goals and Threat Perceptions in Europe

According to Russia's 2035 Strategic Forecast, the United States seeks to deter Russia by implementing policies in three primary domains: military-political, economic, and information-communication.[22] As a result, over the next 15 years, Russia foresees possible threats emanating from each of these areas.

The primary military-political threat that was identified by the forecast is the breakdown of the arms control architecture that characterized the late-Soviet and early post–Cold War era and the instability it causes. The end of both the Anti-Ballistic Missile Treaty and the INF Treaty has created an environment in which each side might develop and deploy arms that could threaten strategic stability, or the assurance of both sides in the ability to inflict unacceptable damage on the other. An arms race or the deployment of previously banned systems could increase tension in the regional military-political situation, which might, at some point in the future, result in a conflict with a reduced nuclear threshold.[23] Other Russian analysts have also expressed concern that Russia could be drawn into an arms race, an outcome that Putin described in 2017 as potentially destructive to the Russian budget, as it once was for the Soviet economy.[24]

---

[22] Nikolai Patrushev, "See the Target [Videt' tsel']," *Rossiiskaia gazeta*, November 11, 2019.

[23] Patrushev, 2019.

[24] Konstantin Sivkov, "Global Strike Against Local Targets [Global'nyi udar po lokal'nym tseliam]," *Military-Industrial Courier* [*Voenno-promyshlennyi kur'er*], July 14, 2020; and "Putin Promised Not to Drag Russia into an Arms Race [Putin poobeshchal ne vtiagivat' Rossiiu v gonku vooruzhenii]," *Rossiiskaia gazeta*, December 14, 2017.

Beyond the breakdown of arms control measures, Russia has identified as threatening several recent changes in U.S. and NATO posture in Europe. In 2017, the Chief of the Russian General Staff, Valerii Gerasimov, summarized a number of recent NATO force posture actions that in his view were "disrupting the balance of forces, increasing the risks of military incidents" and were of a "provocative nature."[25] Such actions included the buildup of formations and command infrastructure across eastern Europe, increases in the volume of useable airfields and ports, the conduct of greater numbers of operational exercises, the creation of weapons and equipment storage facilities, and the alleged possibility to launch cruise missiles from missile defense sites.[26]

A separate Ministry of Defense forecast of military-political threats in Europe to 2030 and 2045 identified several other sources of possible tension: The most problematic areas are in the Baltic region, Ukraine, and southern Caucasus.[27] The forecast specifically highlighted possible future U.S. and NATO support of Ukrainian and Georgian attempts to reconstitute lost territories, such as Crimea, Abkhazia, and South Ossetia.

Despite these assessments of military-political risks, Russian strategic planning documents and official statements have been consistent since 2014 in stating that there is a low probability of large-scale war in Europe. In a 2020 speech, Putin asserted that "Russia's defence capability is ensured for decades to come" as a result of the modernization of its strategic nuclear arsenal.[28] Defense Minister Sergei Shoigu similarly maintained that Russia had achieved "strategic parity" with NATO as a result of increased combat potential of the country's Armed Forces and the "buildup of [Russian] deterrence potential."[29] It is not clear from these statements how much of this confidence in deterrence parity is based on Russia's modernized nuclear forces, improvements to conventional forces (which are qualitatively and quantitatively still inferior to NATO's collective force posture), or a mixture of both.

Present and future threats to Russia in the economic sphere center on Western economic and financial sanctions. Some Russian military experts view the imposition of sanctions as a form of economic warfare intended as part of a broader effort to weaken Russia to the point of abandoning a foreign policy at odds with Western objectives or even as a prelude to future military attack in support of Russian opposition seeking to take advantage of domestic dis-

---

[25] Valerii Gerasimov, "'Tomahawks at the Ready ['Tomagavki' na nizkom starte]," *Military-Industrial Courier* [*Voenno-promyshlennyi kur'er*], May 3, 2017.

[26] Gerasimov, 2017.

[27] Sambu Tsyrendorzhiev, "Forecast of Military Dangers and Threats to Russia [Prognoz voennykh opasnostei i ugroz Rossii]", *Defense and Security* [*Zashchita i bezopasnost'*], Vol. 4, 2015.

[28] Vladimir Putin, "Presidential Address to the Federal Assembly," Moscow, January 15, 2020.

[29] Ministry of Defense of the Russian Federation, "The Minister of Defense Spoke at the Meeting of the Federation Council During the 'Government Hour' [Ministr oborony vystupil na zasedanii Soveta Federatsii v ramkakh 'pravitel'stvennogo chasa]," March 25, 2020.

content with a deteriorating economic situation.[30] Sanctions-based pressure and exclusion from aspects of the international economy have forced Russia into other options, such as acquiring larger percentages of gold and ridding itself of holdings in U.S. dollars or, in a few cases, accepting barter for some goods or services abroad. The Russian economy might provide an attractive partner for other countries, parastatal organizations, or oligarchs who find themselves under strict sanctions regimes or who want to avoid financial regulation.

The employment of psychological and cyber information operations is seen by Russia as an acute national security threat. Senior Russian officials and military officers continuously highlight their use by the United States and its Western allies of social media and other forms of global communication to support opposition groups or manipulate target populations to rise up against national leadership.[31] Such actions are often accompanied with economic, diplomatic, and military measures as ways of applying maximum pressure on an unfriendly regime to alter its behavior or to affect regime change.[32] It is worth noting that Russia applies many of these tactics against its adversaries in Europe and the United States.

Russian Concepts of Competition and the Role of Military Force

Russian documents make clear that the current strategic competition is primarily nonmilitary in nature, although there is a baseline of military capability that is required to be competitive. Putin stated this clearly in 2012, when he justified the resources to be spent on military modernization:

> There should not be such even hypothetical possibilities in relation to [the sovereignty of] Russia. This means that we should not lead anyone into temptation with our weakness. That is why we will, under no circumstances, give up the potential for strategic deterrence and will strengthen it. It was [strategic deterrence potential] that helped us to preserve state sovereignty in the most difficult period of the [19]90s, when we, frankly, did not have any other serious material arguments . . . [and] we will not be able to strengthen our international positions . . . if we are not able to defend Russia.[33]

---

[30] S. G. Chekinov and S. A. Bogdanov, "Particularities of Assuring the Military Security of Russia in the 21st Century in Conditions of Globalization [Osobennosti obespecheniia voennoi bezopasnosti Rossii v XXI stoletii v usloviiakh globalizatsii]," *Military Thought* [*Voennaia mysl'*], No. 6, 2016.

[31] Valerii Gerasimov, "Vectors in the Development of Military Strategy [Vektory razvitiia voennoi strategii]," *Red Star* [*Krasnaia zvezda*], March 4, 2019.

[32] S. P. Belokon', "Technological Aspects of Modern Armed Conflicts and the Military Security of Russia [Tekhnologicheskie aspekty sovremennykh vooruzhennykh konfliktov i voennaia bezopasnost' Rossii]," *Bulletin of Moscow State University* [*Vestnik Moskovskogo gosudarstvennogo universiteta*], Seriia 25, No. 4, 2015.

[33] Vladimir Putin, "Being Strong Is a Safeguard of Russian National Security [Byt' sil'nymi: garantii natsional'noi bezopasnosti dlia Rossii]," *Rossiiskaia gazeta*, February 20, 2012.

The possession of strategic nuclear and nonnuclear weapons by the United States and Russia creates significant downward pressure on the conflict escalation ladder. Each is far more likely to compete to achieve national security objectives below the threshold of direct military conflict, which was similarly the case during the Cold War. Even in *normal conditions*, when the level of tension is relatively low, states employ a wide range of measures to compete "for influence, for resources, to improve their economic and political positions, and to ensure their national security."[34] Credible military deterrence potential reinforces these noncombat measures of great powers in competition.

Senior Russian military officers and analysts have described the means of modern competition against Russia and its strategic interests as "hybrid war," "new type war," and "information war," which, in the case of great powers, are not wars in the traditional sense of inflicting damage with military means.[35] Within each of the aforementioned terms, the primary theme is the idea that the pursuit of national interests is primarily done using *nonmilitary* measures—political, diplomatic, economic, ideological, scientific-technical, and noncombat military actions—that are backed by nuclear and conventional deterrence potential.[36] Western financial sanctions and information operations are two of the primary tools most often discussed by Russian analysts describing the forms and methods of new-type war. The former head of the Russian Academy of Military Sciences, General Makhmut Gareev, and his coauthors noted, "The modern geopolitical and geostrategic confrontation between Russia and the Western coalition has seen a transition in defense objectives and tasks from the military-political to the information and economic domains."[37] Particularly in the context of nuclear armed competition, the military is used to deter, coerce, or intimidate the adversary until some political solution can be achieved—direct military action against a great power like the United States or a NATO ally is a last resort. As retired Major-General Vasilii Burenok, the president of the Russian Academy of Missile and Artillery Sciences, put it: "What, then, is the point of such a war [resulting in catastrophic loss]? There is no point other than to play on

---

[34] A. A. Kokoshin, "National Interests, Real Sovereignty, and National Security [Natsional'nye interesy, real'nyi suverenitet i natsional'naia bezopasnost']," *Questions of Philosophy* [*Voprosy filosofii*], No. 10, October 2015, p. 6.

[35] Timothy Thomas, "The Evolution of Russian Military Thought: Integrating Hybrid, New-Generation, and New-Type Thinking," *Journal of Slavic Military Studies*, Vol. 29, No. 4, 2016; Rod Thornton, "The Russian Military's New 'Main Emphasis,'" *RUSI Journal*, Vol. 162, No. 4, August/September 2017.

[36] There is clear overlap here between the Russian concept of strategic deterrence and the Russian understanding of the way in which states compete without actually going to war.

[37] M. A. Gareev, E. A. Derbin, and N. I. Turko, "Methodology and Practice of Improving the Strategic Management of the Country's Defense, Taking into Account the Character of Future Wars and Armed Conflicts [Metodologiia i praktika sovershenstvovaniia strategicheskogo rukovodstva oboronoi strany s uchetom kharaktera budushchikh voin i vooruzhennykh konfliktov]," *Bulletin of the Academy of Military Sciences* [*Vestnik Akademii voennykh nauk*], Vol. 1, No. 66, 2019, p. 4.

the nerves of your opponent, to try and create fear and force him to retreat without taking it to the point of an actual war."[38]

The former Chief of the Main Operations Directorate of the Russian General Staff, Andrei Kartapolov, explained in 2015 that Russia was developing its own methods to compete in such an environment.[39] The approach was, in part, based on *asymmetric principles* that included the development of traditional and nontraditional military capabilities to threaten weak points of a superior opponent.[40] With regard to the former, Russian analysts have emphasized the need to disrupt the critical connective nodes that facilitate network-centric warfare to include sites from which long-range strikes can be launched.[41] In the nontraditional realm, in 2016, a year after Kartapolov's speech, Russia participated in a cyber campaign to influence the U.S. presidential election, an effort described by the U.S. intelligence community as "the most recent expression of Moscow's longstanding desire to undermine the U.S.-led liberal democratic order, but *these activities demonstrated a significant escalation in directness, level of activity, and scope of effort compared to previous operations* [emphasis added]."[42] Although we have not yet identified this specific line of thinking in Russian discourse, Russian behavior suggests the Kremlin might view the methods of noncombat interstate competition in the same way it views conflict escalation: Increase or decrease the level of "damage" on an opponent in an attempt to alter the opponent's decisionmaking to proceed further.

Russian Understanding of How Force Posture in Europe Yields Advantage in Competition

There is little theoretical discourse in Russian military literature on the role of force posture in state competition. In fact, there is not a direct terminological equivalent to force posture in the Russian language. There are general terms such as *voennoe prisutstviie*, which translates to *military presence*, but that term does not have a clear connotation without additional con-

---

[38] V. M. Burenok, "Conceptual Deadend [Kontseptual'nyi tupik]," *Arms and Economics* [*Vooruzhenie i ekonomika*], Vol. 3, No. 49, 2019, pp. 4–5.

[39] Andrei Kartapolov, "Lessons of Military Conflicts, Perspectives on the Development of Means and Methods to Conduct Them. Direct and Indirect Actions in Modern International Conflicts [Uroki voennykh konfliktov, perspektivy razvitiia sredstv i sposobov ikh vedeniia. Priamye i nepriamye deistviya v sovremennykh mezhdunarodnykh konfliktakh]," *Bulletin of the Academy of Military Sciences* [*Vestnik Akademii voennykh nauk*], Vol. 2, No. 51, 2015, p. 35.

[40] Former Soviet military intelligence officer Colonel Vitalii Tsygichko argued that possessing the capability to threaten the destruction of the information infrastructure that is the backbone of Western economies—in addition to other critical targets—would likely have a significant deterrent effect against an attack on Russia. See Vitalii Tsygichko, "On the Category, the Ratio of Forces and Means [O kategorii sootnosheniie sil i sredstv]," *Military Thought* [*Voennaia mysl'*], No. 5, 2002, p. 57.

[41] I. M. Popov and M. M. Khamzatov, *Future War* [*Voina budushchego*], Moscow: Kuchkovo pole, 2018, p. 498.

[42] National Intelligence Council, *Assessing Russian Activities and Intentions in Recent US Elections*, ICA 2017–01D, Washington, D.C.: Office of the Director of National Intelligence, January 6, 2017, p. ii.

text. Thus, we must discern Russian views on force posture as defined in this report on the basis of its behavior. The desire of Moscow during the Cold War to establish bases around the globe, sell arms, and train and support friendly forces—among other actions—clearly demonstrated a belief that force posture translates into influence and makes it more difficult for a competitor state to achieve foreign policy objectives in a given country or region.[43] Although Russia largely retreated from the world stage after the collapse of the Soviet Union because of financial limitations, it has maintained or enhanced its military presence in the breakaway territories of Transnistria, Abkhazia, and South Ossetia, as well as in Belarus, Armenia, and Kazakhstan, among others. In 2014, Defense Minister Shoigu announced that Russia intended to establish military bases further afield in several countries, including Cuba, Venezuela, Nicaragua, and Vietnam, although the remarks, in hindsight, appear to have been aspirational or limited to more common access rights as opposed to permanent infrastructure.[44]

In Europe, Russia has long argued that NATO enlargement eastward and the buildup of military infrastructure along its border represents a threat to its national security. Some military analysts have more specifically assessed a Western objective to "eliminate a potential geopolitical opponent [Russia] and create an uninterrupted zone of vassal states in eastern Europe."[45] A similar view was reflected in recent comments by the Russian political scientist Fedor Lukianov, who argued that "neither Merkel nor Macron . . . have any idea what the security policy of Europe could be without the United States."[46] Extrapolating from these and other remarks to some extent, Russia seems to believe that once a country falls under the U.S. security umbrella, that country becomes a military and political *platsdarm*, or bridgehead, that not only could house military infrastructure for a future conflict but that would likely embrace Washington's objectives and rarely acknowledge Russian interests.[47] Because much of Europe is either in NATO or inclined to cooperate with the alliance, the United States has the advantage of being able to deploy its military forces across a large swath of territory, thereby increasing its influence to potentially shape the policies of its allies and partners.

---

[43] Karl P. Mueller, Timothy Heath, Clint Reach, Lyle Morris, and Adam R. Grissom, *Great Power Competition in Africa: Chinese and Russian Strategies and Their Implications for the United States*, Santa Monica, Calif.: RAND Corporation, 2020, Not available to the general public.

[44] "Russia Close to Signing Military Base Agreements with a Number of Countries [RF blizka k podpisaniiu soglashenii o voennykh bazakh srazu s riadom stran]," RIA Novosti, February 26, 2014.

[45] Tsyrendorzhiev, 2015, p. 12.

[46] "Political Scientist: Europe Does Not Know How to Build a Foreign Policy Without the United States [Politolog: Evropa ne znaet, kak postroit' vneshniuiu politiku bez SShA]," *The View* [*Vzgliad*], May 28, 2020.

[47] The apparent Russian involvement in a coup attempt in Montenegro prior to 2016 elections with ramifications for NATO accession lends credence to this idea.

Conclusion

Although Russia predominantly views competition as taking place through nonmilitary tools, military capabilities and posture play critical roles in Russian thinking about competition. Indeed, the potential use of military force is particularly important for Russia because, to date, it lacks alternative integration mechanisms (i.e., "soft power") that are more appealing than the European Union and NATO.

Comparing U.S. and Russian Perspectives

In comparing the U.S. and Russian visions of strategic competition as articulated in their national security documents, the first thing that becomes apparent is the broad and apparently irreconcilable way in which they each frame their goals and the threats posed by the other actor. The United States seeks to maintain the current international order and sees Russia as implacably hostile to that order and actively working to undermine it. Russia sees the United States as seeking to impose its model globally, including on Russia and Russia's neighbors and allies. This articulation of their respective goals and threat perceptions almost ensures a high level of mutual hostility.

It is also apparent that military instruments have a role to play in such high-stakes competition, but they can be only one part of a much larger strategy. And indeed, both sides emphasize the importance of whole-of-government approaches, and both consider that direct armed conflict with the other would entail almost unimaginable costs. "Winning without fighting" is the objective.

Focusing more narrowly on the ways in which military instruments might advance the goals of each actor in competition below the level of armed conflict, several themes frequently reappear. Specifically, military forces can influence strategic competition by providing a symbol of the commitment of each country to resist aggression by the other, such as capabilities for irregular and/or unconventional warfare, capabilities to neutralize an adversary's efforts at military intimidation, and capabilities to support nonmilitary instruments of national power.[48] The extent to which military forces are effective in any of these respects, however, remains highly uncertain.

Similar levels of uncertainty characterize the risk of escalation in competition. Do escalation dynamics function similarly when military forces are directed toward competition goals as they do when focused more narrowly on deterring armed conflict? Or do the different ways in which armed forces are employed in competition also suggest that escalation dynamics might differ in important respects? At least some escalation dynamics should be ones familiar from more-traditional analyses of deterring armed conflict (e.g., neutralizing a

---

[48] Military forces can also potentially strengthen allies' and partners' resolve and enhance their capabilities. Although important, these effects are related to how U.S. actions affect allies and partners rather than how they deter or provoke U.S. adversaries and thus are outside the scope of this report.

competitor's ability to use military intimidation). Given the ranges of distance at which war with a near-peer adversary would be waged in the contemporary era, these escalation dynamics potentially have implications for U.S. force posture across a large area of Europe. But the discussion of competition also suggests that some escalation dynamics might be different. In particular, insofar as most of the objectives of competition involve influencing other countries, third-party countries—those other than the United States and Russia—are likely to play an even more important role in escalation than they do in studies of armed conflict more narrowly.

CHAPTER THREE

A Framework for Understanding Deterrence in Competition

Most existing work on deterrence focuses on armed conflict. It is unclear the extent to which these same deterrent dynamics apply in competition. This chapter draws on the large body of deterrence theory to develop propositions about the ways in which forward posture influences malign activities in strategic competition. The following two chapters will examine which of these propositions is supported by historical evidence.

Clearly, U.S. forward posture in Europe has failed to deter a wide variety of Russian hostile measures over the past several years. U.S. forward posture has not prevented Russia from engaging in disinformation and other influence operations throughout Europe (and in the United States itself). Nor has it prevented Russia from undertaking assassinations of Russian political dissidents living in the United Kingdom and Germany, nor deterred Russia from using natural gas shut-offs as a tool of economic coercion against NATO member-states and others.[1] All of these malign activities unambiguously speak to the limits of using military instruments as a means of deterring hostile measures below the level of armed conflict.

But none of these examples speaks to the counterfactual of what would have happened in the absence of U.S. forward posture in Europe. Forward posture, in conjunction with other tools of national power, might have deterred Russia from undertaking even more aggressive measures. For example, Russia appears to have attempted to foment a coup in Montenegro to prevent its accession to NATO, but Moscow does not appear to have used similarly aggressive measures within NATO member-states, including in the Baltic states, where many have expressed concerns about the risk of so-called "hybrid warfare."[2] Russia has sought to inflame political tensions in the fragile Western Balkans; in the absence of the U.S. commit-

---

[1] Raphael S. Cohen and Andrew Radin, *Russia's Hostile Measures in Europe: Understanding the Threat*, Santa Monica, Calif.: RAND Corporation, RR-1793-A, 2019; Doug Klain, "Russian Assassinations Send Chilling Message of Impunity," blog post, Atlantic Council, March 12, 2020; Mikhail Korchemkin, "With Gazprom's Nord Stream 2, Putin Is Getting Ready to Put the Screws on Europe," *Foreign Policy*, October 7, 2019; and Dimitar Bechev, "Russia's Pipe Dreams Are Europe's Nightmare," *Foreign Policy*, March 12, 2019.

[2] For an overview of Russian malign measures, see, for instance, Zeigler et al., 2021. For a discussion of how U.S. and NATO posture might be used to prevent escalation in the Baltics, see, for example, Ulrich Kühn, *Preventing Escalation in the Baltics: A NATO Playbook*, Washington, D.C.: Carnegie Endowment for International Peace, 2018.

ment to Kosovo Forces (KFOR) and similar measures, Russia's actions might have taken on an even harder edge.[3]

On the other hand, a number of observers have argued that the expansion of the NATO alliance and U.S. forward posture in Europe—such as the United States' anti-ballistic missile defenses in Romania (and planned defenses in Poland), troop presence in the formerly Soviet Baltic republics, and military sales to countries such as Georgia and Ukraine—were, in part, responsible for Russia's turn to hostile measures in competition.[4] If the United States were to deploy additional capabilities to Europe, Russia might respond by attempting to impose costs in the competition space by ratcheting up the intensity of its malign activities.

In this chapter, we adapt the logic of traditional deterrence theory to understand how forward posture *might* influence the conduct of strategic competition. We begin by defining what malign activities are to be deterred. We then provide an overview of the ways in which forward posture might deter malign activities below the level of armed conflict—or, alternatively, why forward posture might be particularly likely to provoke such activities. The next section of the chapter breaks apart the concept of forward posture to understand why its different elements—forces, activities, footprint, and agreements—might have different effects. Next, we discuss how different characteristics of posture changes—including continuity with prior forward posture, the introduction of novel and destabilizing capabilities, and the location of posture changes—might influence the risk of escalation. We conclude with a summary of the factors discussed in this chapter and an overview of how the original research in the remainder of the report will be used to evaluate the effectiveness of forward posture in deterring malign activities.

Malign Activities: What Is to Be Deterred?

Our analysis focuses on the United States' ability to deter *malign activities* or *hostile measures*, terms which we use interchangeably and which we define as state activities other than direct conventional or nuclear attacks against other states, conducted with hostile intent and some degree of coercion.[5] Malign activities can include measures in any of the following categories:

- **Military intimidation:** States may seek to influence others' policies through clear demonstrations of military strength, indicating the potential to inflict high costs through military operations without directly attacking other states. Large-scale and/or "snap" military exercises on the borders of target states, harassment of competitor warships

---

[3] On Russian hostile measures in the Balkans, see Paul Stronski and Annie Himes, *Russia's Game in the Balkans*, Washington, D.C.: Carnegie Endowment for International Peace, January 2019.

[4] See, for instance, John J. Mearsheimer, "Why the Ukraine Crisis Is the West's Fault: The Liberal Delusions That Provoked Putin," *Foreign Affairs*, Vol. 93, No. 5, September/October 2014.

[5] This definition is similar to one used in Connable et al., 2020.

or warplanes operating in international waters or airspace, and similar activities fall within this category.

- **Proxy warfare:** States have long sought to impose costs on their competitors by providing support to violent nonstate actors (e.g., insurgent groups) who oppose their competitors. Although these actors frequently engage in armed conflict against the target state because the armed conflict is not waged directly between the two competitor states, such proxy wars are considered an instrument of competition below the level of armed conflict.[6]

- **Economic coercion:** We use this term synonymously with *economic sanctions*, defined in one frequently cited study as "the deliberate, government-inspired withdrawal, or threat of withdrawal, of customary trade or financial relations."[7] Such measures can involve the use or threat of force (such as blockades) but frequently do not (for instance, Russia's threats to shut off access to natural gas). They can be formal (such as sanctions backed by a United Nations Security Council resolution) or informal and subtle (such as restricting guest-worker visas in a deliberate attempt to reduce worker remittances, a common source of income for many poorer countries).

- **Competitive arms transfers:** States transfer arms and other military materiel to allied or partner states for a wide variety of reasons, from a desire to strengthen these states' defenses to simple commercial motives. Such transfers are not necessarily a form of strategic competition. But arms transfers also can be used to signal military support for an ally or partner, gain influence at the expense of a competitor, or strengthen allies and partners relative to a competitor's allies and partners. These latter uses of arms transfers can be considered forms of strategic competition and indeed pose a risk of arms races and escalation to armed conflict.[8]

- **Influence operations, misinformation, and electoral interference:** Unlike traditional diplomatic activities or public diplomacy, this category includes activities that are illegal, covert, or both, including bribing political leaders, deliberately injecting false information into public debates, and stealing true but private information for public release. At the same time, it is important to note that activities that U.S. observers generally

---

[6] Joint Doctrine Note 1-19, 2019, p. 2.

[7] Gary Clyde Hufbauer, Jeffrey J. Schott, Kimberly Ann Elliott, and Barbara Oegg, *Economic Sanctions Reconsidered*, 3rd ed., Washington, D.C.: Peterson Institute for International Economics, June 2009, p. 3.

[8] Keren Yarhi-Milo, Alexander Lanoszka, and Zack Cooper, "To Arm or to Ally: The Patron's Dilemma and the Strategic Logic of Arms Transfers and Alliances," *International Security*, Vol. 41, No. 2, Fall 2016; Roseanne W. McManus and Mark David Nieman, "Identifying the Level of Major Power Support Signaled for Proteges: A Latent Measure Approach," *Journal of Peace Research*, Vol. 56, No. 3, 2019; and Stephen Blank and Edward Levitzky, "Geostrategic Aims of the Russian Arms Trade in East Asia and the Middle East," *Defence Studies*, Vol. 15, No. 1, 2015. Competitive arms transfers can also be driven by states that feel threatened by military support that the United States is providing to its ally or partner. On such dynamics, see, for instance, Andrew Kydd, "Game Theory and the Spiral Model," *World Politics*, Vol. 49, No. 3, April 1997.

consider licit and even beneficial—such as supporting independent investigative journalism in such countries as Russia and its allies—corrupt or repressive governments often consider hostile measures.

Overall Logic of Deterrence and Escalation in Competition

There is an extensive body of literature on how states can use their armed forces to deter armed aggression either against themselves or their allies and partners. There is nowhere near such a well-developed body of literature on to what extent (if at all) and how armed forces might be used to deter hostile measures below the level of armed conflict.[9]

This gap in the deterrence literature is unfortunate because based solely on logical deduction from deterrence principles, it is equally possible to make arguments suggesting that conventional forces can deter hostile measures or provoke them. Writing during the Cold War, the political scientist Robert Jervis famously argued that there are two paths to escalation: the deterrence model and the spiral model. In the *deterrence model*, when one state increases its military capabilities, it *reduces* the risk of escalation by an aggressive state by deterring it. In the *spiral model*, when one state increases its military capabilities, it *increases* the risk of escalation by so threatening other states that they feel the need to take more-extreme measures to defend themselves.[10] In the remainder of this chapter, we map out how the logic behind both of these pathways applies in the competition space. In the following two chapters, we analyze the extent to which and conditions under which an increase in U.S. forward posture increases the risk of escalation and when it reduces the risk.

The Logic of Deterrence in Competition

Scholars of international relations have long argued that military forces can have powerful effects in peacetime.[11] Even when not made explicit in words or actions, the balance of mili-

---

[9] In recent years, a literature has begun to emerge on so-called cross-domain coercion or cross-domain deterrence. Much of this literature has been exploratory, mapping out key concepts and how cross-domain dynamics have played out in recent events. See, for example, King Mallory, *New Challenges in Cross-Domain Deterrence*, Santa Monica, Calif.: RAND Corporation, PE-259-OSD, 2018; and Dmitry (Dima) Adamsky, "From Moscow with Coercion: Russian Deterrence Theory and Strategic Culture," *Journal of Strategic Studies*, Vol. 41, Nos. 1–2, 2018.

[10] Robert Jervis, *Perception and Misperception in International Politics*, Princeton, N.J., and Oxford, U.K.: Oxford University Press, 1976, chapter three.

[11] In his seminal work *The Twenty Years' Crisis*, originally published in 1939, E. H. Carr argued that the militarily predominant state in the international system can set the terms for economic relations between countries, shaping the rules and norms of the system in ways that favor its own growth and prosperity. Later landmark works, such as Robert Gilpin's *War and Change*, further developed these arguments. See E. H. Carr, *The Twenty Years' Crisis, 1919–1939: An Introduction to the Study of International Relations*, New

tary power can shape both the rules and norms of the international system and the outcome of specific negotiations between states.[12] Indeed, some scholars argue that, while subtler, the peacetime effects of military power might be even more profound than those in war.[13]

It is one thing to argue that military power can influence rule-making and bargaining outcomes generally; it is another to argue that it can deter specific acts of aggression launched by a hostile state below the level of armed conflict. But, as we suggested in Chapter Two, there are at least four reasons to believe that armed forces generally—and forward-postured forces specifically—can have such deterrent effects in strategic competition; they are as follows:

- Armed forces can serve as signals of a great power's commitment to its allies and partners.
- They can provide "irregular" capabilities (such as for intelligence or foreign internal defense).
- They can provide conventional capabilities to neutralize attempts at military intimidation.
- They can provide support to other instruments of national power.

Signal of Commitment

Because fighting wars or engaging in other acts to defend an ally or partner is costly, there is always a risk that a defending state will choose not to do so or will be perceived as unwilling by a potential aggressor. Consequently, the defending state must provide unambiguous signals of its commitment to successfully deter. In international relations, talk is often cheap; national leaders often say one thing and do another. An effective signal of commitment, therefore, will be one that only a truly committed defender would provide. The more costly the signal, the better symbol of political will it provides.[14] Clearly and publicly staking the

---

York: Palgrave, 2001; and Robert Gilpin, *War and Change in World Politics*, New York: Cambridge University Press, 1981.

[12] For analysis and historical examples, see Michael Mastanduno, "System Maker and Privilege Taker: U.S. Power and the International Political Economy," *World Politics*, Vol. 61, No. 1, January 2009; Carla Norrlof, "Dollar Hegemony: A Power Analysis," *Review of International Political Economy*, Vol. 21, No. 5, 2014; Stephen G. Brooks and William C. Wohlforth, *America Abroad: The United States' Global Role in the 21st Century*, New York: Oxford University Press, 2016; Christina L. Davis, "Linkage Diplomacy: Economic and Security Bargaining in the Anglo-Japanese Alliance, 1902–23," *International Security*, Vol. 33, No. 3, Winter 2009; and Doug Stokes and Kit Waterman, "Security Leverage, Structural Power and U.S. Strategy in East Asia," *International Affairs*, Vol. 93, No. 5, September 2017.

[13] Robert Art, for instance, writes, "The war-waging use of military power is akin to a powerful flood: it washes away all before it. The peaceful use of military power is akin to a gravitational field among large objects in space: it affects all motion that takes place, but it produces its effects imperceptibly" ("American Foreign Policy and the Fungibility of Force," *Security Studies*, Vol. 5, No. 4, Summer 1996, p. 10).

[14] See, for instance, James D. Fearon, "Signaling Foreign Policy Interests: Tying Hands Versus Sinking Costs," *Journal of Conflict Resolution*, Vol. 41, No. 1, February 1997.

defending country's prestige on the defense of allies and partners is one way to signal commitment. Stationing substantial numbers of forces overseas in or near the allies and partners to be defended might be a stronger signal—especially if such forces are heavy forces that could not easily be repositioned elsewhere, and if they would be placed at risk by an act of aggression by a hostile power.[15]

The signaling value of forward-based forces has been a staple of traditional deterrence theory. But such forces might also provide a potent symbol of commitment to defend against acts of aggression below the level of armed conflict. The cost of maintaining such forces overseas provides a symbol of commitment independent of such forces' actual capabilities for defending against a specific type of threat. Of course, the presence of forward-stationed forces might not be the most effective or efficient way to signal commitment to deter malign activities. But even if U.S. forces are primarily present for other purposes (such as deterring acts of conventional military aggression), their signaling value in competition should not be overlooked.[16]

Irregular Capabilities

Besides overseas forces' symbolic value, however, they also possess a wide variety of military capabilities, some of which are particularly well-suited for competition. These capabilities can be considered *irregular* in that they are principally about trying to strengthen the resilience of allies and partners to political subversion and other forms of malign activity other than overt uses of conventional military power.[17] These capabilities include

---

[15] Frederick et al., 2020.

[16] The symbolic importance of U.S. forces became apparent during an initiative to substantially reduce U.S. troop presence in Germany. Former National Security Council official Philip Gordon argued that the loss of capabilities in Europe was not the primary issue; there is, he said, "no magic number of U.S. troops needed" to defend Europe and undertake other missions. Instead, "[w]hat could be catastrophic is an unplanned and unilateral withdrawal . . . *that sends a message to allies and adversaries* alike that the United States is no longer committed to European defense" (Gordon, 2020).

[17] In its Irregular Warfare Joint Operating Concept, DoD defines *irregular warfare* as "contests for influence and legitimacy over relevant populations." The concept further indicates that the appropriate countermeasures to irregular threats included working "in concert with other governmental agencies and multinational partners, and, where appropriate, the host nation to understand the situation in depth, plan and act in concert, and continually assess and adapt their approach in response to the dynamic and complex nature of the problem. This will be achieved through a sustained and balanced approach aimed at both the threats themselves as well as the population and the causes conditions that give rise to the threats. The goal is to enhance a local partner's legitimacy and influence over a population by addressing the causes of conflict and building the partner's capacity to provide security, good governance, and economic development." Finally, the concept indicates the military activities entailed in irregular operations:

> There are principally five activities or operations that are undertaken in sequence, in parallel, or in blended form in a coherent campaign to address irregular threats: counterterrorism (CT), unconventional warfare (UW), foreign internal defense (FID), counterinsurgency (COIN), and stability operations (SO). In addition to these five core activities, there are a host of key related activities including strategic communications, information operations of all kinds, psychological operations, civil-military opera-

- **Building partner capacity:** The U.S. military can help to build allied and partner capacity for foreign internal defense or emergency response and strengthen the defense institutions of fragile allies and partners against subversion (such as the reported Russian effort to foment a coup in Montenegro in 2016).
- **ISR:** The U.S. military has capabilities to surveil illicit transit routes, detect malign cyber operations, conduct counter-network analysis of foreign operatives, share intelligence with allies and partners, and conduct similar activities.
- **Strategic communication:** The U.S. military has capabilities to communicate U.S. commitment to partners, counter hostile messages about the U.S. role, engage vulnerable populations (e.g., through civil affairs operations), and play a variety of other roles in the information environment.[18]

Although the most visible manifestation of NATO's solidarity with the Baltic states takes the form of the Enhanced Forward Presence (eFP) battlegroups, other efforts aim to enhance irregular capabilities to make it more difficult for Russia to sow unrest, potentially by capitalizing on the presence of ethnic minority Russians in Estonia and Latvia in particular. Ensuring allied and partner resilience to unconventional threats is a core role for U.S. special operations forces, but conventional units also offer relevant expertise, including in such areas as cyberspace. Through the National Guard's State Partnership Program, the state of Maryland and Estonia partner to exchange best practices on cyber defense among other capabilities central to irregular environments.[19] Conventional forces also have roles in communicating with local populations and countering hostile messages, including to prevent Russia from undermining the case for the eFP's presence and exercises.[20] Provision of technology for enhanced ISR—or, more broadly, situational awareness—offers another avenue for cooperation.[21]

Lighter conventional forces, in particular, can serve as a complement to special operations forces. An infantry brigade combat team (BCT), for example, has a variety of organic capabil-

---

tions, and support to law enforcement, intelligence, and counterintelligence operations in which the joint force may engage to counter irregular threats.

Although this concept was developed with counterterrorism and counterinsurgency operations in mind, it generally applies to nonconventional threats in strategic competition. See U.S. Department of Defense, *Irregular Warfare: Countering Irregular Threats, Joint Operating Concept*, version 2.0, Washington, D.C., May 17, 2010.

[18] See, for instance, Connable et al., 2020, p. 66; and Watts et al., 2021.

[19] Kurt Rauschenberg, "National Guard Marks 25 Years of State Partnership Program, Ensures Defense Capabilities in Europe," blog post, U.S. Army, May 17, 2018.

[20] See for example, Anna Churco, "Defender 2020: 418th Civil Affairs Soldiers Meet with Local Leaders in Zagan, Poland," blog post, U.S. Army Reserve, February 18, 2020.

[21] Recent RAND research offers a range of options, some of which will require conventional forces for implementation (Stephen J. Flanagan, Jan Osburg, Anika Binnendijk, Marta Kepe, and Andrew Radin, *Deterring Russian Aggression in the Baltic States Through Resilience and Resistance*, Santa Monica, Calif.: RAND Corporation, RR-2779-OSD, 2019).

ities that are relevant to irregular environments, including human intelligence, short-range signals intelligence collection, small unmanned aerial vehicles, and military information support operations teams.[22] In addition to serving as a signal of U.S. commitment, lighter forces can be employed during steady-state competition, potentially without the escalatory risks that are associated with heavy forces and their greater warfighting potential.

Conventional Capabilities to Neutralize Military Intimidation

As suggested in Chapter One, states can seek to influence the foreign policies of other states through military intimidation even if no shots are ever fired. In his discussion of the risk of nuclear escalation, the political scientist Robert Jervis succinctly summarized a logic that applies more broadly in the competition space: "What . . . brings pressure to bear on the adversary . . . is less the immediate product of the action than the fear of where both states could end up."[23] Even if national decisionmakers believe that the risk of outright military conflict is remote, its very possibility causes them to engage in hedging actions, a sort of geostrategic insurance policy.[24] Where the risk of armed conflict is greater, military imbalances can have even greater effects. In the Czechoslovak coup of 1948, for instance, the military preponderance of the Soviet Union in Eastern Europe might have played a crucial role in the consolidation of power by the Czechoslovak communists.[25] A U.S. State Department memorandum at the time argued that the lack of "any sign of friendly external force was undoubtedly a major factor in the limp Czech collapse."[26] By reducing the likelihood that an armed act of aggression will succeed, U.S. forward posture can neutralize the influence of an unequal balance of military power.

Conventional Capabilities to Support Other Instruments of National Power

Finally, military power generally and forward posture specifically can enhance the power of other instruments of national power, such as diplomacy and economic statecraft. Even if these other instruments are the primary tools through which strategic competition is waged, military force can provide an important "backstop" supporting the use of such instruments. Indeed, Robert Art argues that military capabilities are essential to understanding the strength of diplomacy: "Lurking behind the scenes, unstated but explicit, lies the military

---

[22] For a broader list and discussion, see Connable et al., 2020. In addition to possessing organic capabilities, BCTs have access to reach-back expertise from higher echelons and U.S.-based organizations.

[23] Robert Jervis, "Arms Control, Stability, and Causes of War," *Daedalus*, Vol. 120, No. 1, Winter 1991, p. 175.

[24] In its more extreme form, this phenomenon is sometimes known as *Finlandization*, although the appropriateness of this term is contested—above all, by the Finns themselves.

[25] See, for instance, Martin Myant, "New Research on February 1948 in Czechoslovakia," *Europe-Asia Studies*, Vol. 60, No. 10, December 2008.

[26] Cited in Peter Svik, "The Czechoslovak Factor in Western Alliance Building, 1945–1948," *Journal of Cold War Studies*, Vol. 18, No. 1, Winter 2016, p. 154.

muscle that gives meaning to the posturing of the diplomats . . . Fear of failure, combined with the knowledge that force can be used if agreement is not reached, help produce agreement. It is the ultimate ability of each state to use its military instrument that disciplines the diplomats."[27]

Art might overstate the relationship between military power and diplomacy, but specific instances of this relationship are not hard to identify. Saddam Hussein, for instance, used the threat of a second invasion of Kuwait in 1994 to try to force such countries as France and Russia to apply pressure on the United States to end its campaign of economic sanctions. A strong U.S. military response (Operation Vigilant Warrior) caused Hussein to back down. But without such a military backstop to its sanctions policy, the United States might have found it more difficult to maintain these sanctions.[28]

The Logic of Escalation in Competition

Although forward-postured forces might deter malign activities for all the reasons described previously, there are also reasons to believe that they could lead to an escalation in competitor activities, which are as follows:

- Forward-postured forces might increase competitors' sense of threat, touching off a security dilemma.
- Their success at deterring conventional aggression could cause partners to undertake aggression at levels below armed conflict.
- They could provide incentives for third parties to act in ways that increase the likelihood of confrontation.

Security Dilemmas

A core concept of deterrence theory is the so-called security dilemma. In this dilemma, actions that one state undertakes to improve its security are interpreted by another state as threats, leading to an action-reaction cycle in which both states—even if acting on the basis of purely defensive motives—ratchet up their preparations for war and risk inadvertent escalation to armed conflict.[29] This security dilemma might apply equally to the competition space, in which case U.S. forward posture that is intended to deter hostile measures in competition might actually provoke increased Russian activities.

---

[27] Art, 1996, p. 10.

[28] Frederick et al., 2020, chapter six. Of note, it was U.S. forward posture in the Persian Gulf—infrastructure, prepositioned equipment and stocks, and forces to facilitate the rapid flow of U.S. forces—that made the massive show of strength feasible.

[29] Robert Jervis, "Cooperation Under the Security Dilemma," *World Politics*, Vol. 30, No. 2, January 1978.

The Stability-Instability Paradox

Even if U.S. forward posture does not lead to escalation generally as the spiral model suggests it might, it could provoke increased hostile measures in the competition space. Indeed, U.S. strategic guidance and military concepts suggest that U.S. success at deterring armed conflict has led to increased aggression at the level of competition.[30] Such dynamics are not new; the argument that successful deterrence of direct armed conflict could lead to increased indirect forms of confrontation—often called the *stability-instability paradox*—was a staple of Cold War–era thinking on deterrence.[31]

Indirect or "Pericentric" Pathways to Escalation

So far, we have discussed deterrence and escalation mechanisms as though the only relevant actors were the United States and its competitors. But as we highlighted in Chapter Two, one of the most notable features of strategic competition is that it is, in large measure, a struggle for influence among third parties—states other than the major-power competitors with their own goals, who may and frequently do attempt to use major-power competition to their advantage.[32] Thus, the hosts of U.S. forces, installations, or other forms of forward posture could become the targets of hostile measures for reasons arising principally out of local dynamics but amplified by the competition between the United States and rival powers.

During the Cold War, for example, the Soviet Union attempted to counter U.S. military posture in Ethiopia with military assistance to neighboring Somalia. With the help of Soviet-provided military capabilities, Somalia stepped up attacks on Ethiopia and supported groups in that country who rebelled against the central government. These attacks, in turn, put more pressure on the United States to increase its military support to Ethiopia. More recently, many observers believe that Georgia became emboldened by U.S. military assistance and exercises—despite repeated and high-level U.S. diplomatic warnings—leading to a spiraling confrontation with Russia that culminated in the 2008 Russo-Georgian War.[33] In one of these cases (Ethiopia), a local rival to the United States' partner instigated the hostile measures. In the other case (Georgia), arguably it was the U.S. partner that took the most-fateful steps in an

---

[30] Mattis, 2018, p. 2; Joint Doctrine Note 1-19, 2019, p. 11.

[31] Glenn Herald Snyder, *Deterrence and Defense: Toward a Theory of National Security*, Princeton, N.J.: Princeton University Press, 1961; and Robert Jervis, *The Illogic of American Nuclear Strategy*, Ithaca, N.Y.: Cornell University Press, 1985. For an empirical test of this proposition, see Robert Rauchhaus, "Evaluating the Nuclear Peace Hypothesis: A Quantitative Approach," *Journal of Conflict Resolution*, Vol. 53, No. 2, April 2009.

[32] In international relations scholarship, the tendency of states to get drawn into the conflicts of their allies is known as *chain-ganging* or *entrapment*. In historical scholarship, a similar dynamic has appeared within the *pericentric* historiography of the Cold War. See, for instance, Robert O. Keohane, "The Big Influence of Small Allies," *Foreign Policy*, No. 2, Spring 1971; Glenn H. Snyder, "The Security Dilemma in Alliance Politics," *World Politics*, Vol. 36, No. 4, July 1984; and Tony Smith, "New Bottles for New Wine: A Pericentric Framework for the Study of the Cold War," *Diplomatic History*, Vol. 24, No. 4, Fall 2000.

[33] These two cases will be discussed at greater length in Chapter Five.

escalation spiral. But in both cases, it was local dynamics that provided the principal driver of escalation, with U.S. posture choices playing a background role.

Taken together, these three dynamics suggest the following five pathways by which U.S. forward posture might lead to escalation:

- **Signal-sending:** Competitors could respond to U.S. forward posture by signaling their willingness to take aggressive action to defend their interests. NATO exercises, for instance, often are followed by even larger Russian military exercises near NATO's borders, which, in turn, is often perceived as an attempt at military intimidation.
- **Cost imposition:** Competitors might seek to impose costs on the governments that host U.S. forces or military activities in an attempt to force a reduction in U.S. presence or to demonstrate to other potential U.S. partners the consequences of close military cooperation with the United States. Russia, for example, has relentlessly targeted the Baltic states with disinformation campaigns intended to inflame public opinion against NATO's eFP.[34]
- **Inadvertent escalation:** The presence of U.S. forces in close proximity to those of competitors creates risks of inadvertent escalation. Observers have feared such escalation in the Baltic Sea region as both Russia and NATO increase their air and naval presence.
- **Heightened threat perceptions:** U.S. forward posture could heighten competitors' overall threat perceptions, causing them to react in ways that are more hostile or aggressive in the future. As will be discussed in Chapter Five, for example, the U.S. confrontation with the Soviet Union over Iran was one factor that prompted the Soviets to later take a harder line in Eastern Europe.
- **Emboldenment or entrapment:** U.S. forward posture could embolden U.S. allies and partners to act more aggressively than they otherwise might, or it might inflame local rivalries, thus entrapping the United States in others' conflicts. Arguably, U.S. assistance to Georgia emboldened the Tbilisi government to take military action against South Ossetia, while U.S. assistance to Ethiopia in the Cold War helped to fuel a spiraling conflict between Ethiopia and Somalia.[35]

How Elements of Forward Posture Deter and Provoke

Up until this point, we have examined forward posture as if it were a single thing with uniform effects. There are reasons, however, to believe that different elements of forward posture could have variable consequences in competition. In this section, we assess the escalatory

---

[34] See, for instance, Marta Kepe, "NATO: Prepared for Countering Disinformation Operations in the Baltic States?" *RAND Blog*, June 7, 2017.

[35] Both examples are the subject of case studies in Chapter Five.

or de-escalatory consequences of each type of posture. Most of the discussion focuses on their effects on the likelihood of armed conflict because these are the effects that have been most widely examined in previous studies. Where we have reason to believe that their effects related to competition could differ from those related to armed conflict, we highlight this distinction.

Forces

According to U.S. defense guidance, the so-called *contact layer*—the portion of U.S. forces stationed overseas, in direct contact with allies, partners, and others—is "designed to help us compete more effectively below the level of armed conflict."[36] But it is not clear that the presence of U.S. forces has the same effects in competition as it is believed to have for deterring armed conflict, and existing literature does little to resolve this ambiguity.

The forward presence of military forces—and especially a preponderance in the local military balance of power—has repeatedly been found to deter armed conflict between states.[37] The details of this relationship between forward-positioned forces and the incidence of armed conflict, however, are important. Some analysts have argued that the local balance of power in-theater at the outset of a potential conflict is what matters for deterrence; if the local balance of power favors an aggressor, then aggressive states might convince themselves that they can win quickly and at low cost through a fait accompli before the victim's allies can send in reinforcements.[38] Others have found that, although the local balance of power is important, the ability of a defender to rapidly send reinforcements to its ally or partner can also exercise powerful deterrent effects.[39] Still others have focused not just on the quantity of forward-positioned forces but also on the types of forces present. In the estimation of one line of studies, heavier forces are associated with a higher deterrent value, potentially because the difficulties involved in moving them to other theaters indicates a very high degree of commitment to defending the countries in which they are stationed.[40]

Many analysts have asserted that the presence of forward-positioned forces can also deter malign activities, such as proxy wars and military intimidation. Johns Hopkins University's Paul H. Nitze School of Advanced International Studies professor Hal Brands, for instance,

---

[36] Mattis, 2018, p. 8.

[37] See, for instance, Curtis S. Signorino and Ahmer Tarar, "A Unified Theory and Test of Extended Immediate Deterrence," *American Journal of Political Science*, Vol. 50, No. 3, July 2006; Huth and Russett, 1988; Angela O'Mahony, Miranda Priebe, Bryan Frederick, Jennifer Kavanagh, Matthew Lane, Trevor Johnston, Thomas S. Szayna, Jakub P. Hlavka, Stephen Watts, and Matthew Povlock, *U.S. Presence and the Incidence of Conflict*, Santa Monica, Calif.: RAND Corporation, RR-1906-A, 2018.

[38] Mearsheimer, 1983.

[39] Signorino and Tarar, 2006.

[40] Barry Blechman and Stephen S. Kaplan, *Force without War: U.S. Armed Forces as a Political Instrument*, Washington, D.C.: Brookings Institution Press, 1978; Frederick et al., 2020.

argued that "initiators of gray zone conflicts often possess local military dominance, which is crucial in deterring the target state from responding to ambiguous provocations by resorting to overt military force."[41] In a paper written for the U.S. Joint Chiefs of Staff, Daniel Goure of the Lexington Institute wrote that "Russia's ability to manage risk in the so-called gray zone is a function of its successful integration of all the instruments of state power. The Kremlin views conventional and nuclear forces as a means for managing risk."[42] A recent Center for Strategic and Budgetary Analyses report made very explicit the linkage between conventional military capability and the potential for Russian hostile measures in the northeastern Europe and so is worth quoting at length:

> U.S. and NATO ground forces could be "out-ranged and out-gunned" by Russian forces, offsetting the traditional superiority of U.S. and allied maneuver forces. This could provide Russia a decisive advantage in close combat, particularly since the traditional advantage of Allied airpower could be greatly reduced, at least initially, by Russian IADS [Integrated Air Defense System]. Collectively, these threats erode the credibility of NATO's ability to deter and defend against Russia [sic] aggression, including aggression at the sub-conventional level in areas covered by Russian area-denial systems. Should this erosion continue, Russia may become less wary of conducting gray zone operations against Poland and the Baltic states. Even if Russian leadership believes such actions could escalate, they may not be deterred from undertaking them if they are confident Russian forces could quickly prevail in a short and limited conventional engagement against NATO.[43]

The potential of forward military posture to deter hostile measures in competition is not a new insight, nor is it specific to contemporary so-called gray zone tactics. In an analysis of potential force drawdowns in Europe in the 1980s, for instance, a declassified Central Intelligence Agency memorandum warned that "moderate North African states—Egypt, Tunisia, and Morocco—would be concerned that a drawdown of U.S. forces in the Mediterranean would leave that region more vulnerable to Soviet and radical Arab influence. They would worry particularly that Libya would be even more active in fomenting subversion in the coming months."[44]

As discussed in the previous section, however, the very strength of forward-positioned forces as a deterrent against conventional war could actually increase the risk of malign activities below the level of armed conflict. When the United States deployed Terminal High Altitude Area Defense systems to the Republic of Korea, for instance, China used economic

---

[41] Hal Brands, "Paradoxes of the Gray Zone," blog post, Foreign Policy Research Institute, February 5, 2016.

[42] Daniel Goure, "Russian Strategic Intentions," in Nicole Peterson, ed., *Russian Strategic Intentions: A Strategic Multilayer Assessment (SMA)*, Washington, D.C.: Joint Chiefs of Staff, May 2019.

[43] Billy Fabian, Mark Gunzinger, Jan van Tol, Jacob Cohn, and Gillian Evans, *Strengthening the Defense of NATO's Eastern Frontier*, Washington, D.C.: Center for Strategic and Budgetary Analyses, 2019, pp. 13–14.

[44] Central Intelligence Agency, National Foreign Assessment Center, "Reactions to a Possible Shift of US Forces to the Persian Gulf/Indian Ocean Area," March 10, 1980.

coercion to attempt to force a change of policy in Seoul, even though the primary state the United States sought to deter was the Democratic People's Republic of Korea.[45] The deployment of U.S. and other NATO forces in eFP battalions in the Baltics has been accompanied by frequent Russian misinformation about these forces directed at the populations of the host countries and increased Russian aerial activity that is arguably designed to intimidate the Baltic states.[46] As discussed in Chapter One, some in the State Department feared that the Soviets would seek to impose costs on the United States for deploying intermediate-range missiles to Europe, potentially including an increased risk of proxy wars in other regions around the globe.

Activities

If the United States does not choose to position large numbers of forces overseas, it can attempt to signal its commitment and demonstrate its military capabilities through a variety of activities, including military assistance (materiel transfers and the training that normally accompanies major U.S. systems) and multilateral military exercises. Recent DoD documents suggest that the United States will, in fact, rely increasingly on such activities.[47] One recent Army study suggested that such activities were the *primary* instrument available for deterrence in Europe[48]

Some recent academic analysis supports the contention that such activities may provide important signals of defender commitment.[49] These activities can also increase the capabilities of local actors in ways that deter. Ukrainian officials, for instance, have repeatedly claimed that U.S. sales of Javelin antitank guided missiles to Ukraine have deterred attacks by Russian-led separatist forces in the Donbas region.[50]

There is inherently a higher degree of uncertainty associated with activities, however, than with forward-positioned forces. The monetary cost of such activities is lower than permanently stationing or deploying large numbers of forces abroad. Moreover, forces permanently positioned in an ally or partner country are constantly at risk if an adversary launches

---

[45] Ketian Vivian Zhang, "Chinese Non-Military Coercion—Tactics and Rationale," blog post, Brookings Institution, January 22, 2019.

[46] See, for instance, "NATO: Russia Targeted German Army with Fake News Campaign," *Deutsche Welle*, February 16, 2017; and Valerie Insinna, "British Air Force Charts a Rise in Russian Activity Around Baltic States," *Defense News*, July 18, 2019.

[47] Mark T. Esper, "Implementing the National Defense Strategy: A Year of Successes," July 2020, p. 8.

[48] R. Reed Anderson, Patrick J. Ellis, Antonio M. Paz, Kyle A. Reed, Lendy "Alamo" Renegar, and John T. Vaughan, *Strategic Landpower and a Resurgent Russia: An Operational Approach to Deterrence*, Carlisle, Penn.: Strategic Studies Institute and U.S. Army War College Press, May 2016, p. 121.

[49] McManus and Nieman, 2019.

[50] Jack Laurenson, "Russian Tank Crews Fear Ukraine's New Javelin Missiles, Says Poroshenko," *Kyiv Post*, January 16, 2019; and Joe Gould and Howard Altman, "Here's What You Need to Know About the U.S. Aid Package to Ukraine That Trump Delayed," *Defense News*, September 25, 2019.

an act of aggression against the host country; forces participating in intermittent activities are not. For both of these reasons, activities might provide a weaker signal of U.S. commitment to its allies and partners. Worse, small-scale activities, or those for which host countries impose substantial restrictions, might actually signal a lack of resolve, security consensus, or both among the United States and its allies and partners.[51]

Unless combined with permanently positioned forces, therefore, activities might be less effective at deterrence. And indeed, some studies have found that arms transfers and the training activities that accompany them provide poor signals of a state's willingness to defend its allies and partners. In one recent statistical analysis of this relationship, the authors found that

> the more heavily the protege relies on the defender for its arms imports, the less likely the defender is to go to war to protect the protege. This suggests that in many cases, a defender sends a lot of arms to its protege precisely when it does not expect to defend the protege if the protege is attacked. An implication of this is that neither a potential aggressor nor a protege should take high levels of defender-protege arms transfers as a credible indicator that the defender will fight to defend the protégé.[52]

Not only do activities have uncertain deterrence effects, they could also lead to increased malign activities. U.S. competitors have sometimes responded directly to U.S. arms sales and training or military exercises with increased malign measures. China, for instance, has

---

[51] Prior to the large-scale exercises planned for Defender 2020, for instance, some observers were scathing in their assessments of NATO multilateral military exercises as a deterrent against Russian aggression:

> [T]hese NATO exercises as they exist certainly do not, in and of themselves, contribute to deterring Russian aggression in any meaningful way. First, they are too small, largely lacking in heavy armor and artillery (where the Russians have a significant advantage), and do not typically involve all combat arms. Second, they do not fully engage the huge logistics train that would be required to move forces of sufficient size to halt a large-scale Russian attack through the Baltic states or Belarus. Further, the alliance persists in entertaining the fiction of forward deploying to fight the Russians in the Baltic region, when every serious study of that scenario indicates this would be militarily unsound unless large, heavy forces were already in place or nearby. Considerable thought has already been given to the enhancement of the U.S. Army's deterrence posture in Europe. But until these and other recommendations are fully implemented and exercised, pretending NATO can engage the Russians early in the Suwałki Gap or Estonia in a manner depicted in current exercises is a dangerous illusion, and to practice it is a waste of time at best (Ralph S. Clem, "NATO's Expanding Military Exercises Are Sending Risky Mixed Messages," *War on the Rocks*, October 10, 2017).

Although this assessment is particularly critical, others have pointed to the shortcomings of current exercises and other forms of security cooperation and have argued for more intensive measures. See, for example, Elisabeth Braw, "NATO Needs More Big Exercises, Too," *Defense News*, June 14, 2018; and Zalmay Khalilzad, "A Strategic Reset for NATO," *National Interest*, July 10, 2018.

[52] Signorino and Tarar, July 2006, p. 594. These results are consistent with those in James D. Fearon, "Signaling Versus the Balance of Power and Interests: An Empirical Test of a Crisis Bargaining Model," *Journal of Conflict Resolution*, Vol. 38, No. 2, June 1994; and Volker Krause, "Hazardous Weapons? Effects of Arms Transfers and Defense Pacts on Militarized Disputes, 1950–1995," *International Interactions*, Vol. 30, No. 4, 2004.

attempted to use economic coercion to force Taiwan to reverse decisions to buy U.S. military systems, such as F-16Vs.[53] Russia targeted Georgia with gas pipeline shut-offs, import bans, and other forms of economic coercion in part as a response to increasing Georgian military cooperation with the United States, including arms transfers, training, and military exercises.[54] North Korea has engaged in acts of military intimidation, such as missile test launches, as signaling devices that are intended to warn the United States and South Korea against undertaking joint military exercises.[55] None of these examples indicates that U.S. military activities are necessarily escalatory. In all of these cases, U.S. competitors might have acted even more aggressively in the absence of U.S. activities. However, these cases do suggest at least the possibility that U.S. military activities incite more hostile measures than they deter.[56]

Military activities can also lead to increased hostile measures indirectly, either through inadvertent escalation or by empowering third parties who might be more risk-accepting than the United States or its competitors. Unlike the forward positioning of U.S. forces, arms transfers and training can provide capabilities to other actors, potentially emboldening them to take aggressive action in some circumstances. Exercises, meanwhile, inject higher levels of uncertainty, sometimes concentrating much larger levels of force than usual near a competitor's borders—a potential source of mistakes and inadvertent escalation.[57]

Footprint

The deterrence literature devotes little attention to non-nuclear physical infrastructure, prepositioned equipment sets and stocks, and other elements of the *footprint* that are necessary to rapidly flow forces toward the front lines of a confrontation.[58] This neglect is unfortunate;

---

[53] Glenn Diesen, "From Economic War to Hot War? U.S., China and the End of Strategic Ambiguity over Taiwan," blog post, Valdai Discussion Club, August 29, 2019.

[54] These measures are discussed at greater length in Chapter Five.

[55] Joyce Lee and Hyonhee Shin, "North Korea's Kim Says Missile Launches Are Warning to U.S., South Korea over Drill: KCNA," Reuters, August 6, 2019.

[56] As discussed elsewhere, this increase in hostile measures might arise because U.S. military activities are seen by competitors as unnecessarily provocative—or they might occur because these activities successfully deter conventional aggression, leaving potential aggressors only with options below the level of armed conflict.

[57] In one recent RAND study of potential conflict scenarios in Europe, military exercises—especially snap exercises close to Russian-NATO borders—were one of the primary pathways leading to war. See Samuel Charap, Alice Lynch, John J. Drennan, Dara Massicot, and Giacomo Paoli, *A New Approach to Conventional Arms Control in Europe: Addressing the Security Challenges of the 21st Century*, Santa Monica, Calif.: RAND Corporation, RR-4346, 2020.

[58] In part, this gap in the literature could be because of data concerns; it is extremely difficult to aggregate data on footprint that are distinct from actual force presence, especially at an unclassified level and over long periods of time.

specific case studies suggest that a well-developed footprint can play a critical role in crisis or "immediate" deterrence.[59]

Russian decisionmakers, however, do not overlook the importance of footprint. Russian official defense documents consistently identify the expansion of NATO infrastructure in close proximity to Russian borders as one of Russia's top-tier national security threats, along with U.S. ballistic missile defense, conventional prompt global strike, and space weapons.[60] According to one recent RAND study that examined escalation scenarios with Russia, "modifications designed to improve reception and onward movement in Europe (for example, hardening of military ports and large NATO airfields, designating main deployment routes and improving bridges or roads along those routes, and expanding logistical hubs to support eastward movement toward the Russian and Belarusian borders) are of particular concern."[61]

From a deterrence perspective, the critical problem with improvements to infrastructure and other elements of a military footprint (distinct from any forward-stationed forces that they support) is that they can interject greater uncertainty into strategic calculations, at least relative to forward-positioned forces. From a competitor's standpoint, a sizeable military footprint allows for a more rapid flow of forces, including forces that might be used for an act of aggression rather than defense. They do not, however, precommit the United States (or other defender) to sending in reinforcements if the ally or partner is attacked. In this way, military footprint could provide a less reliable deterrent than would maintaining forces in the path of likely attack while still threatening a competitor.

The greater levels of uncertainty associated with infrastructure is highlighted by Saddam Hussein's behavior in the Persian Gulf. The United States had invested considerable resources during the latter part of the Cold War in building out an enormous military infrastructure in the Persian Gulf to defend against potential Soviet aggression. This infrastructure by itself, however, was not enough to convince Saddam Hussein that the United States would defend Kuwait if he attacked it. On the other hand, the presence of this infrastructure made possible the surge of U.S. forces in Operation Vigilant Warrior that could have deterred a subsequent act of aggression by Saddam.[62]

Agreements

We divide military agreements into two principal types: alliance treaties and other military agreements, such as SOFAs, agreements to support military contracting, and similar arrangements. In some ways, the deterrent value of these agreements parallels the distinc-

---

[59] See, for example, Frederick et al., 2020, Chapter Six.

[60] Ministry of Defense of the Russian Federation, *Military Doctrine of the Russian Federation*, Pr-2976, Moscow, December 25, 2014; Ministry of Defense of the Russian Federation, *National Security Strategy*, Presidential Edict 683, December 31, 2015.

[61] Charap et al., 2020, p. 29.

[62] Frederick et al., 2020.

tion between the forward-positioning of U.S. military forces on the one hand and activities and footprint on the other. Alliances represent a standing commitment in which the United States (or another ally) indefinitely places its credibility at risk should it fail to honor its pledges to defend its allies.[63] Other military agreements, in contrast, are typically much more contingent. They provide a legal basis for certain U.S. military activities if and when they occur, or they facilitate logistical and sustainment support for U.S. forces when present. When combined with alliances, such agreements may further bolster credibility by showing concrete preparations for military actions. In the absence of alliances, such agreements might show some degree of commitment by the United States to its partners and could support the rapid introduction of U.S. military capabilities into the partner country—if the United States chooses to act. But the uncertain nature of the U.S. commitment to defend the partners with whom it brokers such agreements is likely to provide less deterrent value than continuous commitments, such as alliances of forward-basing troops.

Of course, as with other instruments of deterrence, alliances and other military agreements potentially can lead to higher levels of conflict. Agreements can either threaten rivals to the members of an alliance (or other agreement) or embolden the signatories of a military agreement.[64]

In the case of contemporary Europe, there have been relatively consistent patterns between military agreements and armed conflict in the recent past, although there is more uncertainty about the future. Russia appears to have found the U.S. commitment to the NATO alliance highly credible.[65] Some observers nonetheless fear that changes in U.S. or Russian political leadership could create greater uncertainty over the strength of that commitment in the future and thus believe that a substantial forward U.S. troop presence is necessary for deterrence.[66] Agreements short of alliances have clearly failed to deter and may have provoked conflict in at least some instances. The Georgian Membership Action Plan (MAP) with NATO and subsequent Russo-Georgian War is the most notable instance, but the alleged Russian-backed coup attempt in Montenegro before its accession to NATO might be another. It is harder to determine whether other military agreements—such as contracts for civilian

---

[63] Fearon, 1997; James D. Morrow, "Alliances: Why Write Them Down?" *Annual Review of Political Science*, Vol. 3, June 2000; Jesse C. Johnson and Brett Ashley Leeds, "Defense Pacts: A Prescription for Peace?" *Foreign Policy Analysis*, Vol. 7, No. 1, January 2011.

[64] Morrow finds that the escalatory or de-escalatory effects of military alliances are contingent on contextual factors. See James D. Morrow, "When Do Defensive Alliances Provoke Rather Than Deter?" *Journal of Politics*, Vol. 79, No. 1, January 2017. Brett Benson makes an important distinction between unconditional alliance commitments and those that promise support only if an ally is attacked; see Brett V. Benson, "Unpacking Alliances: Deterrent and Compellent Alliances and Their Relationship with Conflict, 1816–2000," *Journal of Politics*, Vol. 73, No. 4, October 2011.

[65] Bryan Frederick, Matthew Povlock, Stephen Watts, Miranda Priebe, and Edward Geist, *Assessing Russian Reactions to U.S. and NATO Posture Enhancements*, Santa Monica, Calif.: RAND Corporation, RR-1879-AF, 2017.

[66] Shlapak and Johnson, 2016.

transport or provision of jet fuel and other stocks necessary to fight a large-scale war—help to reinforce the deterrent effects of alliances or another deterrent signal.

Conclusion

All of the elements of forward posture reviewed in this section have the potential to deter armed aggression or to provoke escalation. Deterrence theory generally suggests that the more "automatically" a particular mechanism triggers a response to an act of armed aggression, the more likely it is to deter. Thus, stationing forces in the line of a likely attack are a particularly strong deterrent, as is staking a country's international reputation to defending other states through an alliance treaty. More-contingent mechanisms—such as demonstrating capabilities and some degree of commitment through multilateral military exercises or

TABLE 3.1

Summary of Propositions on Deterrence and Escalation

Element of Forward Posture	Deterrent Logic	Escalatory Logic
	All elements of posture, even if they deter armed conflict, could lead to escalation of malign activities in competition as competitors either seek to force the reduction of capabilities that they perceive to be threatening or seek to gain competitive advantage.	
Forces	• Relatively strong signal of commitment • Could provide important capabilities to deny competitors their objectives	• Can be perceived as either a threat of direct attack or an attempt at armed intimidation • Capabilities at the level of armed conflict could displace aggression to level of competition
Activities	• Some signal of commitment, although weaker than forward-positioned forces • Can strengthen allied or partner capabilities	• Exercises introduce greater uncertainty because of fluctuating force levels • Activities could embolden allies or partners by strengthening their capabilities through materiel transfers and training
Footprint	• Provides some signal of commitment, although weaker than forces • Could provide opportunity to introduce capabilities as needed, although time to reinforcement attenuates these effects	• Capabilities for rapid reinforcement introduce greater uncertainty about future U.S. force levels
Agreements	• Alliances provide relatively strong signal of commitment by putting defender's reputation at risk • Other agreements provide weaker signals than alliances • Could provide opportunity to introduce capabilities as needed, although time to reinforcement attenuates these effects	• Agreements can embolden allies or partners by perceived U.S. commitment

overseas military footprint—have less deterrent value, although they might be no less likely to provoke a hostile reaction from competitors. These propositions about the potential effects of forward posture are summarized in Table 3.1. The key question for this report—and the subject of the following chapters—is whether these same patterns hold true for hostile measures short of armed conflict.

How Intervening Factors Deter and Provoke

The elements of posture and their specific characteristics influence whether they play an escalatory or de-escalatory role. In this section, we briefly discuss three such characteristics or intervening factors—continuity, proximity, and capability—that prior analyses of international relations generally and Russia specifically have suggested are particularly influential.

Continuity

Although large changes in forward posture can send a particularly strong signal of U.S. commitment and can provide new capabilities in theater, they can also be particularly destabilizing as the U.S. competitor attempts to interpret and adjust to a rapidly changing situation. This destabilizing potential may be particularly strong when new capabilities (as opposed to only agreements) are introduced into a theater.[67] In general, deterrence theory suggests that predictability contributes to stable deterrence, while uncertainty tends to be destabilizing.

Proximity

There is some debate about the consequences of geographic proximity. For those who believe that deterrence requires the ability to deny a potential adversary the opportunity to launch a successful fait accompli, it may be essential for U.S. military capabilities to be positioned as far forward (toward areas that are vulnerable to adversary attack) as possible.[68] On the other hand, such geographic proximity has a high likelihood of threatening potential adversaries and greatly increases the risk of "friction" or inadvertent escalation.[69] In a recent RAND study of potential inadvertent escalation in Europe, geographic proximity played a major

---

[67] The U.S. Deterrence Operations Joint Operating Concept, for instance, warns, "Without forward presence, a U.S. decision to deploy major combat forces to a region in anticipation of (or in response to) adversary coercion or aggression could be seen as a more threatening American response than the alert or reinforcement of forward-based forces" (Joint Chiefs of Staff, *Deterrence Operations Joint Operating Concept*, version 2.0, Washington, D.C.: U.S. Department of Defense, 2006, pp. 34–35). These escalatory risks and their implications for the U.S. military concept of DFE are discussed at greater length in the concluding chapter of this report.

[68] Mearsheimer, 1983, is perhaps the strongest statement of this perspective.

[69] Barry R. Posen, "Crisis Stability and Conventional Arms Control," *Daedalus*, Vol. 120, No. 1, Winter 1991.

role in the most escalatory scenarios.[70] Other recent RAND studies found that the deterrent effects of U.S. forces appeared to be most consistent when they were stationed near—but not necessarily in—the countries to be defended.[71]

Capability

Different military capabilities have different implications for deterrence and escalation. Scholars have long observed that capabilities that provide first-strike advantages are particularly likely to lead to inadvertent escalation: If two rival states fear that a war is likely to be decided in the initial phases, they might feel that they have no choice but to take preemptive action when they see their rival undertaking an activity that looks like preparation for war.[72] A variety of evolving military capabilities—including long-range precision strike, hypersonic weapons, and cyber weapons—all could be used to deal devastating damage to an adversary's ISR capabilities and command and control structure in a surprise attack and, thus, could pose a particularly high risk of inadvertent escalation.[73] And indeed, Russian official documents and statements have highlighted several of these capabilities as among the greatest threats to Russian security. For example, in 2013, Russian Deputy Foreign Minister Sergei Ryabkov warned of the escalatory nature of conventional prompt global strike: "If we are talking about existing ballistic carriers with conventional equipment, it is clearly the path to the escalation of the conflict with the hardest, in fact, apocalyptic consequences."[74] More recently, in its "Basic Principles of State Policy of the Russian Federation on Nuclear Deterrence," released in June 2020, Russia stated, "The main military risks that might evolve into military threats (threats of aggression) to the Russian Federation . . . and that are to be neutralized by implementation of nuclear deterrence" included deployment "of missile defense systems and means, medium- and shorter-range cruise and ballistic missiles, non-nuclear high-precision and hypersonic weapons, strike unmanned aerial vehicles, and directed energy weapons."[75]

Of course, escalation in competition works differently than in armed conflict. Positional advantage in competition typically accumulates slowly, over many years, rather than being

---

[70] Charap et al., 2020.

[71] O'Mahony et al., 2018; and Frederick et al., 2020.

[72] Charles L. Glaser and Chaim Kaufmann, "What is the Offense-Defense Balance and Can We Measure It?" *International Security*, Vol. 22, No. 4, Spring 1998.

[73] The independent escalatory role of these new technologies, however, should not be overstated. They more likely exacerbate underlying dynamics than serve as independent sources of inadvertent escalation. See Caitlin Talmadge, "Emerging Technology and Intra-War Escalation Risks: Evidence from the Cold War, Implications for Today," *Journal of Strategic Studies*, Vol. 42, No. 6, 2019.

[74] Konstantin Bogdanov, "Should Russia Fear the U.S. 'Prompt Global Strike'?" *Russia Beyond the Headlines*, December 16, 2013.

[75] Ministry of Foreign Affairs of the Russian Federation, "On Basic Principles of State Policy of the Russian Federation on Nuclear Deterrence," Decree of the President of the Russian Federation No. 355, June 2, 2020.

seized in a single strike.[76] Many capabilities required for this sort of years-long competition—such as improved ISR and advisors and trainers—may pose little or no risk of a devastating preemptive strike and thus are not a threat to strategic stability. To the extent that forward posture helps to deter malign activities by neutralizing fears of military intimidation and acting as a military "backstop" to other instruments of national power, however, it must be a posture that is capable of fighting and winning wars. Consequently, even forward posture intended primarily to deter malign activities below the level of armed conflict can pose the same risk of escalation as a posture designed primarily to deter armed conflict.

In support of its multi-domain operations vision, the Army plans to field the precision strike missile (PrSM), which has a range of approximately 500 km.[77] Several developmental programs reportedly seek to provide the Army with long range precision fires (LRPF) at 1,000 to 2,500 km or beyond.[78] This includes hypersonic missiles, whose advancements in speed and maneuverability will make them extremely difficult to defend against.

To the extent that physical proximity is provocative and/or increases the risk of inadvertent escalation, positioning LRPF in the European theater has the potential to be destabilizing. Figure 3.1 demonstrates the ever-longer ranges that will complicate efforts to position field artillery brigades (FAB) or LRPF held at echelons above the brigade level. The squares represent sensitive Russian locations. The concentric circles indicate 500-, 1,000-, and 2,500-km ranges for missiles based in Grafenwoehr, Germany, the U.S. Army's training hub in Europe and currently home to the 41st FAB, which was activated in 2018 and now includes three Multiple Launch Rocket Systems (MLRS) battalions in Europe.[79] Because LRPF remains in a developmental state, its impact on escalation dynamics—and particularly any effects in competition—has been underexplored.[80] However, the stationing of such systems in Europe appears likely to trigger Russian hostile measures designed to weaken alliance cohesion, impose costs on the host nations, and more generally to signal Russia's hostility to these deployments. Russia has reacted in similar ways to other actions that it saw as

---

[76] Joint Doctrine Note 1-19, 2019.

[77] The original requirement was technically for 499 km to enable compliance with the now-defunct INF Treaty. A follow-on version might provide a somewhat longer-range capability (Kyle Rempfer and Joe Gould, "U.S. Army Completes Third Test of Lockheed's Precision Strike Missile," *Defense News*, April 30, 2020).

[78] For an overview, see Sydney J. Freedberg, Jr., "Army Says Long Range Missiles Will Help Air Force, Not Compete," *Breaking Defense*, July 16, 2020. A ground-launched version of the Tomahawk land-attack missile is also possible (Joseph Trevitchick, "Marines Set to Be the First to Bring Back Land-Based Tomahawk Missiles Post-INF Treaty," *The Warzone*, March 5, 2020).

[79] MLRS currently fires cruise missiles with ranges of up to 300 km, but will be capable of firing the 500 km PrSM (Lacey Justinger, "41st Field Artillery Brigade Returns to Germany," blog post, U.S. Army, November 30, 2018).

[80] For a viewpoint that supports LRPF, see Luis Simón and Alexander Lanoszka, "The Post-INF European Missile Balance: Thinking About NATO's Deterrence Strategy," *Texas National Security Review*, Vol. 3, No. 3, Summer 2020.

FIGURE 3.1

Depiction of Notional LRPF Ranges from Grafenwoehr

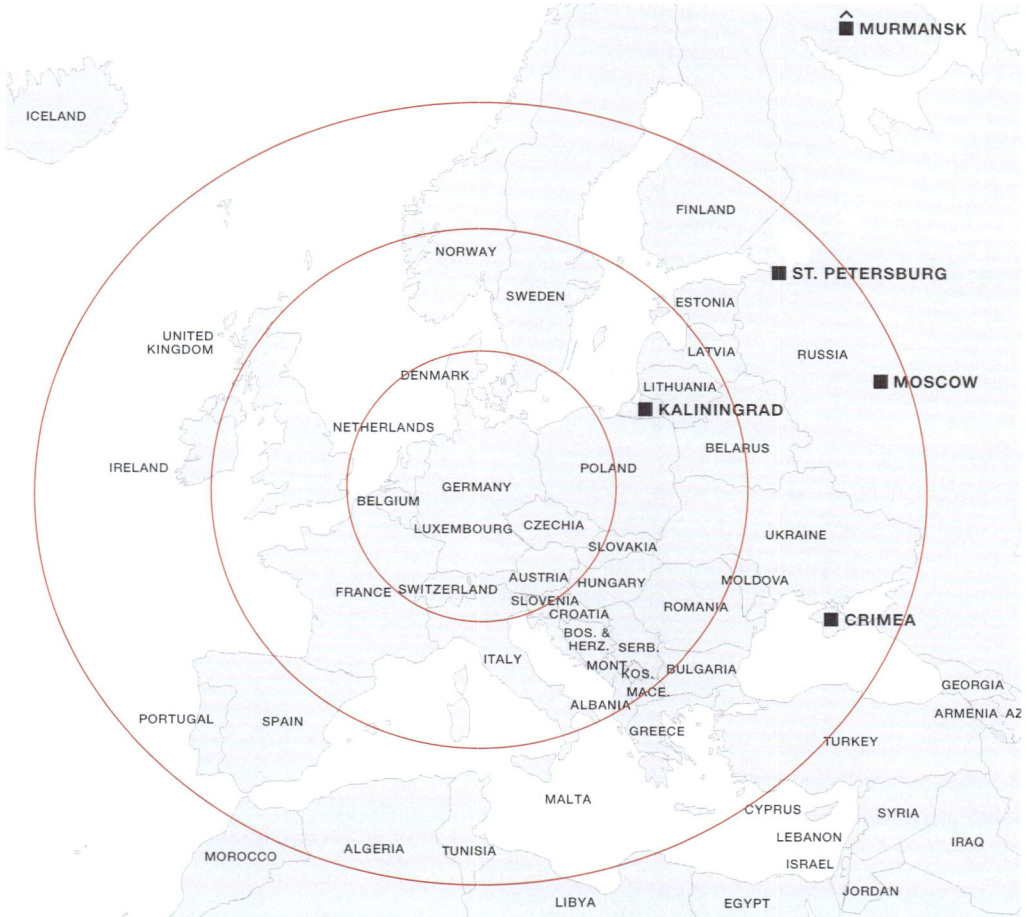

NOTE: The positioning of systems with notional ranges (shown with circular rings) does not, in itself, mean that the system can successfully prosecute LRPF. ISR and targeting would be required; this is one of several considerations that makes range rings suitable for illustrative purposes only.

highly threatening (e.g., the potential extension of such Western international organizations as NATO and the European Union to Georgia and Ukraine), and the Soviet Union reacted to very similar deployments of U.S. missiles in the 1980s (the so-called Euromissiles) with a variety of hostile measures. Beyond the risk of escalation within the realm of competition, these systems also pose risks of inadvertent escalation to armed conflict. These themes will be explored in Chapter Five in a case study on the Euromissile crisis.

TABLE 3.2
Summary of Propositions on Intervening Factors

Intervening Factors	Deterrent Logic	Escalatory Logic
Continuity	• Continuous presence reduces uncertainty and therefore strengthens deterrence	• Large, rapid changes in posture could be destabilizing
Proximity	• Close proximity might prevent faits accompli	• Close proximity could be seen as threatening, triggering countermeasures • Close proximity increases opportunities for friction, inadvertent escalation
Capability	• Warfighting ability deters military intimidation, provides a backstop to other instruments of national power	• Capabilities that provide first-strike advantage could be destabilizing

Conclusion

Each of the factors discussed in this section—capability, proximity, and continuity—has the potential to either offset or amplify the risks and rewards of forward posture. These conditioning effects are summarized in Table 3.2.

Summary of Framework for Understanding Deterrence and Escalation

As the discussion in this chapter has made clear, there is considerable debate within the policy community and among deterrence theorists about how to deter armed conflict. When attempting to understand what deters hostile measures in strategic competition—a topic that has been much less studied—there is even less consensus.

One of the reasons for the lack of consensus within the defense community is the complexity of interrelated factors that determine whether a given element of forward posture is likely to be escalatory or deterring. Figure 3.2 summarizes the factors discussed in this chapter. Each of the blocks in the figure represents a factor that can increase or decrease. Thus, an increase in any of the elements of posture could lead to an increase in any of the hostile measures in the figure (and escalatory outcome) or a decrease (a deterrent outcome).

Because deterrence takes place within the minds of competitors or potential adversaries, it can be difficult to determine in any specific instance whether deterrence was successful. In different contexts and with different actors, any of the logics summarized in Tables 3.1 and 3.2 might be accurate. If U.S. decisionmakers had perfect information on the thought processes of the leaders of competitor states, it might be possible to know which logic was operative for a particular policy decision. Even in the present, however, they lack perfect information. When decisionmakers are trying to anticipate the future consequences of their decisions, looking out as much as 15 years in the future, they have even less information. It

FIGURE 3.2

Summary of Analytic Framework for Understanding Deterrence in Competition

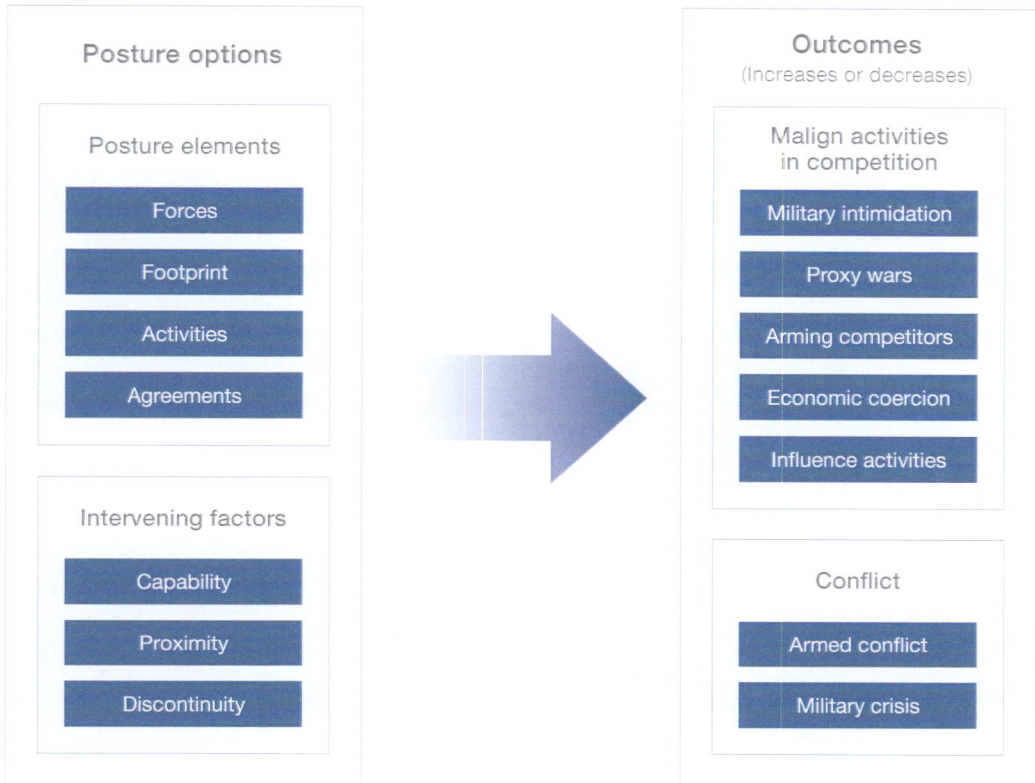

is therefore important to understand general trends to provide a baseline set of expectations. The following section details the strategy by which we assess these various propositions.

Research Design: Evaluating Propositions on Deterrence and Escalation in Competition

The discussion in this chapter has hinted at some of the reasons why it can be extremely difficult to determine the effects of military power, and forward posture specifically, on strategic competition. Two challenges in particular are worth highlighting because they influence the plan of research documented in the remainder of this report.

First, strategic competition is largely a contest for influence among third parties; that is, countries other than the two primary competitors. But these third parties have their own strengths, weaknesses, and agendas, which can obscure action-reaction cycles between the two main competitors. The State Department memo on Soviet reactions to U.S. INF deployments highlighted in Chapter One emphasized this dynamic. Any action requires both motive and opportunity. But "Soviet opportunities," the memo noted, "are defined, above all, by local circumstances."[81] Thus, it is entirely possible that U.S. posture changes provoked the Soviets (a change in motive), but without an appropriate opportunity to impose costs on the United States, the Soviets would not act. This inaction, in turn, could be misread by U.S. decisionmakers, at least some of whom might have interpreted inaction as the result of successful U.S. deterrence rather than as a (potentially temporary) lack of opportunity. As discussed in this chapter, the inverse is also true. Just as third parties can forestall competitor reactions by not providing an opportunity for action, they can also trigger competitor actions where the competitor would have preferred not to act.

Second, even if appropriate opportunities present themselves, action-reaction cycles between competitors might not be tightly linked. That is, competitors might not respond to provocations in a clear tit-for-tat manner. Instead, perceived acts of aggression in the competition space could slowly accumulate. Each action by itself may only marginally shift a competitor's calculus toward either escalation or de-escalation. Again, the State Department memo cited in Chapter One made this logic clear. The Policy Planning Staff warned, "Soviet assessments of their opportunities could conceivably be affected *at the margin*. On any occasion where they face a choice between being more or less constructive, the Soviet leadership may lean toward even less cooperation with us."[82] A specific change in U.S. posture could have a tangible effect on the decisionmaking calculus of its competitors, but that effect might be imperceptible. Indeed, because any one U.S. action is only one factor among many influencing a competitor's decisionmaking process, competitor decisionmakers themselves might not even be aware of how their perceptions were influenced by specific U.S. actions. But over time, the effects could become noticeable as opportunities for competitor aggression accumulate or as the effects of multiple U.S. posture changes or other actions accumulate.[83]

This understanding of action-reaction cycles as (1) a three-way (or more) competition between the United States, Russia, and other countries and (2) the slow accumulation of marginal effects has two important implications for how we analyze deterrence and escalation dynamics, which are as follows:

- The consequences of changes in U.S. posture should be understood probabilistically. Typically, a posture shift will not by itself cause a reaction from a competitor. Instead, it will be one factor among many that influences an adversary's reaction. Even a relatively small change in the probability of escalation or de-escalation for any given instance,

---

[81] Bosworth, 1983.

[82] Bosworth, 1983, emphasis added.

[83] The Iran crisis of 1946 illustrates these dynamics. Although many observers—both at the time and later—saw U.S. actions during the crisis as a triumph of deterrence, others have noted that the Soviet perception that the United States acted unfairly and aggressively in Iran helped to set the stage for later confrontations in Europe. See Chapter Five for more details.

however, can have important consequences over time as opportunities for crises accumulate.

- The consequences of a change in U.S. posture might not be proximate in time or space to the posture change itself. The State Department memo, for instance, warned that Soviet reactions to U.S. posture changes in Europe might manifest in southern Africa or Central America. These more-distant consequences are more difficult to detect, usually requiring intensive analysis of particular cases.

Statistics are a useful tool for understanding changes in probabilities over large numbers of interactions. Consequently, in the following chapter (Chapter Four), we use statistical analysis to evaluate patterns of escalation and de-escalation across decades of strategic competition between the United States, Russia (and previously the Soviet Union), and other competitors. Besides its utility in understanding changes in probabilities, statistical analysis offers at least some insight into the large number of cases for which we do not have access to archival records that would shed light on how decisionmakers made their decisions about whether to undertake malign activities in the competition space.

In Chapter Five, we use case studies to complement the statistical analysis. Case studies can increase our confidence that the patterns that are revealed through statistical analysis are actually causal—that is, that competitors' observed actions were responses to U.S. posture rather than simply being correlated with it. (Alternatively, if they are not consistent with statistical results, they can offer important caveats or other limitations to the quantitative analysis.) They can also be used to evaluate whether competitors respond in places and at points in time far removed from the initial posture change precipitating a reaction.

Our analyses in Chapters Four and Five begin in the period immediately after World War II and extend nearly to the present.[84] Past patterns can provide a useful baseline by which to judge the likely consequences of future policy decisions. They do not, however, substitute for weighing the particulars of a specific case. Policymakers should approach a policy decision with an understanding of the historical probabilities of success or failure, then adjust their expectations about the outcomes of the policy decision at hand based on specific contextual factors.[85] In Chapter Six, we detail the results of a scenario analysis that we conducted in an effort to better understand the implications of our historical analysis for future U.S. posture decisions in Europe and its immediate periphery. The scenarios were chosen to stress different aspects of deterrence and escalation dynamics discussed in this chapter, and they were evaluated both by applying lessons from our historical analysis and through expert elicitation. The results of the empirical analyses in Chapters Four through Six then inform our conclusions and recommendations in Chapter Seven.

---

[84] Our statistical analyses typically extend to 2008–2010, depending on the model. One of our case studies focuses on 2014–2019.

[85] Daniel Kahneman, *Thinking, Fast and Slow*, New York: Farrar, Straus, and Giroux, 2011.

CHAPTER FOUR

Quantitative Historical Analysis

Introduction

In this chapter, we describe our statistical models for evaluating the role of U.S. posture in escalating or reducing competitive state behavior. The purpose of this chapter is to uncover patterns of behavior in the historical record. Understanding how and when competitive responses recur repeatedly over time will allow us to set expectations for future behavior.

The first half of this chapter provides an overview of the research design for our statistical analysis, provides sources of data for key concepts, and briefly explains our modeling strategy.

The second half of this chapter summarizes the results of our statistical analysis, which examines U.S. and adversary behavior toward all potential U.S. partners in the post–World War II time frame.[1] We find evidence of the following:

- U.S. forces are most likely to be associated with a deterrent effect on competitor behavior, although frontline nations are sometimes targeted for malign activities in response to the presence of U.S. forces.
- U.S. agreements are associated with deterring violent competitor responses.
- U.S. activities are associated with greater levels of escalation by competitors.
- Proximity is associated with increased hostile measures: U.S. forward posture located close to a competitor or adversary is associated with greater escalatory risk.
- Discontinuity is also associated with increased hostile measures: U.S. forward posture that changes rapidly is associated with greater escalatory risk.
- Deterrence appears to be enhanced by forward posture that is structured in such a way as to provide a physical or geographic buffer area in the immediate vicinity of a competitor and that is persistent and predictable.

---

[1] The largest samples in our data run from 1946 through 2010. Missing data preclude us from examining the time before or after these markers. In addition, some data are missing for cases within this time frame.

This overview of our statistical research design and findings was written for a general audience. A more-detailed, technical explanation of the analysis and results can be found in Appendix B of this report.

Analytic Framework

To identify broad historical patterns, we translated key aspects of the deterrence relationship into the following quantifiable factors or variables:

- the behavior that is to be deterred (in social-science terms, the *dependent variables*)
- the types of U.S. forward posture that are intended to deter (the *independent variables*)
- important intervening factors that condition the relationship between U.S. forward posture and the behavior to be deterred (the *intervening variables*)
- contextual factors that might also influence the incidence of the behavior that the United States seeks to deter (the *control variables*).

In the following four sections, we explain how we quantified these variables and our sources of data for each.

The fifth section reviews our statistical modeling strategy. The type of statistical analysis we conducted cannot, by itself, demonstrate causal relationships; it can identify patterns between U.S. forward posture and the behavior that the United States seeks to deter, but it cannot clearly demonstrate that U.S. forward posture was the cause of the observed changes in competitors' behavior. Our modeling strategy discusses (in general terms) the types of statistical analysis employed and ways in which we tried to rule out alternative explanations for the patterns we observed. Despite the many strategies that we employed to screen for spurious relationships, we cannot be certain that the relationships were causal through this statistical analysis. We can, however, rule out many alternative explanations for the patterns observed, and we can further strengthen our confidence in our results through the qualitative analysis of specific cases that we discuss in Chapter Five.

What Is to Be Deterred: Malign Activities in Competition (Dependent Variables)

The United States seeks to prevent or deter competitor states from targeting U.S. allies and partners with a variety of hostile measures in competition. Our models seek to identify patterns between changes in U.S. posture and the incidence of these hostile measures. In this chapter, we examine the relationships between U.S. posture changes and all potential competitors' behavior; that is, any state that might reasonably target a U.S. ally or partner with hostile measures, including great powers and states contiguous to a U.S. ally or partner.[2]

The types of behavior to be deterred are the same as those in Chapter Three with two exceptions. First, we are unable to assess the effects of various force posture options on influence operations, misinformation, and electoral interference over time because of data limitations.[3] Second, in addition to considering competitors' use of military intimidation, we also consider military responses that escalate to include the use of military force to better understand the full range of escalation dynamics. Data for the outcomes of interest were derived from several sources:

- **Competitive arms transfers:** To assess competitive arms transfers, we measure the aggregate level of arms that all states directly relevant to the U.S. ally or partner import from sources other than the United States. We rely on the widely used Arms Transfer Database of the Stockholm International Peace Research Institute (SIPRI) to measure this outcome.[4] Our analyses include arms transfer data from 1950 to 2010.
- **Economic coercion:** To measure economic coercion used against U.S. allies and partners, we used data on economic sanctions from the Threat and Imposition of Economic Sanctions (TIES) dataset.[5] In this data set, *sanctions* are defined as actions that countries

---

[2] Academic studies of international relations refer to a pair of states as *politically relevant* if one of the states in the pair is a major power or if the two states share a border (Douglas Lemke and William Reed, "The Relevance of Politically Relevant Dyads," *Journal of Conflict Resolution*, Vol. 45, No. 1, February 2001). In Appendix B, we expand on our analysis, examining particular subgroups of potential competitors, including U.S. rivals, the rivals of the United States' allies and partners, and specifically Russia and the Soviet Union. There are advantages and disadvantages to looking at these narrower subgroups of states. On the one hand, they are the states that the United States most seeks to deter, so they are most relevant from a policy perspective. On the other hand, by reducing the number of states that we examine, we have fewer cases for statistical analysis, making it more likely that a small number of sui generis events might influence particular findings. Moreover, by focusing only on these states, we are missing many instances of indirect pathways to escalation—that is, ways in which the United States' forward posture influences third-party states, which might react in ways that later draw in U.S. rivals or Russia specifically. Fortunately, the broad themes that emerge from our research are consistent across these different samples of states. Readers who wish to better understand certain exceptions to those broad themes should consult Appendix B for an in-depth discussion of the results broken down by each of these types of states (or, in statistical terms, samples).

[3] Existing data on electoral interference are limited to the Soviet Union and the United States, and contain very few cases (Dov H. Levin, "When the Great Power Gets a Vote: The Effects of Great Power Electoral Interventions on Election Results," *International Studies Quarterly*, Vol. 60, No. 2, June 2016).

[4] SIPRI measures arms transfers in units called *trend-indicator value* (TIV). The TIV is calculated either from the production cost of the weapon, or, if it is not known, through a comparison with core weapons based on size and performance characteristics; type of electronics, loading or unloading arrangements, engine, tracks or wheels, armament and materials; and the year in which the weapon was produced. For details, see Stockholm International Peace Research Institute, "SIPRI Arms Transfers Database," webpage, undated.

[5] T. Clifton Morgan, Navin Bapat, and Yoshiharu Kobayashi, "Threat and Imposition of Economic Sanctions 1945–2005: Updating the TIES Dataset," *Conflict Management and Peace Science*, Vol. 31, No. 5, 2014.

take to limit or end their economic relations with a target country in an effort to persuade that country to change its policies. Our statistical models examine both the threat of sanctions (such as through verbal statements or draft legislation) and those that are actually imposed (through such actions as embargos, import and export restrictions, blockades, asset freezing, aid termination, travel bans, and the suspension of existing agreements). The data range from 1946 to 2005 in our models.

- **Proxy warfare:** Our measure of rebel proxy support captures the provision of military support to a violent nonstate actor in the midst of an ongoing intrastate conflict from 1946 through 2010.[6] In each model, we consider the likelihood that a potential competitor will provide support to a proxy group within a U.S. partner state.

- **Military intimidation and the direct use of force:** We account for military intimidation and the use of force using the initiation of a Militarized Interstate Dispute (MID). MIDs comprise historical cases of conflict in which the threat, display, or use of military force short of war by one state is explicitly directed toward the government, official representatives, official forces, property, or territory of another state.[7] We derive two competitor responses from these data. First, we capture military intimidation using low-hostility MIDs. *Low-hostility MIDs* include all cases involving threat or display of force, such as troop mobilization or the fortification of a border. Second, we capture the use of military force using high-hostility MIDs. *High-hostility MIDs* include cases of territorial occupation or seizure, blockades, and minor military clashes. MID data range from 1946 to 2010 in our analyses.

Types of U.S. Military Posture (Independent Variables)

We seek to understand whether and how potential competitors respond to U.S. forward military posture decisions. As we have discussed previously, forward military posture is determined by the *forces* that the United States stations abroad, the *footprint* that supports these forces (that is, the logistics and sustainment arrangements for these forces and potential follow-on forces), the *activities* that these forces conduct (in particular, security cooperation activities with U.S. allies and partners), and the *agreements* that permit their presence.[8]

---

[6] Our measure of state military support for violent nonstate actors is drawn from previous work that synthesized multiple databases to provide a more complete and reliable measure (Stephen Watts, Bryan Frederick, Nathan Chandler, Mark Toukan, Christian Curriden, Erik Mueller, Edward Geist, Ariane Tabatabai, Sara Plana, Brandon Corbin, and Jeffrey Martini, *Proxy Warfare as a Tool of Strategic Competition: State Motivations and Future Trends*, Santa Monica, Calif.: RAND Corporation, 2020, Not available to the general public).

[7] Glenn Palmer, Vito D'Orazio, Michael R. Kenwick, and Roseanne W. McManus, "Updating the Militarized Interstate Dispute Data: A Response to Gibler, Miller, and Little," *International Studies Quarterly*, Vol. 64, No. 2, June 2020.

[8] Although U.S. posture choices often come in bundles, we examine them separately. Therefore, we cannot speak to multidimensional patterns.

Unfortunately, we do not have accurate and complete quantitative data for all of these aspects of military posture. Specifically, we have insufficient data to capture the changing U.S. footprint over time. As a result, our measures of U.S. military posture (our *independent variables*) capture the three other types of U.S. military posture. For each indicator, we examine U.S. posture toward the partner one year prior to the outcome of interest.[9] The types of posture are as follows:

- **Forces (in-country and in-region):** We measure U.S. forces using data from the Pentagon's Defense Manpower Data Center (DMDC). The DMDC provides data on the number and service of military U.S. personnel stationed overseas.[10] These data run from 1948 to 2010 in our sample. Building on prior RAND work, we measure U.S. forces in two ways. The first measure captures all personnel positioned within the borders of a U.S. ally or partner. The second measure captures those troops that are outside a given state but within the same region.[11] We refer to these two types of forces as *in-country forces* (meaning the U.S. personnel are in the country that the statistical analysis is examining for changes in hostile measures) and the second as *in-region forces* (meaning that U.S. forces are stationed in the same region as the country of interest in the analysis but not in that country itself).
- **Activities:** We capture U.S. security cooperation activities using two measures: arms transfers and multilateral military exercises. As with the measure of "competitive arms transfers," our measure of arms imports from the United States comes from SIPRI data. The use of this measure is intended to capture not only the materiel transfer but the training and related activities that usually accompany U.S. arms transfers. These data run from 1950 to 2010 in our sample. Our data on multilateral military exercises come from a data set compiled by the political scientist Vito D'Orazio from an examination of major news sources between 1970 and 2010.[12] Although the SIPRI data provide a mea-

---

[9] This is what is referred to as a *lagged* independent variable. In general, we examine the relationship between our outcome of interest and U.S. posture in the prior year (a one-year lag). For models on proxy support, we examine the year before the episode of conflict begins. For potential U.S. partners, we examine all states that are politically relevant to the United States.

[10] We make use of these data as collected in previous RAND research (O'Mahony et al., 2018; Frederick et al., 2020). We adjust each measure for outliers using the inverse hyperbolic sine function (IHS).

[11] For this measure, we divide the world into nine distinct regions. The regions are Central America and the Caribbean, South America, Europe (excluding Eastern Europe), Eastern Europe and Eurasia, West Africa, Eastern and Southern Africa, the Middle East and North Africa, South Asia, East and Southeast Asia, and Oceania.

[12] Vito D'Orazio, "Joint Military Exercises: 1970–2010," webpage, undated. The existing data do not have information on exercise characteristics, such as information on target, frequency, or size of exercises; therefore, we are unable to distinguish between types of exercises.

sure of the scale of U.S. assistance, the data on military exercises only indicate whether an exercise took place and where; they do not include details on the scale or purpose.[13]

- **Agreements:** We consider two forms of security-related agreements with the United States: alliances and SOFAs. Alliance data come from the Correlates of War Project and include defensive security pacts from 1946 to 2008.[14] Data on status of force agreements come from previous RAND research on security-related agreements.[15] These data run from 1955 to 2010 in our sample.

Intervening Factors (Intervening Variables)

As discussed in Chapter Three, the effects of U.S. forward posture might be conditioned by the specific characteristics of U.S. posture choices—the capabilities that posture introduces into theater, the proximity of the posture to potential adversaries, and the degree of continuity in U.S. posture. Unfortunately, we do not have good quantitative measures for specific military capabilities that posture options introduce into theater over time. We can, however, examine the effects of continuity and proximity through statistical analysis.

Continuity

A key factor identified in our analytical framework is the continuity of U.S. posture. Although our measures of agreements between the United States and its partners inherently capture discontinuity because they are newly formed alliances and newly signed SOFAs, our other measures do not distinguish between continuous and discontinuous U.S. presence and activities.[16] To capture continuity, we perform additional analyses, including of two separate variants of each U.S. force posture option. The first is the measure of a particular type of U.S. posture (forces and activities) in a given year. The second is the average of the same type of U.S. force posture in the preceding three years.[17] The difference between the first measure and the second indicates the degree of discontinuity in that type of U.S. posture. Although

---

[13] It is of course possible—and indeed likely—that the scale and purpose of exercises influences how other actors react to them. Unfortunately, the data available do not allow us to differentiate among exercises. Developing improved data on multinational military exercises is an important objective for future research.

[14] Douglas M. Gibler, *International Military Alliances, 1648–2008*, Vol. 2: *Correlates of War Series*, Washington, D.C.: CQ Press, 2009.

[15] Jennifer Kavanagh, *U.S. Security-Related Agreements in Force Since 1955: Introducing a New Database*, Santa Monica, Calif.: RAND Corporation, RR-736-AF, 2014.

[16] We can use the results from the control variable for U.S. alliances in each model to make inferences about the long-term effects of U.S. alliances. We find that alliances largely deter malign activities but can make the U.S. partner a target of U.S. adversaries.

[17] This measure can also be seen as capturing long-term effects of U.S. posture choices.

this is not a perfect measure, it allows us to capture how the effect of continuous U.S. posture could be different from sharp changes in U.S. posture.[18]

Proximity

A second key factor identified in our analytical framework is the location of U.S. posture. As noted in previous chapters, we expect that U.S. forward posture will be particularly threatening to potential competitors when it is more proximate to those competitors. One way to account for the relationship between proximity and perceived threat in a quantitative model is to introduce a statistical control for the geographical distance between a given U.S. partner hosting U.S. forces or military activities and a potential adversary. We do so by using an interaction term between each of our posture options and distance from the competitor, where *distance* is measured as the border-to-border distance in kilometers between a U.S. partner and its potential adversary.[19]

Contextual Factors (Control Variables)

U.S. forward military posture is one of many factors that could lead to escalatory or de-escalatory responses by competitor states. Furthermore, there are theoretical reasons to believe that U.S. forward military posture might be more or less escalatory in some states or environments than in others. To better isolate the effects of U.S. force posture on behavior by competitor states, we incorporated these other factors in our models as statistical controls. We organize these contextual factors into the following seven categories:[20]

- **Levels of cooperation between the United States and the partner:** U.S. forward posture is not the only signal that competitors use to assess the likelihood that the United States will intervene to protect an ally or partner. A high level of visible cooperation between the United States and its allies and partners also indicates U.S. commitment to these countries. Consequently, we include measures of this cooperation. Because the full range of cooperative activities is difficult to capture quantitatively, we rely on two simple measures that are often used in academic studies: the degree of voting similarity between the United States and its ally or partner in the United Nations General Assembly (UNGA) and whether the two states are in a defense pact.[21]

---

[18] This measure would be ill-suited to capture continuity if our posture measures were relatively rare and cyclical events. The data suggest that this is not the case. Given that this is a theoretical concern when measuring U.S. exercises, we also examine two- and four-year averages with similar results.

[19] We take the IHS of this measure to account for skew.

[20] We provide a discussion of each individual control variable in Appendix B.

[21] On UNGA voting records as a measure of foreign policy similarity or cooperation, see Erik Voeten, Anton Strezhnev, and Michael Bailey, "United Nations General Assembly Voting Data," data set, 2009; and Michael A. Bailey, Anton Strezhnev, and Erik Voeten, "Estimating Dynamic State Preferences from United Nations Voting Data," *Journal of Conflict Resolution*, Vol. 61, No. 2, 2017. Defense pacts are a subset of alli-

- **Partner and competitor cooperation and conflict patterns:** The likelihood that a U.S. ally or partner will be targeted for hostile measures by another state obviously depends, in part, on the nature of the relationship between those two countries. States that enjoy friendly diplomatic relations or are highly economically interdependent may be less likely to target one another with hostile measures. On the other hand, states with a high degree of mutual animosity may be much more likely to target one another. We capture the quality of relations between a U.S. ally or partner and potential competitors through a variety of measures, including joint alliances, joint membership in intergovernmental organizations, joint trade, and a history of conflict or an ongoing conflict.

- **Partner and competitor governance systems:** Democracies can be either more susceptible or more resilient to certain types of malign activity. The United States also might be more predisposed to support other democracies. For this reason, we include a measure of the ally or partner's level of democracy. Democracy might also condition the relationship between a U.S. ally or partner and its potential competitors; countries that are both democracies might be less inclined toward acts of aggression toward one another, including aggression below the level of armed conflict. Consequently, we include a measure of whether the U.S. ally or partner and its potential competitor are both democratic.[22]

- **Partner and competitor power projection, threat, and military strength:** Stronger and more–militarily powerful states might themselves deter hostile measures, aside from any U.S. military presence in the region. We therefore include measures of a U.S. ally or partner's overall material capabilities, the balance of military power between the U.S. ally or partner and a potential competitor, the ally or partner's level of defense spending, and the total number of alliances to which the ally or partner belongs as a measure of the potential for countries other than the United States to come to the state's defense.[23]

- **Partner economic power and political development:** Countries at a high level of economic and political development might be more resilient to a variety of hostile measures, and their economic might may serve as a deterrent. Consequently, we include

---

ances that includes only those alliances that commit states to intervene militarily on the side of any treaty partner that is attacked. See Gibler, 2009.

[22] To measure democracy, we use the well-known Polity IV data set. See Monty G. Marshall and Keith Jaggers, *Polity IV Project: Political Regime Characteristics and Transitions, 1800–2002*, College Park, Md.: Integrated Network for Societal Conflict Research, Program Center for International Development and Conflict Management, University of Maryland, 2002.

[23] Military capabilities and spending data are taken from the Correlates of War project (J. David Singer, Stuart Bremer, and John Stuckey, "Capability Distribution, Uncertainty, and Major Power War, 1820-1965," in Bruce M. Russett, ed., *Peace, War, and Numbers*, Thousand Oaks, Calif.: SAGE Publications, 1972). Data on alliances are taken from Brett Ashley Leeds, *Alliance Treaty Obligations and Provisions (ATOP) Codebook*, Houston, Tex.: Rice University, Department of Political Science, 2005.

measures of a state's income levels (gross domestic product [GDP] per capita), economic growth, trade openness, and state capacity.[24]

- **Demographic characteristics of partner and competitor:** Larger partner states might provide a more threatening presence to opponents because of their latent capacity for warfighting, because these states might be able to substitute a large number of forces for other military capabilities. Conversely, larger states may be particularly susceptible to such behaviors as proxy warfare, leading adversaries to increase behavior under the threshold of armed conflict. In addition, states may be seen as both more valuable partners and more desirable targets if they contain natural resources.

- **Regional and time-period effects:** We also account for systematic differences that occur because of geography or changes that occur over time. We include region-fixed effects in our models, which account for any systematic differences between regions. Because U.S. behavior toward both allies and competitors might be in the Cold War period and in the post–Cold War era, we also control for this with a dummy variable for the Cold War.

In addition, we acknowledge that certain aspects of the context might be especially important for conditioning the relationship between individual types of U.S. posture choices and competitor responses. Specifically, we note that security cooperation activities occur with a wider group of U.S. partners than other U.S. posture choices. As a result, it might be the case that U.S. security cooperation with less-stable partner states is threatening to potential competitors, while security cooperation with more-stable partner states does not lead to escalation or even increases deterrence. To account for this possibility, we interact U.S. posture options with GDP per capita data to determine whether the partner's economic stability conditions our results.[25]

Modeling Approach

We conduct a quantitative analysis that examines relations between all potential U.S. partners and all of their potential competitors in the post–World War II period. We analyze only cases in which we have data for the full complement of our included variables, meaning that the exact time frame and number of cases can vary by model. The unit of analysis is the *dyad-year*. A *dyad* indicates a pair of countries such that one country is the potential recipient of

---

[24] Robert Inklaar, Herman de Jong, Jutta Bolt, and Jan Luiten van Zanden, "Rebasing 'Maddison': New Income Comparisons and the Shape of Long-Run Economic Development," *GGDC Research Memorandum*, No. GD-174, 2018; World Bank, "World Development Indicators," data set, last updated May 25, 2021; and Jacek Kugler and Marina Arbetman, "Relative Political Capacity: Political Extraction and Political Reach," in Marina Arbetman and Jacek Kugler, eds., *Political Capacity and Economic Behavior*, Abingdon, U.K.: Routledge, 2018.

[25] GDP per capita is a commonly used measure both of economic health and of state capacity in the political science literature. See Cullen S. Hendrix, "Measuring State Capacity: Theoretical and Empirical Implications for the Study of Civil Conflict," *Journal of Peace Research*, Vol. 47, No. 3, 2010.

U.S. posture choices (*the partner*) and the second country in the pair is the partner's competitor. Our statistical method is based on our outcome of interest. For binary variables, such as the imposition of sanctions, we use a probit regression. For our continuous measure, such as arms transfers, we use ordinary least squares (OLS) regression.

In such statistical analyses as this one, there is always a risk of reverse causation (or what social scientists refer to as *endogeneity*). It could be, for instance, that a given type of U.S. posture appears associated with higher levels of malign activity, in which case it might appear escalatory. But it could be that U.S. decisionmakers anticipated a high risk of hostile measures and so they increased U.S. forward posture to try to deter such threats. In this case, the increased risk of hostile measures is what would be driving changes in U.S. forward posture rather than forward posture being the cause of increased hostile measures. There is no perfect solution to such challenges to causal inference. We do, however, account for such possibilities by using two-stage propensity-weighting models. Such models attempt to provide statistical controls against the possibility of reverse causation and similar problems. Although this statistical technique cannot fully solve such challenges to causal inference, it again increases our confidence in our results.[26] The qualitative case studies in the following chapter provide additional evidence in favor of the proposition that the patterns we observe are, in fact, causal. But because we cannot be certain that our statistical analysis is identifying a causal relationship, we consistently refer to certain competitor behaviors as *being associated with* changes in U.S. forward posture or being an *apparent outcome* of those changes,

There are two other limitations in this analytic approach that we want to highlight. First, we are limited in this report by the quality of existing data sources. Some of these sources provide much less detail than we would like (e.g., the lack of historical data on the scale and purpose of multilateral military exercises).

Second, in each model, we are looking at average relationships across large numbers of cases. The results in any particular setting may diverge from this average. Our use of intervening variables helps to reduce the extent of this limitation: By examining how continuity and proximity condition the relationship between U.S. forward posture and the incidence of hostile measures, we can show how two of the most important contextual factors lead to different relationships in different circumstances. Obviously, however, these intervening factors are only two among a large number that might matter. Consequently, the patterns uncovered in this analysis are best understood as a set of baseline expectations that will have to be adjusted depending on specific circumstances.

---

[26] In particular, there might be iterative dynamics or positive feedback loops that this statistical analysis would be unable to disentangle. As with the rest of this chapter, a much more in-depth explanation of our two-stage modeling approach can be found in Appendix B.

Results

We divide the discussion of our results into two sections. The first section provides the results of our baseline models—that is, the extent to which different types of U.S. forward posture are associated with changes in the incidence of malign activities. The second section focuses on how the intervening factors of continuity and proximity condition the apparent effects of U.S. forward posture. As will be seen in this discussion, the apparent consequences of U.S. forward posture vary—sometimes dramatically—depending on the location and rapidity of change of U.S. posture.

Baseline Results

In this section, we summarize the results of our statistical analysis by U.S. posture type. In each section, we analyze whether the U.S. posture choice is associated with an increase or a decrease in hostile measures targeted at U.S. allies and partners. An increase in such activities suggests that U.S. posture might be having an escalatory effect, while a decrease in such activities suggests that U.S. posture could be having a deterrent effect.

To facilitate interpretation of our results, we begin this discussion by summarizing our findings in Table 4.1.[27] We denote statistically significant findings using a simple color scheme. Posture options associated with increased malign activity (i.e., posture options that appear escalatory) are marked in red. Posture options associated with decreased malign activity (i.e., options that appear to deter) are marked in green. We also summarize our statistical confidence in the results, dividing our findings into those that are most robust and those that are weaker. Stronger results are marked by darker shaded colors, while weaker results are marked with lighter shades.[28] When there are too few cases of a particular type to make sound statistical inferences, we shade the cell gray.

Forces

The effects of U.S. forces are complex and depend heavily on the forces' location. Prior RAND analysis found that U.S. forces had very inconsistent effects on deterrence and escalation to the level of armed conflict *in the countries in which they were positioned*. In contrast, U.S. forces stationed *nearby* were relatively consistently associated with deterrent outcomes. One interpretation of these results is that forward-positioned U.S. forces both deter and provoke. On the one hand, such forces provide important capabilities and represent a very strong signal of U.S. commitment to defending the host country, thus potentially reducing the likelihood of militarized disputes. On the other hand, the presence of U.S. forces in a particular

---

[27] In each summary table, we incorporate information from both the baseline model results and those using propensity weighting, although we note that the results for the baseline models and the propensity-weighted models, while varying in terms of our statistical confidence in the results, generally follow the same pattern.

[28] For full details on the statistical confidence associated with our results, see Appendix B.

TABLE 4.1

Baseline Relationships Between U.S. Forward Posture and the Incidence of Hostile Measures

Type of U.S. Posture		Competitor Response Options					
		Competitive Arms Transfers	Threatened Sanctions	Imposed Sanctions	Proxy Wars	Military Intimidation	Use of Force
Forces	In-country forces	green (light, deterrent)	red (dark, escalatory)	red (light, escalatory)		red (dark, escalatory)	red (light, escalatory)
	In-region forces	green (dark, deterrent)			green (dark, deterrent)	green (light, deterrent)	
Activities	Arms transfers	red (light, escalatory)	red (dark, escalatory)	red (dark, escalatory)	red (dark, escalatory)	red (dark, escalatory)	red (dark, escalatory)
	Military exercises	red (light, escalatory)		red (light, escalatory)	red (dark, escalatory)		red (light, escalatory)
Agreements	SOFAs	red (dark, escalatory)					
	Defense treaties						green (dark, deterrent)

↘ (green) indicates that increased U.S. posture is associated with a decrease in the incidence of a given type of hostile measure (an apparently deterrent relationship).

↖ (red) indicates that increased U.S. posture is associated with an increase in the incidence of a given type of hostile measure (an apparently escalatory relationship).

Gray shading indicates that there are insufficient data to conduct statistical analysis for this type of relationship.

Darker arrow (↑) symbols represent greater statistical confidence; lighter arrow symbols (↑) represent less statistical confidence.

country might threaten other nearby countries, leading to an increased risk that the host country could become involved in militarized disputes, whether intentional (such as shows of military force designed to signal an adversary's willingness to fight) or inadvertent (such as military incidents that occur from the inevitable friction of hostile forces operating in close proximity to one another). In the countries that host U.S. forces, the escalatory consequences seem to outweigh the deterrent ones. Nearby U.S. forces, on the other hand, were associated much more consistently with deterrent outcomes—potentially because they also conveyed U.S. resolve and provided capabilities in-theater, but without the same risks of escalation.[29] This prior analysis, however, focused only on the effects of U.S. forward posture on armed conflict.

In the research conducted for this report, we found similar patterns in the competition space, as depicted in Table 4.1. *In-country* U.S. personnel (that is, those positioned in the same country that is being analyzed for the incidence of hostile measures) appear to have inconsistent statistically significant effects on the incidence of malign activities. Increases in in-country personnel are associated with a *decrease* in competitive arms transfers, although the substantive significance of this relationship is small (that is, states that are relevant to the host country do not appear to import substantially less after an increase in U.S. forces). On the other hand, in-country U.S. forces are associated with an increased likelihood of economic coercion (although, again, the substantive significance of this relationship is small), military intimidation, and limited uses of force. Overall, the lack of consistency in the results suggests that in-country troop presence has ambiguous effects on malign activities in competition, just as it does on the likelihood of armed conflict.

In contrast, the presence of U.S. personnel *nearby* the potential target of hostile measures (*in-region forces*) is associated with a reduction in the likelihood of many types of malign activities, including competitive arms transfers, proxy wars, and military intimidation. Unlike with in-country forces, there are no types of malign activity that appear to increase as a result of in-region U.S. forces. As with deterrence of armed conflict, it appears that the deterrent consequences of in-region U.S. forces outweigh the potential escalatory consequences in the competition space.

Activities

Our statistical analysis suggests that activities performed by the United States with a partner state do not have substantial deterrent value. Instead, they are associated with higher levels of escalation by potential competitors and likely adversaries, as depicted in Table 4.1. The strongest evidence of competitor escalation is in our models of the provision of U.S. security cooperation that includes U.S. arms transfers. We find that arms transfers are associated with a significant increase in the likelihood of every type of hostile measure—competitive arms transfers, economic coercion, proxy wars, military intimidation, and limited uses of force.

---

[29] O'Mahony et al., 2018; Frederick et al., 2020.

This finding is consistent with several previous studies that have found that arms transfers fail to deter armed aggression against partners. Our analysis builds on this earlier work, however, illustrating that arms transfers could also provoke a wide variety of aggressive actions beneath the level of armed conflict.

We do not find that multilateral exercises with the United States are as consistently associated with escalatory outcomes as U.S. arms transfers. However, we do find evidence suggesting that multilateral exercises could provoke a competitor response. As can be seen in Table 4.1, U.S. multilateral military exercises are associated with increases in competitive arms transfers, economic coercion, proxy wars, and limited uses of force. In the aggregate, multilateral exercises do not appear to deter competitive responses and instead are often associated with adversary escalation. This finding, however, must be interpreted with some caution. The available data do not indicate the size or content of multilateral military exercises. It is possible that our results would become more complex if we had access to better data. It could be, for instance, that large exercises (involving division-level or larger forces) strongly deter (or provoke), while smaller exercises have the opposite effect. Moreover, exercises specifically focused on combat operations could have different effects than ones focused on humanitarian assistance or disaster relief. In addition, exercises that are known far in advance or conducted perennially might not lead to an escalatory response. Finally, our analysis examined only the direct deterrent (or provocative) effects of military exercises. It could be that such exercises contribute to long-term improvements in ally and partner military capabilities, and our models would not detect the deterrent effects of such improvements.

As discussed in the previous chapter, however, scholars of international relations have articulated a clear logic for why exercises might be escalatory, and there are both historical examples and wargaming results that bolster this logic. Our statistical results thus contribute to a wider body of evidence warning of the potential unintended consequences of multilateral military exercises. They also extend these results from the risk of escalation to war—where most previous studies have focused—to examine the risks of escalation in the competition space (i.e., an increase in malign activities below the level of armed conflict).

In addition to our baseline analysis of U.S. security cooperation activities and competitor response options, we also examine how partner stability can condition this relationship. We find evidence that partner stability is associated with a decrease in the escalatory effect of arms transfers for all competitor responses except for proxy support. We similarly find that partner stability dampens the escalatory impact of multilateral exercises. Although these results are less consistent, we see that partner stability is associated with a decrease in the apparently escalatory effect of multilateral exercises with the United States for all competitor responses except for arms transfers. To place these results in a more concrete context, we find that while U.S. cooperation with even the poorest Western European countries does not appear likely to provoke escalation, certain Eastern European states might not be stable enough for the escalatory effects to disappear, and many countries on the periphery of Europe (such as in the Levant and Maghreb regions) appear to pose a much higher risk of escalation in the competition space.[30]

Agreements

As can be seen in Table 4.1, the establishment of a new formal alliance with the United States is associated with a substantial decrease in limited uses of force directed at the United States' new treaty ally. This result is consistent with prior theorizing on deterrence, which suggests that such alliances represent a strong signal of U.S. commitment and thus are more likely to deter.

There is some suggestive evidence that SOFAs may also reduce the likelihood of limited uses of force, although the statistical relationship is weak.[31] With less intense forms of malign activities, however, we find evidence that military agreements may inspire competitors to respond with some forms of malign activity. In particular, new SOFAs are associated with an increase in instances of military intimidation directed at the U.S. partner and with competitive arms sales. The evidence suggests that while these agreements may provide some protection against the most dangerous forms of malign activity, competitor states still find ways to compete below the threshold of force in response to increasing U.S. commitments.

Intervening Factors

Up until now, we have only discussed the broadest trends between U.S. forward posture and potential competitor responses at levels below armed conflict. Posture may have different consequences under different conditions, however. U.S. decisionmakers and military planners are sensitive to these contextual differences, but their implications are not always clear. In this section, we examine how two factors, the degree of continuity in U.S. posture and the proximity of that posture to competitors, conditions the apparent competitor response to U.S. posture.

Continuity

As discussed in Chapter Three, existing deterrence theory suggests that a continuous U.S. forward presence reduces uncertainty and therefore strengthens deterrence. Conversely,

---

[30] This relationship between partner stability and the apparent effects of U.S. military activities raises an important point: The United States can engage in activities with states that are already more likely to experience hostile measures, in which case the relationship would be spurious. Alternatively, lower levels of security cooperation may be chosen to avoid the possibility of entanglement by the U.S. in even higher levels of conflict. Although our statistical analysis included a procedure to account for such endogenous relationships by weighting U.S. posture choices by the probability of each country receiving forward-positioned U.S. military forces, we did not implement a similar procedure for all elements of U.S. posture, including arms transfers and exercises. Prior unpublished RAND work by Watts et al., 2018, however, did use such procedures in analyses of U.S. security assistance and did not find that the association between U.S. arms transfers and higher levels of conflict was endogenous.

[31] In this model, we achieve significance only at the 0.20 level.

rapid, sizeable changes in U.S. forward posture increase uncertainty, which is believed to undermine deterrence. When we examine the relationship between continuity in U.S. forward posture and the incidence of hostile measures targeted at U.S. allies and partners, we find that discontinuity appears to undermine deterrence in competition just as it is believed to undermine the deterrence of armed conflict.[32]

Forces

The sustained presence of U.S. in-country forces is associated with decreases in competitive arms transfers, economic coercion, and military intimidation. Similarly, the continuous presence of U.S. in-region forces is associated with decreases in competitive arms transfers, economic coercion, and proxy wars. Both sets of results are consistent with the expectation from deterrence theory that continuity enhances deterrence. Importantly, while in-country U.S. forces were associated with contradictory or ambiguous outcomes when all such forces were examined, when we focus only on a continuous in-country U.S. force presence, the results are consistently associated with deterrent outcomes.

In contrast, newly introduced in-country U.S. forces are consistently associated with escalatory outcomes—increased competitive arms transfers, economic coercion, and military intimidation. The results for a rapid increase in regional U.S. presence largely mirror those results for the in-country U.S. presence. Newly introduced in-region U.S. forces are associated with an increased likelihood of competitive arms transfers and economic coercion. Only in the case of proxy warfare do we find that newly introduced in-region U.S. forces are associated with deterrent outcomes.

Activities

The results for U.S. activities are less clear. As expected, a sudden increase in U.S. military activities is associated with escalatory outcomes, including an increase in proxy warfare, military intimidation, and limited uses of force. Unlike with the presence of U.S. forces, continuity in U.S. military activities is not associated with deterrent outcomes. In fact, even continuous U.S. military activities are associated with an increase in competitive arms transfers and economic coercion. Although continuity is not associated with deterrence in the case of U.S. military activities, it does appear to shift the nature of competitor responses. Competitors appear to respond to sudden increases in U.S. military activities with the most-dangerous forms of malign activity (proxy warfare, military intimidation, and limited uses of force). In contrast, competitors appear to respond to continuous (and thus more predictable) U.S. mili-

---

[32] As with other parts of our statistical analysis, we summarize the main patterns here and explore each individual model in Appendix B. Because we must make use of an imperfect measure of continuity, we note that the lack of statistically significant results should not be taken as definitive evidence that there is no difference between discontinuous and continuous presence.

tary activities with milder forms of malign activity (competitive arms transfers and economic coercion).[33]

Agreements

Our baseline measure of U.S. military agreements used *new* defense treaties and SOFAs—agreements that were signed in the year prior to a hostile measure that did not previously exist. Consequently, our baseline analysis already examined the apparent effects of discontinuity in military agreements, and thus we include no additional analysis in this section.

Table 4.2 summarizes the apparent effects of continuity on U.S. forward posture using the same symbols for apparently deterrent or escalatory outcomes as in Table 4.1. As expected from the existing deterrence literature, continuity in U.S. force presence—both in-country and in-region—is associated with deterrent outcomes, while sudden increases in U.S. force presence are almost consistently associated with escalatory outcomes. As in our baseline analysis, U.S. military activities are repeatedly associated with escalatory outcomes. But continuity at least appears to reduce the intensity of competitors' hostile responses. In short, our statistical analysis suggests that continuity functions much the same in the deterrence of hostile measures as it does in the deterrence of armed conflict. By creating uncertainty about U.S. commitment and capabilities in-theater, discontinuity may undermine deterrence in the competition space.

Proximity

As discussed in Chapter Three, positioning forces close to a potential adversary can help to deter short-warning attacks, such as faits accompli, for which forces positioned farther away might not arrive in time. But physical proximity to a potential adversary also has the potential to threaten a potential adversary, causing it to signal its hostility to the presence of U.S. forces or to impose costs on the host countries.

Our statistical analysis suggests that these latter, escalatory effects appear to be dominant, at least in the competition space. In our baseline models, we find that greater distance between a U.S. ally or partner and a potential competitor is almost always associated with lower levels of malign activity.[34] But it is not just the distance between a potential target state and a competitor that matters; the distance between U.S. forward posture and the competitor also matters. To examine how proximity conditions the apparent effects of U.S. forward posture, we introduced into our statistical models an interaction term between U.S. forward posture and distance from the host country to a potential competitor. Interpreting the interaction of two continuous variables is notoriously complex; it does not lend itself to the sorts of

---

[33] As a robustness check, we expand our analysis to look at the running average of U.S. posture in years *t–3* through *t–5* and *t–4* through *t–6*. We find that the results are quite similar to the earlier periods. However, we do note as well that several of the effects appear to dissipate over time.

[34] Several of the models find no significant effect, particularly those capturing proxy warfare. The sole instance in which distance is escalatory is in terms of sanctions, where distance from the partner's rival makes them more likely to be targeted by a sanction.

TABLE 4.2

Conditioning Influence of Continuity on the Apparent Effects of U.S. Forward Posture

Type of Forward Posture	Posture Subtype	Competitor Response Options					
		Competitive Arms Transfers	Threatened Sanctions	Imposed Sanctions	Proxy Wars	Military Intimidation	Use of Force
Continuous forces	In-country forces	↓		↓		↓	
	In-region forces	↓	↓	↓	↓ (lighter)		
Discontinuous forces	In-country forces	↑	↑	↑		↑	
	In-region forces	↑	↑ (lighter)	↑	↓		
Continuous activities	Arms transfers		↑				
	Military exercises	↑		↑			
Discontinuous activities	Arms transfers				↑	↑	
	Military exercises					↑	↑

↓ Indicates that increased U.S. posture is associated with a decrease in the incidence of a given type of hostile measure (an apparently deterrent relationship).

↑ Indicates that increased U.S. posture is associated with an increase in the incidence of a given type of hostile measure (an apparently escalatory relationship).

Darker arrow (↑) symbols represent greater statistical confidence; lighter arrow symbols (↑) represent less statistical confidence.

summary tables that we have provided previously.[35] Consequently, we summarize the clearest patterns here and explore them in greater depth in Appendix B.

---

[35] Interpreting an interaction term using a continuous variable such as distance is notoriously complex. See Thomas Brambor, William Roberts Clark, and Matt Golder, "Understanding Interaction Models: Improving Empirical Analyses," *Political Analysis*, Vol. 14, No. 1, Winter 2006. As a result, we summarize the identifiable patterns here and explore them in greater depth in Appendix B.

Forces

As the distance between a U.S. ally or partner and a potential competitor increases, in-country U.S. forces appear less likely to provoke competitive arms races.[36] They also appear more likely to deter the use of force and proxy warfare by at least certain types of competitors.

Activities

U.S. activities show a less-consistent pattern. Distance reduces the escalatory association between multilateral military exercises and the most-violent forms of conflict—proxy wars, military intimidation, and the use of force—but shows no consistent deterrent effects for arms transfers or economic coercion. The effect of distance on arms transfers does not strongly match the theoretical framework. Although the escalatory effect of U.S. arms transfers on competitor arms transfer decreases as distance between the competitor and the U.S. partner increases, we find evidence that more-violent outcomes and economic coercion are more likely when states at greater distances from their competitors obtain this type of cooperation. Given these inconsistencies and the limitations noted previously, we are hesitant to over-interpret our results.

Agreements

We find that the apparent effect of distance is most pronounced in the case of U.S. military agreements. These agreements are associated with greater deterrence and less escalation the farther away the U.S. partner is from the competitor. We find strong statistical results for U.S. SOFAs. These results are most consistent for proxy funding and military intimidation, but we see some evidence of enhanced deterrence for arms transfers, threatened sanctions, and the limited use of force as well. In addition, as the distance between a new U.S. ally and a potential competitor increases, the likelihood of the ally being targeted with military intimidation decreases.

Because proximity is a continuous variable, it is difficult to easily summarize its conditioning effects in tables similar to the others provided in this chapter. Instead, we offer a single illustration of how this factor can condition the relationship between U.S. forward posture and Russian malign activities. Figure 4.1 illustrates how the probability of Russian support for a proxy war in response to U.S. multilateral military exercises appears to decline when these exercises are conducted farther from Russian borders. To help readers visualize this relationship in concrete terms, we have plotted the relationship on a map of Europe. The horizontal axis represents the distance from Russian borders at which a U.S. military exercise takes place. The vertical axis represents the extent to which Russian support for proxy wars increases or decreases from its average likelihood in apparent response to U.S. military exercises. The curve plotting the relationship is color-coded; when Russia appears more likely to support a local proxy war in reaction to U.S. military activities, the curve is red; when Russia

---

[36] Because the U.S. regional presence variable includes troops that are at different distances from both the partner and the adversary, we cannot conclude how distance conditions that relationship and so we do not examine that variable in this analysis.

FIGURE 4.1

Conditioning Influence of Proximity on the Size of the Relationship Between U.S. Multilateral Military Exercises and Incidence of Russian-Supported Proxy Wars

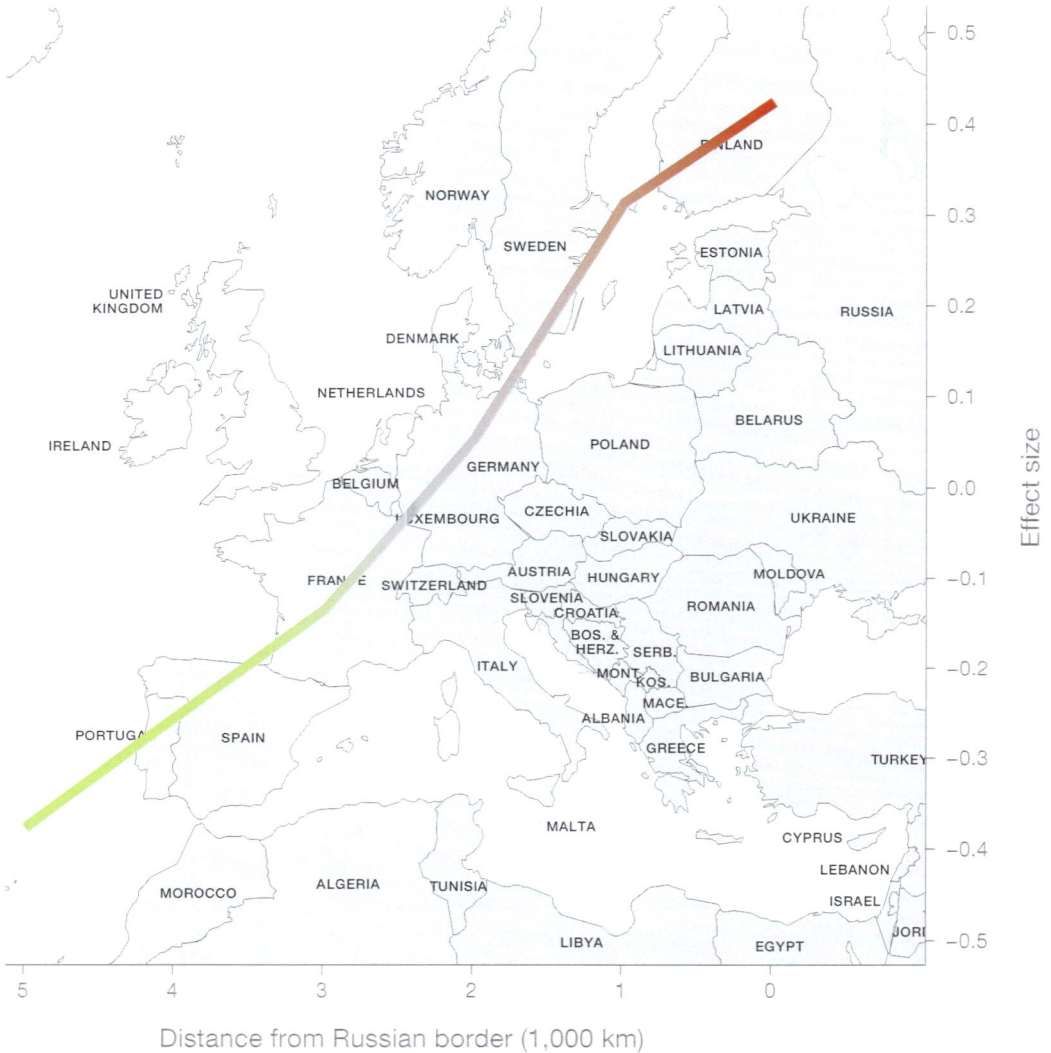

appears less likely to support such a war in reaction to U.S. actions, the curve is green. As can be seen in the figure, U.S. military exercises appear to provoke when conducted relatively close to Russian borders. But as the distance from Russia increases, the relationship reverses, and U.S. military exercises appear to deter such Russian hostile measures. In terms of European geography, the escalatory risk is greatest in Eastern Europe, but that risk is mitigated (and deterrence reinforced) when the exercises take place farther away.

Conclusion

We draw several conclusions from this quantitative analysis of historical trends:

- **Forces:** U.S. troop presence has the potential to deter a variety of hostile measures in competition. The countries that host U.S. forces sometimes appear to be targeted for hostile measures with greater intensity. This escalatory outcome, however, appears primarily associated with newly introduced U.S. forces. When U.S. forces are positioned in a country for an extended period (i.e., several years), they appear to be associated with a reduction in many types of malign activities with little escalatory risk. More generally, U.S. forces are associated with a reduction in malign activities in the broader region in which they are positioned. Escalatory risk appears to increase when U.S. forces are positioned close to a potential competitor or adversary. These patterns suggest that deterrence can be maximized by maintaining a U.S. forward presence in regions of critical interest to the United States but not necessarily in countries highly proximate to a competitor and not in countries that are more vulnerable to hostile measures.

- **Activities:** Security cooperation activities with the United States generally do not appear to directly deter competitive responses by U.S. competitors. Indeed, there is evidence that suggests that these activities are associated with escalatory effects, although the change in malign activities associated with U.S. military activities is typically modest. As with the longer-term presence of U.S. forces, the escalatory risks associated with short-term U.S. military activities can often be ameliorated by conducting these activities farther away from potential competitors and ensuring that these activities have a relatively high degree of continuity and thus predictability. Escalatory risk also appears highest when the United States conducts military activities in less–politically stable allied and partner countries. In contrast, these activities appear to have generally deterrent consequences when conducted in more-stable allied and partner countries.

- **Agreements:** U.S. defense treaties are associated with a reduction in the most-violent forms of competitive behavior against U.S. partners by potential competitors (i.e., limited uses of force). However, there is some evidence that lesser military agreements (such as SOFAs) could make U.S. partners targets of other forms of malign activities, including competitive arms transfers and military intimidation. As with forces and activities, however, this escalatory risk is ameliorated with distance from the potential competitor; in fact, both kinds of agreements are associated with a lower incidence of hostile measures when they are made with countries at some distance from the competitor or potential adversary.

We conclude with a caveat. Throughout this analysis, we examined only the direct relationships between U.S. forward posture and competitors' hostile measures. We did not examine U.S. posture's effects on U.S. allies or partners. Many observers believe that U.S. forward posture can help to reassure allies and partners and can help to build their capabilities, which, in turn, could have deterrent value. These indirect effects might be at least as important as the direct effects and are an important topic for future research.

CHAPTER FIVE

Case Studies

Introduction

Chapter Four provided a statistical overview of competitor activities associated with changes in U.S. forward posture. Despite using a number of techniques designed to bolster our confidence that competitor actions really were reactions to U.S. posture changes (rather than actions taken for other reasons), it is important to examine individual cases in more detail. Such qualitative analysis helps to ensure that the patterns that we detect are occurring for the reasons suggested in Chapters Two and Three—that is, that U.S. forward posture changes the calculus of competitor decisionmakers.

In this chapter, we briefly review five historical cases of U.S. posture changes and Russian or Soviet reactions. The five cases are as follows:

- the Iran Crisis (1946–1947)
- spiraling competition in the Horn of Africa (1962–1974)
- INF missile deployments to Western Europe (1982–1984)
- escalation to the Russo-Georgian War (2002–2008)
- U.S. posture changes in northeastern Europe following the Russian invasion of Ukraine (2014–2020).

Including both older Soviet and more recent Russian cases offers advantages and disadvantages. By going back farther in time, we can benefit from the greater availability of archival materials. We can also observe dynamics across a wider variety of background conditions, thus helping to understand whether some patterns of strategic competition persist despite changes in contextual factors. The five cases were chosen to provide variation in the following three key conditions:

- the overall level of tensions in U.S.-Russian (or Soviet) relations (including episodes from the very beginning of the Cold War, the height of the Cold War, and the recent past)
- geographical location (including incidents within NATO member-states, in countries that Moscow believed to be firmly within its sphere of influence, and in more-peripheral countries)

- the four elements of posture (forces, activities, footprint, and agreements).[1]

Of course, over such a long period of time, many other background factors can change as well. We highlight some of these background factors in the case study, and we return to the importance of context in the final chapter.

Each case study is composed of five sections. Each begins with a brief narrative overview of the case. In the next three sections, each case study summarizes U.S. posture in the region of interest, the Russian or Soviet responses to that posture (and reasons for those responses) with a particular focus on malign activities in competition, and the outcomes of the case. A final section discusses which quantitative findings were supported or not by the qualitative evidence and the broader policy implications of the case.

The Iran Crisis, 1946–1947

The Iran Crisis of 1946–1947 was one of the first crises of the post–World War II period and arguably the one that, more than any other, began the long period of strategic competition known as the Cold War. U.S. forward posture was one critical element that ultimately led Moscow to back down in Iran; however, the United States' victory in the short term appears to have reinforced Soviet perceptions of the United States as an aggressive, expansionist state that could not be trusted.

Background

During World War II, the United States, United Kingdom, and Soviet Union occupied Iran, making the country a de facto protectorate and thus securing an essential transit route from the Western allies to the Soviet Union. This occupation was given legal status by a treaty signed in 1942, which stated that the occupying powers would withdraw their military forces within six months of the end of the war. Following the end of the war, the United States began to rapidly draw down its military presence. The Soviet Union, on the other hand, reinforced its military presence in the country for the first few months following the war.

---

[1] Perhaps the best discussion of approaches to case selection for such studies as this one is John Gerring's *Case Study Research: Principles and Practices* (2nd ed., Cambridge, U.K.: Cambridge University Press, 2017). Using his terminology, these case studies can be considered diagnostic (that is, they assess the validity of our hypotheses—in this case, the theoretical propositions in Chapter Three and the quantitative findings in Chapter Four). Roughly half of our cases were chosen to be *influential* cases—that is, we used the results of our statistical tests to find instances of some of the strongest relationships between our independent and dependent variables, then we examined those cases to determine whether there were good reasons to believe the relationship was causal. But the quantitative data was limited by period and other factors. To make sure that these data limitations were not blinding us to dynamics outside our range of data, we also selected out-of-sample cases for examination. Within these two broad categories of cases, our selection of specific cases was guided by other factors highlighted by Gerring, including the *intrinsic importance* of a case and *logistics* (the accessibility of evidence for a case).

Behind the cover of its military forces, the Soviet Union provided both political and material (including military) support to the pro-Soviet leadership of political movements in northern Iran. These movements used this support to create two breakaway republics, the Autonomous Republic of Azerbaijan and the Kurdish Republic of Mahabad. One message to the head of the Soviet secret police, Lavrentiy Beria, reported,

> Twenty-one experienced NKVD [Narodny Kommisariat vnutrennikh del, or People's Commissariat for Internal Affairs] and NKGB [People's Commissariat for State Security] operatives of the Azerbaijan SSR [Soviet Socialist Republic] have been selected who are capable of organizing work to liquidate people and organizations interfering with the development of the autonomy movement in Iranian Azerbaijan (gendarmes, policemen, officers of the Iranian Army, et al). All these comrades are to organize armed partisan detachments from the local population.[2]

Through these local proxies, the Soviet Union hoped to exercise influence over Iran as a whole—a country rich in oil that could offer both warm-weather ports and a buffer against potential Western aggression—even after its troops withdrew.[3] From the U.S. perspective, these Soviet actions threatened U.S. interests. In a memorandum to the State Department, the Joint Chiefs of Staff warned that "possible Soviet domination of Iran by means other than war" threatened vital oil supplies in Iran and more broadly in the Middle East.[4]

The Soviet Union ultimately withdrew its troops by April 1946, in part because of pressure exercised by the United States and in part because of concessions by Tehran. But by this point, the Autonomous Republic of Azerbaijan and the Kurdish Republic of Mahabad had developed their own militias. Several clashes with Iranian government forces ensued.

After the government of Iran had secured U.S. support for arms sales on concessionary terms and with the United States' full diplomatic support, Tehran made preparations for a major offensive against the Autonomous Republic of Azerbaijan in December 1946. According to U.S. diplomatic reporting, the Soviet ambassador to Iran warned the Iranian prime minister that such actions would lead to "clashes of arms" and "partisan warfare" to which "the Soviet Government cannot be indifferent."[5] Despite this warning, Tehran moved for-

---

[2] "Message from Bagirov and Maslennikov to Beria on Arming the Autonomous Movement in Iranian Azerbaijan," webpage, Wilson Center Digital Archive, October 21, 1945.

[3] A. Polushchuk, "Problems of Iranian Azerbaijan During the Years of the 2nd World War (1941–1946)," in N. M. Mamedova, ed., *Iran and the Second World War*, Moscow: Russian Academy of Sciences Institute of Oriental Studies, 2011; and Fred H. Lawson, "The Iranian Crisis of 1945–1946 and the Spiral Model of International Conflict," *International Journal of Middle East Studies*, Vol. 21, No. 3, 1989.

[4] Cited in Richard Pfau, "Containment in Iran, 1946: The Shift to an Active Policy," *Diplomatic History*, Vol. 1, No. 4, Fall 1977, p. 365.

[5] U.S. Department of State, Office of the Historian, "Memorandum of Telephone Conversation, by the Director of the Office of Near Eastern and African Affairs (Henderson)," *Foreign Relations of the United States, 1946, The Near East and Africa*, Vol. VII, Washington, D.C., December 7, 1946.

ward with its offensive, and Moscow declined to intervene on behalf of its proxies despite their pleas for assistance. Tehran rapidly consolidated its control of the region and soon thereafter gained control of Mahabad as well.

U.S. Forward Posture

U.S. forward posture during the crisis consisted of three elements. First, the United States had some troops (primarily logistical) left in the country after the end of World War II, but these forces rapidly drew down after the end of the war.

Second, in 1946, the United States abandoned its previous commitment to neutrality in Iran and committed to providing substantial military equipment transfers and training. The United States made these commitments to Tehran after the Soviet Union had begun providing aid to its proxies in northern Iran but before the Iranian government undertook its major offensive against the Autonomous Republic of Azerbaijan in December 1946. Washington promised more aid as soon as the offensive began. Indeed, the Soviet Union accused Iran of "inviting American experts to run the army," in addition to other parts of the government and economy.[6]

Finally, and likely most importantly, the United States had built a series of air bases in the region, perhaps none more important than the Dhahran airport in Saudi Arabia. This airfield was one of the facilities capable of supporting U.S. nuclear-capable, long- and medium-range bombers.[7] The airfield represented both an "immovable symbol of Washington's commitment to preserve the status quo in regional affairs . . . while also providing U.S. forces with a secure staging point for any action that might become necessary to support America's beleaguered allies in Tehran."[8]

Soviet Response

As Iranian forces moved north to reconsolidate control of the Autonomous Republic of Azerbaijan, the Azerbaijani leader Jafar Pishevari begged Soviet Premier Joseph Stalin to use Soviet forces in the region to protect the movement. Stalin refused. Although archival copies exist of the note in which Stalin refused to intervene, there are still no authoritative accounts of why he did so.

Historians have proposed some possible answers. The Soviets believed that they had secured the Iranian government's agreement to exploit the oil fields in the northern regions, making physical control less important. They harbored reservations about the reliability of

---

[6] Stephen L. McFarland, "A Peripheral View of the Origins of the Cold War: The Crises in Iran, 1941–47," *Diplomatic History*, Vol. 4, No. 4, October 1980, p. 350.

[7] James L. Gormly, "Keeping the Door Open in Saudi Arabia: The United States and the Dhahran Airfield, 1945–46," *Diplomatic History*, Vol. 4, No. 2, April 1980.

[8] Lawson, 1989, p. 317.

their surrogates in northern Iran. And they worried that by maintaining Soviet forces in Iran, they would be legitimating the presence of American and British forces elsewhere around the world.[9]

All of these factors likely featured in Stalin's calculus. But so, too, did U.S. military superiority in the region. By 1946, the large majority of the Soviet Union's heavy industrial plants and a considerable proportion of its oil production capability lay within striking distance of U.S. bases to the south—particularly the Dhahran airfield. A memorandum from the U.S. Joint Intelligence Staff noted, "Destruction by air of the Caucasian and Ploesti oil fields and the Ukraine and Ural industrial centers would prevent Soviet prosecution of war."[10] Several historians have argued that these capabilities gave the United States considerable leverage over the outcome of the Iran crisis.[11]

Outcomes

The Iran crisis was settled on terms heavily favorable to the United States. The Soviet Union ceased providing military and other assistance to proxies in Iran, and the Shah and prime minister of Iran were able to consolidate control of the country. The Iranians reputed their oil deal with the Soviet Union and instead signed one with the United States; the United States, through these terms, forged a close military relationship with a strategically important country along the Soviet Union's flank. The United States' actions were critical to all of these outcomes. Not only did U.S. military capabilities appear to play a role in forcing the Soviet Union to reconsider its support for its proxies, U.S. military assistance and training was a part of what convinced the Shah and the Iranian prime minister to take resolute action against the breakaway regions in the north—action that they had previously hesitated to take. According to U.S. diplomatic reporting from the time, the Shah claimed that the "most important" reason for these outcomes was the "conviction by all concerned (Soviets, Iranians and Azerbaijanis) that United States was solidly supporting Iranian sovereignty."[12]

In the longer term, the Iran crisis had more-complex consequences. It appears to have represented a "turning point" in U.S.-Soviet relations, one in which the Soviet Union became

---

[9] Jamil Hasanli, *At the Dawn of the Cold War: The Soviet-American Crisis over Iranian Azerbaijan, 1941–1946*, Lanham, Md.: Rowman and Littlefield Publishers, 2006, p. 368; and Geoffrey Roberts, "Moscow's Cold War on the Periphery: Soviet Policy in Greece, Iran, and Turkey, 1943–8," *Journal of Contemporary History*, Vol. 46, No. 1, January 2011, pp. 68–69.

[10] Cited in Lawson, 1989, pp. 319–320.

[11] Lawson, 1989; Polushchuk, 2011; and Hasanli, 2006, p. 369. Of course, U.S. forward posture was not solely responsible for Moscow's calculation of the potential consequences of continuing or escalating its activities in Iran. At the time, the United States possessed a monopoly on nuclear weapons and a global defense infrastructure. The United States' forward posture in the region, however, did offer it specific capabilities relevant to a contingency in Iran above and beyond its overall military potential.

[12] Pfau, 1977, p. 371.

convinced that the United States was an implacable adversary.[13] The crisis bolstered Soviet resolve to consolidate its gains in Eastern Europe, setting the stage for the most tense theater of the Cold War. And, of course, U.S. military support to the regime of the Shah would come to haunt it three decades later in the Iranian Revolution. The Iran crisis was only one contributing factor in all of these longer-lasting consequences. Moreover, it is impossible to know what would have happened had the United States not used its military posture for competitive advantage in Iran in 1946–1947. But the United States' clear success in the short-term gave way to a much more complex, nuanced outcome over the longer term.

Conclusion

The dynamics of the Iran crisis are largely consistent with the findings of the statistical analysis in the previous chapter. Forward-positioned forces and facilities in the region—in particular, the U.S. airfield at Dhahran—appear to have been important factors (combined with U.S. military capabilities more generally) in convincing the Soviet Union to abandon its surrogates by posing a credible threat of escalation if the Soviets continued to destabilize Iran. U.S. arms transfers and training to the Iranian government did not prompt Soviet support to proxies in the country (U.S. military assistance only began after the Soviets initiated their covert aid program). It does appear to have emboldened Tehran to commit to a forcible resolution of the dispute in northern Iran.

This case study also highlights the importance of looking beyond Moscow's immediate responses to understand the longer-term consequences of U.S. actions in the competition space. Strategic competition between the United States and the Soviet Union likely was inevitable following the end of World War II. The intensity of that competition and risks of escalation, however, were determined, in part, by the early actions and perceptions of each side. In denying the Soviets any influence in Iran, the United States strengthened Soviet perceptions that compromise with the United States was unrealistic, and it appears to have strengthened Moscow's resolve to compete aggressively against the United States in other theaters.

Spiraling Competition in the Horn of Africa, 1952–1977

Strategically located at the mouth of the Red Sea, Ethiopia provided the United States access for a communications and listening post for nearly a quarter of a century. As the price for its access agreement, the United States provided millions of dollars of military assistance to Ethiopia annually. This security cooperation, however, touched off an arms race between Ethiopia and Somalia that led to an intensifying series of conflicts in the Horn of Africa, culminating in the disastrous Ogaden War in 1977. In the process, Ethiopia switched allegiances

---

[13] Roberts, 2011; and McFarland, 1980, p. 334.

in the superpower competition, and the United States lost access to the strategically located country.

Background

In 1952, the United States and Ethiopia signed a Defense Installations Agreement and Mutual Defense Assistance Agreement. In these agreements, the United States traded military assistance for access to a former Italian naval radio facility, which it renamed the Kagnew Station. Located near the equator and at over 7,000 feet in elevation, the site of the Kagnew Station provided a critical location for U.S. naval communications, monitoring radio transmissions throughout Eastern Europe and Southwest Asia and eventually tracking U.S. satellites. The United States initially offered the Ethiopians $5 million in military assistance in an explicit quid pro quo for Kagnew. Over time, however, the amount would increase, eventually totaling hundreds of millions of dollars and accounting for nearly half of all U.S. military assistance to Africa.[14]

In 1960, neighboring Somalia gained its independence. Somalia was unique among sub-Saharan African countries in that the Somali nation was well-defined long before the country gained its independence. Because many Somalis lived in neighboring countries, the government in Mogadishu had irredentist ambitions—including in Ethiopia—from the time of Somalia's founding. Numerous, mostly small-scale border clashes between Somalia and Ethiopia began almost as soon as the country gained independence, as did violence within the heavily Somali region of Ogaden in Ethiopia.

Somalia had assumed a posture of nonalignment at the time of its independence. But after Somalia received what it felt to be an inadequate military assistance package from the West, it turned to the Soviet Union, which, in 1963, offered it military assistance worth several times what Ethiopia received. Emboldened by this assistance, Somalia ratcheted up the intensity of its attacks on Ethiopia.[15]

By the latter part of the 1960s and the first half of the 1970s, the United States faced a dilemma. On the one hand, Ethiopia was becoming increasingly unstable. In addition to ongoing border clashes and violent uprisings in the Ogaden, Addis Ababa faced a major armed revolt in Eritrea, where Kagnew was located. Emperor Haile Selassie, with whom the United States had enjoyed relatively strong relations since the 1950s, was aging, and there was widespread concern about what would happen to Ethiopia when he died.[16] The United

---

[14] Jefferey A. Lefebvre, *Arms for the Horn: U.S. Security Policy in Ethiopia and Somalia, 1953–1991*, Pittsburgh, Penn.: University of Pittsburgh Press, 1991; Jeffrey A. Lefebvre, "The United States, Ethiopia and the 1963 Somali-Soviet Arms Deal: Containment and the Balance of Power Dilemma in the Horn of Africa," *Journal of Modern African Studies*, Vol. 36, No. 4, 1998; Terrence Lyons, "The United States and Ethiopia: The Politics of a Patron-Client Relationship," *Northeast African Studies*, Vol. 8, No. 2/3, 1986; and Peter Schwab, "Cold War on the Horn of Africa," *African Affairs*, Vol. 77, No. 306, January 1978.

[15] Lefebvre, 1991, p. 114.

[16] Lyons, 1986, p. 66.

States also had concerns about the way that its military assistance was being used to put down internal political discontent.[17] On the other hand, especially by the 1970s, Ethiopia's strategic importance was also increasing. The Soviet Union sought to increase its influence in the region, and Soviet dominance in the Horn potentially would allow the Soviets to militarily threaten the vital oil shipping lanes in the Indian Ocean and possibly even the Arabian Peninsula.[18] Politically, the United States feared the pressure that the Soviet Union could exert on countries throughout the region if it gained a predominant position in the Horn. According to Henry Kissinger, the Soviets sought "to outflank the Middle East, to demonstrate that the U.S. cannot protect its friends, to raise doubts in Saudi Arabia right across the Red Sea, in Egypt, in the Sudan and in Iran."[19] Thus, the United States feared becoming overly committed in Ethiopia but also feared the consequences of terminating its commitment.

U.S. fears of Ethiopian instability were well-founded. In 1974, the Provisional Military Administrative Council (more commonly known as the *Derg*) overthrew the government of Haile Selassie and seized control. In 1976, the council declared Ethiopia to be a people's republic, and in 1977 it severed all military ties with the United States, which included the closure of Kagnew Station. A few months later, the Western Somali Liberation Front, heavily supported by Somali troops and weapons, seized nearly the entire Ogaden province. To prevent disaster, Ethiopia welcomed thousands of Cuban troops and Soviet advisors to fight off the Somalis.

U.S. Forward Posture

The U.S. military presence in Ethiopia comprised Kagnew Station and U.S. military assistance, including training activities. At its peak manning levels, 3,200 U.S. personnel were stationed at Kagnew, although their principal functions were limited to communications and intelligence.[20] Military assistance was initially valued at approximately $5 million annually, although this amount increased following the announcement of Soviet military aid to Somalia. Ultimately, the United States provided over $200 million of military assistance between the establishment of Kagnew in 1953 and the Derg's seizure of power in 1974, including the provision of small counterinsurgency training teams as conflicts in the Ogaden and Eritrea escalated.[21]

---

[17] See, for example, U.S. Department of State, Office of the Historian, "281. Telegram from the Department of State to the Embassy in Ethiopia," *Foreign Relations of the United States, 1964–1968*, Vol. XXIV, *Africa*, Washington, D.C., February 20, 1964b.

[18] Schwab, 1978; Lefebvre, 1991, p. 15.

[19] Quoted in Lawrence Freedman, "Military Power and Political Influence," *International Affairs*, Vol. 74, No. 4, October 1998, pp. 772–773.

[20] Schwab, 1978, p. 12.

[21] Schwab, 1978, p. 12.

During the 1960s, doubts grew within the U.S. government about the advisability of maintaining the relationship with Ethiopia. The immediate costs of the relationship—in terms of the amount of military assistance required to maintain access to Kagnew—were increasing. But there were also longer-term concerns: Many in Washington sensed "a dangerous resentment [of the emperor] among the younger generation of educated officers and bureaucrats [and] feared that this dissatisfaction would lead to an anti-American reaction when a new government eventually replaced" him.[22] Then–Under Secretary of State Nicholas Katzenbach warned that "the price of our tenure [could] involve us more deeply in the Horn of Africa than our vital interests warrant."[23] The military importance of Kagnew, however, trumped these concerns. In 1967, the Joint Chiefs of Staff prepared a contingency plan in case withdrawal from Kagnew became necessary, but they simultaneously advocated for retaining the facility. Withdrawal, they warned, "would seriously prejudice U.S. security interests and would seriously reduce U.S. military capability in the Middle East, South Asia, and Indian Ocean areas."[24] The United States continued to support the Ethiopian regime for another decade.

Soviet Response

The Soviet decision to provide Somalia with assistance was a complex one. Aside from Kagnew Station, Ethiopia was clearly the greatest "prize" for superpower competition in the Horn because of its size, strategic location, and diplomatic clout. But with Ethiopia at least temporarily out of its reach, Moscow began to invest in Somalia, in part to establish a position in the Horn and, in part, to put pressure on the Ethiopian government. The Soviets did not encourage Somali irredentism; indeed, Moscow feared that a Somali war against Ethiopia would almost certainly be a losing enterprise, and it risked alienating Ethiopians with whom Moscow hoped to cultivate relationships.[25] Military assistance for Somalia, however, might provide the Soviet Union with leverage to force Ethiopia to distance itself from the United States.[26] Indeed, the U.S. State Department feared precisely this outcome, warning, "Inadequate U.S. support for Ethiopia in the current crisis could tempt the Ethiopians to offer to remove Kagnew in exchange for reduced Soviet support of Somalia."[27]

---

[22] Lyons, 1986, p. 66.

[23] Cited in Walter S. Poole, *The Joint Chiefs of Staff and National Policy, 1965–1968*, Washington, D.C.: Office of Joint History, Office of the Chairman of the Joint Chiefs of Staff, 2012, p. 207.

[24] Cited in Poole, 2012, p. 208.

[25] Lefebvre, 1991, pp. 43–44; Radoslav A. Yordanov, *The Soviet Union and the Horn of Africa During the Cold War: Between Ideology and Pragmatism*, Lanham, Md.: Lexington Books, 2016.

[26] Lefebvre, 1991, p. 114.

[27] U.S. Department of State, Office of the Historian, "290. Circular Airgram From the Department of State to Certain African Posts: U.S. Policy in the Horn of Africa," *Foreign Relations of the United States, 1964–1968*, Vol. XXIV: *Africa*, Washington, D.C., March 21, 1964c.

The Soviet Union began this competition at a disadvantage. Compared with the United States and the other countries of the West, it had comparatively little to offer as an economic partner. To make up for these weaknesses in other fields, the Soviets had to outbid the United States and other Western countries by offering considerably more military support to Somalia than the West would. Indeed, Moscow's initial military assistance package to Somalia was worth approximately $30 million—roughly six times what the United States had been offering annually to Ethiopia and one of the largest packages of Soviet military support to any developing country.[28]

Outcomes

What is perhaps most notable about these events on the Horn is that both the United States and the Soviet Union sought to avoid armed conflict in the region. At each step along the way, however, both superpowers took incremental steps in reaction to the decisions of local actors. The end result was much higher costs than either superpower had anticipated and a devastating series of wars in the Horn.

The United States' principal focus in Ethiopia was on economic development, not military assistance.[29] And indeed, the United States repeatedly resisted pressures from Addis Ababa to increase its military aid, fearing that this support reinforced the government's preference for military solutions to the political problems in the Ogaden and Eritrea. The United States provided military assistance explicitly as a quid pro quo for access to Kagnew Station.

This assistance, however, pushed Somalia toward the Soviet Union—a fact that was recognized by the State Department and intelligence community.[30] The United States attempted to dissuade Mogadishu from seeking Soviet support, working with various allies to offer the regime a military aid package. But the size of the package had to remain small for fear of antagonizing Ethiopia. In the end, this effort only pushed Mogadishu further toward Moscow. The Somali government perceived the Western offer

> as a thinly disguised plot to perpetuate Ethiopia's military predominance, thereby bringing to an end the Somali irredentist quest in the Horn. In light of Washington's commitment to support an Ethiopian Army of some 40,000, along with the provision of two squadrons of F-86 Sabre jets during the preceding three years, Mogadishu certainly had

---

[28] Yordanov, 2016, p. 46.

[29] Paul B. Henze, *Is There Hope for the Horn of Africa? Reflections on the Political and Economic Impasses*, Santa Monica, Calif.: RAND Corporation, N-2738-USDP, June 1988, pp. 9–10.

[30] U.S. Department of State, Office of the Historian, "346. Memorandum from the Under Secretary of State (Katzenbach) to President Johnson: Your Meeting with Prime Minister Mohamed Ibrahim Egal of the Somali Republic," *Foreign Relations of the United States, 1964–1968*, Vol. XXIV, *Africa*, Washington, D.C., March 12, 1968; and U.S. Department of State, Office of the Historian, "287. National Intelligence Estimate 75/76–701," *Foreign Relations of the United States, 1969–1976*, Vol. E–5, Pt. 1, *Documents on Sub-Saharan Africa, 1969–1972*, Washington, D.C., May 21, 1970.

reason to feel that the Western aid package was not only inadequate, but anti-Somali in nature. Given such a military imbalance, Addis Ababa would have little motivation to negotiate with Mogadishu over the fate of the Somalis in the Ogaden. Thus, in October 1963 Somalia accepted an unconditional offer from the Soviet Union for $30 million in military aid to expand the Somali Army from 4,000 to 20,000 soldiers, and to assist in the development of an air force.[31]

Because of this Soviet support for the Somalis, the United States found itself under severe pressure from Addis Ababa to increase its assistance to Ethiopia. The United States clearly feared the consequences of increasing its assistance. The State Department, for instance, warned, "Full support of Ethiopia in a conflict with a Soviet-armed Somalia would only aggravate the basic ethnic and tribal tensions in the area without solving them."[32] But as tensions between Ethiopia and Somalia spiraled, the United States felt helpless to persuade Addis Ababa to defuse tensions and unable to refuse continued Ethiopian demands for increased military support:

> Through our Ambassador in Addis, we have been trying persuade [Haile Selassie] that purely military solution not answer to Ogaden question, that economic and social measures to improve lot of Ogaden Somalis, coupled with effort seek areas of agreement, however small, with [the Government of the Somali Republic], offer superior chances achieving long-range solution. Increasing reports of arms support to Ogaden Somalis from [the Somali] side of border can only undermine such attempts on part [of the U.S. government], creating situation in which we cannot afford be unresponsive to pressure for further military assistance from [the Ethiopian government].[33]

The Soviet Union similarly sought to restrain its proxies. According to a U.S. National Intelligence Estimate at the time, "It would be as awkward for the USSR [Union of Soviet Socialist Republics] as for the U.S. if open war broke out in the Horn. Hence we judge that the Soviets will try to restrain the Somalis."[34]

Despite the efforts of both superpowers, war *did* break out on the Horn. In the Ogaden War of 1977, both Ethiopia and Somalia switched superpower patrons. By that point, both superpowers had invested vastly more in military aid than either had intended. For the Soviet

---

[31] Lefebvre, 1991, pp. 113-114.

[32] U.S. Department of State, Office of the Historian, 1964c.

[33] U.S. Department of State, Office of the Historian, "277. Telegram from the Department of State to the Embassy in Somalia, "*Foreign Relations of the United States, 1964–1968*, Vol. XXIV, *Africa*, Washington, D.C., January 21, 1964a.

[34] U.S. Department of State, Office of the Historian, 1970. The Soviets' true motives are disputed by historians, and archival records available since the end of the Cold War have not fully resolved the question. On balance, however, records appear to indicate that while the Soviet Union did engage in political subversion against the Selassie regime, it saw these activities as a long-term investment and was not seeking a rapid and violent overthrow of the government. See Yordanov, 2016.

Union, its commitment was only beginning; to defend its newfound allies in Addis Ababa, it was forced to commit thousands of Cuban forces and Soviet military advisors. For the people of the Horn itself, the wars and ensuing chaos would be more costly still.

Conclusion

This case provides robust evidence in support of the proposition that materiel transfers and training can have destabilizing consequences. In line with the statistical results presented in Chapter Four, U.S. military assistance to Ethiopia appears to have helped touch off competitive arms sales by the Soviets to the Somalis. Soviet military assistance, in turn, appears to have emboldened the Somalis to launch direct cross-border attacks on Ethiopia and ratchet up the intensity of Somali support for armed proxies in the Ogaden.

The evidence on other relationships is more ambiguous. The analysis in Chapter Four suggests that the presence of U.S. forces in a country seems to have mixed effects, having no strong patterns one way or the other. In the case of Ethiopia, Kagnew Station did not appear to have deterred Somali aggression against Ethiopia. On the other hand, the facility was a listening and communications post, not designed for combat roles, and thus the failure to deter either direct armed attacks or proxy warfare is not surprising. Military agreements appear to have no effect on malign activities in competition, although they are associated with a lower likelihood of conventional armed aggression. The U.S. military agreements with Addis Ababa did not deter such aggression. Again, however, the agreements simply exchanged access for a listening and communication facility for limited U.S. military assistance and did not pledge the United States to defend the host country (an early Ethiopian request that the United States had refused). Thus, its deterrent effects were understandably minimal.

The case has broader implications for our understanding of the relationship between U.S. forward posture and competition outcomes. The tone of State Department documents at the time is striking: The United States clearly felt trapped in its relationship with Ethiopia, fearing the consequences of its military assistance but unable to terminate such aid for fear of losing access to Kagnew. The United States was able to maintain access to the station until the widespread use of satellites made the facility less strategically important in the 1970s. But in the process, the United States was drawn into a damaging local competition that it had tried to avoid with negative consequences for all of the actors involved.

The Euromissile Crisis, 1979–1983

By the late 1970s, both the United States and the Soviet Union were making sizeable increases in their defense capabilities, and the Cold War's period of détente was in jeopardy. In the midst of these escalating tensions, NATO committed to the deployment of U.S. intermediate-range nuclear missiles to several countries in Western Europe in response to the Soviet Union's modernization of its own intermediate-range missile systems. The modernization of the Soviet Union's intermediate-range nuclear capabilities and NATO's subsequent deployment of the so-called "Euromissiles" provoked massive popular discontent in Europe and a period of dangerous confrontation between the two blocs. The crisis sheds light on several hostile measures that Moscow has used to combat U.S. forward posture in highly developed allied countries. It also hints at the possible arc of confrontation between the United States and Russia today as both sides again work to develop long-range weapons systems that might threaten strategic stability.

Background

The latter half of the 1970s represented a period of rising tensions in the superpower relationship. On the one hand, the Soviet Union was engaged in an unprecedented period of intervention in the so-called Third World. U.S. National Security Advisor Zbigniew Brzezinski famously declared that détente had been "buried in the sands of the Ogaden"—a reference to the deployment of Soviet and Cuban forces to Ethiopia, discussed in the previous case study. Shortly thereafter, the Soviet Union invaded Afghanistan, thus appearing to threaten the Middle East from both the east (Afghanistan) and the west (the Horn of Africa). Meanwhile, the Soviet Union was improving its capabilities for high-intensity warfare— both quantitatively and qualitatively—in Europe, all during a period when the United States military was recovering from the war in Vietnam. These events presaged the arrival of what is frequently called "the second Cold War" in the following decade. Then–Soviet General Secretary Mikhail Gorbachev later observed of this period, "Never perhaps in the postwar decades was the situation in the world as explosive, and hence more difficult and unfavourable, as in the first half of the 1980s."[35]

It was against this backdrop that the Euromissile crisis played out. In 1977, the Soviet Union began to deploy the SS-20 missile, an advanced nuclear-armed intermediate-range ballistic missile capable of reaching all of Europe. As described in Chapter One, these missiles posed a political challenge to NATO. Because the missiles could be used to attack all of the United States' European allies without posing a direct danger to the United States itself, many European leaders feared that these missiles would "decouple" the security interests of the United States from those of Europe. If doubts arose about the credibility of the United States' commitment to the security of its allies, Moscow could potentially use nuclear intimidation to sway the foreign policies of the Western European states.

In consultation with its European allies, particularly then–West German Chancellor Helmut Schmidt, the United States committed to produce and deploy its own intermediate-range systems in Europe to offset the Soviet advantage and mitigate the risk of strategic decoupling. In December 1979, member-states of the NATO alliance agreed to what was known as the *dual-track strategy* in which it would simultaneously commit to the deployment of these

---

[35] Cited in Ben B. Fisher, *A Cold War Conundrum: The Soviet War Scare*, Washington, D.C.: Central Intelligence Agency, Center for the Study of Intelligence, CSI 97-10002, September 1997.

INF and to pursuing arms control aimed at restoring parity in this category of weapon at the lowest possible level of forces.[36]

Nearly four years elapsed between NATO's announcement of this initiative and the ultimate deployment of the two intermediate-range systems the United States developed: the ballistic Pershing II missiles and the ground-launched cruise missiles (GLCMs) known as Gryphons. The intervening four years were four of the most difficult in the history of the transatlantic alliance. The INF deployments were extremely unpopular in large parts of Europe. In the countries that were ultimately to host these weapon systems—West Germany, Italy, Belgium, the Netherlands, and the United Kingdom—antinuclear groups organized massive demonstrations, some with participants numbering in the hundreds of thousands. Hundreds of thousands more activists went door-to-door in a campaign to rally opposition to the deployments. Despite this popular opposition and the political upheavals that it caused in many of these countries, the deployments of the Pershing IIs and Gryphons began as scheduled in November 1983.

U.S. Forward Posture

In December 1979, NATO reached the decision to deploy 108 Pershing II ballistic missiles and 464 Gryphon GLCMs, with ranges sufficient to reach sensitive sites in the Soviet Union. The Soviets perceived these missiles as highly threatening:

> In the eyes of the Soviet political and military leaders, the threat posed by these systems— primarily the Pershing II—lay in their short flight time to targets in the European Soviet Union. Soviet military experts believed the Pershing II to be a greater danger than ICBMs [intercontinental ballistic missiles] deployed in the United States . . . The supreme leadership viewed the combination of short flight time and high accuracy inherent in the Pershing II to be the most serious threat to the USSR . . . A major consideration was the fact that the decision to use Pershing II or any Euromissiles had to be easier to take, as the Soviet side viewed it, because the missiles would not be launched from American territory.[37]

The risk to critical Soviet targets—in particular, top command and control nodes— became all the more credible after December 1981, when the Soviet Union discovered that a Soviet defector had provided NATO details of the Soviet command bunkers from which it would direct a war in Europe.[38]

---

[36] Later, U.S. strategy sought the elimination of this category of nuclear weapons, the so-called *zero option*.

[37] Aleksandr' G. Savel'yev and Nikolai N. Detinov, *The Big Five: Arms Control Decision-Making in the Soviet Union*, Dmitry Trenin, trans., and Gregory Varhall, ed., Westport, Conn. and London, U.K.: Praeger, 1995, p. 57; see also Brendan R. Green and Austin Long, "The MAD Who Wasn't There: Soviet Reactions to the Late Cold War Nuclear Balance," *Security Studies*, Vol. 26, No. 4, 2017.

[38] Gordon Barrass, "*Able Archer* 83: What Were the Soviets Thinking?" *Survival*, Vol. 58, No. 6, December 2016–January 2017, p. 13.

Soviet Response

NATO's decision to move forward with the INF deployments was motivated by the perception that the Soviets were pressing their military advantages on several fronts. By the early 1980s, however, the Soviets saw themselves as reacting to a multifaceted campaign by the United States to intimidate and "blackmail" the Soviet Union. In 1981, Yuri Andropov (then-chairman of the Committee for State Security [KGB]) reportedly told an ally that the United States was "striving for military superiority in order to 'check' us and then declare 'checkmate' against us without starting a war."[39] The West's attempt to develop and maintain long-term military superiority, in part through the deployment of the Pershing IIs and Gryphons, was supposedly one critical part in this broader offensive.[40] The United States, meanwhile, was unaware of how genuinely Moscow perceived itself to be facing an existential threat. As one senior Soviet expert at the Central Intelligence Agency later admitted, "We didn't realise just how [expletive]ing scared Soviet leaders were of us."[41]

The Soviets launched a multipronged campaign to try to head off the INF deployments. When NATO leaders first began to debate the proposed deployments, Moscow responded with diplomatic pressure. Soviet leaders offered to make reductions in the country's own intermediate-range nuclear capabilities, as well as reductions in the number of Soviet troops and tanks in East Germany. At the same time, they warned that if NATO continued on the path to INF deployments, it would place détente in jeopardy. Then-President Jimmy Carter dismissed the Soviets' offer as propaganda designed to weaken NATO cohesion.[42] The Soviet Union also appears to have offered economic inducements to Europeans whom it perceived receptive—again, without success.[43]

As their diplomatic overtures failed to create cracks within the NATO alliance, the Soviet Union increasingly turned to hostile measures to prevent the deployments. The primary line of effort was an influence campaign designed to turn both European leaders and populations against the INF deployments. The Soviets funded and, in some cases, helped to organize several nongovernmental organizations in Western Europe as part of an attempt to place pressure on Western European leaders, including such organizations as "Generals for Peace" and

---

[39] Cited in Barrass, 2016–2017, p. 10. See also Gerhard Wettig, "The Last Soviet Offensive in the Cold War: Emergence and Development of the Campaign Against NATO Euromissiles, 1979–1983," *Cold War History*, Vol. 9, No. 1, February 2009, p. 98.

[40] Vojtech Mastny, "How Able Was 'Able Archer'? Nuclear Trigger and Intelligence in Perspective," *Journal of Cold War Studies*, Vol. 11, No. 1, Winter 2009, p. 12.

[41] Cited in Barrass, 2016–2017, p. 24.

[42] Charles G. Crupper, Jr. and Richard T. McDonald, *The Ground-Launched Cruise Missile in NATO: Political Aspects*, Montgomery, Ala.: Air Command and Staff College, 1988.

[43] U.S. House of Representatives Permanent Select Committee on Intelligence, *Soviet Active Measures: Hearings Before the Permanent Select Committee on Intelligence*, Washington, D.C., July 13–14, 1982, p. 44.

the "Democratic Front Against Repression."[44] The majority of Soviet funds in this campaign, however, went to the World Peace Council, which received an estimated $63 million from the Soviets.[45] Because many of these organizations had relatively few financial resources of their own, such assistance greatly magnified their ability to communicate with and organize large numbers of potential followers.[46] The Soviets also engaged in a campaign of disinformation, fabricating forged "official documents" from the United States and other Western governments that were designed to heighten war fears and drive wedges between NATO governments.[47] Archival records suggest Soviet leaders took considerable pride in this campaign.[48]

When these influence campaigns failed to stop the deployment of the Pershing IIs and Gryphons in November 1983, the Soviets turned to more-menacing measures in an apparent attempt to intimidate the Western European host countries. In the spring of 1984, the Soviet Union staged the largest naval exercises it had ever held in the Atlantic. Soon thereafter, it conducted the largest Soviet field exercise ever held—and held it in East Germany, just across the border from the European state that had pressed most strongly for the INF deployments. The Soviets also engaged in military intimidation with nuclear weapons. Before the INF deployments, the Soviet Union had never acknowledged that it had stationed short-range nuclear forces in Eastern Europe. But just as NATO was preparing to deploy the Pershing IIs and Gryphons, Moscow revealed that it did indeed have such short-range nuclear weapons stationed throughout Eastern Europe and went further, deploying additional short-range SS-21, SS-22, and SS-23 missiles, claiming that these actions were "necessary to restore the balance allegedly overturned by the cruise missile and Pershing II deployments."[49]

There is some limited evidence to suggest that Moscow considered using violent measures as part of its campaign to politically subvert the INF deployments. According to one former British intelligence official, "in early 1983 the KGB set about identifying places near U.S. bases to conceal explosives that, when detonated, would have appeared to be a terrorist attack. When, in October 1984, [then–East German General Secretary Erich] Honecker discussed with [then–Soviet Foreign Minister Andrei] Gromyko the failure of the peace movement to prevent the deployment of the Euromissiles, Honecker said this was due to the fact

---

[44] Thomas Rid, *Active Measures: The Secret History of Disinformation and Political Warfare*, New York: Farrar, Straus, and Giroux, 2020, Chapter Nineteen.

[45] Lesley Kucharski, *Russian Multi-Domain Strategy Against NATO: Information Confrontation and U.S. Forward-Deployed Nuclear Weapons in Europe*, Livermore, Calif.: Lawrence Livermore National Laboratory, 2018, p. 21.

[46] Wettig, 2009, p. 92.

[47] Rid, 2020, chapter nineteen; Kucharski, 2018, p. 21.

[48] Simon Miles, *Engaging the Evil Empire: Washington, Moscow, and the Beginning of the End of the Cold War*, Ithaca, N.Y. and London, U.K.: Cornell University Press, 2020, p. 79.

[49] John Van Oudenaren, *Soviet Policy Toward Western Europe: Objectives, Instruments, Results*, Santa Monica, Calif.: RAND Corporation, R-3310-AF, 1986, pp. 45–50.

that the protests had remained non-violent."[50] Interestingly, it was in this same period in the 1980s that the East German Stasi worked most intensively with West German terrorist organizations, such as the Red Army Faction, including providing training in weapons and tactics similar to those used in a failed Red Army Faction assassination attempt against U.S. General James Kroesen in Heidelberg.[51] These links suggest that similar violent measures related to the INF deployments were not only considered, but could have been implemented had Moscow chosen to do so.[52] The likely U.S. and NATO reaction if such violent acts were discovered, however, appears to have dissuaded the Soviet Union from undertaking them.[53]

This case study began with a discussion of the debates within the U.S. State Department about the potential for Moscow to launch or intensify proxy wars in developing countries to punish the United States for the INF deployments. In the course of the research for this case study, we found no indication that the Soviets actually did so. At one level, the fact that the Soviets did not turn to violent malign activities during the Euromissile crisis is reassuring. On the other hand, it was little more than a year after the first INF deployments that Mikhail Gorbachev became General Secretary of the Soviet Union. It is not clear what might have happened had a more hawkish leader assumed power.

The Euromissile crisis produced one other "dog that didn't bark"—the infamous Able Archer episode of 1983. Every year, NATO conducted its Autumn Forge exercises to prepare for a potential war in Europe. In 1983, for the first time, these exercises were to conclude with an exercise intended to rehearse procedures for the transition from conventional to nuclear war. This exercise, named Able Archer, by happenstance took place in November 1983—the same month that the United States was scheduled to deploy its Pershing IIs and GLCMs to Europe. Speaking after the end of the Cold War, former Soviet General Viktor Yesin of the Strategic Missile Forces explained that large-scale military exercises, such as Autumn Forge, were "fraught with possibilities that under the cover of such an exercise an unexpected nuclear missiles strike could be launched."[54] But Able Archer-83 took on a much more menacing appearance with the impending INF deployments.

---

[50] Barrass, 2016–2017, p. 12.

[51] David Vielhaber, "The Stasi–Meinhof Complex?" *Studies in Conflict and Terrorism*, Vol. 36, No. 7, 2013; Marian K. Leighton, "Strange Bedfellows: The Stasi and the Terrorists," *International Journal of Intelligence and CounterIntelligence*, Vol. 27, No. 24, 2014; and Catherine Belton, *Putin's People: How the KGB Took Back Russia and Then Took On the West*, New York: Farrar, Straus and Giroux, 2020.

[52] Reportedly, the former head of the KGB's foreign intelligence, General Alexander Sakharovsky, had declared on more than one occasion, "In today's world, when nuclear arms have made military force obsolete, terrorism should become our main weapon" (Belton, 2020).

[53] Barrass, 2016–2017, p. 12.

[54] Cited in Barrass, 2016–2017, p. 17.

For a time, many observers believed that the Able Archer exercise in 1983 was the closest the United States and Soviet Union came to a nuclear war since the Cuban Missile Crisis.[55] Subsequent scholarship that is based on broader access to national security archives from the former Soviet bloc has disputed this conclusion, finding that the Soviets did go into a heightened state of alert but did not come close to launching a preemptive nuclear strike.[56] For at least some of these historians, however, this outcome was not to be taken for granted; had circumstances been different, the Soviets might have interpreted this exercise as an existential threat.[57]

Outcomes

Despite the political turmoil that accompanied the INF deployments, they were completed and transatlantic unity held. The crisis is generally considered a failure of Soviet foreign and defense policy. Not only did the Pershing II and Gryphon deployments restore the theater-level nuclear parity that NATO had lost after the development of the Soviet SS-20s, but the U.S. missiles were actually more capable than the SS-20s, leaving the Soviets militarily worse off.[58] In his memoirs, Gorbachev offered a devastating critique of the SS-20 decision:

> [T]he Soviet leadership failed to take into account the probable reaction of the Western countries. I would even go so far as to characterize it as an unforgivable adventure, embarked on by the previous Soviet leadership under pressure from the military-industrial complex. They might have assumed that, while we deployed our missiles, Western counter-measures would be impeded by the peace movement. If so, such a calculation was more than naïve.[59]

It would be wrong, however, to be sanguine about the costs and risks associated with the Euromissile crisis. The deployments, for instance, galvanized a peace movement in West Germany that (with some degree of help from Soviet "active measures") destroyed what had

---

[55] See, in particular, the declassified memorandum of the President's Foreign Intelligence Advisory Board, "The Soviet 'War Scare,'" Washington, D.C., February 15, 1990.

[56] See, for instance, Barrass, 2016–2017; Mastny, 2009; and Dmitry Adamsky, "'Not Crying Wolf': Soviet Intelligence and the 1983 War Scare," in Leopoldo Nuti, Frederic Bozo, Marie-Pierre Rey, and Bernd Rother, eds., *The Euromissile Crisis and the End of the Cold War*, Washington, D.C.: Woodrow Wilson Center Press with Stanford University Press, 2015.

[57] Vojtech Mastny, for instance, wrote, "If neither side jumped into action on any of the frequent ominous but murky situations that may have been close calls, this attested to a critical margin of willingness to give the enemy the benefit of the doubt—an important side effect of the otherwise ambivalent East-West détente" (Mastny, 2009, p. 120).

[58] Van Oudenaren, 1986, p. v.

[59] Mikhail Gorbachev, *Memoirs*, London, U.K.: Doubleday, 1996, p. 443.

been a broad-based post-war political consensus on security policy in that country.[60] With the end of the Cold War and collapse of the Soviet Union only a few years after the INF deployments, the potential consequences of that political polarization were never tested. Under other circumstances, German political developments may have caused considerable problems within the transatlantic alliance. Similarly, most historians now appear to believe that Able Archer-83 was not the nuclear near-miss that it was once believed to have been. But some of the same historians have expressed concern about what might have happened during that exercise had Soviet leadership been different or had the Soviets not had the same high quality of intelligence available.

Conclusion

The Soviet response to the deployment of the Euromissiles broadly conforms with the findings of the quantitative analysis in the previous chapter. Those findings suggest that U.S. forward-positioned forces generally deter malign activities in the regions in which they are positioned. The host countries for those forces, however, may be targeted by competitors seeking to signal their opposition to U.S. presence or to impose costs on the host countries in an effort to undermine political support for cooperation with the United States. Such hostile measures should be particularly likely when the presence of U.S. forces represents a sharp change in U.S. policy, when they are positioned close to a competitor or adversary, and/or when they possess sensitive capabilities. The INF deployments were provocative for all three reasons. They introduced a new category of U.S. nuclear weapons into Europe, just on the edge of the Soviet bloc. The missiles were particularly feared by the Soviets because of their precision guidance systems and rapid flight times—capabilities that together made a surprise attack on key Soviet command and control nodes seem plausible. It is thus not surprising that these deployments attracted Soviet hostile measures. At the same time, the Soviets appear to have been deterred from undertaking more-aggressive actions, such as provoking violence at mass demonstrations against the deployments.

The case study also conforms with the expectation that U.S. military activities—especially ones that involve novel elements and exercise sensitive capabilities close to U.S. competitors—can be escalatory. Able Archer-83 was precisely such an activity, making use of new procedures and communications channels for an exercise that involved a simulated escalation to nuclear war and inadvertently was timed to coincide with the arrival of the Pershing IIs and Gryphons. Able Archer-83 did not lead to escalation, but had circumstances been different (for instance, if the Soviets had lacked the extremely sophisticated intelligence capabilities that allowed them to correctly interpret the purpose of the exercise), the risk could have been much greater.

---

[60] Alexander R. Alexiev, *The Soviet Campaign Against INF: Strategy, Tactics, and Means*, Santa Monica, Calif.: RAND Corporation, N-2280-AF, 1985, pp. 42–43.

The Euromissile crisis bears a number of similarities to ongoing debates in the United States about the development and deployment of LRPF capabilities. The lessons of the crisis, however, are complex. On the one hand, the INF deployments were an important demonstration of NATO unity (a "costly signal" of its resolve to respond to the Soviet military build-up of the 1970s). The deployments also neutralized the potential threat posed by the Soviet SS-20s, both in competition as well as in a possible armed conflict. Soviet leaders perceived the outcome of the crisis as a defeat.

But the events of this period might have transpired very differently under other circumstances. Had the Soviets not invaded Afghanistan just after NATO announced its decision on INF deployments in 1979, it is possible that NATO member-states would not have perceived the Soviet Union as sufficiently threatening to warrant the political costs of its INF policy. Had the Soviets and East Germans not had such excellent intelligence on U.S. and NATO decisionmaking, they might have interpreted Able Archer-83 differently. Had Soviet leadership not first been thrown into turmoil by the death of Andropov and the brief chairmanship of Konstantin Chernenko and then turned more reformist under Gorbachev, Moscow might have responded more aggressively to the INF deployments. And if the Cold War had not ended only a few years after the INF deployments, the rejuvenated European peace movement and the political polarization of defense policy issues in Europe could have had more severe consequences for alliance cohesion.

The events of 1979–1983 suggest that the United States can forward position even highly sensitive capabilities when military and foreign policy requirements demand it. But the success of such posture decisions is likely to rest on the political resilience of the host countries, the skill of U.S. and allied and partner diplomats, and the ability of U.S. and competitor governments to mitigate the heightened risk of inadvertent escalation through improved communication and transparency.

Escalation to the Russo-Georgian War, 2001–2008

Background

The United States and Georgia had engaged in very minor security cooperation activities during the first decade following Georgia's independence in 1991. It was not until 2002, however, following the September 11, 2001, attacks, that these activities accelerated, initially under the Georgian Train and Equip Program (GTEP). The United States was concerned that Georgia potentially harbored radical Islamists in the Pankisi Gorge, located in northern Georgia. The United States then engaged in security cooperation programs aimed at increasing Georgian military capacity to enable Georgia to deal with such problems internally.[61]

---

[61] Rick Fawn, "Russia's Reluctant Retreat from the Caucasus: Abkhazia, Georgia, and the US After 11 September 2001," *European Security*, Vol. 11, No. 4, 2002.

Security cooperation between the United States and Georgia increased following the 2003 Rose Revolution, which placed Mikheil Saakashvili's pro-Western government in power.[62]

U.S.-Georgian security cooperation activities, however, threatened to further strain the relationship between Russia and Georgia. These two countries had maintained rocky relations since the collapse of the Soviet Union. As Georgia declared its independence from the Soviet Union, the Georgian regions of Abkhazia and South Ossetia, located on the Georgian-Russian border, broke away from Georgia and declared themselves independent. Russia supported these separatist movements in the 1990s and then increased its support of the separatist regions as relations between Georgia and Russia worsened during the 2000s.[63] Relations between Russia and Georgia, already volatile, worsened after the Rose Revolution and Mikheil Saakashvili's rise to power. Saakashvili emphasized Western integration and the reunification of separatist regions with Georgia, goals that ran counter to Russia's intentions for the region and led to worsening relations.[64]

Tensions between the countries, which had been building since the collapse of the Soviet Union, reached their nadir during the 2008 war in Georgia, which ran from August 8–12, 2008. Although U.S. military involvement in the region did not directly lead to the 2008 war, it might have contributed to the escalating tensions between the two countries. On the one hand, Russia feared that U.S.-Georgian military cooperation and Georgia's ascension to NATO would (1) displace Russian interests in what it considered to be its sphere of influence and (2) threaten Russia's southern border. These fears spurred Russia toward more-aggressive actions against Georgia. On the other hand, U.S. military cooperation with Georgia might have emboldened the country's leadership by strengthening Georgian military capabilities relative to those of the separatist forces in South Ossetia and Abkhazia and, in conjunction with U.S. political statements, helped create the false impression that the United States would support Georgia in the event of a conflict with Russia. Although the causes of and responsibility for the Russo-Georgian War are hotly disputed, most observers believe Georgia's active pursuit of a NATO MAP, U.S. public support for such a plan in April 2008, and joint U.S.-Georgian military exercises were all parts of the complex set of factors that led to the August 2008 conflict.[65]

[62] Ivan Ivanov, "Train and Equip . . . For Aggression [Obucheneye I osnashchennye . . . dlya agressii]," *On Guard of the Arcti [Na strazhe Zapolyar'ya]*, No. 65, 2008; Vyacheslav Tseluiko, "Reformation of the Georgian Army Under Saakashvili Prior to the 2008 Five Day War," in Ruslan Pukhov, ed., *Tanks of August: Collected Papers*, Moscow: Center for the Analysis of Strategies and Technologies, 2009, pp. 14–15.

[63] Stylianos A. Sotiriou, "The Irreversibility of History: The Conflicts in South Ossetia and Abkhazia," *Problems of Post-Communism*, Vol. 66, No. 3, 2019.

[64] Ghia Nodia, "The War for Georgia: Russia, the West, the Future," blog post, Open Democracy, August 15, 2008; Tseluiko, 2009, pp. 14–15.

[65] John Feffer and Stephen Zunes, "U.S. Role in Georgia Crisis," blog post, Foreign Policy in Focus, August 14, 2008; Ivanov, 2008.

U.S. Forward Posture

The first major security cooperation program between the United States and Georgia was GTEP, which ran from 2002 to 2004 and spanned the administrations of both Eduard Shevardnadze and Saakashvili. GTEP provided $64 million to the Georgian government for the training of 2,700 troops by U.S. personnel and the acquisition of modern military equipment.[66] Although the United States' stated purpose for GTEP was to train Georgian forces to counter Islamist terrorism, many Georgian officials reportedly believed that the assistance provided by the United States would allow the Georgian military to prepare for a potential conflict in Abkhazia.[67] These conflicting views of the ultimate purpose of U.S. assistance were apparent in later programs as well, including those undertaken to help train and equip Georgian forces that participated in the U.S.-led operations in Iraq and Afghanistan.

Georgia strengthened its relations with the United States and NATO following the Rose Revolution, which ushered the pro-Western government into power. From Saakashvili's ascent to power in 2003 to the start of the 2008 war, Georgia received over $300 million in military aid from the United States, which represented 21 percent of U.S. aid to the states of the former Soviet Union.[68] Programs included the Georgia Sustainment and Stability Operations Program, which ran from spring 2005 to autumn 2006, and various programs that provided aid for the purchase of arms by the Georgian military.[69] U.S. arms acquisition programs provided Georgia with funding to purchase armored personnel carriers, helicopters, artillery systems, and light arms. The majority of these arms were purchased from former Soviet or Warsaw Pact states that had poor relations with Russia, such as the Czech Republic (now Czechia) or Ukraine.[70] Eventually, more than 12,000 Georgian military personnel participated in U.S. training programs.[71] The United States also participated in several multilateral military exercises with Georgia, sometimes involving 1,000 or more U.S. troops, such as the exercise Immediate Response, which took place shortly before the 2008 war.[72]

---

[66] Tseluiko, 2009, p. 13; and Aleksandr Ganin, "What Does Georgia Want? [Chego khochet Gruziya?]" *On Guard of the Motherland* [*Na strazhe Rodiny*], No. 91, November 18, 2008.

[67] Fawn, 2002, p. 137; Paul Quinn-Judge, "Down but Not Out: The Breakaway Republic of Abkhazia Braces for Another Attack from Georgia," *Time International*, May 20, 2002, quoted in Fawn, 2002; and Anna Badkhen, "Georgia Has Its Own Agenda: U.S. Trainers Seen as Allies Against Secessionists," *San Francisco Chronicle*, March 21, 2002, updated January 30, 2012.

[68] Ivanov, 2008; and A. Novik, "Georgia. Instead of Russia—The U.S. and NATO? [Gruziya. Vmesto Rossii—SshA i NATO?]" *Guardian of the Baltic* [*Strazh Baltiki*], No. 171, October 13, 2005.

[69] Ivanov, 2008.

[70] Ivanov, 2008.

[71] Feffer and Zunes, 2008.

[72] In an article published immediately following the 2008 war, a Russian military analyst stated that the Immediate Response 2008 military exercise served as a spark for the larger conflict. See Ivanov, 2008.

Russian Response

Russia has consistently expressed discontent with U.S. actions in Georgia, arguing that these actions increased the aggressiveness of Georgian governmental policies against the separatist regions of Abkhazia and South Ossetia and interfered in Russia's sphere of influence in the Caucasus.

Negative Russian reactions to U.S. forward posture in Georgia predate the 2008 Georgian war by several years. Russia reacted negatively to GTEP from the outset, despite the relatively low level of U.S. assistance to Georgia and the less-strained status of relations between Russia and Georgia before the Rose Revolution. Russian military experts claimed that, by improving Georgian military readiness, the United States was implicitly supporting Georgia's militant policies against Abkhazia and South Ossetia.[73] Furthermore, Russian military experts viewed U.S. presence in Georgia as an intrusion into Russia's sphere of influence—one that threatened its prestige in the region and thus potentially its influence over other post-Soviet states beyond Georgia.[74] Russia's negative assessment of GTEP suggests that discontent with U.S. security cooperation in Georgia at least initially stemmed neither from Mikheil Saakashvili's anti-Russian foreign policy nor the threat of immediate NATO membership (although both of those factors would later intensify Russian hostility).

Although security cooperation with Georgia represented a small fraction of global U.S. military assistance, Russia viewed the amount of this aid as outsized relative to Georgia's geographic size, population, and economy.[75] Military aid provided by the United States to Georgia during this period nearly equaled the defense budget of Georgia, which, at its highest, represented 9.2 percent of total Georgian GDP.[76]

In the years following the launch of GTEP, Russia increasingly targeted Georgia with hostile measures. First, Russia instituted a campaign of economic coercion against its tiny southern neighbor, including sanctions against Georgian wine and mineral water (two of Georgia's leading exports), restrictions on work permits for Georgians working in Russia (which placed pressure on wage remittances back to Georgia—a major source of income for the country), restrictions on travel to Georgia (which remained a major vacation destination for Russians), and pipeline shut-offs. In combination, these measures inflicted considerable damage on the Georgian economy.[77]

---

[73] V. Gubrii, "Is Georgia Preparing for War? [Gruziya gotovitsya k voine?]" *Military Bulletin of the South of Russia [Voennyi vestnik iuga Rossii]*, No. 10, March 7, 2005.

[74] Vladimir Kuzar', "Geopolitics. NATO's Transcaucasian Route," *Red Star*, No. 113, June 24, 2004.

[75] Novik, 2005.

[76] Gubrii, 2005; and Gerard Toal, *Putin, the West and the Contest over Ukraine and the Caucasus*, New York: Oxford University Press, 2017, p. 145.

[77] One observer noted, "Economic intimidation has proved to be a very successful way for Moscow to exert pressure on Georgian civilians and therefore exploit domestic political tensions in Georgia, undermining the government" (Tracey German, "David and Goliath: Georgia and Russia's Coercive Diplomacy," *Defence Studies*, Vol. 9, No. 2, June 2009, p. 229). See also Sergi Kapanadze, "Georgia's Vulnerability to Russian Pres-

Second, Russia launched various efforts at political subversion, such as policies of "passportization" and other measures in Abkhazia and South Ossetia that had the effects of reinforcing uncompromising stances by the leadership of the two breakaway republics and undermining Georgia's efforts to join NATO.[78]

Third, Russia engaged in numerous acts of military intimidation, sometimes immediately following specific Georgian actions to move closer to NATO. Following the April 2008 Bucharest Summit, for instance, Russia increased its activity in South Ossetia and Abkhazia, moving additional forces into the region and violating Georgian airspace.[79]

Determining the precise causes of these various hostile measures is difficult. Shortly after security cooperation between the United States and Georgia increased, the Rose Revolution led to a more anti-Russian bent in Georgian foreign policy. For the most part, neither the Russian government nor Russian observers close to the Russian government attempted to clarify the extent to which various measures were responses to U.S. military activities rather than other factors. Observers writing in Russian government–linked publications, for example, did not tie Russia's economic pressure campaign to specific U.S. or NATO actions in Georgia, although they did indicate that the campaign was tied to increased political and economic tensions between the two countries.[80] Many observers, on the other hand, were very direct in asserting that U.S. military activities were at least in part responsible for the 2008 war. Gorbachev, for instance, asserted, "Western assistance in training Georgian troops and shipping large supplies of arms had been pushing the region toward war rather than peace."[81]

Aside from the direct ways in which U.S. military activities in Georgia contributed to inflaming tensions between Moscow and Tbilisi, they might have contributed in indirect ways as well. No amount of U.S. military assistance to Georgia could have made the tiny country a direct threat to its massive neighbor (although it may well have represented a symbolic threat to Russia's preeminence in the former Soviet space). American military assistance did, however, lead to a massive shift in the balance of power between the Georgian military and the forces of the two breakaway republics of South Ossetia and Abkhazia. Before the

---

sure Points," blog post, European Council on Foreign Relations, June 19, 2014; and Givi Gigitashvili, "Russian Sanctions Against Georgia: How Dangerous Are They for Country's Economy?" blog post, Emerging Europe, July 17, 2019.

[78] Because the conflicts in Abkhazia and South Ossetia continued to be stumbling blocks on Georgia's path to NATO membership, Russia viewed the escalation of tensions between the separatist regions and Georgia as a way to prevent the republic's NATO accession. See Shota Utiashvili, "Ten Years Since August 2008: Was It Possible to Avoid the War?" Rondeli Foundation, Georgian Foundation for Strategic and International Studies, 2018, pp. 4–5.

[79] Utiashvili, 2018, p. 4.

[80] Malkhaz Matsaberidze, "Georgia—Russia: The Search for a Civilization Model of Relations [Gruziya—Rossiya: Poisk tsivilizovannoi modeli otnoshenii]," *Central Asia and the Caucasus* [*Tsentral'naya Aziya i Kavkaz*], Vol. 5, No. 53, 2007, p. 53.

[81] Cited in Derek S. Reveron, *Exporting Security: International Engagement, Security Cooperation, and the Changing Face of the U.S. Military*, 2nd ed., Washington, D.C.: Georgetown University Press, 2016, p. 218.

introduction of GTEP, levels of professionalism in the Georgian military were extremely low. Given the small numbers of Georgian forces, even relatively small amounts of U.S. assistance (relative to its global security assistance budget) had a dramatic impact on levels of professionalization in the Georgian military. Several journalistic accounts indicate that some Georgian military officers were straightforward in their assessments that U.S. assistance made the Georgian military much more capable of an offensive against the forces of South Ossetia and Abkhazia. Leaders from the two breakaway republics also reached the same conclusion.[82]

Beyond the concrete changes in the local balance of power wrought by U.S. assistance, U.S. military activities in Georgia might also have inadvertently emboldened Georgian leaders. Some Georgian leaders reportedly believed that Russia would not come to the aid of South Ossetia or Abkhazia in the event of a war because of Russia's military embarrassment only a few years earlier in Chechnya. But many observers—including one former Georgian defense minister who served under Saakashvili—believe that Georgian leaders were certain that the United States would come to the aid of Georgia if Russia attacked, forcing a diplomatic end to any such war and the withdrawal of Russian forces.[83] However, not even warnings by U.S. President George W. Bush and cabinet-level U.S. officials were enough to dissuade Saakashvili from entering into the 2008 conflict.[84]

Outcomes

Russia's actions in Georgia are frequently viewed as the beginning of Russia's resurgence as a major global power, a status that it largely lost following the collapse of the Soviet Union. The 2008 war indicated that Russia could influence the countries in its periphery and counter U.S. and NATO goals within the region.[85] This allowed Russia to portray itself as a great power internationally.

The 2008 war also demonstrated to Russia the limits of U.S. and NATO support to non-NATO states on Russia's periphery. Following the start of the 2008 conflict, neither the United States nor NATO member-states provided support to Georgia, despite providing military aid to the country prior to the conflict.[86] The reticence of the United States and European countries to become involved in a conflict in Russia's so-called near abroad (that is, the states of the former Soviet Union other than the Baltic states) reinforced Russia's status as a resurgent great power.

Although efforts to broker a durable settlement on the status of South Ossetia and Abkhazia had foundered long before the 2008 war, their quasi-independent status was reinforced by

---

[82] Fawn, 2002.

[83] See, for instance, Reveron, 2016, pp. 217–218; Feffer and Zunes, 2008; Brian Rohan, "Saakashvili 'Planned S. Ossetia Invasion': Ex-Minister," Reuters, September 14, 2008.

[84] Toal, 2017, pp. 148, 156–157.

[85] Utiashvili, 2018, pp. 4–5.

[86] Utiashvili, 2018, pp. 4–5.

the conflict. Meanwhile, as of this writing, Georgia still has not received a MAP, suggesting that Russian actions against Georgia have hindered the country's efforts to gain NATO membership.[87] Moreover, the damage that Russia inflicted on Georgia through its campaign of economic coercion, as well as in the 2008 war, might have played a role in bringing the more pro-Russian Georgian Dream party to power in the 2012 elections in Georgia.

U.S.-Georgian security cooperation might well have helped to professionalize the Georgian military, and it might have helped to secure Georgian force contributions to U.S.-led operations in Iraq and Afghanistan. But security cooperation also appears to have been at least one contributing factor in a spiraling series of events that ultimately left Russia demonstrably better off and Georgia worse off, all while further inflaming tensions between Russia and the United States.

Conclusion

The 2008 Russo-Georgian War was the culmination of nearly two decades of escalating tensions. Although these tensions began long before the United States increased its military activities in Georgia and had many sources unrelated to the United States' actions, U.S. military activities were one potentially significant contributor to the spiraling pattern of confrontation between Moscow and Tbilisi. These activities contributed to tensions directly by posing a symbolic threat to Russian preeminence within its self-declared sphere of influence in the former Soviet space and potentially indirectly by changing the local balance of power within Georgia and possibly emboldening Georgian leaders.

The events of this case study are largely consistent with the analytic framework described in Chapter Three and the historical patterns described in Chapter Four. Military activities, including materiel transfers, training, and multilateral military exercises, do appear to have been escalatory, as we would expect based on the previous findings on the relationship between military activities and escalation in the competition space. Moreover, these activities took place in close proximity to Russia, and they represented a significant break from prior U.S. practice, which had been to exercise a high degree of caution in security cooperation with the non-Baltic states of the former Soviet Union. All of these factors would have suggested a high risk that Russia would target the U.S. partner with malign measures, as, in fact, happened.

Beyond the direct relationship between U.S. military activities in Georgia and Russia's response, the case study lends at least some support for the concept of third-party risk. In this case, although Russia bears a large share of the blame for the events that led to the 2008 war, there is some evidence to suggest that U.S. military activities in Georgia at the least might

---

[87] Archil Gegeshidze, "New Realities after August 2008," in Archil Gegeshidze and Ivlian Haindrava, eds., *Transformation of the Georgian-Abkhaz Conflict: Rethinking the Paradigm*, London, U.K.: Conciliation Resources, 2011, p. 20.

have made then-President Saakashvili less inclined to reach an accommodation with Russia and may have emboldened him to take military action in South Ossetia.

U.S. Posture Changes in Northeastern Europe, 2014–2019

Background

In March 2014,[88] Russia illegally annexed Crimea and started supporting an insurgency in eastern Ukraine. Although Ukraine had been experiencing political turmoil and tensions with Russia prior to these events, Russia's aggression was still largely perceived as a surprise.[89] These events made clear that Russia could resort to force and seek to redraw internationally accepted borders when it found itself challenged—or its influence contested—in states in its neighborhood. Russia's move was met with broad international condemnation; trade and financial sanctions, which were still in place as of 2020; and a clear response, on the part of the United States, stating that it would deter Russia from undertaking further aggression and reassure U.S. European allies that it is committed to their defense. This commitment took the form of important changes in U.S. (and NATO) forward posture in northeastern Europe that included troop deployments, supporting activities (such as prepositioning of supplies) and agreements, exercises, and arms transfers.

U.S. Forward Posture

On June 3, 2014, then–U.S. President Barack Obama announced the European Reassurance Initiative, which was aimed at bolstering the defense capabilities of Eastern European countries and strengthening their defense relationships with the United States. The program covered five domains: increased bilateral and multinational exercises between the United States and its allies and partners, improved military infrastructure in Europe, enhanced prepositioning of equipment and supplies, capacity-building of U.S. allies and partners, and an increased U.S. military presence in Europe.[90] The European Reassurance Initiative—which was renamed the European Deterrence Initiative in 2018—represented a major U.S. investment in European security, with an initial funding of approximately $1 billion, later increas-

---

[88] In this report, we use the term *Northeastern Europe* to refer to the states in this region that border Russia: Estonia, Latvia, and Lithuania (the three Baltic states); Poland; Finland; and Norway.

[89] See for instance, Michael Kofman, Katya Migacheva, Brian Nichiporuk, Olesta Tkatcheva, and Jenny Oberholtzer, *Lessons from Russia's Operations in Crimea and Eastern Ukraine*, Santa Monica, Calif.: RAND Corporation, RR-1498-A, 2017, p. 20.

[90] Office of the Undersecretary of Defense (Comptroller), *European Reassurance Initiative: Department of Defense Budget, Fiscal Year (FY) 2016*, Washington, D.C.: U.S. Department of Defense, February 2015.

ing to over $5 billion.[91] It also represented a major reversal of U.S. military policy in Europe, which had previously been characterized by gradual disengagement.[92]

Two years later, at NATO's Warsaw Summit (July 8–9, 2016), the alliance announced that it would establish an eFP in Estonia, Latvia, Lithuania, and Poland, with four battalion-sized battlegroups led by different framework countries (Canada in Latvia, Germany in Lithuania, the United Kingdom in Estonia, and the United States in Poland).[93] In 2017, the United States also started positioning U.S. marines on a rotational basis in Norway.[94] This new posture was supported or supplemented by new activities and agreements, such as the creation of NATO Force Integration Units in Estonia, Latvia, Lithuania, and Poland and the establishment of new Army prepositioned stocks (APS) sites in Germany, Belgium, and the Netherlands.

The pace and scale of multinational exercises in Europe increased as well. Some existing routine exercises grew in size: For instance, the annual land forces exercise SABER STRIKE had 4,500 participants in 2014; the 2013 exercise only had 2,000.[95] Some national exercises opened up to the United States or other NATO members. For instance, in 2016 the U.S. Army took part for the first time in the Finnish ARROW exercise.[96] Perhaps of most significance, NATO exercises began to grow in scope, scale, and sophistication. Trident Juncture 2018, NATO's largest collective defense in over two decades, took place in Norway and included over 50,000 personnel. In addition to U.S. ground forces, six multinational brigades participated.[97]

The United States also bolstered the security of its allies and partners in northeastern Europe by authorizing a number of sales of sophisticated defense systems to its allies. Such sales include, for example, P-8A Patrol Aircraft to Norway in 2016, and high mobility artillery rocket systems M142 launchers to Poland in 2018.

In sum, the United States and its allies transitioned their posture from one focused primarily on expeditionary missions (well outside NATO territory) toward one oriented toward deterring Russian aggression (on NATO's borders).

---

[91] White House, "Fact Sheet: European Reassurance Initiative and Other U.S. Efforts in Support of NATO Allies and Partners," Washington, D.C.: Office of the Press Secretary, June 3, 2014.

[92] Michelle Shevin-Coetzee, *The European Deterrence Initiative*, Washington, D.C.: Center for Strategic and Budgetary Assessment, 2019, p. 3.

[93] NATO, "Warsaw Summit Communiqué," press release, July 9, 2016, para. 40.

[94] Dan Bilefsky and Henrik Pryser Libell, "Cold War Jitters Resurface as U.S. Marines Arrive in Norway," *New York Times*, January 16, 2017.

[95] Matt Millham, "Russian Maneuvers Don't Alter NATO Plans for Baltics War Games," *Stars and Stripes*, June 18, 2014.

[96] Jennifer Bunn, "Arrow '16 Brings 2nd Cavalry Regiment and Finnish Army Together," blog post, U.S. Army, May 6, 2016.

[97] NATO, "LANDCOM Participants in Exercise Trident Juncture 2018," press release, 2018.

Russian Response

The scope of Russian direct responses to U.S. and NATO posture changes has ranged from null to relatively sharp. While there was, for instance, no clear responses to the sale of Patriot PAC-3 missile defense system to Poland or the announcement of various military mobility initiatives, Russia responded to the Baltic Operations exercises in the Baltic Sea in 2014 and 2019 by launching snap exercises. When NATO forces participated in the exercise Trident Juncture 2018, Russia jammed their Global Positioning System and communications links.

It is much more difficult to assess the extent of Russia's nonproximate responses, if any. Russia might have reacted to a more forceful NATO posture in northeastern Europe by altering its behavior in Ukraine or in Syria, for instance. In the northeastern European theater, however, Russian direct, short-term responses have been overall mild as of 2020. Arms sales in particular rarely, if ever, seemed to trigger a clear, direct response from Russia. Exercises tended to fall into extreme categories—either Russia ignored them or responded forcefully; for instance, with a snap exercise or activities intended to disrupt the U.S. or NATO exercise. Forces positioned close to Russia frequently triggered a Russian response, although these responses ranged from very mild to sharp. Russia appeared to be particularly sensitive to the quasi-permanent deployment of ground and air forces close to its borders, although it did not systematically respond forcefully to such deployments.[98]

Russia's hostile measures in reaction to a U.S. or NATO change in military posture do not always take place in the military realm. Russia has often expressed its condemnation of U.S. or NATO's actions through diplomatic means or in the media. Some disinformation campaigns also could have been prompted by U.S. or NATO posture changes. For instance, a month prior to the signing of a bilateral statement of intent reinforcing defense cooperation between the United States and Finland, Finland experienced what appears to be a campaign launched by the Russian government, in which Russian media accused Finnish authorities of taking away the children of a Russian family living in Finland—allegations that were denied by Finnish authorities.[99] Another example is the false accusation of rape against German troops in Lithuania that appeared in the media in 2017 and that is believed to have originated in Russia.[100]

Russia's response can be slow-developing and happen in phases. Norway's decision to upgrade its radar in Vardø with U.S. support, for example, was publicized in the spring of

---

[98] That said, Russia was already in the process of adjusting its posture as a result of the 2014 breakdown in relations with the West. Steps included additional air and ground forces in the exclave of Kaliningrad as well as measures in the Western and Southern Military Districts that were most likely intended to strengthen Moscow's hand in Ukraine.

[99] Jussi Rosendahl and Tuomas Forsell, "Finland Sees Propaganda Attack from Former Master Russia," Reuters, October 19, 2016.

[100] "Lithuania Looking for Source of False Accusation of Rape by German Troops," Reuters, February 17, 2017; and Teri Schultz, "Why the 'Fake Rape' Story Against German NATO Forces Fell Flat in Lithuania," *Deutsche Welle*, February 23, 2017.

2016, but substantial Russian reactions (including simulated attacks against the installation and moving coastal missiles closer to it) took place later on—in March 2017, February 2018, and August 2019. This suggests that Russia does not necessarily respond immediately to changes in U.S. and NATO posture. Instead, it responds to irritants such as the Vardø radar—which a news source described as having "long been a thorn in the side of Russia's security relations to Norway"—at the time of its choosing.[101]

Conclusion

Because the situation in northeastern Europe remains fluid, we cannot determine the ultimate outcome of U.S. and NATO posture changes. We can, however, examine the extent to which Russian responses conform with patterns of behavior observed in Chapter Four and the earlier case studies in this chapter. We can also draw some longer-term lessons for U.S. policy.

Since 2014, the United States and NATO have been continually hardening their posture in northeastern Europe and have overall triggered limited Russian direct reactions (with a few notable exceptions). Most of the immediately observable reactions have taken the form of either disinformation campaigns or tit-for-tat military exercises; harassment of U.S. and NATO troops, warplanes, and warships; shifting Russian forces closer to its borders with NATO; or other activities that could be considered forms of military intimidation—or, at a minimum, signal-sending. On the one hand, these outcomes are consistent with earlier findings that security cooperation activities (such as training and exercises) seem to have little ability, in and of themselves, to deter malign activities below the level of armed conflict (although they could increase the resilience of allied and partner countries to these sorts of activities). On the other hand, these Russian responses have been relatively mild, despite the fact that they represent a sharp change in direction for NATO and have occurred in close proximity to Russian borders—conditions that our framework and earlier findings suggest pose relatively high risk

How should we interpret these outcomes and their broader implications for U.S. and NATO deterrence efforts? Do relatively mild Russian responses suggest that the United States and its allies and partners can further increase their efforts to strengthen their posture in the region with little fear of escalation? Or do the results suggest that deterrence has already been enhanced at relatively low levels of friction—the outcome that NATO has been seeking? Much depends on how events in Moscow and elsewhere evolve in the coming years. But a few points should be highlighted.

First, the outcomes in the region are consistent with the claim that regional forces have deterrent effects, although there is no specific evidence indicating that U.S. forces positioned in Europe have deterred Russia from any particular act of aggression in northeastern Europe.

---

[101] Thomas Nilsen, "Russia Deploys Missile System 70km from Norway's Vardø Radar," *Barents Observer*, August 7, 2019.

Some observers have pointed out that the Russian invasion of Ukraine happened shortly after the United States withdrew combat brigades from Germany and have asserted that Moscow was emboldened by this signal of relatively less U.S. commitment in Europe.[102] Such arguments, however, are purely speculative. There is no way of knowing at this time (and perhaps ever) if Russia would have behaved more aggressively without the larger U.S. presence in the region. So, although this case is generally consistent with the claim that regional forces deter, it does not offer strong evidence in support of the proposition.

Second, it is important to note that NATO has carefully calibrated its posture in the region to highlight its resolve while avoiding a build-up of capabilities that might threaten Russia. The numbers of forces on eFP rotations are relatively small and are far inferior—in both quantity and capability—to Russian forces in the region. NATO forces in eFP also bring with them none of the capabilities that most concern Moscow, such as long-range fires that could potentially reach sensitive sites within Russia. Most materiel transfers from the United States to its allies and partners have been relatively routine. The few exceptions (such as the sale of Joint Air-to-Surface Standoff Missile [JASSM-ER] munitions to Poland) thus far have been in relatively low quantities. Military exercises have been planned well in advance, and their purposes have been clearly communicated to Moscow. Most exercises have been relatively small, although a handful have involved more than 10,000 combined forces operating in states adjacent to Russia. Given this relative restraint by NATO, it is perhaps not surprising that Russia has not reacted more forcefully. These relatively mild Russian reactions, however, do not indicate how Russia would respond if the United States and NATO greatly increased their military presence in the region or if the United States transferred large numbers of sensitive military systems to its allies in the area.

Third, the United States and NATO benefit from a relatively stable structure in this region. Most of the countries in northeastern Europe had been NATO allies for at least a decade at the time of the Russian invasion of Ukraine. Borders were clearly delineated and generally accepted. The governments in this region are also relatively well-functioning democracies. The region is therefore at much lower risk of having third parties pull the United States and Russia into a confrontation as occurred in the much less stable circumstances of Georgia in the post-Soviet period or of the Horn of Africa in the 1960s and 1970s. This same level of stability does not exist in some other regions of Europe (such as the Western Balkans) or its immediate periphery (such as in the Levant and Maghreb regions).

Fourth, one of the clearest conclusions to emerge from this case is that Russia often does not signal its reactions to NATO posture changes in a clear, unambiguous fashion. In some cases, Russia reacted to nearby NATO forces or military exercises with military activities intended to harass NATO forces and otherwise communicate Moscow's displeasure. But in several very similar exercises, Russia did not react in a readily observable way. This inconsis-

---

[102] The editorial board of the *Wall Street Journal*, for instance, wrote, "The Obama Administration in 2012 and 2013 withdrew U.S. combat brigades from Germany, and Vladimir Putin responded by invading Ukraine in 2014"; see "Trump's Spite-Germany Plan," *Wall Street Journal*, July 30, 2020.

tency highlights the challenges involved in attempting to parse Russia's reactions to U.S. and NATO actions.

Fifth, it is important to acknowledge that many potential consequences of U.S. and NATO posture changes in the region are, as of yet, unobservable. We simply do not know whether Western actions have been critical to preventing more-aggressive Russian activities in this part of Europe or if, conversely, these actions are furthering Russian leaders' perception of the United States as a power determined to impose its control right up to Russia's borders—and potentially beyond.

Conclusion: The Case Studies in Comparison

Without access to complete and accurate archival records, it is extremely difficult to determine whether a state was deterred from an act of aggression. Even with access to such records, such a determination can be challenging. Decisionmakers themselves might not be aware of the extent to which particular prior actions or capabilities of other actors have influenced their decisions. Nonetheless, the five case studies in this chapter combine to form a picture that is broadly consistent with the quantitative analysis of Chapter Four, even if we cannot be certain of the exact decisionmaking process of leaders in Moscow. Key points from the case studies are summarized in Table 5.1.

Forward-positioned U.S. forces appear to have contributed to deterring malign activities in competition with the Soviet Union and later Russia, although the pattern is complex. In the case of the Iran crisis, it is clear that Moscow initially believed that it had considerable freedom of maneuver in a country that bordered the Soviet Union. It used this perceived latitude for action to stoke a proxy conflict in northern Iran, similar in many respects to the manner in which Moscow has used so-called frozen conflicts to gain influence over such countries as Georgia and Ukraine in the post-Soviet era. But when the United States signaled that Iranian security was an important U.S. national interest, Soviet fear of U.S. nuclear superiority—including several U.S. nuclear-capable air bases near Iran and along the Soviet Union's southern flank—appears to have played a role in causing Stalin to reverse course and back down. The Euromissile crisis was more complex. On the one hand, it was the impending presence of U.S. forces—in particular, INF missile systems—that sparked the crisis. Countries that agreed to host the Euromissiles were targeted for influence campaigns, including disinformation and covert funding of advocacy groups in Western Europe. After the missiles were deployed, the Soviets also engaged in military intimidation—again, with an apparent focus on the states hosting the U.S. weapons. On the other hand, the Soviets appear to have been deterred from more-extreme measures, including efforts to turn the demonstrations violent (despite contemplating such measures and having the capabilities to execute them). In broad terms, these outcomes are consistent with the finding that forward-positioned forces generally deter in the regions in which they are deployed, although the host countries for these forces can become targets of some malign activities.

TABLE 5.1

Summary of Case Studies

Case	U.S. Posture	Short-Term Outcomes	Longer-Term Outcomes
Iran crisis (1946–1947)	• Nearby airfields (nuclear-capable) • Military assistance	The Soviet Union withdrew support from proxy forces in Iran, a major diplomatic victory for the United States.	The Iran Crisis might have heightened Soviet suspicions of and hostility toward the United States.
Horn of Africa (1962–1974)	• Listening/ communications post (Kagnew Station) • Military assistance	The Soviets responded with competitive arms sales to Somalia.	The Ethiopian-Somali disputes spiraled into the collapse of a U.S. partner regime and the Ogaden War.
Euromissile crisis (1979–1983)	• INF missile deployments	The Soviets engaged in large-scale information operations and military intimidation.	The Soviets negotiated the INF Treaty, a major diplomatic victory for the United States.
Russo-Georgian disputes (2001–2008)	• Military assistance • Military exercises	Russia placed steadily increasing pressure on Georgia, ultimately leading to war.	Defeat in war and the economic costs of Russian hostile measures appear to have been major contributors to electoral defeat of anti-Russian government.
Competition in Northeast Europe (2014–2019)	• eFP • Military assistance • Military exercises	Russia engaged in information operations and frequent but relatively low-level military intimidation.	N/A

NOTE: N/A = not applicable.

U.S. military activities also generally conformed to the same patterns we observed in Chapter Four. Materiel transfers and training appear to have contributed to the pattern of malign activities against both Ethiopia and Georgia, including competitive arms transfers, economic coercion, military intimidation, and proxy wars. In both cases, U.S. activities seem to have generated third-party dynamics that undermined U.S. national interests. In the Horn of Africa, U.S. military assistance to Ethiopia threatened Somalia, leading it ultimately to embrace the Soviet Union as a defense partner, and U.S. military assistance appears to have made Addis Ababa less likely to seek a negotiated settlement of the conflicts within its own borders—conflicts that Somalia and the Soviet Union exploited. In Georgia, U.S. military assistance shifted the local balance of power between Tbilisi and the breakaway republics of South Ossetia and Abkhazia, and it might have led Georgian leaders to believe that the United States would come to its support in the event of a conflict with Russia. In both cases, without the deterrent presence of substantial U.S. forces to prevent an escalating spiral of confrontation, the two U.S. partners became targets of ever more aggressive hostile measures and eventually armed conflict. Military exercises were similarly a part of the pattern of U.S. activities in Georgia that seems to have provoked greater Russian hostility. The infamous exercise Able Archer-83, on the other hand, did not lead to escalation, but the exercise nonetheless is broadly seen as a cautionary tale of the potential dangers of exercising sensitive military capabilities in proximity to U.S. adversaries.

Our analysis did not focus on the effects of U.S. military agreements but, here again, the patterns were generally consistent with the findings of our quantitative analysis. The quantitative analysis suggested that such agreements do not deter hostile measures below the level of armed conflict, although they might contribute to deterring conventional aggression. On the one hand, the U.S. military agreement with Ethiopia did not deter either hostile measures or armed conflict. On the other hand, the United States had very specifically refused the inclusion of any language in the agreement that suggested that the United States had an obligation to defend its partner, so it is perhaps not surprising that the agreement failed to deter Somalia. In the case of Georgia, the United States also had in place military agreements, but at the Bucharest Summit in 2008, NATO member-states postponed any action toward Georgia's accession to NATO. Military agreements with Georgia thus also sent only a very weak signal of U.S. (or NATO) commitment, making it unsurprising that such agreements did not deter either malign activities or ultimately armed conflict.

The case studies also generally reinforce our findings about the intervening role of continuity, proximity, and capability. As expected, Moscow tended to be most sensitive about U.S. military forces, activities, and agreements in close proximity to its borders, whether that be in Iran, Georgia, or the Baltic Sea region. Moscow was also extremely sensitive to military capabilities that posed a threat to its command and control nodes and other critical elements of regime and state security, as the Euromissile crisis demonstrated. And it was particularly sensitive to what it saw as sharp breaks in U.S. policy, such as encroaching on its perceived sphere of influence in Iran in the immediate aftermath of World War II or Georgia in the post-Soviet era.

The case study of Northeastern Europe in the period since the Russian invasion of Ukraine in 2014 appears to be an instance in which the United States and its NATO allies have successfully reestablished deterrence (if such was required) without provoking escalation. In this case, U.S. and NATO posture enhancements were made in countries neighboring Russia. But decisionmakers in Washington and other NATO capitals carefully calibrated these posture changes. They strengthened (and continue to strengthen) their military capabilities in the region gradually. They have not introduced sensitive capabilities into the region, deploying relatively modest numbers of ground forces that pose no threat of aggression to Russia. With only a handful of exceptions (e.g., Trident Juncture 18), NATO has carefully scoped military exercises to prevent a concentration of large numbers of forces close to Russian borders. Russia has engaged in some hostile measures targeting the countries that host U.S. forces, including disinformation activities and some acts of military intimidation. For the most part, however, a relatively stable equilibrium appears to have developed.

It is important to note one final theme from the case studies, which has potential implications for ongoing efforts at deterrence in Northeastern Europe and elsewhere. In many cases, the consequences of U.S. posture decisions were not immediately apparent. In the Iran crisis, the United States was able to deter Soviet proxy warfare, but its actions in the crisis might have hardened Soviet positions on the evolving partition of Europe. In Ethiopia, the United States gained an important listening and communications post—but the price was a security assistance program that might have helped to fuel a spiral of competition in the Horn over the following two decades. When the United States deployed the Pershing IIs and Gryphons to Europe in 1983, it did not realize just how much these deployments fed into escalating Soviet threat perceptions at the time. In Georgia, even a relatively small-scale train and equip program with counterterrorism goals helped to feed a broader escalatory spiral. None of these examples are intended to imply that the United States should not take robust action where needed to protect U.S. national interests. These examples do, however, offer a warning about the difficulties of anticipating the longer-term escalatory consequences of posture decisions.

CHAPTER SIX

Scenario-Based Analysis

The previous chapters explored how changes in U.S. forward posture affected prior competitions. Our quantitative and case study analyses reveal broad historical trends and, in the Northeastern Europe case, more-recent insights on how different types of forward posture deter or provoke Russian behavior, including both hostile measures and armed conflict. The scenario-based analysis detailed in this chapter offers a means to explore the implications of our historically oriented analysis for future decisionmaking about U.S. forward posture in Europe and its immediate periphery. Scenario-guided discussions with experts and practitioners also enable us to weigh how some of the specific capabilities emphasized in recent Army plans and concepts, if introduced into the European theater, might deter or provoke Russia in the course of the evolving competition.

This chapter has two major sections. First, we detail three scenarios designed to stress different aspects of deterrence and escalation dynamics that were discussed in the previous chapters. Second, we present insights derived from scenario-guided workshops and interviews with current and recently retired government officials.[1] We conclude with an overview of implications for future force posture.

Before proceeding, it is important to note the inherent limitation of scenario-based analysis: It is highly speculative. We cannot know the precise diplomatic and security context under which forward posture will actually evolve, how technological trends might affect competition, or how third parties will approach their relations with the two competitors. Scenario analysis (with appropriate assumptions to bound the problem) can, however, provide an additional layer of observations to strengthen, add nuance to, or challenge our historical analysis and provide some indication of their applicability to future contingencies.

---

[1] The workshops took place in July 2020 over a virtual platform. Participants included RAND experts in deterrence, European security, Army operations, and Russian strategy for competition. The group included former ambassadors, ground commanders, and intelligence community professionals. Phone interviews were conducted in summer 2020 with an array of current and recently retired civilian and military officials from both U.S. embassies and civilian and military headquarters; their ranks ranged from lieutenant colonel to lieutenant general (or the civilian equivalent). Several RAND experts on deterrence and Army capabilities also participated in the interviews. Although we took care to elicit expertise from an array of stakeholders with various experiences, the workshop and interviewee pool included more military expertise than diplomatic, economic, and informational. See Appendix A for an anonymized list of interview participants.

Scenario Design

Researchers designed three scenarios positing alternative logics for U.S. forward posture for the 2025–2028 period. This period was selected based on the Army's objective to implement its Multi Domain Task Force construct by 2028, and secondarily by the analytic need to disentangle our forward-looking analysis from ongoing force posture deliberations at the time of the writing of this report. Table 6.1 describes the inputs and approach to arriving at scenarios for examination during the workshops and interviews.

Using the inputs as the foundation from which to design alternative posture logics, we outlined three scenarios: a posture focused on in-theater forces, one that emphasizes the DFE construct, and a third that focuses on lighter ground forces, principally in Southeastern Europe.[2] The scenarios are illustrative and, by design, not mutually exclusive. In actual planning, aspects of one posture logic might be combined with those of another to deter Russian hostile measures, Moscow's escalation to armed conflict, or both. Figure 6.1 depicts our methodology.

TABLE 6.1

Input and Approach to Scenario Development

Input	Approach
Army plans for forward posture	Scenarios emphasize capabilities most influential in emerging Army concepts and plans. This was a key motivation for featuring LRPF and cyber electromagnetic (CEMA) and information operations (IO) capabilities.
Northeastern Europe case study	Scenarios incorporate similar but more-aggressive changes in forward posture than what occurred in 2014–2019. For example, we asked workshop participants about Russia's potential reactions to a Trident Juncture 2018–scale exercise being held primarily from the territory of a partner instead of an ally.
Recent gaming and analytic reports	Scenarios include recommended changes in posture from recent RAND and non-RAND reports. For example, the emphasis on in-theater forces derives from a body of work that claims that deterrence would be enhanced with more-persistent presence.
Russian threat perceptions	Scenarios include aspects of posture known to be most threatening to Russia. For example, we inquired whether Army LRPF might be interpreted in a similar fashion to how Moscow has traditionally viewed U.S. and NATO missile defense.

NOTE: Unless otherwise specified, sources that were consulted to design scenarios were cited in Chapters Two, Three, and Five.

---

[2] The first two posture logics resemble choices analyzed in a recent study on Army posture in Europe, although that work explores issues well beyond our primary focus on competition and hostile measures. See J. P. Clark and C. Anthony Pfaff, *Striking the Balance: US Army Force Posture in Europe, 2028*, Carlisle, Penn.: Strategic Studies Institute and Army War College Press, June 2020.

FIGURE 6.1
Scenario-Based Analysis Methodology

Assumptions and Variables Across Scenarios

Examining future security environments requires plausible assumptions that enable the analysis to focus on a primary topic of interest; in this case the impact of changes in U.S. forward posture on Russian employment of hostile measures and potential escalation up to the level of armed conflict. In support of this objective, we established the following four assumptions:

1. Emerging advanced capabilities will work as intended. LRPF technologies and concepts will appear in the early 2020s and steadily mature thereafter.
2. U.S. Army formations will be well-trained, equipped, and enabled. Key examples include higher-echelon headquarters and joint targeting and other technical integration.[3]
3. U.S. Army LRPF systems will not be designed for nuclear munitions (although Russia may believe that these systems will be dual-capable).[4]
4. Security cooperation will work as intended, at least initially. Allies and partners will support U.S. proposals to a degree that makes the considered postures viable. The main caveat is that Russian reactions and potential interference in third-party states need to be considered as part of the competition.

After presenting these assumptions, informed by key factors found through historical and case study research, we asked the experts with whom we consulted to consider three variables when assessing each posture logic: geographic proximity, specific parameters of capabilities and individual weapon systems, and the geopolitical trajectory of the U.S.-Russian competition.

---

[3] This might include a Theater Fires Command as envisioned in the multi-domain operations concept, for example.

[4] In the course of our workshops and interviews, several military and intelligence professionals noted that Russia is highly likely to assume that LRPF will be dual purpose regardless of U.S. efforts to demonstrate otherwise.

Scenario One: Emphasis on In-Theater Forces

This scenario imagines a future in which the U.S. Army prioritizes increasing the number of units and sophistication of capabilities with a persistent presence in Europe, through a combination of permanently stationed and rotational forces. This logic consists of the following four changes in forward posture compared with today's ground force presence in Europe:[5]

1. Major increase in maneuver forces, with at least a division of combat power in the theater at any given time. The force increase would include an overall increase in armor and corresponding air defense, aviation, and sustainment packages.
2. Fielding of LRPF in the form of PrSM, assumed to have a range of 500 km with the possibility of a 750 km version. LRPF systems could belong to one or more FABs or the envisioned Multi Domain Task Force organization.
3. Introduction of LRPF in the form of systems capable of substantially greater distances than PrSM (1,000-2,500 km), including a hypersonic capability with unprecedented speed and maneuverability.[6]
4. Increase in the number and sophistication of units capable of managing and executing CEMA- and IO-related capabilities. Possibilities include a new type of BCT that is focused on information warfare and a theater-level command that oversees an increasingly mature architecture that is capable of technical and nontechnical means of operating across the cognitive domain.

Figure 6.2 is the map used to assist workshop and interview participants in visualizing the theater. The dots represent sensitive locations in Russia. The orange and yellow lines provide a scale for discussions about geographic proximity in general and LRPF ranges in particular. The three subregions—west, southeast, and northeast—enable a dialogue about which specific capabilities might deter or provoke in which of Europe's environs.[7]

The logic of increasing the U.S. Army's persistent presence in the European theater raises several important questions. Will this deter or provoke new Russian hostile measures, and could some of the more sensitive capabilities lead to a military crisis or armed conflict? Do dynamics differ by subregion? Which capabilities might be helpful in the competition if inte-

---

[5] The core elements of today's posture include a rotational armored BCT that operates out of Poland, one forward-stationed Stryker BCT in Germany, and one forward stationed airborne infantry BCT in Italy. In terms of fires, the 41st FAB in Germany currently has three MLRS battalions. Higher-echelon command and control organizations, aviation, air defense, sustainment, and enablers constitute the remainder of the U.S. Army's forces in Europe.

[6] Workshop participants were reminded that ranges are notional and maximum; ISR and target acquisition, among other factors, will be key to achieving desired effects at longer ranges.

[7] Our analysis did not include a country-by-country review, which might be a suitable line of inquiry for security cooperation–related research and analysis. That being said, a frequent topic of deliberation centered on the distinction of locating specific capabilities in Germany (designated as west) versus Poland or the Baltic states (designated as northeast).

FIGURE 6.2

Scenario One, Emphasis on Forces in the Theater

Northeast = Poland, Baltics, Scandinavia, Belarus, Czechia, Slovakia
Southeast = Black Sea Nations, Western Balkans, Hungary
West = Remaining countries

grated as part of a whole-of-government approach? More broadly, how might a forward posture that emphasizes forces unfold as part of the strategic competition?

Scenario Two: Emphasis on Dynamic Force Employment

Our second scenario explores the logic of DFE, a concept introduced by the 2018 NDS, which aims for operational unpredictability while maintaining stability and transparency at the strategic level. Although some amount of persistent overseas presence does not conflict with DFE, the concept generally places a premium on episodic, short-term deployments as accompaniments to a relatively modest in-theater posture. In other words, at least as constructed here, the focus of DFE shifts somewhat from the forces themselves to the activities that they conduct. This posture logic included the following five changes in forward posture compared with the U.S. Army's current activities in Europe:

1. An increase in the number and sophistication of expansive exercises that rehearse surging heavy forces based outside the theater. The envisioned exercises include air defense, aviation, and sustainment packages alongside maneuver forces. An important element of this change in forward posture is that it would be accompanied by an expansion of efforts to enhance reception, staging, onward movement, and integration and military mobility in Europe.[8]
2. An increase in APS on top of current plans and programs. Exercises would rehearse APS drawdowns.[9]
3. Limited-duration LRPF deployments. These would be tailored to the system in consideration but might resemble how the U.S. Air Force deploys bomber task forces at the request of combatant commanders.[10]
4. Arms transfers of LRPF to allies, partners, or both. The rationale for examining arms transfers in this scenario stems from the presumed desire for NATO to maintain a permanent LRPF presence if the U.S. Army does not provide this as envisioned in the first scenario.
5. Periodic displays of CEMA- and IO-related capabilities in the theater, with an emphasis on reach-back to organizations based in the continental United States (CONUS).

Figure 6.3 depicts the map that we used to assist workshop and interview participants in visualizing the theater. Current APS sites (orange), several important seaports of debarkation (SPOD) (green), and notional exercise areas (light blue) are added to the previous map.

The posture logic of relying on DFE raises the issues of consistency, predictability, and permanence: How important are these attributes to deterring Russian hostile measures? Which capabilities, in which subregions, might prove to have more deterrent (or provocative) value when not persistently in the theater?

Scenario Three: Emphasis on Lighter Forces

The third scenario examines the role of lighter forces in competition, specifically in Southeastern Europe. We limited this scenario to Southeastern Europe to ensure consideration of

---

[8] For an analysis of steps needed to enhance military mobility, see for example, Curtis M. Scaparrotti and Colleen B. Bell, *Moving Out: A Comprehensive Assessment of European Military Mobility*, Washington, D.C.: Atlantic Council, April 22, 2020.

[9] For an overview of current APS, see U.S. Army Europe and Africa Public Affairs Office, "Fact Sheet: Army Prepositioned Stock," last updated November 20, 2020.

[10] See, for example, U.S. Air Forces in Europe and Air Forces Africa, "Bomber Task Force Returns from Flights in Black Sea Region," blog post, U.S. Strategic Command, October 23, 2019.

FIGURE 6.3

Scenario Two, Emphasis on Dynamic Force Employment

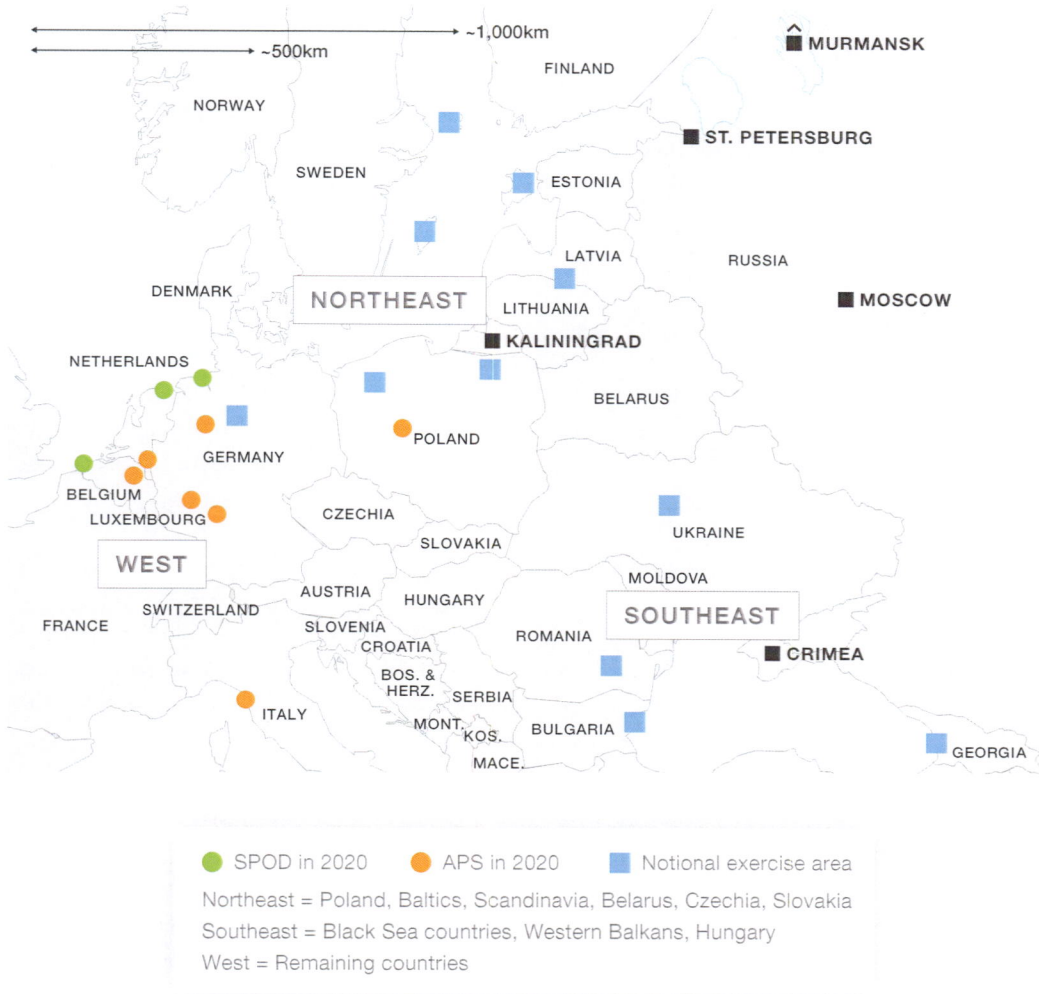

~1,000km

~500km

SPOD in 2020   APS in 2020   Notional exercise area

Northeast = Poland, Baltics, Scandinavia, Belarus, Czechia, Slovakia
Southeast = Black Sea countries, Western Balkans, Hungary
West = Remaining countries

all three subregions; the first two scenarios involved much discussion about the West and Northeast. Additionally, current force posture in Southeastern Europe consists predominantly of lighter forces.

Theoretically, lighter forces could provide capabilities that support whole-of-government efforts to compete with Russia but do so without the attention and potential provocation that comes with heavier forces (e.g., tanks) or highly advanced capabilities (e.g., LRPF). Instead of postulating an increase in forces (Scenario One) or activities (Scenario Two), this scenario explored both an increase and a decrease in the presence and use of lighter forces.[11] Using the map in Figure 6.4 to orient themselves, workshop participants considered the following four potential changes from today's posture in Southeastern Europe:

1. Increase in the number of lighter units persistently in the region.
2. Increase in the number of activities conducted by lighter units. This includes an emphasis on arms sales and related training activities.
3. Decrease in the number of lighter units persistently in the region.
4. Decrease in the number of activities conducted by lighter units. This includes a deemphasis of arms sales and related training activities.

Bolstering or removing elements of forward posture centered on lighter ground forces could have important implications for competition. Would eliminating KFOR, for example, provide an opportunity for Russian exploitation of the Western Balkans? Conversely, could introducing new training facilities in the region complement U.S. government efforts to compete in the region without provoking unintended escalation?

Insights from Scenarios

Workshop and interview discussions revealed a wide diversity of views regarding the alternative posture logics examined in the three scenarios. This is not surprising: Examining the future necessarily requires a degree of speculation and is sensitive to individual experiences and areas of expertise. Where scenario-based analysis does reveals convergence—and to the extent to which this convergence conforms to historical patterns—potentially powerful observations could be at play. In cases in which there is divergence among experts or discrepancies with quantitative and historical research, additional nuance might be revealed. The following sections describe several areas in which there was convergence, as well as the most pertinent areas of divergence. This summary parallels our workshops and interviews, focusing primarily on deterring hostile measures and potential escalation spirals to armed conflict and less so on conventional deterrence considerations. The following sections primarily reflect expert judgements from the workshops and interviews.

The Subtle Impact of Forward Posture on Competition

Workshops and interviews revealed an underlying theme. Throughout the dialogue, most experts cautioned that forward posture—and, even more so, U.S. Army posture as a subset of joint posture—more often than not has a subtle and indirect relationship with competi-

---

[11] Currently, lighter ground forces include KFOR, the 173rd airborne infantry BCT in Italy, bilateral State Partnership Program (SPP) activities, and various forms of assistance to Ukraine and Georgia.

FIGURE 6.4

Scenario Three, Emphasis on Lighter Forces

NOTE: IBCT = infantry brigade combat team.

tion and the prevalence of Russian hostile measures. Diplomacy, economics, and whole-of-government informational efforts represent the primary tools in the competition toolbox.[12] There was consensus that, in most cases, any forward posture's impact on competition will be long-term and cumulative. Nonetheless, there was broad acknowledgement that, under specific circumstances, changes in forward posture can either be advantageous for competition or pose escalation risks in a more direct, if not immediate, manner.

Potential Contributions to Deterring Hostile Measures

Lighter Forces

An armored division can only do so much for competition. As broadly agreed in the workshops and interviews, heavy forces mainly provide a backbone that makes it more difficult for a competitor to militarily intimidate U.S. allies and partners. More broadly, heavier conventional capabilities can serve to underpin diplomatic efforts and in some cases offer ancillary benefits for competition. Other types of forces might be of more practical use when the priority is competing with Russia, deterring or preventing further hostile measures, and doing so

---

[12] Several experts went so far as to predict that virtually no U.S. actions would catalyze a significant escalation as long as there was effective communication and solidarity among the United States, its allies, and its partners. An important consideration in this regard is that forward posture can provide a narrative for exploitation by the competitor.

with limited risk of escalation. Workshop participants and experts posited several capabilities and activities—most of which nest under the broader category of lighter forces—that they felt were more effective for competition.

Standing missions, such as KFOR, represent one manifestation of lighter forces. This NATO force, now two decades into its existence, has at its core a rotational U.S. Army National Guard brigade headquarters. Although KFOR's United Nations (UN)-endorsed mission explicitly centers on facilitating a stable Kosovo and freedom of movement, the U.S. and NATO presences also deter Russia's and others' hostile measures. Most experts and practitioners noted that KFOR provides a powerful symbol of U.S. and NATO commitment and a high return on the relatively modest investment.[13] One senior State Department official emphatically stated that a U.S. withdrawal from KFOR would be highly destabilizing for Kosovo and might even contribute to instability in Bosnia by feeding into a narrative that the United States is abandoning the Western Balkans.[14]

A number of our interlocutors favored potential steps to expand the use of lighter forces in Southeastern Europe: For example, adding additional training for lighter forces in North Macedonia, NATO's newest member-state.[15] Operating on the territory of an ally or partner establishes key relationships and provides vital information that can inform the U.S. government's broader competition efforts. Indeed, this is part of the logic behind the heralded SPP, which several of our interviewees framed as the most important and often most effective U.S. military engagement tool in the Western Balkans. Continuing to rely on the SPP's pairing of U.S. states with countries in the region will be helpful from a competition standpoint, in that this arrangement capitalizes on long-standing partnerships that are widely supported by populations and elites alike.[16] Beyond SPP, lighter ground forces (e.g., training teams, infantry platoons or companies, logistics forces) could be used as important military contributions

---

[13] This is consistent with February 2020 congressional testimony from the commander of U.S European Command, Tod D. Wolters ("Statement of General Tod D. Wolters, United States Air Force, Commander, United States European Command," testimony before the United States Senate Committee on Armed Services, Washington, D.C., February 25, 2020). In his testimony, Wolters stated, "The principal stabilizing force in Kosovo remains NATO's KFOR, which includes a small, but significant U.S. contribution. KFOR's presence will remain essential to stability while Serbia and Kosovo pursue a stable relationship through the planned 10-year transition of the Kosovo Security Forces" (pp. 6–7).

[14] RAND interview with senior State Department official, August 25, 2020.

[15] The U.S. and North Macedonia governments have discussed this potentiality (C. Todd Lopez, "3 Things to Know: The U.S.-North Macedonia Defense Relationship," blog post, U.S. Department of Defense, March 7, 2019).

[16] An increase in the use of this specific type of lighter force, however, might not be advisable: Many U.S. states conduct a fairly robust set of annual activities that approach the absorptive capacity of countries in the region.

to whole-of-government competition, an observation consistent with the SPP experience and past findings on the role of special operations forces.[17]

Intelligence Forces

Intelligence support—including intra-theater ISR—to broader U.S. government efforts in competition represents another type of military activity beneficial to competition. Generally, simply knowing about the competitor's capabilities and intentions for competition can inform changes in U.S. forward posture. In some cases, the U.S. government could elect to declassify imagery or take other proactive steps based on capabilities provided by intelligence organizations.

Routine Arms Transfers

Finally, some arms transfers offer a pathway for influence without escalation. The process of socializing, negotiating, transferring, and assisting with the stand-up and maintenance of relatively benign, low-profile capabilities (e.g., communications equipment) can provide important opportunities. Interview participants noted how these types of arms transfers can establish a greater understanding of the competitive landscape within a third-party country, drive institutional reforms within and beyond a military, and help cement relationships with senior leaders who will have a large say in their country's geopolitical trajectory. However, the transfer of more-offensively oriented capabilities does have a potential to provoke hostile measures, a dynamic we return to in the following section.

Potential Escalatory Risks

Large-Scale Exercises

Of the capabilities that were explored in the scenarios, workshop participants and interviewees noted several that could significantly increase the risk of escalation under certain conditions. Major military exercises stand at the top of the list of traditional escalatory concerns, and our interlocuters reinforced that introducing a great number of U.S. forces in a short amount of time and demonstrating their interoperability with other NATO forces naturally will interest the Russian military and influence Moscow's political deliberations.[18] The linkage to hostile measures remains vague, but it is likely that a significant increase in the scope, scale, and sophistication of exercises would engender some level of malign response, be it as an immediate reaction to the exercises or as part of a longer-term, cumulative effect. While exercises will remain an important aspect of conventional deterrence, they come with escala-

---

[17] Stephen Watts, Bryan Frederick, Nathan Chandler, Mark Toukan, Christian Curriden, Erik Mueller, Edward Geist, Ariane Tabatabai, Sara Plana, Brandon Corbin, and Jeffrey Martini, *Proxy Warfare as a Tool of Strategic Competition: State Motivations and Future Trends*, unpublished RAND Corporation research, 2020.

[18] Another possibility is that disparate, uncoordinated maneuvers might appear to the competitor as massive, coordinated exercises.

tory risks, including in competition.[19] As relayed next, these risks might be particularly acute if the exercises include sensitive, threatening capabilities or are conducted without sufficient transparency and coordination.

Forces or Activities with Sophisticated Capabilities

Regardless of the posture logic relied on (in-theater forces or DFE), another area of concern relates to the potential introduction of high-end, sensitive capabilities *in some circumstances*. Discussions at the workshops centered on how the U.S. Army's potential introduction of LRPF into the European theater might be interpreted in Moscow. Weapon systems placed in the northeast or southeast and even portions of the west (depending on system capabilities) would be seen as a direct threat to the Russian homeland, its major population centers, and its most-sensitive military capabilities. Russia also most likely would assume that any LRPF systems will be nuclear-capable, and any U.S. or NATO efforts to convince the Kremlin otherwise will have to counter deeply rooted Russian skepticism. This does not necessarily mean that the U.S. Army should or should not deploy LRPF, only that certain types of deployments could contribute to an increase in hostile measures and possibly an unintended escalation—risks that need to be compared with the warfighting value of any given capability. Workshop participants and interviewees identified the following ways in which advanced and unambiguously offensive capabilities could be most problematic in terms of the escalation side of that equation:

- **Introduction of advanced capabilities into sensitive locations.** Sensitive locations are countries that fall into one of three categories: Those whose proximity would pose a direct threat to Russia, those that Russia considers in its current or historical sphere of influence, and/or those where Russia maintains a capacity to undertake waves of hostile measures. For example, an announcement to deploy LRPF into a sensitive location would almost certainly engender immediate efforts to portray the action as provocative, and Moscow could follow this narrative with more-substantial efforts to undermine the partner government through a variety of stepped-up hostile measures, such as support to political parties in opposition, increases in energy prices, and others.
- **Short-term deployments that lack transparency or introduce discontinuity, especially during times of heightened tensions in the competition or vis-à-vis Russia's domestic or international situation.** The main advantage of DFE is its operational unpredictability, but at a certain point this feature can become more of a problem by undermining strategic stability. Most experts advised that, notwithstanding Russia's

---

[19] Two participants offered interesting mitigation measures. The first was to employ "muscular HA/DR" [humanitarian assistance and disaster relief], whereby exercise events are oriented toward humanitarian assistance and disaster relief but involve rehearsing skills that are also relevant to combat. The other was to conduct major exercises away from Russia's periphery, which appears to have been the case for NATO's Trident Juncture 2015, held in Portugal, Spain, and Italy (NATO, "A View from the Ground: The Land Component of Trident Juncture 2015," webpage, November 3, 2015).

own mixed record on notification, continued U.S. and NATO forthrightness regarding deployments of advanced capabilities dampens escalation risk and should remain a cornerstone of U.S. policy in the region. This relates to both multinational exercises and other forms of deployments, such as sending a battery with LRPF to demonstrate that the U.S. Army has the means and access to swiftly introduce high-end capabilities.[20]

- **Arms transfers to countries that could become emboldened actors.** Some allies or partners might have strategic cultures or governments that could lead them to believe that they can undertake increasingly aggressive actions, including unilaterally. If the arguably mundane arms transfers of the early 2000s, in concert with U.S. official statements, indeed contributed to the Georgian government's sense of increased freedom of action leading up to the 2008 conflict, providing highly threatening systems to potentially aggressive allies could have similar or more severe effects. Although the Northeastern Europe case study in Chapter Five suggests that arms sales in 2014–2019—including of such sensitive capabilities as JASSM-ERs to Poland—did not elicit any unusually strong responses, it also noted that Russia might be biding its time to respond and that the sale could be contributing to unobservable or future dynamics in the competition. Although our workshops focused on LRPF transfers, the transfers of any other particularly advanced or sensitive technologies would most likely follow a similar logic.[21]

This does not mean that well-organized, ally-supported, transparent deployments of advanced capabilities to Western European countries would be frictionless. Indeed, many workshop participants stated that placing ground-launched hypersonic missiles or other weapons with ranges between 1,000 and 2,500 km could indirectly or even directly lead to a militarized dispute. One participant predicted "another Euromissile crisis, this time in the age of social media."

Experts had fewer concerns with the 500 km PrSM, which corresponds with our historical insights about how greater novelty and proximity were factors in escalation dynamics.[22] The ranges of the weapon systems that the Army is developing also expand the notion of what it means to be "proximate." Some of the ground-based systems currently being discussed in U.S. defense circles could reach sensitive sites within Russia from locations in Germany or even farther west. Russian concerns could be particularly acute if it is not confident that it could detect movements of such launchers.

---

[20] U.S. Air Force's bomber task force model and U.S. Navy's increasingly nonroutine, shorter notice deployments of carrier and amphibious ready groups may offer insights. For an example of the latter, see David B. Larter, "The U.S. Navy Returns to an Increasingly Militarized Arctic," *Defense News*, May 12, 2020.

[21] Of course, the level of sensitivity perceived by Russia might differ from U.S. expectations. A drone intended for counterterrorism purposes, for instance, might be viewed as a capability meant to collect intelligence on Russian forces on the proximity its border.

[22] The PrSM will be an enhanced capability, but not a revolutionary leap-ahead over the Army's current 200–300-km range cruise missile and rocket capabilities, although in countries bordering Russia or the Black Sea, this increase might be more problematic.

The CEMA and IO category of capabilities could also pose escalatory risk, but here, our findings are much less conclusive. Some interlocuters viewed actions, such as standing up new organizations or commands in Europe to conduct CEMA and IO throughout the theater, as relatively benign, particularly if it was clear that the activities were limited to preparations for a conventional conflict. Conversely, several experts argued that a visible manifestation of CEMA and IO, perhaps in the form of a theater information command or the deployment of a new type of BCT oriented on the cognitive domain, might cause alarm if it was interpreted as an effort to undermine the Russian government's and its partner governments' legitimacy as a sort of militarized version of U.S. government democracy-promotion efforts. Under these conditions, unintended escalation would be unsurprising.

Introducing advanced, potentially highly threatening capabilities may be the right course of action to enhance deterrence, but case-by-case evaluations will need to consider the specifics of the capability, the partner or host nation involved, and the timing and messaging associated with any deployments.

Footprint and Agreements

One area of significant disagreement among workshop participants and interview subjects deserves mention: the role of footprint and agreements that facilitate movement of forces. Some participants claimed that these issues lie entirely outside the competition space. Others advised that aspects of posture, such as infrastructure and prepositioning—although they are necessary for conventional deterrence—could reinforce Russian beliefs about Western intentions and, over the long term, contribute to heightened tensions and escalation.

Conclusion

The macro implications of this scenario-based analysis are twofold. First, our examination here conforms with historical and case study analysis in that the impact of posture will primarily be ancillary, subtle, and often unobservable. Important exceptions to this rule nonetheless point to the need for careful screening and long-term monitoring of the impact of changes in forward posture on competition. Second, there are simply too many variables to declare that an in-theater, DFE, or any other type of posture logic would be optimal for competition across a wide variety of contexts. Throughout the course of our workshops and interviews, it became clear that, although certain principles can be helpful in informing a deterrence strategy, they do not substitute for a case-by-case evaluation of changes to forward posture. The existence of these ambiguities conforms with our historical research.

CHAPTER SEVEN

Conclusion

The research in this report has helped to highlight a number of trade-offs between different types of posture, where that posture is introduced, and how rapidly U.S. posture changes. The research has provided evidence that U.S. forward posture has important effects on deterrence of malign activities in competition as well as deterring armed conflict. In general, U.S. forward posture is one contributing factor to competition outcomes but is seldom the primary driver.

This analysis provides a baseline set of expectations about aggregate relationships—what tends to be associated with deterrence more often than not, and where the greatest risks for escalation lie. This baseline does not substitute for expert judgment on specific policy decisions. It does, however, suggest that the United States would be accepting high risk if it frequently adopts policies at odds with these past trends and analysis.

In most cases, when U.S. decisionmakers and military planners elect to accept risk, either by enhancing forward posture or reducing it, there will likely be no obvious negative repercussions. Other than information and influence operations, most of the malign activities that we have examined in this report are relatively rare events. Even small increases in the likelihood of rare events, however, accumulate. If the United States repeatedly accepts risk across large numbers of countries over extended periods of time, it is likely to provoke several episodes of escalation that otherwise would not have occurred.

In this chapter, we take stock of the risks and rewards associated with U.S. forward posture changes, focusing particularly on competition in Europe. We begin with an overview of our findings. We then apply these findings to specific posture options for Europe. We conclude with recommendations for DoD as a whole and for U.S. European Command and U.S. Army Europe.

Summary of Findings

Forward-Positioned Forces Play an Important Role in Deterring Aggression in Both Competition and Conflict

Regional U.S. force presence was consistently associated with deterrent outcomes in both our quantitative and qualitative research. Typically, this presence was most effective when it was persistent. These findings are consistent with earlier research suggesting that forward-positioned forces play an important role in deterring armed conflict. Our research here suggests that these deterrent effects could extend to the level of competition as well. Because forward-positioned forces send a signal of U.S. commitment, provide certain capabilities for countering hostile unconventional activities, help reduce the risk of military intimidation, and support the activities of other U.S. government agencies, they have an important role to play in deterring hostile measures. This role in the competition space might not be as central as other instruments of national power (such as diplomacy, information activities, or economic statecraft), but forward-positioned, at the very least, offer ancillary benefits in competition while deterring armed conflict.

The location of these forces matters. Relying on flowing forces forward from CONUS in times of crisis does not visibly commit the United States to the defense of its allies and partners and thus sends a weaker deterrent signal. CONUS-based forces also cannot employ their capabilities to build resilience to unconventional aggression, and they could arrive too late to defeat armed aggression at the time of attack. On the other hand, positioning U.S. forces directly in the states that are most vulnerable to malign activities or direct armed attack carries its own risks. Competitors often target the host countries for U.S. overseas forces with a variety of hostile measures, including military intimidation, economic coercion, disinformation, and occasionally proxy conflicts. These measures appear to be efforts by competitors to signal their opposition to nearby U.S. forces, impose costs on the host countries in the hopes of having them withdraw access for U.S. forces, and/or demonstrate to other potential host countries the consequences of close military cooperation with the United States. When U.S. forces are stationed near a competitor, in vulnerable states, or in the most likely targets of aggression, these escalatory consequences could predominate. Consequently, deterrence appears most reliably associated with U.S. forces that are positioned in an at-risk region, but nearby rather than within the most likely targets of aggression.[1]

Finally, the precise capabilities of forward-positioned U.S. forces matter. These forces potentially have a wide variety of capabilities that can increase the resilience of allies and partners to hostile measures, including capabilities for ISR, information operations, and training and capacity-building.[2] It would be wrong, however, to focus just on the unconventional or irregular aspects of competition. Forward-positioned U.S. conventional forces can be potent symbols of U.S. commitment to the security of its allies and partners. They also reduce the risks of conventional military overmatch, which, in turn, reduces competitors' freedom of action even in nonmilitary spheres and increases that of the United States and its partners.

Despite these potential advantages (especially when combined with other elements of power), certain conventional capabilities carry higher risks of escalation. These risks are typically dependent on context. In the case of Russia, Moscow appears most concerned about

---

[1]   Again, these results are consistent with previous RAND research, but the research in this report extends these findings to the level of hostile measures below the level of armed conflict.

[2]   Connable et al., 2020.

information and cyber capabilities that might threaten its domestic political control and LRPF that could threaten its homeland, to include its nuclear deterrent. The former might not be as significant a consideration for U.S. forward presence in Europe; U.S. capabilities for information and cyber operations exist across a number of U.S. actors beyond DoD, and physical proximity of U.S. military forces is not a major determinant of U.S. offensive capabilities in this area. On the other hand, LRPF are a critical consideration as the United States continues to shape its force posture in Europe, especially as ground-based systems are introduced with ranges that could easily threaten sensitive sites within Russia.

Military Activities and Dynamic Force Employment Cannot Replace Persistent Presence

The 2018 NDS emphasized that the United States would shift to a more flexible force posture in which U.S. forces and activities would be shifted around the globe in ways that are "strategically predictable, but operationally unpredictable."[3] The practical details of this concept are still evolving. At a broad level, it seems to indicate that the United States will attempt to compensate for lower numbers of forces permanently stationed overseas with greater levels of activity, including short-term deployments, military exercises, and small-scale engagements.

The United States typically has multiple objectives for such activities, including enhancing U.S. forces' readiness (especially for operating in unfamiliar terrain and with foreign militaries), developing allies' and partners' capabilities and ability to interoperate with U.S. forces, testing agreements and logistical networks, experimenting with new operating concepts under variable conditions, and so on. Frequently, such activities are used as signals to deter competitors or adversaries from initiating acts of aggression at the level of armed conflict or below.

The research in this report, including the quantitative analysis and some of the case studies, suggests that *on average* the risks of escalation from these activities are greater than their immediate deterrent value. This pattern holds across both hostile measures and armed conflict.

These results are consistent with the broad body of deterrence theory, reaching back several decades. From the perspective of deterrence theory, such activities are subject to two limitations. First, these activities represent a less "costly"—and thus weaker—signal of the United States' commitment to protect an ally or partner than permanently stationed forces. Second, they can introduce greater strategic uncertainty into adversaries' calculations. Under the DFE concept, adversaries sometimes have to react rapidly to sudden increases in U.S. military capabilities, sometimes near their territory, and decisionmaking under short timelines is prone to higher rates of mistakes and thus higher potential for inadvertent escalation. It is notable that large exercises held in the vicinity of Russia-NATO borders were a frequent

---

[3] Mattis, 2018, p. 5.

source of escalation to armed conflict in scenario work previously undertaken by RAND.[4] The Western reaction to the Zapad military exercises in 2017 should also provide some indication of the potential for misperceptions and increased tensions inherent in some of these events.[5]

These findings are not intended to suggest that such activities have no deterrent value or that the United States should avoid them. Although their *net* effects are escalatory, many such activities can provide useful deterrent signals, especially when they are conducted in relatively more-stable countries at some distance from a U.S. competitor, such as Russia. Moreover, as discussed above, the United States engages in such activities for many reasons besides deterrent signaling. The findings *do* suggest that the United States should not broadly assume that exercises and similar sorts of activities contemplated under the DFE concept can broadly substitute for forward-positioned forces. They also suggest that the United States should take concerted efforts to minimize the escalatory risk these activities pose (a subject to which we return in the following section).

Materiel Transfers and Training Can Build Capabilities but Provide Weak Signals and Introduce Third-Party Risks

The United States engages in materiel transfers and training with allies and partners to improve their capabilities, increase interoperability, build relationships, reduce costs of acquisitions through economies of scale, and (in the case of training) improve U.S. forces' familiarity with operating environments around the world. All of these objectives are defensible reasons for engaging in these activities.

The United States also engages in these activities to send deterrent signals to competitors and potential adversaries. Our research suggests that materiel transfers (and the training that normally accompanies them) are a poor deterrent signal—especially if they are attempting to *substitute* for the forward-positioning of U.S. forces rather than being *additive* to them. Prior research has suggested that materiel transfers—because they do not by themselves "tie the hands" of U.S. decisionmakers or precommit them to the defense of their partners—can inadvertently signal weak U.S. commitment. Therefore, they might actually increase the likelihood of armed aggression. Our research extends on this previous finding, suggesting that a similar logic appears to be at work in the competition space. Our case studies illustrate this relationship: Although the United States provided military assistance to Ethiopia and Georgia, it did not come to their aid when those countries were attacked.

Beyond being problematic signaling devices, materiel transfers and training introduce the risk that U.S. allies and partners could feel emboldened, or, alternatively, that the local rivals of U.S. allies and partners could feel threatened and therefore lash out at those allies and part-

---

[4] Charap et al., 2020.

[5] See, for instance, Keir Giles, "Russia Hit Multiple Targets with Zapad-2017," blog post, Carnegie Endowment for International Peace, January 25, 2018.

ners. Again, such third-party risks are apparent in the cases of Ethiopia and Georgia. Both governments appear to have adopted more-uncompromising positions with regards to internal conflicts, in part because they believed that they could rely on U.S. support. And in both cases, these countries' local adversaries (Somalia and Russia, respectively) felt threatened by U.S. aid to their neighbors and reacted accordingly. Beyond these specific cases, our statistical results show that materiel transfers are associated with an increased risk of escalation across a wide variety of hostile measures, and this escalation risk extends to the local rivals of U.S. allies and partners and to U.S. rivals.

These third-party risks are likely highest in cases of weak and poorly governed states that face a wide variety of threats beyond interstate war. But our workshops and interviews also highlighted the potential for transfers of sensitive capabilities (such as LRPF) to reduce U.S. control over an escalating crisis even in strong states.

Many Escalatory Consequences Are Not Proximate in Space or Time

As discussed in Chapter Three, there are many paths that escalation in competition might take. The most direct and obvious is signal sending: A competitor reacts to a change in U.S. posture by signaling its opposition to an increase in U.S. posture or by taking advantage of a decrease in U.S. posture to intimidate or impose costs on U.S. allies and partners. Depending on how aggressively the competitor responds, such signals (e.g., snap exercises conducted on the borders of these countries) might further ratchet up tensions. But as the case study on recent posture changes in Northeastern Europe revealed, Russia does not always respond in a straightforward manner to U.S. posture changes. If Moscow seeks to impose costs on either the United States or a U.S. ally or partner for its close military cooperation with the United States, it might need to wait for a promising opportunity. Alternatively, Moscow might not respond at all in the short term. But U.S. choices that it considers to be illegitimate or provocative could feed Russian perceptions of the threat posed by the United States and thus encourage it to avoid compromise or act more aggressively on future occasions, as happened in the aftermath of the Iran crisis. Finally, U.S. actions might not provoke Russia directly, but they could embolden third parties, who, in turn, take actions at a later point in time that do provoke Moscow, as arguably occurred in Georgia in the run-up to the 2008 Russo-Georgian war. Or U.S. actions might threaten third parties, who subsequently turn to Moscow for support, as occurred in the Horn of Africa in the 1960s and 1970s.

Critically, where escalation occurs because of an increase in U.S. posture, the consequences of U.S. actions are not immediately apparent. Indeed, they may not be apparent to U.S. observers for years afterward (if ever). Instead of U.S. actions feeding a clear action-reaction cycle, there appears to be considerable latency (long lags before Russian reactions) and considerable opportunity for miscommunication and misunderstanding. These dynamics make it extremely difficult to judge the deterrent or escalatory consequences of U.S. actions, especially in real time.

Escalatory Consequences of Forward Posture Can Often Be Mitigated

Despite the potential for unintended consequences, there are many measures that U.S. decisionmakers and military planners can take to minimize the risk of escalation. The primary considerations are the factors that we have repeatedly stressed—proximity, continuity, capability.[6] In general, changes in posture that occur closer to Russia, represent sharp changes in policy for the United States or its allies and partners, and involve capabilities that pose the highest threat to Russia pose the highest risk of escalation. For materiel transfers and training, support to inherently weak or fragile regimes also poses substantial risks. The United States can—and indeed frequently does—mitigate risk by manipulating one or more of these factors. Mitigating the risks posed by third parties can be more challenging, but here, too, there are measures that the United States can take.

In the case of military exercises, for instance, the United States can reduce the risks posed by sharp discontinuities in the scale, location, capabilities, purpose, or participants in an exercise by planning the events well in advance and repeatedly communicating to Moscow the precise goal of the event.[7] The United States can reduce the risks posed by exercising sensitive capabilities by holding those events farther from Russian borders. Additionally, the United States can closely coordinate with allies and partners to ensure that they are not simultaneously conducting national exercises that might further concentrate military capabilities in a way that Russia could perceive as threatening.[8]

In the case of U.S. materiel transfers and training of allies and partners, the United States can mitigate risk by manipulating these same factors. Such transfers and training pose little risk and likely enhance deterrence when the allies and partners are stable countries at some distance from Russian borders. These activities become more problematic when they occur close to Russia, involve sensitive capabilities in substantial quantity, involve politically unstable allies or partners, or some combination thereof. On the one hand, a buildup of stocks of long-range precision munitions in countries close to Russia, for instance, would likely be considered threatening by Russian decisionmakers and might provoke an increase in hostile measures.[9] The sale of modest numbers of JASSM-ERs to Poland, on the other hand, repre-

---

[6] For materiel transfers and training, the political stability of the ally or partner is also important.

[7] RAND virtual interviews with multiple current and former defense attachés in the region in July 2020 and with a retired three-star general officer in August 2020. This view was also expressed by most participants in RAND's workshops, as detailed in Chapter Six.

[8] RAND virtual interviews with multiple current and former defense attachés in the region in July 2020 and with a retired three-star general officer in August 2020. This view was also expressed by most participants in RAND's workshops, as detailed in Chapter Six.

[9] Clint Reach, Vikram Kilambi, and Mark Cozad, *Russian Assessments and Applications of the Correlation of Forces and Means*, Santa Monica, Calif.: RAND Corporation, RR-4235-OSD, 2020, pp. xi–xiii; and S. R. Tsyrendorzhiev and S. A. Monin, "Assessment of the Contribution of Defense Capability to the Military Security of the Russian Federation [Otsenka vklada oboronsposobnosti v voennuiu bezopasnost' Rossiiskoi Federatsii]," *Military Thought* [*Voennaia mysl'*], No. 1, 2020, p. 66.

sented only a change at the margins in NATO's capabilities, especially because other NATO member-states already had used similar missiles (such as the German-Swedish Taurus KEPD 350). A greater challenge is mitigating the risk of indirect paths to escalation, such as when U.S. allies or partners use the military capabilities that are provided by the United States in ways contrary to U.S. policy or are emboldened by a perception of a U.S. security guarantee.

The United States can also mitigate the risks posed by forward-stationing U.S. forces. The findings in this paper suggest that location appears to be a critical variable; forces positioned nearby but not necessarily in the most-vulnerable countries offer a generally preferred means of managing risk. So-called tripwire forces are one possible exception to this generalization. In our quantitative analysis, both the deterrent and escalatory effects of forces tended to increase with increases in the number of U.S. troops. Because regional forces were consistently associated with deterrence, larger forces are not problematic. For in-country forces, the results were more ambiguous. Small numbers of forces could offer an important symbol of U.S. commitment to a vulnerable state. Because their numbers are small, such forces carry less escalatory risk. But if their presence would almost inevitably trigger the deployment of the much larger number of nearby forces, they might play an important deterrent role.

Decisionmakers in the United States and its NATO allies have been acutely aware of the risks of deploying large numbers of forces in vulnerable countries contiguous to Russia. The eFP forces represent precisely such a tripwire commitment. There has been considerable debate, however, over whether the number of U.S. and other NATO forces in these frontline states should be increased. Our research suggests that a substantial increase in the numbers of these forces risks making the frontline states targets of intensified Russian hostile measures.[10]

Application of the Analysis to Specific Posture Options

To make the discussion more concrete and indicate how our analysis might be applied to future posture decisions, we developed a list of illustrative U.S. posture options throughout Europe and its periphery. This list was derived from official U.S. policy documents and debates in the broader U.S. defense community (such as papers and reports from think tanks and U.S. military research institutes). This list builds on the analysis that is throughout this report, including the scenario analysis, but it develops a fuller and more specific list of policy measures than were discussed elsewhere.

Although our statistical, case study, and scenario analyses are broadly consistent with one another, there were some discrepancies on specific points. Consequently, there is some degree

---

[10] We did not analyze in-depth critical questions, such as the time required to surge forces to these states from rear positions in the event of a crisis. Consequently, there are limits to what we can say with confidence about the ability of forces in rear areas (e.g., Germany) to deter armed conflict with Russia in frontline states such as the Baltics. Our research does suggest, however, that enhancing the abilities of U.S. and NATO forces to defeat a short-notice act of conventional Russian armed aggression in the Baltics would make these states—and potentially others nearby—targets for increased hostile measures.

of judgment involved in using our findings to project the likely outcomes of some measures. For the most part, however, our findings can be translated directly into clear guidance on a variety of posture decisions.

Table 7.1 summarizes these posture options, their values on our key factors, and the projected outcomes for each decision. Throughout the table, we use color-coded arrows to summarize what we believe the research in this report indicates are the likely effects of a given posture decision.[11]

The projected outcomes in Table 7.1 represent the direct consequences of a given U.S. posture decision on Russian hostile measures in the competition space.[12] A green, downward arrow indicates lower risk of Russian hostile measures (greater deterrent value); a red, upward arrow indicates greater risk of Russian hostile measures (greater escalatory risk); and a gray, horizontal arrow indicates neutral or ambiguous implications.

The projected outcomes are based on the interaction of the *type of force posture* (forces, activities, and agreements) with the *intervening factors* in the framework (proximity, continuity, and capability). For each posture option, each of the intervening factors is described as being more prone to enhance deterrence (distant, continuous, and/or nonsensitive posture) or more prone to escalatory risk (proximate, discontinuous, and/or sensitive). As with the outcomes, these descriptors are color-coded: More-escalatory values are depicted in red and more-deterrent values are depicted in green.

In the subsections that follow, we discuss the projected outcomes for each category of posture—forces, activities, and agreements. It is important to note that the outcomes discussed here are relative—that is, they indicate a somewhat higher or somewhat lower degree of risk or reward. As the analysis throughout this report has indicated, U.S. forward posture is only one factor that influences outcomes; typically, it will be a contributing factor but not decisive. In many cases where escalatory risk is indicated—especially for specific activities rather than large-scale repositioning of forces—the United States likely will be able to undertake such actions without observable negative consequences. If the United States repeatedly accepts risk in its posture choices, however, the opportunities for escalation will accumulate. While consequences may be invisible in the short term, over the course of the 15-year time

---

[11] In approximately two-thirds of the rows of Table 7.1, the findings from both the quantitative and qualitative research have clear implications for the expected outcome of a given posture decision—higher or lower Russian malign activity. In some cases, the intervening factors work in countervailing directions, such as when sensitive capabilities (an escalatory factor) are deployed, but not in close proximity to Russia (a factor which should reduce the likelihood of escalation). In these cases, we had no formal weighting scheme to determine which factor would likely predominate—and, given our qualitative analysis of the effects of sensitive capabilities, no such formal weighting scheme was possible. In these cases, some degree of judgment was necessary. These judgments were reached by consensus among the research team using their interpretations of the implications of the research.

[12] They do not indicate longer-term outcomes that might include indirect effects, such as the building of relationships with or capabilities and capacity in allies and partners over time.

TABLE 7.1

Illustrative Posture Options and Projected Implications for Likelihood of Russian Malign Activities in Competition

Option	Proximity	Discontinuity	Capability	Projected Direct Outcome	Rationale
Forces (Augment)					
Maintain or modestly increase U.S. forces in Western Europe	Distant	Continuous	Nonsensitive	↓	Existing U.S. forces in Western Europe deter malign activity and conflict with little escalatory risk.
Augment U.S. forces in Western Europe with PrSM	Distant	Discontinuous	Sensitive	↕	PrSM could help to deter conflict and escalation risk that would be mitigated by stationing to the West, but could invite hostile influence operations or worse.
Augment U.S. forces in Northeast Europe (e.g., Poland) to division or more	Proximate	Discontinuous	Neutral	↑	Ground forces generally possess fewer sensitive capabilities than air forces, although large numbers could result in outsized Russian reactions.
Deploy LRPF to Northeastern Europe	Proximate	Discontinuous	Sensitive	↑	Deployment of such sensitive capabilities close to Russia would be highly likely to make host countries targets of Russian hostile measures.
Forces (Reduce)					
Modestly reduce U.S. force levels in Western Europe	Distant	Discontinuous	Nonsensitive	↑	Reductions in U.S. forces would, at a minimum, signal decreasing U.S. commitment to Europe.
Withdraw US forces from KFOR	Distant	Discontinuous	Nonsensitive	↑	Withdrawal of U.S. forces would signal U.S. disengagement and invite potential crises that Russia could exploit.
Downsize Operation Atlantic Resolve	Proximate	Discontinuous	Nonsensitive	↑	After years of bolstering defenses, a change in U.S. direction without reciprocal change from Russia could be seen as weakening commitment.

Table 7.1—Continued

Option	Proximity	Discontinuity	Capability	Projected Direct Outcome	Rationale
Activities					
Routine materiel transfers and training in Western Europe	Distant	Continuous	Nonsensitive	↗ (green)	Such routine behavior is highly unlikely to provoke Russia and could signal continued U.S. commitment.
Materiel transfers to make Northeastern Europe "hedgehogs" or "poison pills"	Proximate	Continuous	Nonsensitive	↔	Activities to make Northeastern European states more-"costly" targets of conventional aggression are unlikely to deter malign activities but are unlikely to provoke.
Transfer of LRPF and training for Western Europe	Distant	Neutral	Neutral	↔	Many Western European states have air- and/or naval-launched LRPF; such transfers are less likely to be problematic, unless they are long range (1,000 km+).
Materiel transfers and partnership activity increase in Southeastern Europe	Distant	Continuous	Neutral	↔	Many such activities would likely have some positive effects, although others (e.g., offensive capabilities for Serbia) would be problematic.
Routine military exercises in Northeastern Europe	Proximate	Continuous	Nonsensitive	↔	Routine exercises might provoke low-level hostile measures, but risks are low if the United States communicates intent and types of forces involved and coordinates with allies.
Repeated exercises in Northeastern Europe, such as Trident Juncture-18 or larger	Proximate	Discontinuous	Neutral	↙ (red)	Large-scale exercises in Northeastern Europe run risks of escalation in competition as well as inadvertent conflict.
Transfer of substantial LRPF and training for Northeastern Europe	Proximate	Discontinuous	Sensitive	↙ (red)	Small-scale transfers (e.g., JASSM-ER sales to Poland) might not be escalatory, but large transfers likely would provoke hostile measures.
Agreements					
Agreements to enhance border transit, military contracting in Western Europe	Distant	Continuous	Nonsensitive	↗ (green)	Although predominantly targeted at conventional conflict, such measures can demonstrate U.S. commitment and reduce the likelihood of intimidation.
Agreements to enhance border transit, military contracting in Northeastern Europe	Proximate	Neutral	Neutral	↔	Such agreements represent only incremental change with NATO allies; with Finland or Sweden, there is a higher risk of hostile measures.

134

Table 7.1—Continued

NOTES: *Projected Direct Outcome*: The outcome that the research in this report suggests is most likely to result from a given change in U.S. posture. These outcomes represent only the direct results of U.S. posture changes; indirect effects (such as assuring allies and partners or increasing their capabilities) are not evaluated.

⬆ (green)	A given U.S. posture decision is projected to result in a decrease in the incidence of a given type of hostile measure (a deterrent relationship).
⬆ (red)	A given U.S. posture decision is projected to result in an increase in the incidence of a given type of hostile measure (an escalatory relationship).

Proximity: The distance between a given U.S. posture change and Russia.

Distant	U.S. forward posture is not located in Russia's immediate environs, including the states of the former Soviet Union and states in Northern and Eastern Europe that are contiguous or nearly contiguous to Russia; the green shading of the word indicates a reduced likelihood of aggressive Russian response.
Proximate	U.S. forward posture that is located in Russia's immediate environs, including the states of the former Soviet Union and states in Northern and Eastern Europe that are contiguous or nearly contiguous to Russia; the red shading of the word indicates an increased likelihood of aggressive Russian response.

Continuity: The extent and rapidity of change in U.S. forward posture.

Continuous	U.S. forward posture that remains the same or changes only gradually, thus increasing its predictability; the green shading of the word indicates a reduced likelihood of aggressive Russian response.
Discontinuous	U.S. forward posture that changes rapidly (either qualitatively or quantitatively), thus increasing its unpredictability; the red shading of the word indicates an increased likelihood of aggressive Russian response.

Capability: The sensitivity of capabilities possessed by forward-positioned U.S. forces or military activities, with *sensitive capabilities* understood as those that Russia perceives as posing severe threats to state or regime security (especially weapon systems that could theoretically give the United States a debilitating first-strike capability, or a large-scale build-up of more traditional capabilities).

Nonsensitive	U.S. forward posture that does not pose a severe threat to Russian state or regime capability.
Sensitive	U.S. forward posture that Russia perceives as posing a severe threat to Russian state or regime capability.

135

horizon in this report, such decisions could ultimately trigger Russian acts of aggression or even major crises.

Projected Outcomes of Posture Options Centered on U.S. Forces Positioned in Europe

Our findings have implications for several policy debates about U.S. force presence in Europe. On one end of the spectrum, some observers have argued that it is essential to place sizeable numbers of U.S. forces (an armored division or more) close to the exposed Baltic states.[13] Others argue that such forces likely would provoke Russia and expose the host countries to intensified malign activities, if not direct armed aggression. Many of these observers and others believe that the small tripwire eFP contingents are sufficient to establish deterrence without provoking Russia.[14] Finally, because China is increasingly assuming the role of the "pacing threat" around which U.S. defense planning is oriented, U.S. forces in Europe might be targeted for reductions as resources are directed to the Indo-Pacific theater.

Our research lends support to the middle option in this spectrum. U.S. forces positioned in Europe play a valuable role in deterring malign activities both in competition and in armed conflict. Drawdowns of U.S. forces, such as the one announced by then–U.S. Secretary of Defense Mark Esper in July 2020, threaten to undermine that deterrent. On the other hand, a sharp increase in the number of U.S. forces—especially if they are present in substantial numbers and positioned in close proximity to Russia (including the Kaliningrad exclave)— are likely to provoke hostile measures directed at the host countries, at least in the short term.

Our research also provides evidence in support of the tripwire concept that undergirds U.S. forces in Operation Atlantic Resolve and KFOR.[15] In general, our quantitative findings are linear—to the extent that forward-positioned U.S. forces provoke hostile measures, they are likely to have mild effects when only small numbers of forces are involved, as is the case in Operation Atlantic Resolve and KFOR. Moreover, especially since U.S. forces have been present in these regions for several years, Moscow has been able to calibrate its expectations accordingly, thus reducing the uncertainty that often fuels misperceptions. Any initiative to reduce or withdraw U.S. forces from these small tripwire deployments likely would signal decreasing U.S. commitment to the region and thus potentially embolden Moscow.

The capabilities of U.S. forces positioned in Europe also have important implications in the competition space. The U.S. Army is developing several LRPF systems. PrSM (with an estimated range of approximately 500 km) is relatively close to being operational, while systems with ranges as far as 2,500 km are being considered. The deployment of PrSM capabilities in Western Europe would be unlikely to arouse much response from Russia; the ranges

---

[13] Shlapak and Johnson, 2016; and Colby and Solomon, 2015.

[14] See, for instance, Kofman, 2018.

[15] Operation Atlantic Resolve, funded through the European Deterrence Initiative, is the name of the ongoing mission to support European allies following Russia's invasion of Ukraine in 2014.

currently anticipated for these systems would represent only an incremental (albeit tactically important) improvement on existing U.S. capabilities. If these systems were positioned in substantial numbers in Northeastern Europe or if longer-range systems were placed in Western Europe, however, they would be capable of striking sensitive sites in Russia. As the INF experience of the 1980s suggests, Russia would be likely to react by targeting host countries with hostile measures.

Projected Outcomes of Posture Options Centered on U.S. Military Activities in Europe

Proposals to enhance deterrence in Europe through increased U.S. military activities fall into several broad categories, including

1. the continuation and incremental expansion of ongoing activities throughout Europe (including efforts to strengthen the irregular or unconventional defenses of the Baltic states—so-called poison pill or hedgehog concepts[16]
2. efforts to greatly increase the capabilities of European allies and partners (including through the development and transfer of LRPF systems)[17]
3. sizeable expansion of multilateral military exercises held in Northeastern Europe[18]
4. intensifying security cooperation activities in Southeastern Europe and potentially in the post-Soviet space to strengthen relationships between the United States and governments in these regions.

The analysis in this report suggests that the first category of activities is unproblematic and, in fact, likely to enhance deterrence in most cases. Western European countries already have advanced military capabilities, so additional materiel transfers from and training or exercising with the United States typically represent only incremental gains on their existing capabilities. These countries are also far enough from Russian borders that they are less likely to provoke hostile measures in response to U.S. military activities. Countries closer to Russia (such as the Baltics) are more sensitive for Moscow, but investments in improving these countries' capabilities to make them so-called *hedgehogs* or *poison pills* (i.e., countries that would impose high costs on an aggressor and occupier through irregular and unconventional national defense concepts) pose little threat to Russian interests. Such investments might do little to deter Russian hostile measures, but they represent important investments

---

[16] See, for instance, Robert M. Klein, Stefan Lundqvist, Ed Sumangil, and Ulrica Pettersson, *Baltics Left of Bang: The Role of NATO with Partners in Denial-Based Deterrence*, Washington, D.C.: National Defense University, Institute for National Strategic Studies, November 2019; and Flanagan et al., 2019.

[17] See, for example, Simón and Lanoszka, 2020.

[18] Clem, 2017.

in deterring armed conflict and are unlikely to incite additional Russian hostile measures beyond what Moscow is already doing.

Activities intended to help European allies and partners develop more-advanced capabilities are more sensitive, particularly in the case of LRPF systems. Again, in the case of Western European allies and partners, their existing capabilities (such as the long-range German-Swedish Taurus KEPD 350) and their distance from Russia suggests a muted Russian reaction to even activities designed to enhance these countries' LRPF capabilities, at least up to the 500-km range associated with intermediate-range missiles. Longer-range systems (e.g., 1,000 or more kilometers), on the other hand, could well provoke Russian hostile measures similar to the INF crisis of the 1980s, even in Western Europe. If such systems were transferred in substantial numbers to countries in Northeastern Europe (and possibly to such countries as Romania along the Black Sea), Russia would almost certainly seek to target hostile measures at the U.S. allies and partners incorporating such systems into their militaries.

Large-scale multilateral military exercises could pose similar risks. Such exercises might well signal U.S. commitment to its allies and partners (especially if they are additive to, rather than substitutes for, a persistent U.S. forward military presence in the region). Such exercises also help to build allies' and partners' warfighting capabilities and interoperability with U.S. forces, test logistics and sustainment systems, and test the system of legal agreements in place that allows for intratheater mobility and various support functions. But these various benefits must be weighed against the escalatory risks. The research in this report suggests that military exercises provoke malign activities in competition more often than they deter them. These risks can be mitigated by planning events well ahead of time and communicating the United States' intentions for the exercise and the capabilities involved, thus enhancing their predictability. The risks can be further mitigated by conducting them farther from Russian borders—or potentially conducting distributed exercises, in which only a portion of U.S., NATO, and partner forces are operating near Russia at any one time. Risks can also be mitigated by investing in measures intended to bolster participating countries' resilience, such as public information campaigns to explain the purpose of such exercises. But there are limits to what such mitigating measures can accomplish. Just as the United States and many European states have been concerned by Zapad exercises, it is reasonable to expect Russian decisionmakers to entertain similar concerns about NATO events. Exercises on the scale of Trident Juncture-18 should be held by exception, at least when they are held within countries neighboring Russia.

Projected Outcomes of Posture Options Centered on Military Agreements in Europe

The risks borne by countries on a path to NATO accession are, by now, well understood (as underscored by Russian activities in Georgia, Montenegro, and North Macedonia). Less well understood are the implications of lesser military agreements, such as agreements designed to enhance intratheater mobility or logistics and sustainment in the region. Our research suggests that the primary benefits of such agreements are to conventional deterrence. They could, however, have ancillary benefits in the competition space by reducing the likelihood of Russian military intimidation and enhancing the confidence of the United States and its partners to undertake strong measures that are designed to resist Russian malign activities and potentially impose costs on Russia for such measures. Such agreements should be unproblematic with existing NATO allies. With countries outside NATO near Russian borders—including Finland and Sweden—such agreements are more likely to elicit hostile Russian responses (as, indeed, Finland and Sweden have already experienced).

Recommendations

Based on the analysis in this report, we offer the following recommendations.

Adopt Specific and Appropriately Scoped Goals for U.S. Forward Posture

Our research suggests that U.S. military posture has a variety of effects on competition. For the most part, however, these effects tend to be subtle. Each posture decision might only incrementally increase or decrease the risk of Russian aggression across the competition continuum. Over the course of the 15-year time horizon adopted for this report, however, these incremental changes can have important effects—both positive and negative.

These outcomes suggest that U.S. decisionmakers should think of U.S. posture primarily as an enabler of a much broader strategy that incorporates the full range of the instruments of national power. Understood in these terms, military posture can be one important contributor to a competition strategy, especially when focused on countering hostile measures for which the military has inherent advantages (such as military intimidation or proxy warfare). But a competition strategy that weights military instruments heavily is almost certain to disappoint.

These outcomes also suggest that U.S. decisionmakers should base U.S. forward posture changes on specific objectives. It is not enough simply to attempt to complicate competitor decisionmaking, impose costs, expand the competition space, or any other vague goals that some observers might suggest. A great many posture changes, on balance, have more escalatory consequences than deterrent ones. Without clear goals, it is difficult to weigh whether the escalation risks can be justified.

Despite these cautions, U.S. decisionmakers might well decide that the risk of escalation is warranted in many cases. When making decisions about forward posture, U.S. senior leaders and military planners must balance multiple considerations, many of which were outside the scope of this analysis. These considerations include the potential of certain activities to strengthen the capabilities of U.S. allies and partners or to reinforce relationships with leaders in those states. Repeatedly accepting such risk, however, could lead to escalating spirals of tit-for-tat measures in the competition space, which have the potential to create highly costly competition that could tip into armed conflict.

Retain U.S. Forces Currently Positioned in Europe

U.S. forces currently positioned in Europe broadly support deterrence—not just deterrence of armed conflict, but also, more subtly, several forms of malign activity. The relationship between U.S. forces and the maintenance of stability is perhaps most obvious in the case of eFP and KFOR—forces that are directly tied to deterring both renewed armed conflict but also subtler forms of destabilization. But our research suggests that U.S. forces that are removed from the frontlines play an important role in making the implicit threat behind these small deployments of U.S. forces much more credible. Not only do U.S. forces positioned near—but not in—the most vulnerable countries play an important deterrent role, but they might be *more* effective than stationing more troops (beyond the current tripwire forces) closer to the front lines. Forces stationed in vulnerable states can make the host countries targets for a variety of hostile measures, from military intimidation (with the ever-present risk of inadvertent escalation) to subtler forms of aggression that are intended to impose costs on or weaken the will of host countries. Forces positioned in less vulnerable countries pose fewer threats to the host nation but could still be repositioned quickly as needed.[19]

Limit Reliance on Dynamic Force Employment

Although still an evolving concept, DFE appears to emphasize short-term deployments and unpredictable military activities over committing to permanent (or at least long-term) forward-stationing of U.S. forces. There are many reasons why the concept is attractive in theory and from a fiscal perspective. Our research nonetheless suggests that there are inherent escalatory risks in relying on military exercises and similar activities to establish deterrence. Some of these risks can be mitigated through manipulation of such factors as proximity, but operational unpredictability implies discontinuity—a factor frequently associated with escalation in our analysis. DFE is best used as a supplement to persistent presence, not a substitute, and only if appropriate measures are taken to mitigate the associated risks.

Place More Emphasis on Rigorous Risk Assessment and Evaluation

There was often little agreement among the experts and practitioners we consulted about what "worked" in competition—a lack of consensus that was also reflected in the scholarly and policy literature that we reviewed for this report. Some of the practitioners whom we

---

[19] In saying that forces can be repositioned quickly, we do not intend to minimize the serious mobility and logistics factors that complicate efforts to reinforce the Baltic states and other vulnerable countries. NATO has made efforts to reduce these challenges, but the alliance is still far from achieving the degree of intra-theater mobility that its forces require. These mobility and logistics challenges, however, need to be weighed against the strategic risks of forward-positioned forces.

consulted recognized this fact and emphasized the need for more-rigorous efforts to assess the consequences of U.S. posture decisions.

These consequences can be assessed prospectively through risk assessments and retro-actively through evaluations. Both are needed to improve U.S. performance in competition. Particularly for those options shown to be high-risk in this report, the United States should adopt rigorous interagency risk assessment processes. When evaluating the consequences of U.S. posture decisions after the fact, the United States should not only look for immediate reactions but should also explore longer-term and indirect dynamics.

Workshop and Interview Participants

As described in Chapter Six, in support of our scenario-based analysis, we conducted workshops and interviews in July and August 2020 over a virtual platform. The following is an anonymized list of participants. Each person is identified by their former or current position or occupation. The parenthetical specifies the individual's expertise that is most pertinent to this report.

Workshop Participants

1. Retired senior diplomat, former U.S. ambassador (diplomacy, Russia and Eurasia)
2. Retired senior diplomat, former U.S. ambassador (diplomacy, Russia and Eurasia)
3. Retired U.S. Army colonel (Army operations and logistics)
4. Retired U.S. Army colonel (Army operations and multidomain operations)
5. Senior political scientist (deterrence and military operations)
6. Senior political scientist (deterrence and military operations)
7. Retired senior defense civilian (European security)
8. Retired senior defense civilian (European security)
9. Retired senior intelligence community civilian (Russia and Eurasia)
10. Researcher (information operations)
11. Researcher (escalation, nuclear)
12. Researcher (European security)
13. Researcher (Russia and Eurasia)

Interview Participants

1. Department of State senior official (European security)
2. Retired three-star general/flag officer (European security)
3. Active duty one-star general/flag officer (Asian and European security)
4. Active duty U.S. Army colonel (European security)

5. Active duty U.S. Air Force lieutenant colonel, defense attaché office in Europe (country-level expertise)
6. Active duty U.S. Army lieutenant colonel, defense attaché office in Europe (country-level expertise)
7. Active duty U.S. Army lieutenant colonel, defense attaché office in Europe (country-level expertise)
8. Retired U.S. Army lieutenant colonel, defense attaché office in Europe (country-level expertise)
9. Senior political scientist (deterrence and escalation)

Technical Discussion of Quantitative Analysis

Our quantitative models examine the impact of identifiable U.S. posture choices on malign activities in the competition space for a variety of potential competitors. In Chapter Four, we provide a nontechnical discussion of our quantitative analysis to provide an overview of our approach and results for readers without a background in statistical research. In this appendix, first, we provide in-depth details on our model specification to supplement the key points made in Chapter Four, addressing the methodological issues inherent to a study of competitive behavior across time. We then discuss the full range of statistical and substantive effects and our models examining the conditional effects of U.S. posture, expanding on the discussion in the main text. Lastly, we present our precise regression results.

Model Specifications

We perform a large-N quantitative analysis that runs from 1945 to 2010.[1] Our unit of analysis is the dyad year. The *dyad year* uniquely identifies a partner-competitor pair for a particular year (e.g. Germany-Russia-2004, Germany-Russia-2005). As discussed in detail in the main report, the included dyads depend on the specific sample that we are examining, moving from the most inclusive sample of politically relevant states—in which all states are included as potential U.S. partners—to more-restrictive samples. Our data form an unbalanced panel in which some dyads appear in the data for the full range of years, while others have only partial coverage.[2]

---

[1] Missing data preclude us from examining the time before or after these markers. There are missing data for each of our variables. Although we do not argue that this missingness is at random, we do not believe that there is any reason to suggest that they are missing in a way that is related to our variables of interest or in a way that would systematically bias our results.

[2] In certain models, we are missing data for some years or dyads such that we do not consider the full time range listed or the full set of cases across these years. This can introduce bias into our results if our models contain missing data that are not missing randomly but rather because they are correlated with our variables of interest. Although there are several methodologies for calculating missing data from existing data, they rely on a specific set of assumptions being true. Often, these methods increase the power of a model without truly reducing bias, and there is no way to determine whether bias has indeed been reduced. Rather than making these assumptions, we present the results without imputing these missing data and allow the reader to place their own weights on the extent of this bias.

Equation 1 represents our model for our continuous dependent variable (arms transfers) using OLS regression. We regress the dependent variable in country i in time t on a one-year lag of U.S. posture $(t–1)$ for country i. Our β for each posture choice captures the change in our dependent variable, on average and in a given sample, for a one-unit shift in our posture choice with all of our control variables held constant. We also include a vector of controls, all lagged by one year, with $\gamma_{i,t-1}$ representing the corresponding coefficients on these variables. Our error is denoted by $\epsilon_{i,t}$ which captures deviations in our sample from the true population values.

$$Y_{i,t} = \alpha + \beta_{i,t-1} \left(Posture \right) + \gamma_{i,t-1} \left(Controls \right) + \varepsilon_{i,t}.$$

Equation 2 represents our model for each binary dependent variable (sanctions, proxy warfare, military intimidation, the use of force) using probit regression.[3] Here $Pr(Y=1)$ denotes the probability that a malign activity will take on a value of 1 for a given dyad-year, and Φ is the cumulative distribution function of the standard normal distribution. The parameters, indexed by dyad, time, and variable (j), whether posture option or control, are estimated for both our posture options and our controls by maximum likelihood.

$$Pr \left(Y_{i,t} = 1 \,|\, X_{i,t-1} \right) = \Phi \left(X_{i,t-1} \beta_{i,t-1,j} \right).$$

Unlike in our specification for equation 1, the probability of a malign activity is not given, with all else held equal, by the β for each posture choice. Rather our probability depends not simply on the value of each posture option but on the value of each control variable in the model as well. Instead of examining each coefficient in isolation, where we can determine only the direction of the effect, we determine the size of the effect of each posture choice (known as a *marginal effect*) by examining the impact of each posture choice when our controls are held at specific values. We summarize these results in our discussion in Chapter Four and explain them in greater technical depth in this appendix.

In each model, our standard errors are clustered by dyad. This clustering method helps adjust standard errors for correlation of residuals within clusters—that is, we account for the correlation of dyad-pairs across time mathematically in our measures of confidence.

---

[3]   The two main statistical models for binary dependent variables are probit regression and logistic regression. Logistic regression (*logit*) is better suited in the case of extreme values for independent variables. However, in our models, all extremity is removed for our variables of interest through our treatment of outliers. As a result, the choice of probit or logit will not likely dictate our results. However, because probit assumes that our errors take a standard normal distribution—a more common real-life distribution than the standard logistic distribution used by logit—we use probit regression here.

Types of Potential Competitors (Samples)

In our statistical analysis, we examine the effect of U.S. posture directed toward a friendly country that we denote as the partner state, on the level of malign activities or hostile measures directed toward the partner by potential competitors. Our analysis does not focus solely on Russia but rather looks at broader patterns of competition. We examine the hostile measures of a broader range of states for two reasons. First, statistical analysis functions by examining patterns in large amounts of data. The smaller the number of observations (such as malign activities), the more likely that the results will be skewed by a small number of potentially idiosyncratic cases. By examining more competitor states, we can more easily detect changes in the probability of malign activities that reflect patterns of state behavior.

Second, as we discussed in Chapter Three, analysis of competition is complicated by the fact that third parties play important roles. Russia might not target a U.S. partner with hostile measures itself; instead, it might provide military capabilities and diplomatic support to the neighbors or rivals of the U.S. partner, and these countries—emboldened by Moscow's support—might be the ones that undertake malign activities.

For both of these reasons, our analysis examines four different types of states:

- **Politically relevant:** The broadest category of potential competitors includes those that are called "politically relevant" in the scholarship on deterrence. Academic studies of international relations refer to a pair of states as politically relevant if one of the states in the pair is a major power or if the two states share a border.[4] This sample includes the broadest range of potential competitors, but it still excludes states that could not realistically pose a threat to the U.S. partner. For example, the Republic of South Korea falls outside the sample of politically relevant countries for Serbia.

- **U.S. adversaries:** We expect that states that have an adversarial relationship with the United States are particularly likely to be threatened by and respond to U.S. posture choices. We define *U.S. adversaries* using the peace scale developed by the international relations scholars Paul Diehl, Gary Goertz, and Yahve Gallegos.[5] The *peace scale* is a measure that captures issues in dispute, violent interactions, communication and transnational ties, diplomacy and areas and levels of agreement using media and historical accounts of state to state interactions. We categorize as a U.S. adversary any state with

---

[4] Randolph M. Siverson and Harvey Starr, *The Diffusion of War: A Study of Opportunity and Willingness*, Ann Arbor, Mich.: University of Michigan Press, 1991. The list of major powers is as follows: United States (1946–present), United Kingdom (1946–present), France (1946–present), Soviet Union/Russia (1946–present), China (1950–present), Germany (1991–present), and Japan (1991–present).

[5] Paul F. Diehl, Gary Goertz, and Yahve Gallegos, "Peace Data: Concept, Measurement, Patterns, and Research Agenda," *Conflict Management and Peace Science*, 2019. Thompson's data better capture the reciprocal nature of enmity that identifies states that are likely to engage in conflict. However, this is harder to identify for a world superpower, such as the United States, which might have many adversaries and face few threats, and therefore we use the more forgiving peace scale to identify U.S. adversaries.

a score in the two lowest categories on this scale.[6] For example, Iran is a U.S. adversary, but Armenia is not a U.S. adversary.

- **Partner's rivals:** In addition to U.S. adversaries, states that share a long historical antipathy with the partner should be particularly likely to respond to U.S. posture choices. We capture these relationships using the concept of interstate rivalry. Rival states are those that view one another as enemies and have engaged in sustained competition with the potential to escalate to military conflict. Pairs of rival states have been identified by international relations scholar William Thompson through an examination of the diplomatic histories of states' foreign policy activities to capture mutual threat and enemy perceptions on the part of decisionmakers.[7] For example, the United States and Russia are rival states but Belarus and Latvia are not rival states.
- **Russia/Soviet Union:** Although the larger analysis is designed to understand underlying trends in behavior between states, we are also interested in better understanding the behavior of Russia and the Soviet Union following changes in various aspects of U.S. force posture.

As will be seen in the discussion of our statistical results later in this appendix, each of these samples of potential competitor states has advantages and disadvantages for understanding competition dynamics. With the largest number of observations, the sample that includes all "politically relevant" states is most likely to detect even subtle patterns of competition, and it is least likely to exclude states that might have been deterred or provoked by U.S. behavior. This allows us to examine competitive behavior between states that are not explicitly defined by their competitive behavior, limiting selection effects. Furthermore, although we are including states that are not explicitly competitors, we are also controlling for cooperative relations between states, such as alliances, meaning that we are able to parcel out our statistical relationships holding all else equal (or constant). For this reason, in the body of the report we present our results for politically relevant dyads.

On the other hand, this sample is most likely to include states that do not resemble Russia and might not even be engaged in what could be considered competitive behavior with U.S. partners. Rival and adversary states are more likely to engage in one of the activities of interest—such as economic sanctions or arms transfers—because of strategic competition with the United States or the U.S. partner. These samples, however, are smaller, so they are more likely to miss important patterns and our statistical results are more likely to be influenced by a handful of unrepresentative cases. Finally, the analysis of Russia and the Soviet Union is most directly relevant to this report but is also the sample most susceptible to idiosyncratic outcomes caused by a small number of cases. When the results of our statistical

---

[6] Scores of 0.25 and 0 on the scale capture the categories of lesser and severe rivalry as identified by the authors.

[7] William R. Thompson, "Identifying Rivals and Rivalries in World Politics," *International Studies Quarterly*, Vol. 45, No. 4, December 2001.

analysis are the same across all of these samples, it provides strong evidence in favor of a particular competitive dynamic. The more inconsistent the results are across the samples, the more tentative the findings are.

Dependent Variables

We describe the data and measurement for our independent and dependent variables in depth in Chapter Four. Here, we reiterate the key points and expand our technical detail as follows:

- **Competitive arms transfers:** To assess competitive arms transfers, we measure the level of arms that all states directly relevant to the U.S. ally or partner import from sources other than the United States using the SIPRI's Arms Transfer Database TIV. The TIV is intended to represent the transfer of military resources rather than the financial value of the transfer. The TIV is calculated either from the production cost of the weapon, or, if it is not known, through a comparison with core weapons using data on size and performance characteristics; type of electronics, loading or unloading arrangements, engine, tracks or wheels, armament and materials; and the year in which the weapon was produced.[8] We measure the flow of arms using the IHS of all arms imports to correct for outliers. The IHS function is commonly used to account for significantly skewed data.[9] These data run from 1950 to 2012.[10]

- **Economic coercion:** To measure economic coercion used against U.S. allies and partners, we used data on economic sanctions from the TIES dataset.[11] In this dataset, *sanctions* are defined as actions that countries take to limit or end their economic relations with a target country in an effort to persuade that country to change its policies. Our statistical models examine both the threat of sanctions (such as through verbal statements or draft legislation) and those that are actually imposed (through such actions as embargos, import and export restrictions, blockades, asset freezing, aid termination, travel bans, and the suspension of existing agreements). These data run from 1945 to 2005.

- **Proxy warfare:** Our measure of rebel proxy support captures the provision of military support to a violent nonstate actor in the midst of an ongoing intrastate conflict. Data on violent nonstate actors cover those groups that were actively engaged in an intrastate conflict with the government of the state in which they were located from 1946 through

---

[8] For details, see SIPRI, undated.

[9] John B. Burbidge, Lonnie Magee, and A. Leslie Robb, "Alternative Transformations to Handle Extreme Values of the Dependent Variable," *Journal of the American Statistical Association*, Vol. 83, No. 401, March 1988.

[10] Although these data have been updated to cover the period from 2013 to 2019, our controls and independent variables do not allow us to make use of these data.

[11] Morgan, Bapat, and Kobayashi, 2014.

2010.[12] Our measure of state military support for violent nonstate actors is drawn from previous work that synthesized multiple databases to provide a more complete and reliable measure.[13] In each model, we consider the likelihood that a potential competitor will provide support to a proxy group within a U.S. partner state. Models of this class are unique in that they include only predictors from prior to the onset of each episode of conflict to ensure that we can separate the effect of U.S. posture before a conflict from that taken in response to the conflict. In addition, cases in which the United States is also supporting a rebel group in the conflict are excluded to further differentiate between the effects of U.S. force posture and U.S. involvement in the conflict.

- **Military intimidation and the direct use of force:** We account for military intimidation and the use of force using the initiation of MID. We capture military intimidation using low-hostility MIDs. We capture the use of military force using high-hostility MIDs.[14] Data on militarized interstate disputes run from 1816–2010, although our analysis only begins in 1945.

Independent Variables

We describe the data and measurement for our independent and dependent variables in depth in Chapter Four. Here, we reiterate the key points and expand our technical detail. For each indicator, we examine U.S. posture toward the partner one year prior to the outcome of interest. We use a one-year lag because this is the standard in the quantitative literature. We acknowledge that this is an imperfect construct, particularly because we believe that there might be both short- and long-term effects. In that sense, this is a stricter test than others would be, and our results likely are biased downward.

- **Forces (in-country and in-region):** We measure U.S. forces using data from the Pentagon's DMDC, which provides data on the number and service of U.S. military personnel stationed overseas.[15] We measure U.S. forces in two ways, building on prior RAND research. The first measure captures all personnel positioned within the borders of a U.S. partner. The second measure captures those troops that are outside a given state but within the same region. For this measure, we divide the world into nine distinct regions. The regions are Central America and the Caribbean, South America, Europe (excluding Eastern Europe), Eastern Europe and Eurasia, West Africa, Eastern and Southern

---

[12] Ralph Sundberg, Kristine Eck, and Joakim Kreutz, "Introducing the UCDP Non-State Conflict Dataset," *Journal of Peace Research*, Vol. 49, No. 2, 2012.

[13] Unpublished research from Watts et al., 2020.

[14] Palmer et al., 2020.

[15] O'Mahony et al., 2018; Frederick et al., 2020.

Africa, the Middle East and North Africa, South Asia, East and Southeast Asia, and Oceania. We adjust each measure for outliers using the IHS function.

- **In robustness checks, we examine two other measures of U.S. forces.** The first distinguishes between three types of ground forces. *Heavy ground forces* include armored, mechanized, artillery, and combat aviation units. *Light ground forces* include light infantry, airborne, and some special forces units. Air defense and artillery forces count only standalone units and not those embedded in larger light or heavy forces. For each measure of ground force types, we also include a measure of nearby U.S. forces, a distance-weighted metric of the U.S. forces that are closest to each state. This loss of strength gradient comes from Frederick et al., 2020. The second is an analysis of threshold effects at the 25th, 50th, and 75th percentile of U.S. troops. Neither measure led us to substantially different results.

- **Activities:** We capture U.S. security cooperation activities using two measures: arms transfers and multilateral military exercises. As with the measure of competitive arms transfers, our measure of arms imports from the United States comes from SIPRI data and captures the inverse hyperbolic sine of all arms transfers from the United States in a given year. Our data on multilateral military exercises comes from a dataset compiled by Vito D'Orazio from an examination of major news sources from 1970–2010. News sources in this dataset include the Associated Press, Agence France Press, Interfax News Agency, and Xinhua General News Agency.[16]

- **Agreements:** We consider two forms of security-related agreements with the United States, alliances, and SOFAs. Alliance data come from the Correlates of War Project.[17] Data on SOFAs come from previous RAND research on security-related agreements.[18]

Control Variables

In this section, we provide further details on the control variables that we used in our analysis and the sources of data that we used. U.S. forward military posture is one of many factors that could lead to escalatory or de-escalatory responses by adversary states. Furthermore, there are theoretical reasons to believe that U.S. forward military posture might be more or less escalatory in some states or environments than in others. To better isolate the effects of U.S. force posture on behavior by adversary states, we incorporated these other factors in

---

[16] D'Orazio, undated.

[17] Gibler, 2009. The United States has 133 formal alliances in the data, and we examine three types of alliance agreements: defense pacts, consultation pacts, and nonaggression pacts. The United States only has 13 agreements that include neutrality or nonaggression provisions that do not also include defense or consultation commitments. We nevertheless include these agreements as a signal of formal U.S. relationships with another state.

[18] Kavanagh, 2014.

our models as statistical controls. First, we discuss the theoretical motivations behind why certain elements of the geopolitical context must be considered when examining the relationship between U.S. force posture and competitor responses, given the extant literature. We then explain the specific realizations in terms of statistical control variables. In each model, we include controls for only those variables that could simultaneously cause the U.S. posture choice and the adversary response. Because our control variables only partially overlap across our models of different competitor response options, Table B.1 provides a full accounting of which control variables are included in which set of models.

Levels of Cooperation Between the United States and the Partner

- **UN voting similarity:** Partners that share foreign policy interests with the United States are more likely to host elements of U.S. forward military posture. Partners that support U.S. foreign policy across the globe also might be more likely to face adversaries. This is, therefore, important to control for, regardless of adversary response. We measure foreign policy similarity using the similarity of UNGA voting profile, where states that cast the same votes in UNGA demonstrate the extent of their overlapping or shared interests. UNGA votes are a standard data source for measures of states' preferences for foreign policy. Our measure uses voting records from UNGA and assesses the similarity of the votes cast by the partner state and the United States in each voting session using the model provided by Bailey, Strezhnev, and Voeten. The model first places all UNGA votes along a preference spectrum where countries vote in a particular way. The model then weights votes by how much they reflect the main preference dimension.[19]
- **U.S. alliance:** Formal obligations that the United States has to defend a partner often coincide with the measures of forward posture that we examined, while the presence of a U.S. alliance itself might be either escalatory or deter adversary escalation at the level of competition below conflict. We control for a formal alliance in all models in which that is not our key variable of interest. Our measure captures whether the partner state has an active defense pact with the United States, where *defense pacts* are those alliances that commit states to intervene militarily on the side of any treaty partner that is attacked.[20]

Partner and Competitor Cooperation and Conflict Patterns

- **Joint alliance:** States that maintain an active alliance might be less interested in taking actions to undermine one another. This should be especially likely for military—as

---

[19] Voeten, Strezhnev, and Bailey, 2009; and Bailey, Strezhnev, and Voeten, 2017.

[20] Gibler, 2009.

TABLE B.1

Contextual Factors (Control Variables)

Variables	Data Availability	MIDs	Arms Imports	Sanctions	Proxy Support
UN voting similarity	1946–2010	X	X	X	X
U.S. alliance	1946–2010	X	X	X	X
Dyadic alliance	1946–2010	X	X		X
Joint trade	1946–2006	X	X	X	
Joint intergovernmental organization membership	1946–2010	X	X	X	
Conflict history	1946–2010	X	X		
Ongoing conflict	1946–2010		X		X
Level of democracy	1946–2010				X
Joint democracy	1946–2010	X	X	X	
Material capabilities	1946–2010				X
Capability balance	1946–2010	X	X	X	
Distance	1946–2010	X	X	X	X
Ally count	1946–2010		X		
Military spending	1946–2010		X		X
GDP per capita	1946–2010		X	X	X
GDP growth	1961–2010			X	X
State capacity	1960–2010				X
Trade openness	1960–2010			X	
Population	1946–2010		X		X
Oil production	1970–2010			X	X

opposed to economic—actions. Our measure captures whether the partner state and its potential competitor have an active defense pact as defined previously.[21]

- **Joint trade:** Trade between states exerts a pacifying effect on relations because states that trade will not want to forgo the gains from trade to engage in conflictual behavior. This has been demonstrated for measures of interstate crises, and states should be less likely to target one another with economic coercion when they have a strong trade relationship. We measure the bilateral flow of trade between each pair of states. This measure is calculated as the IHS of imports plus exports between a partner state and an adversary.[22]

- **Joint intergovernmental organization membership:** Scholars also often argue that intergovernmental organizations have a pacifying effect on behavior between states.

---

[21] Gibler, 2009.

[22] Katherine Barbieri, Omar M. G. Keshk, and Brian M. Pollins, "Trading Data: Evaluating Our Assumptions and Coding Rules," *Conflict Management and Peace Science*, Vol. 26, No. 5, 2009.

This is especially true for measures of direct conflict. In addition, membership in shared economic organizations might prevent states from using sanctions against one another. Our measure counts the international governmental organizations of which both states in a dyad are participants. The dataset provides information on state membership of all international organizations that have at least three nation-states as their members.[23]

- **Conflict history:** States that have engaged in a conflict in the past are more likely to do so in the future. The United States might seek to intervene to prevent this. As a result, we must account for previous military disputes when examining the probability of future military disputes. We measure conflict history in a dyad using a running count of previous militarized interstate disputes in the dyad. As noted in Chapter Four, MIDs comprise united historical cases of conflict in which the threat, display, or use of military force short of war by one state is explicitly directed toward the government, official representatives, official forces, property, or territory of another state.[24]

- **Ongoing conflict:** States might engage in behaviors short of armed conflict when they are already engaged in an ongoing military dispute. States might directly seek to combat the U.S. partner by importing arms, and adversaries might seek to undermine their opponents when they are involved in a conflict with a third party by supporting proxies within their opponent's borders. We account for three types of ongoing conflicts. As a result, the United States could take actions to support their partner in its conflicts. We measure MIDs with any state, MIDs with a direct rival, and MIDs with any state outside a direct rivalry.[25]

Partner and Competitor Governance Systems

- **Level of democracy:** Historically, the United States has demonstrated a commitment to defending democracy, and the United States might intervene to prevent such partner states from collapsing in the event of structural difficulties by the government. We measure the level of democracy within a partner state with Polity scores. Polity scores approximate a state's level of democracy based on the level of competitiveness and openness of elections, the nature of political participation, and the extent of checks on executive authority. In our models of proxy warfare, we control for the partner's democracy score alone because this will be most relevant for the possibility that a state can

---

[23] Jon C. W. Pevehouse, Timothy Nordstrom, Roseanne W. McManus, and Anne Spencer Jamison, "Tracking Organizations in the World: The Correlates of War IGO Version 3.0 Datasets," *Journal of Peace Research*, Vol. 57, No. 3, 2020.

[24] Zeev Maoz, Paul L. Johnson, Jasper Kaplan, Fiona Ogunkoya, and Aaron P. Shreve, "The Dyadic Militarized Interstate Disputes (MIDs) Dataset Version 3.0: Logic, Characteristics, and Comparisons to Alternative Datasets," *Journal of Conflict Resolution*, Vol. 63, No. 3, 2019.

[25] Maoz et al., 2019.

be undermined by a proxy. This measure runs from –10 to 10, where higher numbers indicate greater levels of democracy.[26]

- **Joint democracy:** Historically, proponents have argued that democratic states are less likely to engage in conflict with one another. As a result, in our dyadic specifications, we include a measure that captures whether both states are democratic. Joint democracy indicates that both in a dyad have a Polity score greater than or equal to 7, the common threshold for democracy.[27]

Partner and Competitor Power Projection, Threat, and Military Strength

- **Material capabilities:** Partners with sufficient military capabilities are better able to credibly threaten to defend themselves from potential adversaries. These partners might have a reduced need for U.S. assistance. However, they might also be considered particularly important partners because they will be able to provide greater assistance to the United States in the event of a conflict. We use the composite indicator of national capabilities (CINC) score, a common measure in the literature for material capabilities. The CINC score captures the share of material power that a state has using six indicators: military expenditure, military personnel, energy consumption, iron and steel production, urban population, and total population. The CINC score measures the sum of these indicators for each state compared with the total in the overall system.[28] As with the measure of democracy, in the proxy warfare case, we consider the partner's military capabilities to be a primary determinant of the likelihood of proxy success and thus an important control variable.
- **Balance of capabilities:** The relative military capabilities of adversaries is commonly believed to be a determinant of military competition and conflict. Adversaries could be unwilling or unable to compete with partners that are substantially stronger militarily. Adversaries might seek to coerce those partners whom they believe to be militarily weak. In addition to the individual capabilities of the partner state, we measure the relative balance of capabilities between the partner and its potential adversary. The capabilities balance measures the ratio of adversary state's CINC score to sum of the adversary and partner's CINC scores.[29]
- **Distance:** States at greater distances are less likely to see one another as threats and are less likely, on average, to experience contentious issues, whereas U.S. posture in nearby

---

[26] Marshall and Jaggers, 2002.

[27] Marshall and Jaggers, 2002.

[28] Singer, Bremer, and Stuckey, 1972.

[29] Singer, Bremer, and Stuckey, 1972.

countries can be viewed as more dangerous. Although we account for this in refining our individual samples, we also account for the specific distance between states in several models. Our measure captures the minimum distance between states in thousands of kilometers.[30] In addition, for the models of Russian behavior, the distance between the U.S. partner and Russia is included.

- **Total alliance count:** Because alliances can substitute for a country's own military strength, partners with a higher number of overall alliances—and thus that are more likely to receive support against potential adversaries—are also better able to defend themselves. Our measure of the partner's ongoing alliances includes obligations of defensive assistance, offensive assistance, neutrality, and nonaggression or consultation, and thus accounts for the likely parties that an adversary must account for when engaging in conflictual behavior with the partner.[31]

- **Military spending:** As with overall capabilities, partners with sufficient military spending and weapon manufacturing are better able to credibly threaten to defend themselves from potential adversaries without being supplemented by outside military capabilities. We include a measure for the IHS of the military expenditures by the partner and adversary.[32]

Partner Economic Power and Political Development

- **GDP per capita:** Partners with higher levels of economic output should be better able to resist coercive actions and therefore should be more costly to influence or coerce. For example, states with greater economic health should be able to better import arms when necessary, to overcome sanctions, and to use domestic tools to suppress combat proxy warfare. Additionally, these partners should serve as better partners for the United States, increasing the willingness of the United States to provide assistance. We measure the economic health of the state using GDP. Our measure is the IHS of a partner state's GDP per capita, a common a measure of a country's economic output that accounts for its population.[33]

---

[30] Kristian Skrede Gleditsch, "Distance Between Capital Cities," dataset, undated.

[31] Leeds, 2005.

[32] Singer, Bremer, and Stuckey, 1972. To account for the possibility that a state's necessity to import arms may depend on its ability to generate its own source of weapons, we include a measure for the total arms exports by each partner and adversary as a robustness check.

[33] Inklaar et al., 2018.

- **GDP growth:** For similar reasons to those mentioned for economic output, we measure the state's economic growth. We measure the partner state's economic growth using the percent rate of increase of its GDP.[34]
- **State capacity:** Partners with higher government capacity and more-stable democratic institutions might be better able to combat external interventions into their political system. State capacity is measured using relative political extraction. This indicator measures the ability of governments to obtain resources from a population using tax effort as a proxy for political capacity. Relative political extraction is constructed as the ratio of the actual tax revenue that a country is able to collect to the predicted amount of revenues given its agricultural output, natural resource revenues, international trade activities, and economic productivity.[35]
- **Trade openness:** Adversaries might be unwilling to take action against partners that are more active in the global economic system because these states could be more likely to respond with economic coercion. In addition, these states will be more likely to receive assistance from outside parties, such as the United States. We measure the extent to which a state's economy depends on trade measured by its exports of goods and services as percentage of its GDP.[36]

Demographic and Other Characteristics of Partner and Competitor

- **Population:** Larger partner states could provide a more threatening presence to opponents because of their latent capacity for warfighting because these states might be able to substitute a large number of forces for other military capabilities. Conversely, larger states might be particularly susceptible to such behaviors as proxy warfare and terrorism. This could lead adversaries to increase behavior under the threshold of armed conflict. We measure the IHS of the population of the partner or adversary state.[37]
- **Oil production:** States might be both more-valuable partners for the United States and others and more-desirable targets for competitive behavior if they have greater natural resource endowments. We measure the of oil revenues of the partner state as a percentage of a state's GDP.[38]

In addition to controlling for contextual factors, as we have noted in Chapter Four, we also account for systematic differences that occur because of geography or changes that occur over

---

[34] World Bank, 2021.

[35] Kugler and Arbetman, 2018.

[36] World Bank, 2021.

[37] Singer, Bremer, and Stuckey, 1972.

[38] World Bank, 2021.

time. We include region-fixed effects in our models, which account for any systematic differences between regions. Because U.S. behavior toward both allies and competitors has shown significant differences between the Cold War period and the post–Cold War era, we also control for this with a dummy variable that takes on a value of 1 for all years during the Cold War and 0 otherwise. Additionally, in our statistical analysis of MIDs, we use peace-year splines to account for the time since pairs of states have last engaged in conflict.

Selection Bias

Examining U.S. posture decisions and adversary competitive responses leads to a problem that is common to statistical analysis. The United States makes posture decisions using several factors, including the reassurance of partners, economic interests, and domestic political pressures. One key determinant of U.S. force posture is the likelihood that a specific partner will be the target of a belligerent state. As a result, the United States might be choosing its force posture based on where adversaries are already particularly difficult to deter, and thus the probability of escalation is already heightened. This makes identifying the true effect of U.S. posture decisions very difficult.

In our baseline specifications, we use our control variables to account for the possibility that a heightened risk of malign activities causes the United States to adjust its posture choices rather than vice versa. For instance, by controlling for joint democracy, we identify dyads that the literature suggests are already significantly less likely to engage in conflictual behavior. There are several ways to further refine this approach that have been identified by scholars. We follow the procedure performed by previous RAND analysis, most directly Frederick et al. (2020), in which the authors seek to account for these selection processes by modeling them directly.

In these models, we take a two-stage approach. We first identify the types of countries in which the United States was most likely to place its forces. We identify U.S. forces as the a priori most definitive sign of U.S. commitment, and thus base our estimation of the likelihood of U.S. force posture off of their presence. We run a series of regressions on each state that predicts the likelihood that this state will be above the 90th percentile of countries hosting noncombat U.S. forces. That is, we predict the likelihood that a state will be the location of the most substantial U.S. presence in our data. We predict this likelihood using a series of variables that are expected to increase the chances that the United States will deploy troops to a country: regional threat, distance from noncombat U.S. troops, U.S. military assistance, partner military strength, the proximity of U.S. rivals, the partner being engaged in a rivalry, GDP per capita, an indicator for the Cold War, and the threat scale index used by Frederick et al. (2020).[39] We present these results (the *first stage* results) in Table B.2.

---

[39] The threat scale index incorporates the aforementioned variables, as well as an alliance with the United States, history of militarized interstate disputes, democracy, an imbalance of capabilities, and a higher-salience territorial claim between the state and one of its neighbors. The initial model by Frederick et al. (2020)

These results largely correspond with expectations. The United States is more likely to station its troops in partners that face a high level of threat and have a low level of military strength with which to defend themselves. In addition, the United States is likely to supplement its forward presence with military assistance and favors placing its troops in more-developed countries and in familiar regions where the United States is already operating. Furthermore, the U.S. troop presence globally was substantially larger during the Cold War. Given that the predictions in our first stage are consistent with extant research, we suggest that this model should provide us with relatively good predictors of U.S. force posture.

From the model, we are able to derive a predicted probability that each partner will be the recipient of a substantial deployment of noncombat U.S. troops in-country. We classify *positive* or predicted cases as all those in which the predicted probability of being in the 90th percentile of U.S. troops is greater than 0.5. The model has a high specificity (99 percent), meaning that there is an extremely low false positive rate. This is unsurprising because of the

TABLE B.2
Propensity Weights: First Stage Results

Factor	90th Percentile of Troops (1)
Threat scale index	0.455**
	(0.204)
Threat scale index for regional states	−0.165
	(0.197)
Nearby U.S. troop presence	0.019***
	(0.006)
U.S. military assistance	0.069**
	(0.029)
Proximity of U.S. rivals	−0.061
	(0.920)
State engaged in rivalry	0.199
	(0.626)
GDP per capita	1.885***
	(0.443)
Military strength	−0.588***
	(0.166)
Cold War	0.796**
	(0.381)
Constant	−16.674***
	(3.698)
N	4,606

uses U.S. alliances as an additional predictor. Because this is one of our key independent variables, we omit this variable in our first stage predictions. For a complete discussion of these variables, see the cited work.

high threshold for inclusion. Our sensitivity is lower because our false negative rate is higher, but still only 33 percent. Overall, the model performs quite well.

We then incorporate these predictions using a method known as *propensity weighting*, in which each individual observation—in our case, each dyad year—is weighted by the individual probability predicted of the potential U.S. partner receiving these substantial troop deployments. These scores are then inverted and used to weight each dyad-year in the second stage regressions. The weights (Ω) are defined as follows: $\Omega = 1/P$ for those states in the 90th percentile of troops and $\Omega = 1/(1-P)$ for those states below this threshold. This method aims to reweight the observations in our analysis to better approximate a sample without selection bias.

Our two methods are combined in our analysis in the main report. The baseline results and the propensity-weighted results are each given equal footing in our analysis.[40] Where models agree in direction and significance, our measure of confidence indicates this shared agreement. Where models disagree on the relative significance of the finding, we downgrade our subsequent confidence in the result. Where models disagree on the direction of the result, we consider our findings to be inconclusive. For readers who are interested in examining the relative effects of the baseline and propensity weighted models, we include our full regression results in the final sections of this appendix.

Regression Results

In Chapter Four, we provide an overview of our quantitative findings that examine the historical relationship between U.S. forward posture and malign competitor behavior. In this section, we discuss our findings in greater depth and discuss differences that arise across the samples that we have examined. We first discuss the statistical significance of our observed effects.[41] In our discussion, we refer to the 0.010 level as a statistically significant finding, with the 0.15 confidence level representing reduced confidence. In our regression tables, we also denote statistical significance at the 0.01 and 0.05 confidence levels.[42] Each of these thresholds of significance might represent meaningful levels of confidence in our results, and we present them each to give the reader a better understanding of the range of our confidence.

Although statistical significance tells us the extent to which the associations we have found could be the result of chance, it does not tell us anything about the size of this relationship. A statistically significant relationship could exist where the impact of U.S. posture change

---

[40] We choose this methodology because although our propensity-weighted models attempt to correct for bias caused by selection effects, they could also result in misspecification, which can introduce its own bias. As a result, a measured approach favors considering both specifications.

[41] That is, the term *effects* does not imply that we take these to be causal effects but rather that they correspond to the term of art for statistical changes within our sample.

[42] This indicates our confidence in the results and represents the probability that the difference between our estimated effect size and no effect could be found by chance.

on competitor response options is either large or small. In addition, many of the events of interest are rare events, so even a doubling in the likelihood of an event could increase the likelihood by only a small amount (e.g., from one percent to two percent). Therefore, it is important to distinguish which posture choices have large, immediate impacts on the likelihood of competitor responses and which posture choices will have effects only cumulatively and in the longer term.

We also note that there are important differences across samples. In the politically relevant category, the sizes of marginal effects tend to be small because the likelihood of any one state acting aggressively toward another in any given year is low. However, given the sizable number of interactions that fall into this category, the cumulative effects are likely large. In the sample of U.S. partners and their direct rivals, the likelihood of competitive behavior is already high. Once states are in a heightened state of competition, they become very reactive,[43] meaning that we are much more likely to observe a direct effect of U.S. posture on adversary responses in this sample.

We demonstrate this pattern visually in Figure B.1 in the case of U.S. arms transfers and corresponding adversary arms imports (what we have called *competitive arms transfers*). We have placed these effects on the same scale to better highlight their differences. Each panel shows the substantive effect of moving from the median level of U.S. arms transfers to the 75th percentile of U.S. arms transfers on arms imports from a potential adversary. The first panel shows the results for the politically relevant sample, and the second panel shows the

FIGURE B.1

Substantive Significance of Arms Transfers Across Samples

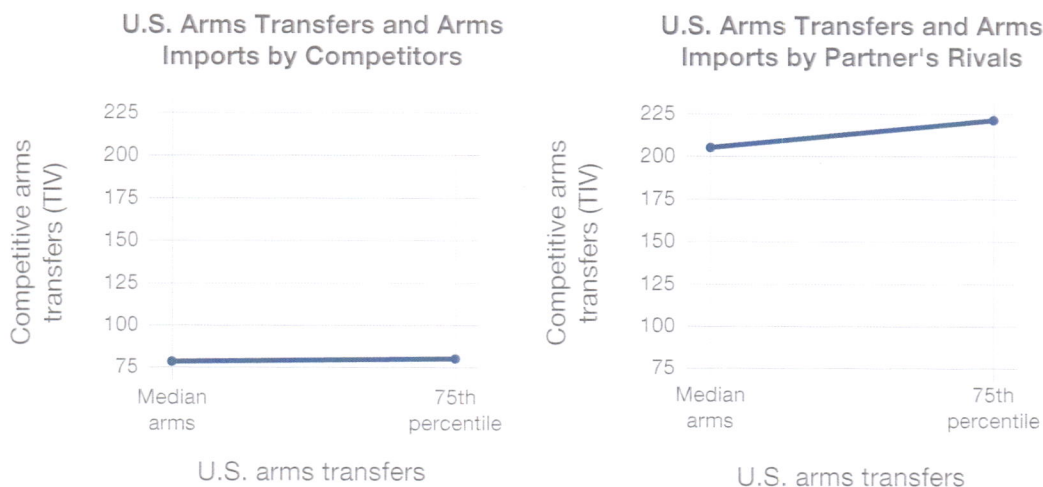

---

[43] See, for example, Michael P. Colaresi, and William R. Thompson, "Hot Spots or Hot Hands? Serial Crisis Behavior, Escalating Risks, and Rivalry," *Journal of Politics*, Vol. 64, No. 4, November 2002.

results for direct rivals. Each model is statistically significant. We find that the marginal effects are greater for the model of direct rivals in relative terms, where arms transfers are associated with an 8 percent increase compared with a 2 percent increase in the politically relevant sample. In absolute terms, this difference is quite pronounced because arms transfers are already likely in the sample of direct rivals. In fact, in comparison with the sample of rival states, the marginal effect in the sample of politically relevant states is barely detectable.

We describe the substantive effects for our OLS regressions in terms of marginal effects. For these models, our calculated effect sizes represent the effect when all control variables are held constant. For our dichotomous variables, we present substantive results in terms of average marginal effects. Average marginal effects calculate marginal effects at every observed value of our posture options and controls and average across the estimates of our effects. Rather than presenting the results at the mean values for each of our controls, which is unlikely to be an observation in our data, this captures the full distribution of the independent variables in our data.

Forces

We find mixed results for in-country U.S. forces (Table B.3).[44] In-country U.S. forces are associated with decreased arms sales in the politically relevant sample and escalation in the sample of direct rivals and Russia. However, the results are substantively meaningful for the partner's direct rivals only. An increase from 25 to 1,000 in-country U.S. personnel is associated with an increase in non-U.S. arms imports by the partner's rivals of 16 percent (198 TIV to 230 TIV) while having a much less significant deterrent association on arms transfers in the politically relevant sample (77 TIV to 74 TIV). The most interesting results are for proxy warfare (Figure B.2). An increase from 25 to 1,000 in-country U.S. troops is associated with an increase from 9 percent to 19 percent in the likelihood of proxy support by a U.S. adversary, while that same shift is associated with a decrease from roughly 10 percent to 3 percent in the likelihood of proxy support by the partner's direct rivals.

We find that increases in the in-country U.S. presence are associated with increases in military intimidation in the politically relevant sample. As in the proxy support sample, however, we find that an in-country U.S. presence is associated with a decrease in the likelihood of proxy support in the sample of the partner's rivals. We also find evidence that the presence U.S. personnel makes partner countries more likely to be the targets of both threatened and imposed economic sanctions in the politically relevant sample, although the absolute size of these effects is quite low. Regarding the use of force, we do not see evidence of a deterrent relationship with an in-country U.S. presence. Instead, in-country U.S. personnel are associated

---

[44] As a robustness check, we examine a variable that distinguishes between any troop presence and no troop presence. We no longer see statistically significant escalatory relationships with the use of force or with threatened sanctions. However, the other relationships do not change substantially. This suggests that this discontinuity is important for explaining behavior, but the continuous measure adds additional information.

FIGURE B.2

Substantive Significance of In-Country U.S. Personnel and Proxy Support for U.S. Rivals and the Partner's Rivals

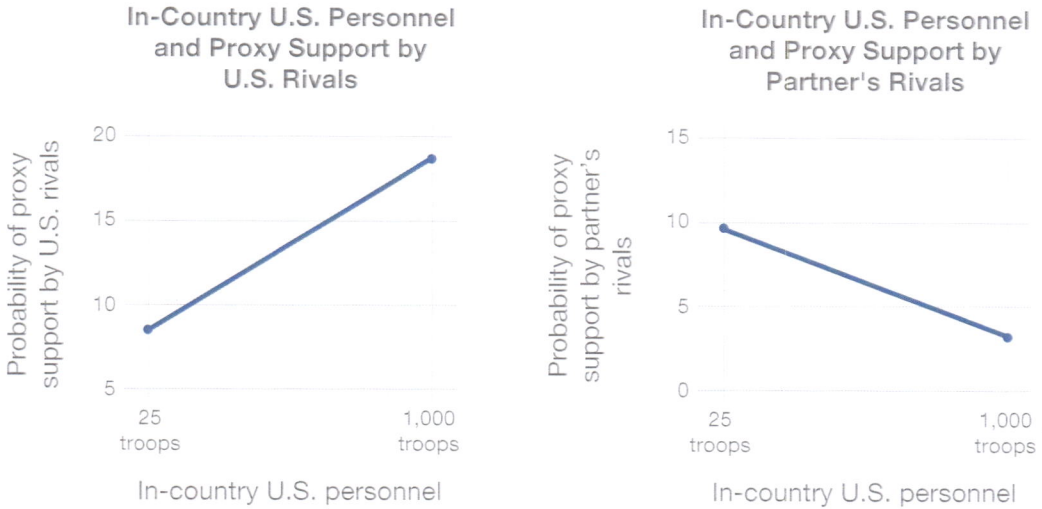

TABLE B.3

In-Country U.S. Personnel and the Incidence of Hostile Measures

States Countering U.S. Posture	Competitor Response Options					
	Competitive Arms Transfers	Threatened Sanctions	Imposed Sanctions	Proxy Wars	Military Intimidation	Use of Force
Politically relevant	⬇	⬆	⬆		⬆	⬆
U.S. rivals				⬆		⬆
Partner's rivals	⬆			⬇	⬇	
Russia/USSR	⬆					

NOTE: Arrow or box color indicates the direction of the relationship, if any. Green indicates a statistically significant deterrent relationship between U.S. posture and competitor response, red indicates a statistically significant escalatory relationship between U.S. posture and competitor response, and no color indicates no statistically significant change to the likelihood of competitor response. Gray indicates that there are insufficient data to draw a firm conclusion. Shading indicates the degree of statistical significance: Darker indicates a higher level of statistical significance.

with increases in the use of force against the partner by both politically relevant states and U.S. adversaries. However, we note that the size of this relationship is quite low.

The findings for regional U.S. personnel are clearer and the substantive results are even stronger than for in-country personnel (Table B.4). This is clearest in the context of proxy

TABLE B.4

U.S. Personnel In-Region and the Incidence of Hostile Measures

States Countering U.S. Posture	Competitor Response Options					
	Competitive Arms Transfers	Threatened Sanctions	Imposed Sanctions	Proxy Wars	Military Intimidation	Use of Force
Politically relevant	↓			↓	↓	
U.S. rivals			↓	↓		
Partner's rivals	↑				↓	
Russia/USSR				↓		↓

NOTE: The box or arrow color indicates the direction of the relationship, if any. Green indicates a statistically significant deterrent relationship between U.S. posture and competitor response, red indicates a statistically significant escalatory relationship between U.S. posture and competitor response, and no color indicates no statistically significant change to the likelihood of competitor response. Gray indicates that there are insufficient data to draw a firm conclusion. Shading indicates the degree of statistical significance: Darker indicates a higher level of statistical significance.

warfare. We find that increases in nearby troops are associated with a decrease in the likelihood of proxy funding in the politically relevant sample for U.S. adversaries and for Russia and the Soviet Union. Similarly, we find that regional U.S. personnel are associated with a decreased likelihood of the use of force by Russia and a decrease in the probability of military intimidation by both politically relevant states and the partner's direct rivals. Moving from a state with 250 nearby troops to one with 5,000 nearby troops is associated with a decrease in the likelihood of a rival engaging in military intimidation from roughly 30 percent to under 10 percent, while the likelihood of proxy support in this sample declines from 12 percent to roughly 6 percent.

We also find that U.S. personnel inside a region are associated with a decrease in the use of economic coercion by U.S. adversaries. Because economic sanctions are already unlikely, the overall substantive effect is small, but an increase in regional troops is associated with a decrease in the probability of an imposed sanction by U.S. rivals. However, while we find that states in the politically relevant sample appear less likely to acquire arms in response to U.S. regional presence, direct rivals appear somewhat more likely to bolster their arms imports. Despite this finding, on the whole, a regional U.S. troop presence is associated with a reduction in potential hostile measures in competition (Figure B.3).

Activities

U.S. arms transfers are associated with a statistically significant increase across the range of malign competitor responses (Table B.5). We find statistically significant increases in both military intimidation and the use of force following U.S. security cooperation that includes arms transfers across virtually all samples. There are particularly strong results for military intimidation. When a state has no preexisting arms relationship with the United States, a one

FIGURE B.3

Substantive Significance of Nearby U.S. Personnel on Rival Military Intimidation and Proxy Support

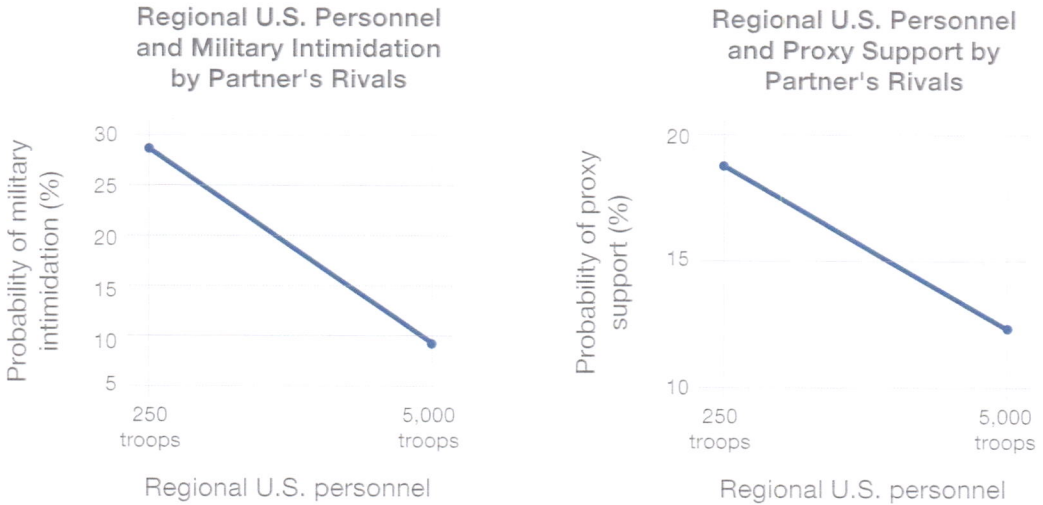

Regional U.S. Personnel and Military Intimidation by Partner's Rivals

Regional U.S. Personnel and Proxy Support by Partner's Rivals

TABLE B.5

U.S. Arms Transfers and the Incidence of Hostile Measures

States Countering U.S. Posture	Competitor Response Options					
	Competitive Arms Transfers	Threatened Sanctions	Imposed Sanctions	Proxy Wars	Military Intimidation	Use of Force
Politically relevant	⬍	⬍	⬍	⬍	⬍	⬍
U.S. adversaries				⬍	⬍	⬍
Partner's rivals	⬍		⬍	⬍	⬍	⬍
Russia/USSR	⬍			⬍	⬍	

NOTE: Box or arrow color indicates the direction of the relationship, if any: Green indicates a statistically significant deterrent relationship between U.S. posture and competitor response, red indicates a statistically significant escalatory relationship between U.S. posture and competitor response, and no color indicates no statistically significant change to the likelihood of competitor response. Gray indicates that there are insufficient data to draw a firm conclusion. Shading indicates the degree of statistical significance: Darker indicates a higher level of statistical significance.

standard deviation increase in U.S. arms transfers is associated with a 34 percent increase in the probability of military intimidation by U.S. adversaries and a 51 percent increase for Russia and the USSR. There is also modest evidence in our models that the probability of proxy funding increases as arms transfers increase. Moving from the median level of arms transfers to the 75th percentile on arms imports is associated with an increase in the probability that a U.S. rival will fund a proxy from 10 percent to 14 percent.

We find that arms transfers are associated with a significant increase in the likelihood of politically relevant states and direct rivals responding by importing their own arms from non-U.S. sources. This includes increases in Russian and Soviet arms exports to those states. This behavior could be indicative of arms spirals, although we also note that the substantive effects are quite small. There is also some evidence that the threat and imposition of economic sanctions is more likely to increase following U.S. arms transfers. We see statistically significant increases in economic coercion in the politically relevant sample and in imposed sanctions by direct rivals of the U.S. partner. However, we again find only moderate-sized relationships for each.

Multilateral exercises are also associated with a statistically significant increase across the range of malign competitor responses (Table B.6). Most significantly, we find that states are more likely to respond with force following an exercise with the United States in the politically relevant sample, for the partner's direct rivals, and for Russia and the Soviet Union. In the sample of the partner's rivals, we find that engaging in a multilateral exercise with the United States is associated with a 42 percent increase the probability of the rival using force against the U.S. partner. Although this is a predicted increase only from 9 percent to 13 percent, given the rarity of the use of force, this is a significant change. The effects outside this sample are not as strong, however. Similarly, although we see statistically significant associations among multilateral exercises and proxy warfare, sanctions, and competitive arms transfers, the substantive effects are very low.

TABLE B.6
Multilateral Exercise with the United States and the Incidence of Hostile Measures

States Countering U.S. Posture	Competitor Response Options					
	Competitive Arms Transfers	Threatened Sanctions	Imposed Sanctions	Proxy Wars	Military Intimidation	Use of Force
Politically relevant	⬆		⬆	⬆		⬆
U.S. adversaries			⬆	⬆		
Partner's rivals						⬆
Russia/USSR	⬆					⬆

NOTE: Box or arrow color indicates the direction of the relationship, if any: Green indicates a statistically significant deterrent relationship between U.S. posture and competitor response, red indicates a statistically significant escalatory relationship between U.S. posture and competitor response, and no color indicates no statistically significant change to the likelihood of competitor response. Gray indicates that insufficient data exist to draw a firm conclusion. Shading indicates the degree of statistical significance: Darker indicates a higher level of statistical significance.

Agreements

We find that both types of novel agreements are associated with a decrease in the likelihood of the use of force. We find that, in general, the substantive effect of signing a new agreement with the United States is low initially but is likely to have dramatic effects over time (Table B.7). The most significant substantive effect we find is for new U.S. alliances (Table B.8). We find that the establishment of a new formal alliance with the United States is associated with a 54 percent decrease in the use of force in the politically relevant sample and a 55 percent decrease in such confrontations between U.S. allies and their direct rivals. We also find that SOFAs are associated with a decrease in the use of force by both U.S. adversaries and by Russia and the Soviet Union.

However, agreements are also associated with some clear adversary responses. Novel SOFAs are associated with a 43 percent increase in arms imports from the partner's rivals, and formal U.S. alliances are associated with a 17 percent increase in arms imports by U.S. adversaries. They also are associated with statistically significant increases in the likelihood of military intimidation from both U.S. rivals and Russia, even as they deter the use of force.

Intervening Factors

In the main text, we summarize the results that explore the effect of our intervening factors. In this section, we explore the impact of the intervening factors in greater detail.

Proximity

Our analytical framework stresses that the relative deterrent or escalatory value of a U.S. posture choice should depend on the partner's distance from its potential adversaries. We

TABLE B.7

New U.S. SOFAs and the Incidence of Hostile Measures

States Countering U.S. Posture	Competitor Response Options					
	Competitive Arms Transfers	Threatened Sanctions	Imposed Sanctions	Proxy Wars	Military Intimidation	Use of Force
Politically relevant	⬆ (red)				⬆ (light red)	
U.S. rivals					⬆ (light red)	⬇ (green)
Partner's rivals	⬆ (light red)					
Russia/USSR					⬆ (light red)	⬇ (green)

NOTE: Box or arrow color indicates the direction of the relationship, if any: Green indicates a statistically significant deterrent relationship between U.S. posture and competitor response, red indicates a statistically significant escalatory relationship between U.S. posture and competitor response, and no color indicates no statistically significant change to the likelihood of competitor response. Gray indicates that insufficient data exist to draw a firm conclusion. Shading indicates the degree of statistical significance: Darker indicates a higher level of statistical significance.

TABLE B.8

Newly Formed U.S. Alliances and the Incidence of Hostile Measures

States Countering U.S. Posture	Competitor Response Options					
	Competitive Arms Transfers	Threatened Sanctions	Imposed Sanctions	Proxy Wars	Military Intimidation	Use of Force
Politically relevant						⬇ (green)
U.S. adversaries	⬆ (red)					
Partner's rivals						⬇ (green)
Russia/USSR						

NOTE: Box or arrow color indicates the direction of the relationship, if any: Green indicates a statistically significant deterrent relationship between U.S. posture and competitor response, red indicates a statistically significant escalatory relationship between U.S. posture and competitor response, and no color indicates no statistically significant change to the likelihood of competitor response. Gray indicates that insufficient data exist to draw a firm conclusion. Shading indicates the degree of statistical significance: Darker indicates a higher level of statistical significance.

account for this in our quantitative analysis by using an interaction term between each of our posture options and distance from the competitor, where distance is measured as the border-to-border distance in kilometers between the U.S. partner and its potential adversary.

In the main text, we summarize the conditional effect of proximity on U.S. posture choices on escalatory or deterrent effects in competition. Here, we describe them in greater depth. We note that these results are complex. Four outcomes are possible: Distance could (1) increase or (2) decrease the deterrent effect of a posture choice. Distance could also (3) increase or (4) decrease the escalatory effect of a posture choice. In addition, we note that when conditioned by distance, the posture choice might be statistically significant only for a portion of the distance variable or we could see nonlinear effects, in which the effect of distance is not uniform for each posture choice. We consider each possibility as we discuss our results.

We present our overall results in Table B.9. We show the marginal effect of U.S. posture when the partner shares a border with the adversary (which is when our distance measure is zero) and the conditional effect of distance on the relationship between U.S. posture and competitor responses.

First, we find that within 1,000 km, U.S. in-country forces increase the likelihood of competitor arms transfers in the politically relevant sample. However, past this distance, we see a statistically significant decrease in competitor arms as in-country forces increase. That is, as distance increases, states are less likely to import non-U.S. arms in response to increases in U.S. personnel. In the politically relevant sample, we also find that states are more likely to threaten economic coercion as distance increases. At less than 2,000 km, this effect is not statistically significant. However, at greater distances it is significant, and the observed effect size increases.

TABLE B.9

Conditional Effect of Distance on U.S. Posture and Competitor Responses

Measure	Posture Type	Competitor Response Options					
		Competitive Arms Transfers	Threatened Sanctions	Imposed Sanctions	Proxy Wars	Military Intimidation	Use of Force
In-country U.S. forces	Effect at border					↑	
	Conditional effect of distance	↓	↑		↑	↓	
Arms transfers	Effect at border	↑		↑			
	Conditional effect of distance	↓	↑		↑	↑	
Military exercises	Effect at border				↑		
	Conditional effect of distance	↑ (light)		↑			
SOFAs	Effect at border	↑					↓
	Conditional effect of distance		↓		↓		
Defense treaties	Effect at border					↑	
	Conditional effect of distance					↓	

↓   indicates that increased U.S. posture is associated with a decrease in the incidence of a given type of hostile measure (an apparently deterrent relationship).

↑   indicates that increased U.S. posture is associated with an increase in the incidence of a given type of hostile measure (an apparently escalatory relationship).

Gray shading   indicates that there are insufficient data for this type of relationship to conduct statistical analysis.

Darker arrow (↑) symbols represent greater statistical confidence; lighter arrow symbols (↑) represent less statistical confidence.

The most interesting results are for proxy wars. We find that as the in-country U.S. presence increases, the likelihood of proxy funding increases in the politically relevant sample, but only for states at relatively extreme distances, for which we have few cases. For the sample of the partner's rivals, the deterrent relationship with a U.S. in-country presence is consistently and largely increasing with distance. Turning to the results for military intimidation, we find evidence that politically relevant states are less likely to initiate a dispute in response to U.S. personnel when the partner is at a greater distance, but that the substantive effect is very small. For rivals of the partner, we see a deterrent relationship with U.S. in-country personnel at greater than 2,000 km, though we also see a slightly escalatory relationship at less than 1,000 km. Alternatively, we also find that at distances greater than 2,000 km, U.S. personnel are actually associated with an increase in the likelihood of the use of force by U.S. rivals.

We find evidence that as distance increases, adversaries are less likely to respond to U.S. arms imports with arms imports of their own in both the politically relevant sample and the Russian sample. At greater than 1,000 km, the observed effect is no longer significant in the Russian sample, while at greater than 3,000 km, the relationship changes from escalatory to deterrent in the politically relevant sample. However, distance does not ameliorate the escalatory associations of U.S. arms transfers and malign activities in other circumstances. Most notably, distance from the partner increases the association between U.S. arms transfers and proxy funding for the politically relevant sample, although only at distances greater than 3,000 km, and there is no consistent conditioning effect outside this sample. The conditional effects on the use of force and military intimidation are nonlinear and inconsistently significant, although arms transfers remain consistently associated with increases in these military responses.

The conditioning effect of distance on multilateral exercises is mixed. As distance increases, the escalatory relationship between exercises and military intimidation by U.S. rivals and Russia decreases, becoming insignificant at 2,000 km. As distance increases, multilateral exercises are also associated with a decrease in proxy warfare from Russia and the Soviet Union beginning at distances greater than 2,000 km. In terms of the use of force, distance has a nonlinear conditioning effect on multilateral exercises in the politically relevant sample, first increasing the escalatory association and then decreasing it. In the Russian sample, the conditioning effect of distance is much more straightforward, as at greater than 1,000 km, a military exercise with the United States is no longer associated with the likelihood of the use of force. Although exercises have a significant deterrent association with arms imports by U.S. rivals at greater than 4,000 km, they have an increasingly escalatory relationship in the politically relevant sample starting at a distance of just 1,000 km. Furthermore, distance increases the likelihood of the imposition of economic coercion following a military exercise. This suggests that distance could lead to different adversary responses rather than uniform deterrence or escalation.

As distance increases, we find evidence that SOFAs and new alliances are more likely to deter malign activities. At greater distances, the conditional effect of distance offsets the unconditional, escalatory effect of status of force agreements on proxy funding, eventually leading to an overall deterrent effect. At greater than 1,000 km, we also see an increase in the deterrent association between SOFAs and the use of force and military intimidation by the partner's rivals. We find that as distance between the U.S. partner and its adversary increases, U.S. alliances are associated with a substantial decrease in the likelihood of military intimidation. At greater than 1,000 km, U.S. alliances are associated with a lower probability of military intimidation in the samples of politically relevant states, U.S. rivals, and the partner's rivals (Figure B.4).

Russian behavior is more interesting. We find evidence that Russia is less likely to use military intimidation following a SOFA at greater distances, particularly over 2,000 km. However, while SOFAs are associated with a decrease in likelihood that Russia will use force overall, this deterrent relationship shrinks in magnitude at greater distances and disappears after 4,000 km. This suggests that both the deterrent and escalatory value of these agreements can decline over distance.

The results we have described are quite complex. However, we note that, while there is greater variability in our findings, on the whole we find that the effect of distance is consistent with our theoretical framework. Increased distance reduces many of the escalatory associations between U.S. force posture and competitor responses.

Continuity

In our framework, we argue that persistent U.S. force posture should have little escalatory impact on adversary responses while providing deterrent value to the U.S. partner. However, significant changes to U.S. posture, particularly those that were not expected by the adversary, should be likely to inspire a competitor response. To capture the apparent effects of continuity, we include two variants of each U.S. force posture option. The first is the measure of

FIGURE B.4

Substantive Significance of Interaction Between Distance and U.S. Alliance Agreements on Military Intimidation by the Partner's Rivals

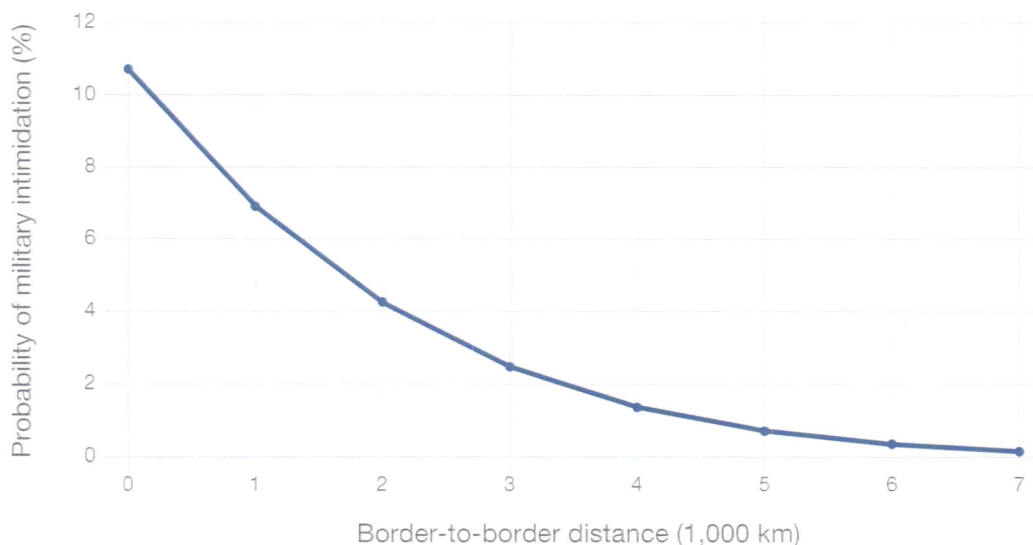

U.S. posture in a given year. The second is the average of each U.S. force posture option in the preceding three years. Including these two variables together allows the first measure to capture changes solely from the previous three-year baseline, encompassing discontinuous U.S. posture choices, while the second measure provides a measure of a persistent U.S. presence. In the main text, we summarize the overall effects of persistence and discontinuity. Here, we discuss the results in greater depth across all samples and potential competitor responses.[45] We present our results in Table B.10.

We find suggestive evidence that a sustained U.S. in-country presence can reduce escalation, while a novel U.S. in-country presence can be escalatory. This is most clear in the politically relevant sample, where we have the largest amount of data and thus can most easily disentangle the impacts of a novel presence and a sustained presence. Here we see that a continuous U.S. presence is associated with decreases in arms transfers, sanctions, and military intimidation, while a discontinuous presence is associated with an increase in each of those forms of malign activities. We further find consistent evidence that a sustained in-country force presence is associated with a reduction in proxy warfare in the samples of both direct rivals and U.S. rivals. A prime example of this is the relationship between in-country U.S. personnel and arms transfers by U.S. rivals. When we increase a persistent U.S. in-country presence from 25 troops to 1,000 troops, we find a 10 percent decrease in arms transfers by U.S. rivals. That is virtually the same magnitude as the escalatory effect of a discontinuous increase in a U.S. in-country presence from 25 troops to 1,000 troops (Figure B.5). There is only one type of competitor response for which the sustained presence of U.S. in-country forces appears to show an escalatory relationship: the use of force. This occurs in both the sample of U.S. rivals and the models that examine Russian behavior. However, given the relatively small sample size in each and the low number of occurrences of the use of force, it could be that this result is simply an artefact of an idiosyncratic conjunction of factors rather than representative of a broader trend.

The results for regional U.S. personnel follow a similar pattern as for in-country personnel. A sustained U.S. regional presence is associated with a reduction in escalation, while an increase in U.S. regional presence is associated with greater escalation. This result is most clear in the politically relevant sample, as in the case of U.S. in-country presence, where a persistent U.S. presence is associated with a decline in competitive arms transfers, sanctions, and the probability of proxy warfare. In fact, we find that a regional U.S. presence is associated with a deterrent effect on proxy warfare whether it is continuous or discontinuous across most samples. A continuous U.S. regional presence is associated with a decreased likelihood of proxy funding by the partner's rivals, with a shift from 250 to 5,000 regional troops corresponding to a decrease from 18 percent to 11 percent in the likelihood of proxy funding

---

[45] As we note in the main text, we can explain persistence only using a measure of the presence of an agreement, which is difficult to causally identify because there are no level changes to exploit. That is, the only direct point of difference for agreements is the discontinuous shift from no agreement to an agreement being present.

TABLE B.10

Conditioning Influence of Discontinuity on the Effects of U.S. Forward Posture

Measure	Posture Type	Competitor Response Options					
		Competitive Arms Transfers	Threatened Sanctions	Imposed Sanctions	Proxy Wars	Military Intimidation	Use of Force
Persistent forces	In-country U.S. forces	↓		↓		↓	
	In-region U.S. forces	↓	↓	↓	↓		
Discontinuous forces	In-country U.S. forces	↑	↑	↑		↑	
	In-region U.S. forces	↑	↑	↑	↓		
Persistent activities	U.S. arms transfers		↑				
	Multilateral military exercises	↑		↑			
Discontinuous activities	U.S. arms transfers				↑	↑	
	Multilateral military exercises						↑

↓ indicates that increased U.S. posture is associated with a decrease in the incidence of a given type of hostile measure (an apparently deterrent relationship).

↑ indicates that increased U.S. posture is associated with an increase in the incidence of a given type of hostile measure (an apparently escalatory relationship).

Gray shading indicates that there are insufficient data for this type of relationship to conduct statistical analysis.

Darker arrow (↑) symbols represent greater statistical confidence; lighter arrow symbols (↑) represent less statistical confidence.

We also find that a continuous U.S. regional presence is associated with a decrease in military intimidation by U.S. rivals, while a discontinuous presence shows the reverse association. The primary exception to this overall pattern concerns Moscow's willingness to export in competitive arms transfers. Again, we are reluctant to overinterpret this one exception because of the smaller sample size.

As we have discussed, arms transfers are almost uniformly associated with escalatory outcomes. In line with our expectations, this pattern becomes somewhat more pronounced when we examine arms transfers that are novel. We find that this is especially true for the partner's direct rivals and Russia, where we see an association between discontinuous arms

FIGURE B.5

Substantive Significance of Continuous and Discontinuous In-Country U.S. Personnel on Arm Transfers by U.S. Rivals

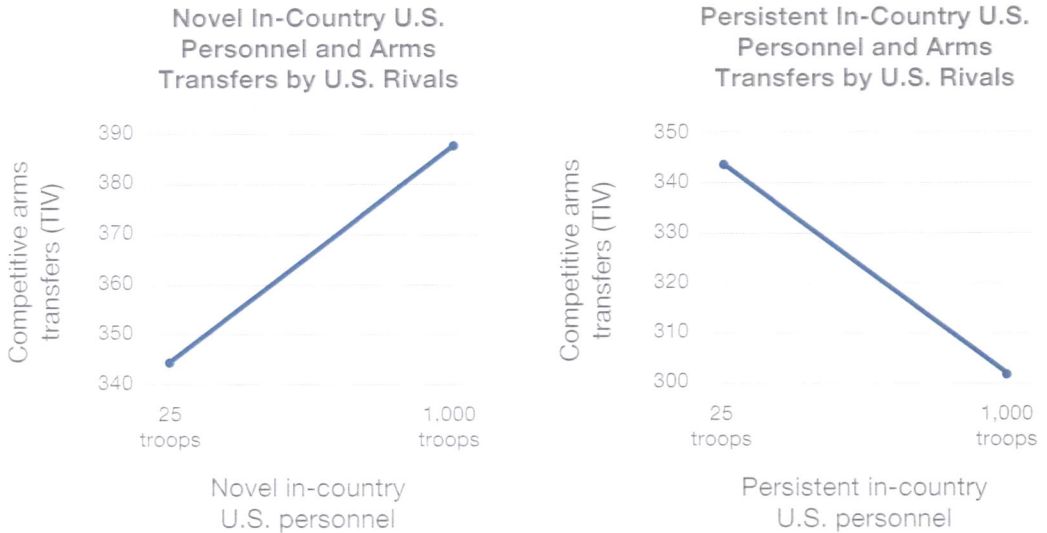

transfers and competitor arms transfers, sanctions, and military intimidation.[46] We also find that discontinuous arms transfers are especially likely to provoke two particularly violent outcomes: proxy warfare, across all samples, and the use of force by politically relevant states and the partner's rivals. However, there are otherwise no clear patterns in our models of U.S. adversaries.

Multilateral exercises with the United States show an interesting pattern. We find that novel exercises with the United States are associated with military responses both at the level of military intimidation and the use of force by politically relevant states, the partner's rivals, and Russia. However, they are not consistently associated with escalation for any other type of competitor response. There is instead evidence that sustained U.S. exercises are associated with an increase in the likelihood of non-U.S. arms imports for the politically relevant sample and for U.S. rivals. The results for U.S. exercises and sanctions are mixed and no clear patterns can be drawn, while discontinuous exercises are associated with an increase in proxy warfare only in the sample of U.S. rivals.

---

[46] There are three exceptions to this pattern. Once again, Russia and the Soviet Union account for most (two) of the exceptions. Moreover, the Russian exceptions concern lethal MIDs, a very rare type of event. Given the small numbers of lethal Russian MIDs, we again do not have a great deal of confidence in these particular findings, although they are important to note.

Analysis of U.S. Activities and Partner Stability

In addition to the intervening factors discussed in our framework, we expect that U.S. force posture choices directed toward less-stable partner states will be particularly threatening to potential competitors. We expect that these results will be particularly important for understanding the effects of U.S. activities, which are conducted with a wider range of states that might be less stable or have lower capacity. Given these expectations, we test the robustness of our results through an examination of this possibility to better understand how partner characteristics may be determinant of the effect of U.S. force posture on malign activities.

We measure partner stability using GDP per capita. GDP per capita is a commonly used measure both of economic health and of state capacity in the political science literature.[47] We interact our measure of stability with each measure of U.S. activities, arms transfers, and multilateral exercises to determine whether partner stability attenuates any escalatory effects or instead heightens them.

It is less straightforward to present a summary of results for economic stability for several reasons. There is no natural interpretation that can be drawn from the regression results themselves. The regression results provide us with an unconditional or noninteracted effect (that is, the effect of U.S. posture when GDP per capita is zero) and the conditional marginal effect (that is, the effect of U.S. posture as GDP per capita increases). The first effect is impossible—GDP per capita is never zero. The second effect is difficult to interpret. Because GDP per capita is a *continuous variable*—meaning that, for specific levels of this variable, we might see an escalatory relationship, while for others, we might see no relationship or a deterrent relationship. It is therefore easier to examine the effects at different thresholds. To put this in concrete policy terms, we examine the threshold of the maximum GDP per capita level found in Eastern Europe in the final year of our data.

In Table B.11, we present the relationship between U.S. activities and competitor responses for states below and above the maximum level of GDP per capita in our data for an Eastern European state, which corresponds to Slovenia. We find that for states above this threshold, there are few effects of U.S. activities on competitor responses. The only significant effect is that for proxy funding, and we note that the magnitude of this effect is very small. There are strong escalatory relationships below this threshold, particularly for U.S. arms transfers.

Although this captures the effect of partner economic stability for just two levels, it is indicative of a larger trend. For partners at the lowest level of economic development in our dataset (as measured by GDP per capita), U.S. activities with partner states are associated with escalatory responses by competitors. As the economic stability of the partner increases (as its GDP per capita rises), this escalatory association becomes weaker, meaning that for more–economically stable partners, U.S. activities are not as escalatory as they are for less stable partners.

---

[47] Hendrix, 2010.

TABLE B.11

Impact of Partner Economic Stability on U.S. Posture and Competitor Responses

Posture Type	Maximum GDP per Capita in Eastern Europe	Competitor Response Options					
		Competitive Arms Transfers	Threatened Sanctions	Imposed Sanctions	Proxy Wars	Military Intimidation	Use of Force
Arms transfers	Below threshold	⬆	⬆	⬆		⬆	
	Above threshold				⬆		
Military exercises	Below threshold			⬆			
	Above threshold				⬆		

⬇   indicates that increased U.S. posture is associated with a decrease in the incidence of a given type of hostile measure (an apparently deterrent relationship).

⬆   indicates that increased U.S. posture is associated with an increase in the incidence of a given type of hostile measure (an apparently escalatory relationship).

Gray shading   indicates that there are insufficient data for this type of relationship to conduct statistical analysis.

Darker arrow (⬆) symbols represent greater statistical confidence; lighter arrow symbols (⬆) represent less statistical confidence.

Detailed Regression Results: Baseline Models

In the following sections, we present the full regression results as described in our modeling approach. We first examine the detailed regression results for our baseline models. We present our results as ordered in the main text, grouped by U.S. posture choice. Model 1 corresponds to the politically relevant sample. Model 2 corresponds to the sample of U.S. rivals. Model 3 corresponds to the sample of the partner's direct rivals. Lastly, model 4 corresponds to the sample of Russia and the Soviet Union and its politically relevant states.

Each row shows the direction and magnitude of the effect for each force posture option and control variable on the indicated malign activity across each sample. We also include our measures of confidence. We indicate statistically significant results with stars, where *** indicates significance at the 0.01 confidence level, ** indicates significance at the 0.05 confidence level, and * indicates significance at the 0.10 confidence level, and we present our standard errors in parentheses.

We do not discuss the individual regression results here because of the sheer magnitude of the models examined (Tables B.12 through B.45). For a summary of our key findings from each model, we direct the reader to Chapter Four in the main text and to our discussion earlier in this appendix.

Forces

TABLE B.12

In-Country U.S. Troops and Imposed Sanctions

Measure	Politically Relevant (1)	U.S. Rival (2)	Partner's Rival (3)	Russia/USSR (4)
In-country U.S. troops	−0.010*	0.003	0.041**	0.009
	(0.006)	(0.007)	(0.020)	(0.006)
Lag arms to adversary	0.727***	0.915***	0.628***	0.161***
	(0.011)	(0.008)	(0.038)	(0.011)
UN affinity to U.S.	−0.050	−0.333***	0.012	−0.109***
	(0.035)	(0.052)	(0.086)	(0.032)
Alliance with U.S.	−0.135***	0.049	−0.512**	−0.053
	(0.050)	(0.041)	(0.232)	(0.057)
Capabilities balance	0.194	0.076	0.400	0.264
	(0.161)	(0.117)	(0.479)	(0.191)
Alliance in dyad	−0.027	−0.105**	0.079	0.087*
	(0.037)	(0.046)	(0.177)	(0.048)
Distance	−0.107***	−0.005	0.019	−0.114***
	(0.029)	(0.007)	(0.112)	(0.028)
Joint democracy	0.040	−0.321***	0.232	−0.180***
	(0.036)	(0.084)	(0.150)	(0.036)
Shared IGOs	−0.000	0.005**	−0.003	−0.004***
	(0.001)	(0.002)	(0.004)	(0.001)
Trade	0.007	0.019**	−0.022	−0.041***
	(0.010)	(0.008)	(0.024)	(0.011)
Military spending (adversary)	−0.021	−0.233***	0.197***	0.008
	(0.017)	(0.020)	(0.050)	(0.014)
Military spending (partner)	0.011	0.001	−0.014	0.004
	(0.013)	(0.011)	(0.033)	(0.015)
Alliance count (adversary)	−0.030***	0.005***	0.008	0.008***
	(0.002)	(0.002)	(0.016)	(0.003)
Alliance count (partner)	0.005**	0.006**	−0.015	0.002
	(0.002)	(0.003)	(0.019)	(0.002)
GDP per capita (adversary)	0.187***	0.133***	0.142*	−0.150***
	(0.024)	(0.028)	(0.077)	(0.031)
GDP per capita (partner)	0.070***	0.005	0.066	0.102***
	(0.023)	(0.022)	(0.070)	(0.028)
Population (adversary)	0.206***	0.202***	0.079	−0.038
	(0.032)	(0.024)	(0.108)	(0.042)
Population (partner)	0.035	−0.021	0.087	0.084***
	(0.028)	(0.019)	(0.087)	(0.029)
Past MIDs	0.005*	−0.001	0.005	−0.002
	(0.003)	(0.002)	(0.007)	(0.003)
Cold War	0.113***	0.157***	0.523***	−0.102***
	(0.027)	(0.048)	(0.109)	(0.031)
Constant	−3.637***	0.294	−4.878***	−0.012
	(0.370)	(0.440)	(0.918)	(0.346)
N	29,838	4,681	2,832	27,229

TABLE B.13

In-Country U.S. Personnel and Threatened Sanctions

Measure	Politically Relevant (1)	U.S. Rival (2)	Partner's Rival (3)	Russia/USSR (4)
In-country U.S. troops	0.025*	0.003	0.004	0.052
	(0.013)	(0.040)	(0.060)	(0.317)
UN affinity to U.S.	0.119	−0.074	0.927***	0.106
	(0.108)	(0.370)	(0.326)	(0.284)
Alliance with U.S.	−0.109	−0.180	−0.328	0.000
	(0.084)	(0.288)	(0.301)	N/A
Capabilities balance	0.449***	−0.094	0.304	4.603
	(0.085)	(0.308)	(0.420)	(4.175)
Distance	−0.004	−0.068*	0.120**	−0.264
	(0.011)	(0.038)	(0.050)	(0.384)
Joint democracy	0.021	0.000	−0.514	0.000
	(0.077)	N/A	(0.441)	N/A
Shared IGOs	−0.002	0.018	0.037**	0.000
	(0.003)	(0.011)	(0.016)	(0.016)
Trade	0.138***	0.035	−0.001	0.221*
	(0.024)	(0.062)	(0.069)	(0.131)
Oil rents (partner)	0.006*	0.001	0.035***	−0.076
	(0.003)	(0.010)	(0.010)	(0.073)
Exports (partner)	−0.004	−0.010*	−0.034**	−0.016**
	(0.003)	(0.006)	(0.014)	(0.006)
GDP per capita (partner)	−0.124**	0.153	−0.018	−0.120
	(0.050)	(0.113)	(0.147)	(0.343)
GDP growth (partner)	0.010*	0.034***	0.015	0.021**
	(0.006)	(0.012)	(0.010)	(0.009)
Cold War	0.116*	−0.002	−0.371	0.000
	(0.067)	(0.219)	(0.359)	N/A
Constant	−2.486***	−4.710***	−3.491*	−6.499***
	(0.401)	(0.982)	(1.864)	(2.352)
N	43,930	6,340	1,619	828

TABLE B.14

In-Country U.S. Personnel and Threatened Sanctions

Measure	Politically Relevant (1)	U.S. Rival (2)	Partner's Rival (3)	Russia/USSR (4)
In-country U.S. troops	0.034**	−0.005	0.001	0.081
	(0.016)	(0.034)	(0.040)	(0.055)
UN affinity to U.S.	0.134	−0.395	0.561	−0.018
	(0.121)	(0.448)	(0.342)	(0.886)
Alliance with U.S.	−0.362***	−0.242	−0.485*	3.373**
	(0.106)	(0.357)	(0.272)	(1.452)
Capabilities balance	0.345***	−0.288	0.267	0.339
	(0.101)	(0.310)	(0.461)	(1.746)
Distance	0.001	−0.064	0.186***	0.336
	(0.014)	(0.039)	(0.038)	(0.272)
Joint democracy	0.116	0.000	0.000	0.000
	(0.087)	N/A	N/A	N/A
Shared IGOs	−0.001	0.011	−0.001	−0.024
	(0.003)	(0.011)	(0.013)	(0.037)
Trade	0.201***	0.175***	0.122**	1.536**
	(0.024)	(0.064)	(0.049)	(0.726)
Oil rents (partner)	0.008*	0.004	0.002	0.099**
	(0.004)	(0.010)	(0.008)	(0.048)
Exports (partner)	−0.006*	−0.006	−0.006*	0.034
	(0.003)	(0.007)	(0.003)	(0.025)
GDP per capita (partner)	−0.146**	0.098	−0.049	−2.530**
	(0.057)	(0.185)	(0.137)	(1.274)
GDP growth (partner)	0.008	0.034***	0.002	0.099**
	(0.008)	(0.010)	(0.013)	(0.047)
Cold War	0.034	0.344	−0.402	0.000
	(0.076)	(0.272)	(0.308)	N/A
Constant	−2.629***	−4.876***	−2.343	6.197
	(0.490)	(1.527)	(1.446)	(4.233)
N	43,930	6,340	1,379	1,256

TABLE B.15

In-Country U.S. Personnel and Proxy Support

Measure	Politically Relevant (1)	U.S. Rival (2)	Partner's Rival (3)	Russia/USSR (4)
In-country U.S. troops	0.035	0.091*	−0.030	0.115
	(0.036)	(0.051)	(0.091)	(0.141)
UN affinity to U.S.	0.126	−0.030	0.650	4.475***
	(0.322)	(0.540)	(0.804)	(1.630)
Alliance with U.S.	−0.144	0.092	0.388	−1.121
	(0.323)	(0.354)	(0.884)	(0.982)
MID (dyad)	1.141***	0.717***	0.831***	2.258**
	(0.081)	(0.216)	(0.269)	(0.963)
Distance	0.038	−0.006	−0.033	1.489**
	(0.028)	(0.047)	(0.241)	(0.657)
Capabilities balance	−6.054*	−13.642	−14.389*	−9.334
	(3.391)	(10.350)	(7.770)	(51.347)
Military spending	0.076**	0.136*	0.043	−0.079
	(0.037)	(0.071)	(0.042)	(0.152)
Polity	0.021	−0.009	0.142***	−0.220**
	(0.022)	(0.037)	(0.041)	(0.099)
GDP per capita	0.020	0.050	−0.031	0.032
	(0.030)	(0.045)	(0.076)	(0.129)
GDP growth	−0.020**	−0.022	−0.018	−0.019
	(0.008)	(0.016)	(0.014)	(0.075)
State capacity	0.340***	0.586***	0.226	2.124***
	(0.113)	(0.172)	(0.255)	(0.776)
Oil rents	−0.007	−0.018	0.015	−0.802
	(0.007)	(0.011)	(0.014)	(0.780)
Population	−0.148***	−0.281***	−0.050	−0.587**
	(0.055)	(0.108)	(0.073)	(0.288)
Cold War	−0.106	0.062	−0.599	−0.712
	(0.122)	(0.245)	(0.422)	(0.512)
Alliance in dyad	0.409***	−0.167	0.294	0.000
	(0.154)	(0.290)	(0.373)	N/A
Constant	−2.204***	−1.806***	−1.217*	−0.040
	(0.155)	(0.271)	(0.687)	(1.357)
N	4,938	837	268	241

TABLE B.16

In-Country U.S. Personnel and Military Intimidation

Measure	Politically Relevant (1)	U.S. Rival (2)	Partner's Rival (3)	Russia/USSR (4)
In-country U.S. troops	0.033***	−0.021	−0.003	0.020
	(0.011)	(0.017)	(0.020)	(0.023)
UN affinity to U.S.	0.001	0.506***	0.236	0.276
	(0.104)	(0.178)	(0.175)	(0.296)
Alliance with U.S.	−0.102	−0.009	0.408	−0.113
	(0.102)	(0.163)	(0.382)	(0.180)
Capabilities balance	0.331***	0.215	0.425**	−0.932
	(0.087)	(0.206)	(0.171)	(1.341)
Alliance in dyad	0.122	−0.007	0.196	−0.313
	(0.081)	(0.142)	(0.131)	(0.279)
Joint democracy	−0.394***	−0.056	0.090	0.000
	(0.123)	(0.272)	(0.133)	N/A
Distance	−0.119***	−0.187***	0.205**	−0.768***
	(0.031)	(0.049)	(0.096)	(0.146)
Shared IGOs	−0.005	0.013**	−0.005	0.028**
	(0.004)	(0.006)	(0.005)	(0.012)
Trade	0.004	0.022	0.031	−0.055
	(0.019)	(0.029)	(0.025)	(0.074)
Past MIDs	0.020***	0.018***	0.010	0.008
	(0.005)	(0.005)	(0.007)	(0.007)
Cold War	−0.265***	−0.104	0.087	0.330
	(0.076)	(0.179)	(0.154)	(0.348)
Constant	−1.709***	−1.846***	−1.779***	1.632
	(0.153)	(0.350)	(0.292)	(1.835)
N	34,174	5,666	3,174	2,301

TABLE B.17

In-Country U.S. Personnel and Use of Force

Measure	Politically Relevant (1)	U.S. Rival (2)	Partner's Rival (3)	Russia/USSR (4)
In-country U.S. troops	0.021*	0.035*	0.028	0.050
	(0.011)	(0.020)	(0.021)	(0.043)
UN affinity to U.S.	−0.171**	−0.363**	−0.008	0.163
	(0.077)	(0.175)	(0.120)	(0.360)
Alliance with U.S.	0.138	0.240	−0.390	−0.078
	(0.136)	(0.191)	(0.279)	(0.356)
Capabilities balance	0.302***	0.004	0.060	−2.587
	(0.113)	(0.235)	(0.262)	(1.742)
Alliance in dyad	0.046	0.140	0.080	0.365
	(0.063)	(0.181)	(0.096)	(0.369)
Joint democracy	−0.323***	−0.105	0.113	0.000
	(0.114)	(0.235)	(0.122)	N/A
Distance	−0.158***	−0.121	−0.094	−0.793***
	(0.047)	(0.105)	(0.075)	(0.269)
Shared IGOs	0.000	−0.004	0.000	−0.030
	(0.002)	(0.005)	(0.004)	(0.021)
Trade	−0.062***	−0.057*	−0.024	−0.121**
	(0.015)	(0.031)	(0.023)	(0.061)
Past MIDs	0.021***	0.022***	0.011**	0.029**
	(0.003)	(0.006)	(0.005)	(0.013)
Cold War	−0.044	0.201	−0.068	−0.025
	(0.065)	(0.159)	(0.114)	(0.510)
Constant	−1.114***	−1.091***	−1.074***	5.556**
	(0.128)	(0.259)	(0.340)	(2.633)
N	34,174	5,666	3,206	2,301

TABLE B.18

Regional U.S. Personnel and Arms Transfers

Measure	Politically Relevant (1)	U.S. Rival (2)	Partner's Rival (3)	Russia/USSR (4)
Regional U.S. troops	−0.012**	−0.001	0.027	−0.005
	(0.006)	(0.006)	(0.017)	(0.009)
Lag arms to adversary	0.727***	0.915***	0.630***	0.161***
	(0.011)	(0.008)	(0.037)	(0.011)
UN affinity to U.S.	−0.047	−0.330***	0.038	−0.091***
	(0.035)	(0.053)	(0.090)	(0.034)
Alliance with U.S.	−0.141***	0.059	−0.445*	−0.024
	(0.050)	(0.040)	(0.236)	(0.061)
Capabilities balance	0.219	0.086	0.455	0.251
	(0.157)	(0.117)	(0.448)	(0.193)
Alliance in dyad	−0.042	−0.111**	0.069	0.076
	(0.041)	(0.049)	(0.175)	(0.051)
Distance	−0.114***	−0.005	−0.019	−0.121***
	(0.030)	(0.008)	(0.119)	(0.030)
Joint democracy	0.057	−0.327***	0.239	−0.183***
	(0.037)	(0.088)	(0.152)	(0.037)
Shared IGOs	−0.001	0.005**	−0.001	−0.004***
	(0.001)	(0.002)	(0.004)	(0.001)
Trade	0.008	0.020**	−0.029	−0.041***
	(0.010)	(0.009)	(0.025)	(0.011)
Military spending (adversary)	−0.019	−0.231***	0.185***	0.010
	(0.017)	(0.020)	(0.050)	(0.014)
Military spending (partner)	0.013	0.001	−0.014	0.005
	(0.013)	(0.011)	(0.033)	(0.015)
Alliance count (adversary)	−0.030***	0.005***	0.009	0.008***
	(0.002)	(0.002)	(0.015)	(0.003)
Alliance count (partner)	0.005**	0.006**	−0.018	0.002
	(0.002)	(0.003)	(0.017)	(0.002)
GDP per capita (adversary)	0.188***	0.131***	0.138*	−0.149***
	(0.024)	(0.027)	(0.078)	(0.031)
GDP per capita (partner)	0.073***	0.008	0.087	0.109***
	(0.023)	(0.021)	(0.066)	(0.028)
Population (adversary)	0.205***	0.199***	0.084	−0.035
	(0.031)	(0.023)	(0.104)	(0.042)
Population (partner)	0.031	−0.020	0.127	0.087***
	(0.028)	(0.019)	(0.080)	(0.030)
Past MIDs	0.005*	−0.001	0.004	−0.002
	(0.003)	(0.002)	(0.008)	(0.003)
Cold War	0.107***	0.160***	0.558***	−0.093***
	(0.028)	(0.050)	(0.107)	(0.028)
Constant	−3.575***	0.283	−5.476***	−0.114
	(0.368)	(0.431)	(0.881)	(0.340)
N	29,838	4,681	2,832	27,229

TABLE B.19

Regional U.S. Personnel and Threatened Sanctions

Measure	Politically Relevant (1)	U.S. Rival (2)	Partner's Rival (3)	Russia/USSR (4)
Regional U.S. troops	−0.004	−0.013	0.004	−0.165
	(0.014)	(0.057)	(0.070)	(0.138)
UN affinity to U.S.	0.134	−0.053	0.931***	0.458
	(0.105)	(0.350)	(0.309)	(0.446)
Alliance with U.S.	−0.040	−0.168	−0.322	0.000
	(0.083)	(0.243)	(0.306)	N/A
Capabilities balance	0.391***	−0.100	0.312	6.441
	(0.087)	(0.304)	(0.431)	(4.250)
Distance	−0.002	−0.068*	0.120**	−0.229
	(0.011)	(0.039)	(0.051)	(0.302)
Joint democracy	0.006	0.000	−0.513	0.000
	(0.075)	N/A	(0.438)	N/A
Shared IGOs	−0.002	0.017	0.037**	0.010
	(0.003)	(0.011)	(0.017)	(0.040)
Trade	0.146***	0.037	−0.001	0.194
	(0.025)	(0.062)	(0.064)	(0.311)
Oil rents (partner)	0.005	0.000	0.035***	−0.186
	(0.004)	(0.014)	(0.013)	(0.202)
Exports (partner)	−0.004	−0.010*	−0.035**	−0.013
	(0.003)	(0.006)	(0.016)	(0.013)
GDP per capita (partner)	−0.104**	0.173	−0.021	0.303
	(0.051)	(0.146)	(0.157)	(0.234)
GDP growth (partner)	0.010	0.035***	0.014*	0.027***
	(0.006)	(0.011)	(0.008)	(0.009)
Cold War	0.126*	0.006	−0.367	0.000
	(0.069)	(0.220)	(0.359)	N/A
Constant	−2.559***	−4.765***	−3.493*	−11.149**
	(0.387)	(0.972)	(1.889)	(4.608)
N	43,930	6,340	1,619	828

TABLE B.20

Regional U.S. Personnel and Imposed Sanctions

Measure	Politically Relevant (1)	U.S. Rival (2)	Partner's Rival (3)	Russia/USSR (4)
In-country U.S. troops	0.034**	−0.005	0.001	0.081
	(0.016)	(0.034)	(0.040)	(0.055)
UN affinity to U.S.	0.134	−0.395	0.561	−0.018
	(0.121)	(0.448)	(0.342)	(0.886)
Alliance with U.S.	−0.362***	−0.242	−0.485*	3.373**
	(0.106)	(0.357)	(0.272)	(1.452)
Capabilities balance	0.345***	−0.288	0.267	0.339
	(0.101)	(0.310)	(0.461)	(1.746)
Distance	0.001	−0.064	0.186***	0.336
	(0.014)	(0.039)	(0.038)	(0.272)
Joint democracy	0.116	0.000	0.000	0.000
	(0.087)	N/A	N/A	N/A
Shared IGOs	−0.001	0.011	−0.001	−0.024
	(0.003)	(0.011)	(0.013)	(0.037)
Trade	0.201***	0.175***	0.122**	1.536**
	(0.024)	(0.064)	(0.049)	(0.726)
Oil rents (partner)	0.008*	0.004	0.002	0.099**
	(0.004)	(0.010)	(0.008)	(0.048)
Exports (partner)	−0.006*	−0.006	−0.006*	0.034
	(0.003)	(0.007)	(0.003)	(0.025)
GDP per capita (partner)	−0.146**	0.098	−0.049	−2.530**
	(0.057)	(0.185)	(0.137)	(1.274)
GDP growth (partner)	0.008	0.034***	0.002	0.099**
	(0.008)	(0.010)	(0.013)	(0.047)
Cold War	0.034	0.344	−0.402	0.000
	(0.076)	(0.272)	(0.308)	N/A
Constant	−2.629***	−4.876***	−2.343	6.197
	(0.490)	(1.527)	(1.446)	(4.233)
N	43,930	6,340	1,379	1,256

TABLE B.21

Regional U.S. Personnel and Proxy Support

Measure	Politically Relevant (1)	U.S. Rival (2)	Partner's Rival (3)	Russia/USSR (4)
Regional U.S. troops	−0.067***	−0.088*	−0.057	−0.469***
	(0.026)	(0.050)	(0.059)	(0.133)
UN affinity to U.S.	0.379	0.444	0.675	7.346***
	(0.340)	(0.577)	(0.730)	(1.896)
Alliance with U.S.	0.055	0.557**	0.196	1.556
	(0.231)	(0.277)	(0.803)	(1.209)
MID (dyad)	1.156***	0.762***	0.872***	5.029***
	(0.080)	(0.221)	(0.283)	(1.594)
Distance	0.037	−0.024	−0.030	1.231**
	(0.028)	(0.047)	(0.239)	(0.566)
Capabilities	−9.168**	−17.077*	−16.049**	−166.035**
	(3.650)	(9.628)	(7.474)	(78.402)
Military spending	0.101***	0.174**	0.055	−0.111
	(0.039)	(0.077)	(0.046)	(0.216)
Polity	0.028	−0.001	0.147***	−0.082
	(0.023)	(0.038)	(0.041)	(0.081)
GDP per capita	0.015	0.051	−0.035	0.111
	(0.032)	(0.050)	(0.074)	(0.167)
GDP growth	−0.018**	−0.018	−0.016	−0.005
	(0.008)	(0.015)	(0.014)	(0.065)
State capacity	0.331***	0.546***	0.212	3.415***
	(0.114)	(0.168)	(0.248)	(1.196)
Oil rents	−0.006	−0.020*	0.017	−3.455**
	(0.007)	(0.011)	(0.013)	(1.463)
Population	−0.119**	−0.231**	−0.034	−0.288
	(0.058)	(0.107)	(0.059)	(0.259)
Cold War	−0.096	0.100	−0.653	−1.283**
	(0.115)	(0.232)	(0.405)	(0.500)
Alliance in dyad	0.410***	−0.164	0.331	0.000
	(0.153)	(0.310)	(0.381)	N/A
Constant	−2.018***	−1.617***	−0.927	0.080
	(0.161)	(0.281)	(0.655)	(1.305)
N	4,938	837	268	241

TABLE B.22

Regional U.S. Personnel and Military Intimidation

Measure	Politically Relevant (1)	U.S. Rival (2)	Partner's Rival (3)	Russia/USSR (4)
Regional U.S. troops	−0.010	0.012	−0.035	0.041
	(0.014)	(0.026)	(0.026)	(0.040)
UN affinity to U.S.	0.039	0.488***	0.232	0.297
	(0.101)	(0.179)	(0.171)	(0.301)
Alliance with U.S.	0.034	−0.098	0.378	−0.052
	(0.099)	(0.165)	(0.342)	(0.170)
Capabilities balance	0.286***	0.239	0.425***	−1.307
	(0.085)	(0.202)	(0.165)	(1.419)
Alliance in dyad	0.109	0.014	0.216	−0.318
	(0.080)	(0.141)	(0.134)	(0.275)
Joint democracy	−0.419***	−0.041	0.101	0.000
	(0.123)	(0.273)	(0.135)	N/A
Distance	−0.111***	−0.189***	0.198**	−0.751***
	(0.029)	(0.050)	(0.092)	(0.152)
Shared IGOs	−0.004	0.012*	−0.005	0.028**
	(0.004)	(0.006)	(0.005)	(0.012)
Trade	0.009	0.019	0.029	−0.056
	(0.018)	(0.028)	(0.025)	(0.076)
Past MIDs	0.021***	0.017***	0.011	0.008
	(0.004)	(0.005)	(0.007)	(0.008)
Cold War	−0.234***	−0.145	0.083	0.342
	(0.075)	(0.184)	(0.154)	(0.322)
Constant	−1.540***	−2.000***	−1.348***	1.514
	(0.229)	(0.489)	(0.409)	(1.779)
N	34,174	5,666	3,174	2,301

TABLE B.23

Regional U.S. Personnel and Use of Force

Measure	Politically Relevant (1)	U.S. Rival (2)	Partner's Rival (3)	Russia/USSR (4)
Regional U.S. troops	−0.006	−0.020	−0.031	−0.017
	(0.016)	(0.030)	(0.036)	(0.032)
UN affinity to U.S.	−0.145*	−0.325*	0.019	0.182
	(0.081)	(0.180)	(0.119)	(0.326)
Alliance with U.S.	0.220*	0.400**	−0.266	0.117
	(0.131)	(0.186)	(0.318)	(0.310)
Capabilities balance	0.273**	−0.041	0.022	−2.738
	(0.114)	(0.249)	(0.260)	(1.783)
Alliance in dyad	0.037	0.108	0.066	0.293
	(0.063)	(0.182)	(0.092)	(0.373)
Joint democracy	−0.334***	−0.119	0.105	0.000
	(0.116)	(0.243)	(0.120)	N/A
Distance	−0.152***	−0.116	−0.103	−0.766***
	(0.048)	(0.102)	(0.075)	(0.265)
Shared IGOs	0.001	−0.004	0.001	−0.024
	(0.002)	(0.005)	(0.003)	(0.021)
Trade	−0.059***	−0.051*	−0.024	−0.124*
	(0.014)	(0.030)	(0.023)	(0.063)
Past MIDs	0.022***	0.024***	0.011**	0.030**
	(0.003)	(0.006)	(0.005)	(0.013)
Cold War	−0.025	0.246	−0.043	0.179
	(0.063)	(0.160)	(0.113)	(0.474)
Constant	−1.013***	−0.802	−0.604	5.729**
	(0.230)	(0.489)	(0.485)	(2.553)
N	34,174	5,666	3,206	2,301

Activities

TABLE B.24

U.S. Arms Transfers and Adversary Arms Transfers

Measure	Politically Relevant (1)	U.S. Rival (2)	Partner's Rival (3)	Russia/USSR (4)
U.S. arms transfers	0.012*	−0.005	0.044**	0.014*
	(0.006)	(0.007)	(0.022)	(0.008)
Lag arms to adversary	0.727***	0.916***	0.628***	0.161***
	(0.011)	(0.009)	(0.039)	(0.011)
UN affinity to U.S.	−0.058	−0.304***	−0.034	−0.111***
	(0.036)	(0.052)	(0.101)	(0.032)
Alliance with U.S.	−0.186***	0.071*	−0.461*	−0.037
	(0.050)	(0.039)	(0.245)	(0.060)
Capabilities balance	0.367**	0.138	0.431	0.265
	(0.165)	(0.122)	(0.463)	(0.204)
Alliance in dyad	−0.033	−0.123**	0.077	0.048
	(0.041)	(0.054)	(0.178)	(0.050)
Distance	−0.093***	−0.004	−0.002	−0.118***
	(0.030)	(0.007)	(0.117)	(0.032)
Joint democracy	0.041	−0.300***	0.218	−0.186***
	(0.036)	(0.081)	(0.157)	(0.037)
Shared IGOs	0.000	0.004*	−0.003	−0.003**
	(0.001)	(0.002)	(0.004)	(0.001)
Trade	0.009	0.023***	−0.024	−0.047***
	(0.011)	(0.009)	(0.025)	(0.011)
Military spending (adversary)	−0.035*	−0.224***	0.191***	0.007
	(0.018)	(0.020)	(0.051)	(0.016)
Military spending (partner)	0.018	0.011	−0.021	−0.006
	(0.015)	(0.012)	(0.034)	(0.017)
Alliance count (adversary)	−0.031***	0.004**	0.007	0.007**
	(0.002)	(0.002)	(0.015)	(0.003)
Alliance count (partner)	0.007**	0.003	−0.007	0.004
	(0.003)	(0.003)	(0.019)	(0.003)
GDP per capita (adversary)	0.186***	0.120***	0.146*	−0.145***
	(0.025)	(0.030)	(0.074)	(0.033)
GDP per capita (partner)	0.057**	−0.000	0.054	0.103***
	(0.025)	(0.021)	(0.074)	(0.030)
Population (adversary)	0.188***	0.177***	0.084	−0.038
	(0.032)	(0.023)	(0.106)	(0.044)
Population (partner)	0.037	−0.019	0.096	0.086***
	(0.028)	(0.018)	(0.088)	(0.030)
Past MIDs	0.006**	−0.001	0.004	−0.001
	(0.003)	(0.002)	(0.008)	(0.003)
Cold War	0.098***	0.137***	0.537***	−0.115***
	(0.030)	(0.050)	(0.105)	(0.032)
Constant	−3.410***	0.438	−4.744***	0.051
	(0.385)	(0.427)	(0.995)	(0.361)
N	28,273	4,415	2,790	25,794

TABLE B.25

U.S. Arms Transfers and Threatened Sanctions

Measure	Politically Relevant	U.S. Rival	Partner's Rival
	(1)	(2)	(3)
U.S. arms transfers	0.037***	−0.018	0.013
	(0.014)	(0.042)	(0.043)
UN affinity to U.S.	0.106	0.116	0.915***
	(0.111)	(0.382)	(0.289)
Alliance with U.S.	−0.082	−0.041	−0.315
	(0.085)	(0.239)	(0.283)
Capabilities balance	0.440***	0.171	0.314
	(0.081)	(0.277)	(0.403)
Distance	0.003	−0.063	0.121**
	(0.011)	(0.043)	(0.051)
Joint democracy	0.033	0.000	−0.522
	(0.078)	N/A	(0.443)
Shared IGOs	−0.001	0.026***	0.037**
	(0.003)	(0.010)	(0.016)
Trade	0.138***	0.048	0.001
	(0.025)	(0.070)	(0.062)
Oil rents (partner)	0.006*	0.009	0.035***
	(0.003)	(0.009)	(0.010)
Exports (partner)	−0.004	−0.012*	−0.033**
	(0.003)	(0.007)	(0.013)
GDP per capita (partner)	−0.150***	0.093	−0.044
	(0.055)	(0.107)	(0.167)
GDP growth (partner)	0.010*	0.039***	0.015*
	(0.006)	(0.011)	(0.009)
Cold War	0.120*	0.135	−0.382
	(0.069)	(0.231)	(0.341)
Constant	−2.285***	−4.751***	−3.291*
	(0.455)	(0.994)	(1.933)
N	41,327	6,027	1,619

TABLE B.26

U.S. Arms Transfers and Imposed Sanctions

Measure	Politically Relevant (1)	U.S. Rival (2)	Partner's Rival (3)	Russia/USSR (4)
U.S. arms transfers	0.038**	−0.024	0.090**	0.226
	(0.017)	(0.055)	(0.040)	(0.148)
UN affinity to U.S.	0.111	−0.260	0.605*	0.834
	(0.126)	(0.516)	(0.341)	(2.002)
Alliance with U.S.	−0.289***	−0.107	−0.523*	4.170
	(0.100)	(0.319)	(0.278)	(3.086)
Capabilities balance	0.344***	0.009	0.343	2.386*
	(0.102)	(0.303)	(0.441)	(1.249)
Distance	0.010	−0.059	0.199***	0.390
	(0.014)	(0.047)	(0.038)	(0.336)
Joint democracy	0.133	0.000	0.000	0.000
	(0.090)	N/A	N/A	N/A
Shared IGOs	−0.000	0.019	−0.004	−0.076*
	(0.003)	(0.013)	(0.014)	(0.045)
Trade	0.209***	0.220***	0.143***	2.329
	(0.025)	(0.065)	(0.047)	(1.487)
Oil rents (partner)	0.008**	0.010	0.009	0.115
	(0.004)	(0.009)	(0.009)	(0.073)
Exports (partner)	−0.006*	−0.007	−0.005*	0.056
	(0.004)	(0.009)	(0.003)	(0.046)
GDP per capita (partner)	−0.181***	0.004	−0.263	−3.629
	(0.065)	(0.210)	(0.167)	(2.320)
GDP growth (partner)	0.009	0.041***	0.000	0.116
	(0.008)	(0.008)	(0.014)	(0.079)
Cold War	0.056	0.591**	−0.535	0.000
	(0.079)	(0.279)	(0.325)	N/A
Constant	−2.421***	−4.945***	−0.644	9.605
	(0.570)	(1.760)	(1.661)	(7.643)
N	41,327	6,027	1,379	1,169

TABLE B.27

U.S. Arms Transfers and Proxy Support

Measure	Politically Relevant (1)	U.S. Rival (2)	Partner's Rival (3)	Russia/USSR (4)
U.S. arms transfers	0.049*	0.126***	0.081	0.346***
	(0.026)	(0.043)	(0.056)	(0.117)
UN affinity to U.S.	0.084	−0.052	0.113	3.767**
	(0.314)	(0.508)	(0.826)	(1.652)
Alliance with U.S.	−0.150	0.152	−0.209	−0.923
	(0.264)	(0.320)	(0.776)	(0.932)
MID (dyad)	1.141***	0.706***	0.924***	3.185**
	(0.081)	(0.217)	(0.283)	(1.248)
Distance	0.039	0.003	0.004	1.613**
	(0.028)	(0.047)	(0.250)	(0.641)
Capabilities	−5.804*	−11.643	−12.367*	−31.219
	(3.180)	(10.300)	(7.162)	(63.750)
Military spending	0.068*	0.099	0.035	−0.174
	(0.037)	(0.073)	(0.044)	(0.116)
Polity	0.021	−0.021	0.142***	−0.246**
	(0.023)	(0.037)	(0.039)	(0.115)
GDP per capita	0.025	0.084*	−0.015	0.168
	(0.030)	(0.051)	(0.073)	(0.133)
GDP growth	−0.020**	−0.022	−0.018	−0.004
	(0.009)	(0.017)	(0.017)	(0.087)
State capacity	0.349***	0.617***	0.214	2.434***
	(0.118)	(0.185)	(0.265)	(0.820)
Oil rents	−0.008	−0.023**	0.014	−1.893*
	(0.007)	(0.011)	(0.014)	(1.069)
Population	−0.141**	−0.266**	−0.089	−0.662**
	(0.055)	(0.114)	(0.067)	(0.268)
Cold War	−0.126	0.068	−0.693*	−1.270**
	(0.116)	(0.221)	(0.372)	(0.506)
Alliance in dyad	0.422***	−0.136	0.302	0.000
	(0.153)	(0.292)	(0.380)	N/A
Constant	−2.198***	−1.777***	−1.038*	0.118
	(0.163)	(0.270)	(0.607)	(1.323)
N	4,938	837	268	241

TABLE B.28

U.S. Arms Transfers and Military Intimidation

Measure	Politically Relevant (1)	U.S. Rival (2)	Partner's Rival (3)	Russia/USSR (4)
U.S. arms transfers	0.028**	0.049*	0.042**	0.068**
	(0.014)	(0.028)	(0.021)	(0.032)
UN affinity to U.S.	−0.037	0.363**	0.208	0.238
	(0.103)	(0.169)	(0.178)	(0.311)
Alliance with U.S.	−0.056	−0.212	0.232	−0.114
	(0.114)	(0.185)	(0.348)	(0.194)
Capabilities balance	0.342***	0.324	0.439***	−0.660
	(0.091)	(0.230)	(0.167)	(1.354)
Alliance in dyad	0.134*	0.074	0.257*	−0.083
	(0.078)	(0.138)	(0.136)	(0.271)
Joint democracy	−0.400***	−0.060	0.091	0.000
	(0.118)	(0.251)	(0.135)	N/A
Distance	−0.104***	−0.190***	0.229**	−0.799***
	(0.032)	(0.051)	(0.098)	(0.171)
Shared IGOs	−0.006*	0.011*	−0.005	0.025**
	(0.003)	(0.006)	(0.005)	(0.013)
Trade	0.007	0.010	0.024	−0.037
	(0.018)	(0.026)	(0.026)	(0.076)
Past MIDs	0.021***	0.016***	0.010	0.006
	(0.004)	(0.005)	(0.007)	(0.008)
Cold War	−0.258***	−0.163	0.073	0.240
	(0.077)	(0.182)	(0.154)	(0.348)
Constant	−1.693***	−1.956***	−1.851***	1.422
	(0.156)	(0.330)	(0.304)	(1.816)
N	31,833	5,304	3,102	2,155

TABLE B.29

U.S. Arms Transfers and Use of Force

Measure	Politically Relevant (1)	U.S. Rival (2)	Partner's Rival (3)	Russia/USSR (4)
U.S. arms transfers	0.035**	0.048**	0.051**	−0.036
	(0.014)	(0.022)	(0.025)	(0.036)
UN affinity to U.S.	−0.212**	−0.467**	−0.054	0.204
	(0.087)	(0.185)	(0.127)	(0.334)
Alliance with U.S.	0.085	0.192	−0.421	0.335
	(0.132)	(0.196)	(0.309)	(0.348)
Capabilities balance	0.307***	−0.184	0.078	−2.593
	(0.119)	(0.232)	(0.278)	(1.840)
Alliance in dyad	0.030	0.126	0.111	0.307
	(0.062)	(0.177)	(0.095)	(0.371)
Joint democracy	−0.318***	−0.155	0.099	0.000
	(0.114)	(0.238)	(0.124)	N/A
Distance	−0.143**	−0.094	−0.072	−0.719**
	(0.061)	(0.107)	(0.079)	(0.318)
Shared IGOs	−0.000	−0.008	0.000	−0.035*
	(0.002)	(0.005)	(0.004)	(0.019)
Trade	−0.061***	−0.038	−0.027	−0.094*
	(0.015)	(0.031)	(0.024)	(0.055)
Past MIDs	0.022***	0.025***	0.010**	0.031**
	(0.004)	(0.006)	(0.005)	(0.012)
Cold War	−0.051	0.348*	−0.052	−0.043
	(0.066)	(0.189)	(0.114)	(0.458)
Constant	−1.100***	−1.142***	−1.088***	5.494*
	(0.135)	(0.279)	(0.348)	(2.920)
N	31,833	5,304	3,131	2,155

TABLE B.30

U.S. Military Exercises and Arms Transfers

Measure	Politically Relevant (1)	U.S. Rival (2)	Partner's Rival (3)	Russia/USSR (4)
U.S. military exercises	0.055*	−0.029	−0.103	0.051**
	(0.032)	(0.045)	(0.123)	(0.024)
Lag arms to adversary	0.721***	0.911***	0.620***	0.159***
	(0.011)	(0.009)	(0.046)	(0.011)
UN affinity to U.S.	−0.086**	−0.317***	0.374***	−0.056*
	(0.041)	(0.057)	(0.111)	(0.031)
Alliance with U.S.	−0.173***	0.093**	−0.231	−0.019
	(0.049)	(0.044)	(0.226)	(0.059)
Capabilities balance	0.192	−0.022	0.447	0.316
	(0.171)	(0.135)	(0.419)	(0.225)
Alliance in dyad	−0.079**	−0.093*	−0.038	0.045
	(0.037)	(0.054)	(0.182)	(0.044)
Distance	−0.104***	−0.006	0.002	−0.124***
	(0.028)	(0.007)	(0.136)	(0.035)
Joint democracy	−0.046	−0.441***	−0.023	−0.188***
	(0.037)	(0.086)	(0.167)	(0.039)
Shared IGOs	0.001	0.004	0.001	−0.003**
	(0.001)	(0.003)	(0.006)	(0.001)
Trade	0.004	0.027***	−0.023	−0.054***
	(0.011)	(0.010)	(0.023)	(0.011)
Military spending (adversary)	−0.041**	−0.295***	0.188***	0.009
	(0.019)	(0.027)	(0.056)	(0.016)
Military spending (partner)	−0.001	−0.007	−0.039	−0.011
	(0.015)	(0.014)	(0.035)	(0.017)
Alliance count (adversary)	−0.030***	0.007***	−0.005	0.005**
	(0.002)	(0.002)	(0.010)	(0.002)
Alliance count (partner)	0.007**	0.003	0.008	−0.000
	(0.003)	(0.003)	(0.017)	(0.003)
GDP per capita (adversary)	0.248***	0.193***	0.241***	−0.127***
	(0.027)	(0.033)	(0.086)	(0.033)
GDP per capita (partner)	0.064***	−0.007	0.062	0.121***
	(0.023)	(0.026)	(0.064)	(0.029)
Population (adversary)	0.231***	0.255***	0.089	−0.039
	(0.033)	(0.026)	(0.109)	(0.048)
Population (partner)	0.032	−0.037	0.121	0.108***
	(0.030)	(0.023)	(0.080)	(0.036)
Past MIDs	0.010***	0.001	0.009	−0.002
	(0.003)	(0.002)	(0.009)	(0.003)
Cold War	0.113***	0.218***	0.463***	−0.101***
	(0.029)	(0.052)	(0.105)	(0.026)
Constant	−3.965***	0.557	−5.615***	−0.391
	(0.369)	(0.485)	(1.005)	(0.359)
N	22,920	3,657	2,047	20,853

TABLE B.31

U.S. Military Exercises and Threatened Sanctions

Measure	Politically Relevant (1)	U.S. Rival (2)	Partner's Rival (3)
U.S. military exercises	−0.053	0.164	0.279
	(0.080)	(0.188)	(0.325)
UN affinity to U.S.	0.085	0.036	1.139***
	(0.117)	(0.364)	(0.315)
Alliance with U.S.	−0.044	−0.137	−0.361
	(0.090)	(0.259)	(0.338)
Capabilities balance	0.300***	0.084	0.423
	(0.104)	(0.332)	(0.497)
Distance	0.004	−0.052	0.100**
	(0.012)	(0.043)	(0.051)
Joint democracy	0.040	0.000	−0.478
	(0.074)	N/A	(0.432)
Shared IGOs	−0.002	0.026**	0.041***
	(0.003)	(0.010)	(0.015)
Trade	0.138***	0.042	0.000
	(0.026)	(0.073)	(0.086)
Oil rents (partner)	0.004	0.008	0.041***
	(0.003)	(0.009)	(0.009)
Exports (partner)	−0.004	−0.012*	−0.038**
	(0.003)	(0.007)	(0.015)
GDP per capita (partner)	−0.104**	0.079	−0.068
	(0.048)	(0.095)	(0.186)
GDP growth (partner)	0.012**	0.040***	0.014
	(0.006)	(0.012)	(0.009)
Cold War	0.109	0.158	−0.282
	(0.069)	(0.228)	(0.362)
Constant	−2.469***	−4.654***	−3.312
	(0.404)	(1.001)	(2.142)
N	39,022	6,075	1,582

TABLE B.32

U.S. Military Exercises and Imposed Sanctions

Measure	Politically Relevant (1)	U.S. Rival (2)	Partner's Rival (3)
U.S. military exercises	0.112	0.336**	0.268
	(0.083)	(0.143)	(0.342)
UN affinity to U.S.	0.129	−0.471	0.819**
	(0.144)	(0.519)	(0.323)
Alliance with U.S.	−0.283***	−0.393	−0.657*
	(0.106)	(0.350)	(0.345)
Capabilities balance	0.282**	−0.321	0.138
	(0.121)	(0.345)	(0.501)
Distance	0.003	−0.031	0.171***
	(0.015)	(0.050)	(0.055)
Joint democracy	0.133	0.000	0.000
	(0.086)	N/A	N/A
Shared IGOs	−0.002	0.017	0.001
	(0.003)	(0.011)	(0.016)
Trade	0.208***	0.221***	0.193***
	(0.027)	(0.056)	(0.058)
Oil rents (partner)	0.008*	0.009	0.010
	(0.004)	(0.010)	(0.008)
Exports (partner)	−0.007*	−0.008	−0.007**
	(0.004)	(0.008)	(0.004)
GDP per capita (partner)	−0.139**	0.008	−0.178
	(0.056)	(0.200)	(0.157)
GDP growth (partner)	0.009	0.043***	0.002
	(0.008)	(0.009)	(0.015)
Cold War	0.064	0.622**	−0.265
	(0.082)	(0.255)	(0.355)
Constant	−2.573***	−4.875***	−1.566
	(0.505)	(1.651)	(1.609)
N	39,022	6,075	1,342

TABLE B.33

U.S. Military Exercises and Proxy Support

Measure	Politically Relevant (1)	U.S. Rival (2)	Partner's Rival (3)	Russia/USSR (4)
U.S. military exercises	0.212	0.229	0.266	−2.176*
	(0.134)	(0.181)	(0.354)	(1.172)
UN affinity to U.S.	0.297	0.305	0.548	7.051**
	(0.317)	(0.519)	(0.697)	(3.232)
Alliance with U.S.	−0.079	0.347	0.109	−0.756
	(0.245)	(0.294)	(0.788)	(0.896)
MID (dyad)	1.141***	0.727***	0.897***	2.410***
	(0.081)	(0.215)	(0.314)	(0.874)
Distance	0.038	−0.011	0.000	1.536**
	(0.028)	(0.048)	(0.268)	(0.632)
Capabilities	−5.548*	−10.191	−13.328**	−15.919
	(2.877)	(8.364)	(6.463)	(53.964)
Military spending	0.064*	0.125*	0.034	−0.012
	(0.038)	(0.072)	(0.041)	(0.212)
Polity	0.016	−0.018	0.127***	−0.275*
	(0.023)	(0.038)	(0.042)	(0.163)
GDP per capita	0.020	0.055	−0.032	−0.038
	(0.030)	(0.046)	(0.073)	(0.132)
GDP growth	−0.020**	−0.022	−0.019	−0.056
	(0.008)	(0.016)	(0.014)	(0.080)
State capacity	0.343***	0.562***	0.219	2.652**
	(0.115)	(0.174)	(0.243)	(1.064)
Oil rents	−0.007	−0.020*	0.017	−0.203*
	(0.007)	(0.012)	(0.013)	(0.104)
Population	−0.127**	−0.241**	−0.057	−0.713*
	(0.057)	(0.110)	(0.063)	(0.366)
Cold War	−0.083	0.137	−0.594	−0.721
	(0.114)	(0.237)	(0.402)	(0.571)
Alliance in dyad	0.407***	−0.154	0.300	0.000
	(0.153)	(0.306)	(0.372)	N/A
Constant	−2.224***	−1.840***	−1.148*	−0.134
	(0.153)	(0.277)	(0.620)	(1.328)
N	4,938	837	268	241

TABLE B.34

U.S. Military Exercises and Military Intimidation

Measure	Politically Relevant (1)	U.S. Rival (2)	Partner's Rival (3)	Russia/USSR (4)
U.S. military exercises	0.045	0.216	0.081	0.402*
	(0.092)	(0.154)	(0.191)	(0.239)
U.S. exercises (three-year average)	−0.034	−0.061	0.149	−0.414
	(0.110)	(0.180)	(0.217)	(0.266)
UN affinity to U.S.	−0.014	0.555***	0.071	0.296
	(0.104)	(0.201)	(0.172)	(0.360)
Alliance with U.S.	0.011	−0.189	0.166	−0.102
	(0.113)	(0.171)	(0.369)	(0.221)
Capabilities balance	0.250**	0.110	0.578***	−0.799
	(0.101)	(0.235)	(0.219)	(1.664)
Alliance in dyad	0.133	0.071	0.203	−0.349
	(0.093)	(0.180)	(0.155)	(0.429)
Joint democracy	−0.417***	0.127	−0.012	0.000
	(0.132)	(0.448)	(0.171)	N/A
Distance	−0.079**	−0.179***	0.426***	−0.727***
	(0.032)	(0.045)	(0.126)	(0.146)
Shared IGOs	−0.006	0.009	−0.006	0.045***
	(0.004)	(0.007)	(0.006)	(0.014)
Trade	0.017	0.008	0.016	−0.123
	(0.018)	(0.028)	(0.025)	(0.086)
Past MIDs	0.024***	0.019***	0.016**	0.014*
	(0.004)	(0.005)	(0.007)	(0.008)
Cold War	−0.207**	−0.053	0.130	0.674**
	(0.081)	(0.184)	(0.162)	(0.306)
Constant	−1.682***	−1.578***	−1.983***	1.158
	(0.181)	(0.383)	(0.328)	(2.158)
N	25,137	4,117	2,230	1,666

TABLE B.35

U.S. Military Exercises and Use of Force

Measure	Politically Relevant (1)	U.S. Rival (2)	Partner's Rival (3)	Russia/USSR (4)
U.S. military exercises	0.121	0.158	0.230**	0.287
	(0.079)	(0.147)	(0.116)	(0.192)
UN affinity to U.S.	−0.279***	−0.660***	0.144	−0.254
	(0.102)	(0.247)	(0.159)	(0.474)
Alliance with U.S.	0.118	0.555*	−0.172	−0.827
	(0.164)	(0.316)	(0.415)	(0.694)
Capabilities balance	0.360***	−0.326	0.171	6.635
	(0.131)	(0.357)	(0.309)	(5.052)
Alliance in dyad	0.001	−0.186	0.116	−0.367
	(0.072)	(0.278)	(0.121)	(0.375)
Joint democracy	−0.323**	−0.484***	−0.049	0.000
	(0.127)	(0.187)	(0.166)	N/A
Distance	−0.193***	−0.218	−0.239	−1.076**
	(0.057)	(0.135)	(0.182)	(0.467)
Shared IGOs	0.001	−0.008	−0.002	0.012
	(0.002)	(0.008)	(0.004)	(0.039)
Trade	−0.069***	−0.020	−0.012	−0.135
	(0.016)	(0.036)	(0.028)	(0.151)
Past MIDs	0.023***	0.025***	0.013**	0.060
	(0.004)	(0.007)	(0.006)	(0.038)
Cold War	0.040	0.321	−0.095	−1.998*
	(0.064)	(0.202)	(0.128)	(1.126)
Constant	−1.205***	−1.251***	−1.415***	−0.275
	(0.158)	(0.406)	(0.385)	(3.890)
N	25,844	4,180	2,297	1,703

Agreements

TABLE B.36

U.S. SOFAs and Arms Transfers

Measure	Politically Relevant (1)	U.S. Rival (2)	Partner's Rival (3)	Russia/USSR (4)
SOFA	0.190***	0.049	0.427***	−0.005
	(0.044)	(0.062)	(0.153)	(0.023)
Lag arms to adversary	0.730***	0.913***	0.638***	0.165***
	(0.011)	(0.009)	(0.039)	(0.011)
UN affinity to U.S.	−0.080**	−0.329***	0.070	−0.097***
	(0.034)	(0.052)	(0.089)	(0.031)
Alliance with U.S.	−0.168***	0.053	−0.404	−0.033
	(0.049)	(0.037)	(0.248)	(0.060)
Capabilities balance	0.168	0.067	0.401	0.241
	(0.159)	(0.123)	(0.473)	(0.194)
Alliance in dyad	−0.022	−0.107**	0.061	0.086*
	(0.038)	(0.049)	(0.181)	(0.048)
Distance	−0.104***	−0.004	−0.026	−0.115***
	(0.028)	(0.007)	(0.117)	(0.029)
Joint democracy	0.020	−0.344***	0.208	−0.180***
	(0.035)	(0.080)	(0.162)	(0.036)
Shared IGOs	−0.000	0.004**	−0.002	−0.004***
	(0.001)	(0.002)	(0.004)	(0.001)
Trade	0.010	0.023***	−0.024	−0.041***
	(0.010)	(0.009)	(0.025)	(0.011)
Military spending (adversary)	−0.025	−0.247***	0.188***	0.008
	(0.017)	(0.020)	(0.050)	(0.014)
Military spending (partner)	0.013	0.001	−0.008	0.003
	(0.013)	(0.012)	(0.034)	(0.015)
Alliance count (adversary)	−0.029***	0.005***	0.007	0.007***
	(0.002)	(0.002)	(0.015)	(0.003)
Alliance count (partner)	0.005**	0.005**	−0.013	0.002
	(0.002)	(0.003)	(0.019)	(0.002)
GDP per capita (adversary)	0.191***	0.145***	0.139*	−0.151***
	(0.024)	(0.028)	(0.080)	(0.031)
GDP per capita (partner)	0.058**	0.002	0.084	0.106***
	(0.023)	(0.021)	(0.069)	(0.027)
Population (adversary)	0.203***	0.207***	0.083	−0.035
	(0.031)	(0.024)	(0.110)	(0.043)
Population (partner)	0.023	−0.025	0.097	0.088***
	(0.028)	(0.018)	(0.090)	(0.030)
Past MIDs	0.006*	−0.000	0.005	−0.002
	(0.003)	(0.002)	(0.008)	(0.003)
Cold War	0.109***	0.170***	0.541***	−0.097***
	(0.027)	(0.050)	(0.103)	(0.028)
Constant	−3.435***	0.419	−5.049***	−0.067
	(0.358)	(0.436)	(0.939)	(0.334)
N	29,317	4,633	2,769	26,733

TABLE B.37

U.S. SOFAs and Threatened Sanctions

Measure	Politically Relevant (1)	U.S. Rival (2)
SOFA	−0.194	0.003
	(0.134)	(0.359)
UN affinity to U.S.	0.135	−0.075
	(0.105)	(0.369)
Alliance with U.S.	−0.033	−0.170
	(0.083)	(0.246)
Capabilities balance	0.391***	−0.098
	(0.081)	(0.300)
Distance	−0.002	−0.068*
	(0.011)	(0.038)
Joint democracy	0.006	0.000
	(0.075)	N/A
Shared IGOs	−0.002	0.018*
	(0.003)	(0.010)
Trade	0.146***	0.036
	(0.024)	(0.059)
Oil rents (partner)	0.005	0.001
	(0.003)	(0.010)
Exports (partner)	−0.004	−0.010*
	(0.003)	(0.006)
GDP per capita (partner)	−0.106**	0.155
	(0.046)	(0.102)
GDP growth (partner)	0.010	0.034***
	(0.006)	(0.011)
Cold War	0.110	−0.002
	(0.067)	(0.223)
Constant	−2.565***	−4.718***
	(0.383)	(0.955)
N	43,930	6,340

TABLE B.38

U.S. SOFAs and Imposed Sanctions

Measure	Politically Relevant (1)	U.S. Rival (2)
SOFA	0.066	0.150
	(0.118)	(0.370)
UN affinity to U.S.	0.134	−0.412
	(0.120)	(0.452)
Alliance with U.S.	−0.263***	−0.267
	(0.094)	(0.331)
Capabilities balance	0.278***	−0.280
	(0.098)	(0.324)
Distance	0.003	−0.065*
	(0.014)	(0.037)
Joint democracy	0.098	0.000
	(0.085)	N/A
Shared IGOs	−0.001	0.011
	(0.003)	(0.011)
Trade	0.211***	0.173***
	(0.024)	(0.060)
Oil rents (partner)	0.007*	0.004
	(0.004)	(0.010)
Exports (partner)	−0.006*	−0.006
	(0.003)	(0.007)
GDP per capita (partner)	−0.123**	0.093
	(0.054)	(0.180)
GDP growth (partner)	0.007	0.034***
	(0.008)	(0.010)
Cold War	0.049	0.355
	(0.075)	(0.272)
Constant	−2.739***	−4.854***
	(0.473)	(1.499)
N	43,930	6,340

TABLE B.39

U.S. SOFAs and Proxy Support

Measure	Politically Relevant (1)	U.S. Rival (2)
SOFA	−0.045	−0.241
	(0.233)	(0.310)
UN affinity to U.S.	0.241	0.245
	(0.320)	(0.528)
Alliance with U.S.	−0.004	0.472*
	(0.244)	(0.281)
MID (dyad)	1.137***	0.711***
	(0.079)	(0.214)
Distance	0.036	−0.017
	(0.028)	(0.047)
Capabilities	−6.109*	−10.862
	(3.183)	(9.217)
Military spending	0.075**	0.141*
	(0.037)	(0.072)
Polity	0.025	−0.008
	(0.022)	(0.038)
GDP per capita	0.018	0.053
	(0.031)	(0.048)
GDP growth	−0.020**	−0.024
	(0.008)	(0.016)
State capacity	0.340***	0.570***
	(0.113)	(0.172)
Oil rents	−0.007	−0.021*
	(0.007)	(0.012)
Population	−0.136**	−0.258**
	(0.056)	(0.113)
Cold War	−0.086	0.129
	(0.117)	(0.244)
Alliance in dyad	0.407***	−0.119
	(0.152)	(0.302)
Constant	−2.230***	−1.841***
	(0.157)	(0.273)
N	4,938	837

TABLE B.40

U.S. SOFAs and Military Intimidation

Measure	Politically Relevant (1)	U.S. Rival (2)	Partner's Rival (3)	Russia/USSR (4)
SOFA	0.127	0.479***	−0.160	0.814***
	(0.098)	(0.139)	(0.233)	(0.139)
UN affinity to U.S.	0.053	0.489***	0.224	0.316
	(0.103)	(0.181)	(0.171)	(0.300)
Alliance with U.S.	0.014	−0.186	0.377	−0.233
	(0.102)	(0.170)	(0.360)	(0.179)
Capabilities balance	0.283***	0.276	0.428**	−0.746
	(0.087)	(0.220)	(0.169)	(1.256)
Alliance in dyad	0.128	0.007	0.244*	−0.388
	(0.083)	(0.143)	(0.146)	(0.263)
Joint democracy	−0.408***	0.050	0.093	0.000
	(0.123)	(0.296)	(0.135)	N/A
Distance	−0.106***	−0.188***	0.239**	−0.782***
	(0.029)	(0.052)	(0.093)	(0.159)
Shared IGOs	−0.004	0.012*	−0.006	0.029**
	(0.004)	(0.006)	(0.005)	(0.013)
Trade	0.009	0.023	0.032	−0.036
	(0.018)	(0.028)	(0.025)	(0.072)
Past MIDs	0.021***	0.017***	0.011	0.009
	(0.004)	(0.005)	(0.007)	(0.008)
Cold War	−0.233***	−0.103	0.072	0.523
	(0.076)	(0.186)	(0.156)	(0.348)
Constant	−1.652***	−1.903***	−1.797***	1.453
	(0.151)	(0.361)	(0.280)	(1.817)
N	33,494	5,555	3,081	2,247

TABLE B.41

U.S. SOFAs and Use of Force

Measure	Politically Relevant (1)	U.S. Rival (2)	Partner's Rival (3)	Russia/USSR (4)
SOFA	−0.147	−0.331**	−0.042	−0.907**
	(0.110)	(0.153)	(0.179)	(0.364)
UN affinity to U.S.	−0.148*	−0.333*	0.001	0.166
	(0.083)	(0.181)	(0.118)	(0.363)
Alliance with U.S.	0.231*	0.472**	−0.298	0.374
	(0.135)	(0.199)	(0.327)	(0.391)
Capabilities balance	0.264**	−0.072	0.000	−3.390*
	(0.116)	(0.249)	(0.267)	(1.828)
Alliance in dyad	0.034	0.114	0.061	0.640**
	(0.064)	(0.193)	(0.097)	(0.308)
Joint democracy	−0.320***	−0.154	0.114	0.000
	(0.115)	(0.235)	(0.121)	N/A
Distance	−0.148***	−0.116	−0.089	−0.759***
	(0.047)	(0.103)	(0.078)	(0.274)
Shared IGOs	0.001	−0.005	0.002	−0.030
	(0.002)	(0.005)	(0.004)	(0.023)
Trade	−0.061***	−0.052*	−0.024	−0.171***
	(0.014)	(0.030)	(0.023)	(0.063)
Past MIDs	0.021***	0.023***	0.010**	0.031**
	(0.003)	(0.006)	(0.005)	(0.013)
Cold War	−0.027	0.227	−0.040	0.025
	(0.063)	(0.160)	(0.116)	(0.493)
Constant	−1.080***	−0.976***	−0.974***	6.405***
	(0.125)	(0.272)	(0.338)	(2.440)
N	33,494	5,555	3,113	2,247

TABLE B.42

U.S. Alliance and Arms Transfers

Measure	Global (1)	U.S. Rival (2)	Partner's Rival (3)	Russia/USSR (4)
New U.S. alliance	−0.005	0.171*	0.015	−0.043
	(0.104)	(0.100)	(0.340)	(0.057)
Lag arms to adversary	0.729***	0.915***	0.640***	0.161***
	(0.011)	(0.008)	(0.035)	(0.011)
UN affinity to U.S.	−0.111***	−0.309***	−0.078	−0.104***
	(0.034)	(0.046)	(0.118)	(0.040)
Capabilities balance	0.202	0.069	0.323	0.244
	(0.158)	(0.120)	(0.451)	(0.190)
Alliance in dyad	−0.067**	−0.121**	−0.047	0.075**
	(0.033)	(0.049)	(0.149)	(0.038)
Distance	−0.113***	−0.002	−0.112	−0.117***
	(0.028)	(0.007)	(0.120)	(0.028)
Joint democracy	0.025	−0.304***	0.107	−0.192***
	(0.035)	(0.077)	(0.185)	(0.034)
Shared IGOs	−0.001	0.006***	−0.005	−0.004***
	(0.001)	(0.002)	(0.005)	(0.001)
Trade	0.006	0.020**	−0.038*	−0.041***
	(0.010)	(0.008)	(0.023)	(0.011)
Military spending (adversary)	−0.016	−0.234***	0.199***	0.010
	(0.017)	(0.021)	(0.050)	(0.013)
Military spending (partner)	0.018	0.001	0.002	0.007
	(0.013)	(0.011)	(0.035)	(0.015)
Alliance count (adversary)	−0.030***	0.004***	0.011	0.008***
	(0.002)	(0.002)	(0.015)	(0.003)
Alliance count (partner)	0.006***	0.006**	−0.008	0.002
	(0.002)	(0.003)	(0.017)	(0.002)
GDP per capita (adversary)	0.183***	0.131***	0.156*	−0.150***
	(0.024)	(0.028)	(0.081)	(0.030)
GDP per capita (partner)	0.046**	0.009	0.058	0.101***
	(0.022)	(0.021)	(0.067)	(0.027)
Population (adversary)	0.200***	0.200***	0.115	−0.036
	(0.032)	(0.023)	(0.105)	(0.042)
Population (partner)	0.017	−0.020	0.090	0.083***
	(0.027)	(0.018)	(0.085)	(0.029)
Past MIDs	0.004	0.000	0.000	−0.002
	(0.003)	(0.002)	(0.006)	(0.003)
Cold War	0.096***	0.171***	0.480***	−0.096***
	(0.027)	(0.049)	(0.095)	(0.028)
Constant	−3.312***	0.292	−5.251***	−0.046
	(0.359)	(0.422)	(1.011)	(0.312)
N	29,908	4,686	2,844	27,296

TABLE B.43

U.S. Alliance and Proxy Support

Measure	Politically Relevant (1)	U.S. Rival (2)
New U.S. alliance	0.355	0.480
	(0.350)	(0.466)
UN affinity to U.S.	0.162	−0.398
	(0.338)	(0.568)
Alliance count	−0.010	−0.017
	(0.010)	(0.019)
MID (dyad)	1.184***	0.700***
	(0.090)	(0.236)
Distance	0.007	−0.059
	(0.029)	(0.050)
Capabilities	−7.429**	−8.287
	(3.301)	(7.365)
Military spending	0.052	0.125*
	(0.034)	(0.070)
Polity	0.039**	0.062*
	(0.018)	(0.032)
GDP per capita	0.025	0.029
	(0.034)	(0.047)
GDP growth	−0.023***	−0.039**
	(0.007)	(0.017)
State capacity	0.363***	0.817***
	(0.141)	(0.241)
Oil rents	−0.005	−0.020
	(0.007)	(0.013)
Population	−0.101*	−0.220**
	(0.053)	(0.112)
Cold War	−0.111	0.177
	(0.124)	(0.278)
Constant	−2.163***	−1.681***
	(0.153)	(0.326)
N	4,304	716

TABLE B.44

U.S. Alliance and Military Intimidation

Measure	Politically Relevant (1)	U.S. Rival (2)	Partner's Rival (3)
New U.S. alliance	0.014	0.415	0.275
	(0.244)	(0.393)	(0.386)
UN affinity to U.S.	0.051	0.449**	0.258
	(0.092)	(0.176)	(0.163)
Capabilities balance	0.275***	0.283	0.391**
	(0.084)	(0.214)	(0.157)
Alliance in dyad	0.306***	0.192	0.454**
	(0.066)	(0.219)	(0.218)
Joint democracy	−0.417***	−0.046	0.104
	(0.123)	(0.268)	(0.134)
Distance	−0.110***	−0.195***	0.203**
	(0.029)	(0.053)	(0.098)
Shared IGOs	−0.004	0.011*	−0.004
	(0.004)	(0.007)	(0.005)
Trade	0.009	0.021	0.031
	(0.018)	(0.029)	(0.025)
Past MIDs	0.021***	0.016***	0.014**
	(0.004)	(0.005)	(0.006)
Cold War	−0.232***	−0.154	0.110
	(0.075)	(0.188)	(0.155)
Constant	−1.663***	−1.911***	−1.816***
	(0.147)	(0.358)	(0.300)
N	34,271	5,679	3,191

TABLE B.45

U.S. Alliance and Use of Force

Measure	Politically Relevant (1)	U.S. Rival (2)	Partner's Rival (3)	Russia/USSR (4)
New U.S. alliance	−0.097	0.211	0.076	−0.126
	(0.192)	(0.320)	(0.301)	(0.452)
UN affinity to U.S.	−0.090	−0.218	0.001	0.215
	(0.080)	(0.168)	(0.123)	(0.329)
Capabilities balance	0.235**	−0.135	0.050	−3.086*
	(0.112)	(0.245)	(0.258)	(1.729)
Alliance in dyad	0.166	−0.026	−0.074	0.153
	(0.143)	(0.213)	(0.253)	(0.413)
Joint democracy	−0.326***	−0.113	0.093	0.000
	(0.114)	(0.250)	(0.118)	N/A
Distance	−0.145***	−0.107	−0.088	−0.743***
	(0.049)	(0.097)	(0.075)	(0.265)
Shared IGOs	0.002	−0.000	0.001	−0.024
	(0.002)	(0.005)	(0.003)	(0.020)
Trade	−0.058***	−0.050	−0.023	−0.133**
	(0.015)	(0.031)	(0.022)	(0.065)
Past MIDs	0.023***	0.027***	0.009**	0.032**
	(0.003)	(0.006)	(0.004)	(0.013)
Cold War	−0.006	0.296*	−0.059	0.214
	(0.063)	(0.163)	(0.110)	(0.423)
Alliance in dyad	−0.117	0.071	0.065	0.151
	(0.148)	(0.257)	(0.270)	(0.328)
Constant	−1.050***	−0.957***	−0.993***	5.766**
	(0.127)	(0.255)	(0.321)	(2.535)
N	34,271	5,679	3,223	2,308

Detailed Regression Results: Propensity Weighted Models

In the following tables (B.46 through B.79), we present our results for these propensity weighted models. As discussed earlier in this appendix, these results account for the possibility that the United States might choose its posture options based on the likelihood of malign activities. We do so by weighting each partner-dyad by the likelihood that the partner will receive a substantial level of posture commitment from the United States.

Each model can be interpreted as before in terms of both the effect itself and the statistical significance of the association. Models again are grouped by posture choice and each column represents the labeled sample. As before, we do not discuss the individual regression results and direct the reader to Chapter Four in the main text or our earlier discussion in the appendix for a summary of our findings.

Forces

TABLE B.46

In-Country U.S. Troops and Imposed Sanctions

Measure	Politically Relevant (1)	U.S. Rival (2)	Partner's Rival (3)	Russia/USSR (4)
In-country U.S. troops	−0.014*	−0.012	0.006	0.004
	(0.008)	(0.012)	(0.022)	(0.008)
Lag arms to adversary	0.739***	0.901***	0.631***	0.171***
	(0.012)	(0.017)	(0.041)	(0.013)
UN affinity to U.S.	−0.117**	−0.289**	0.028	−0.176***
	(0.057)	(0.128)	(0.154)	(0.049)
Alliance with U.S.	−0.088*	0.097	−0.213	0.015
	(0.053)	(0.064)	(0.216)	(0.052)
Capabilities balance	−0.047	0.151	−0.186	0.132
	(0.225)	(0.292)	(0.717)	(0.259)
Distance	−0.119***	−0.015	0.229*	−0.126***
	(0.026)	(0.010)	(0.129)	(0.034)
Joint democracy	0.028	−0.218**	0.105	−0.165***
	(0.045)	(0.110)	(0.214)	(0.048)
Shared IGOs	0.001	0.000	−0.001	−0.003
	(0.001)	(0.004)	(0.004)	(0.002)
Trade	0.008	0.038***	−0.027	−0.058***
	(0.014)	(0.014)	(0.027)	(0.018)
Military spending (adversary)	−0.015	−0.226***	0.205***	−0.007
	(0.021)	(0.053)	(0.066)	(0.020)
Military spending (partner)	0.023	0.011	0.056	−0.002
	(0.022)	(0.018)	(0.052)	(0.021)
Alliance count (adversary)	−0.028***	0.002	0.013	0.009***
	(0.002)	(0.003)	(0.014)	(0.003)
Alliance count (partner)	0.006**	0.007*	−0.019	0.006*
	(0.002)	(0.004)	(0.016)	(0.003)
GDP per capita (adversary)	0.161***	0.136***	0.077	−0.149***
	(0.036)	(0.048)	(0.092)	(0.040)
GDP per capita (partner)	0.049	−0.005	−0.018	0.127***
	(0.036)	(0.043)	(0.095)	(0.035)
Population (adversary)	0.237***	0.194***	0.163	0.006
	(0.051)	(0.050)	(0.143)	(0.059)
Population (partner)	0.002	−0.027	−0.099	0.077**
	(0.035)	(0.042)	(0.124)	(0.035)
Past MIDs	−0.001	0.004	0.003	−0.000
	(0.004)	(0.003)	(0.007)	(0.003)
Cold War	0.162***	0.163**	0.551***	−0.055
	(0.037)	(0.077)	(0.135)	(0.040)
Constant	−3.388***	0.312	−3.377**	−0.293
	(0.479)	(0.764)	(1.302)	(0.502)
N	28,416	4,486	2,718	25,901

TABLE B.47

In-Country U.S. Troops and Threatened Sanctions

Measure	Politically Relevant (1)	U.S. Rival (2)	Partner's Rival (3)	Russia/USSR (4)
In-country U.S. troops	0.031**	−0.026	0.050	−0.002
	(0.014)	(0.035)	(0.057)	(0.318)
Regional U.S. troops	−0.023	−0.062	0.029	−0.177***
	(0.017)	(0.064)	(0.059)	(0.053)
UN affinity to U.S.	0.169	−0.553	0.323	0.373
	(0.126)	(0.442)	(0.430)	(0.344)
Alliance with U.S.	−0.191*	0.110	−0.059	0.000
	(0.103)	(0.319)	(0.329)	N/A
Capabilities balance	0.642***	0.055	0.424	6.038
	(0.121)	(0.321)	(0.542)	(4.512)
Distance	0.019	−0.042	0.191***	−0.230
	(0.014)	(0.031)	(0.053)	(0.320)
Joint democracy	−0.122	0.000	−0.850*	0.000
	(0.105)	N/A	(0.493)	N/A
Shared IGOs	0.003	0.001	0.031*	0.004
	(0.004)	(0.014)	(0.017)	(0.020)
Trade	0.161***	0.031	−0.021	0.222
	(0.030)	(0.053)	(0.056)	(0.160)
Oil rents (partner)	0.005	−0.013	0.031*	−0.193
	(0.005)	(0.018)	(0.019)	(0.160)
Exports (partner)	−0.004	−0.012*	−0.025	−0.007
	(0.003)	(0.007)	(0.017)	(0.013)
GDP per capita (partner)	−0.068	0.394**	−0.170	0.245
	(0.071)	(0.185)	(0.200)	(0.301)
GDP growth (partner)	0.020***	0.037***	0.018**	0.029***
	(0.008)	(0.013)	(0.007)	(0.009)
Cold War	0.232**	−0.135	−0.614*	0.000
	(0.108)	(0.221)	(0.323)	N/A
Constant	−3.422***	−5.913***	−2.558	−10.356***
	(0.493)	(1.187)	(1.821)	(2.993)
N	43,046	6,157	1,613	798

TABLE B.48

In-Country U.S. Troops and Threatened Sanctions

Measure	Politically Relevant (1)	U.S. Rival (2)	Partner's Rival (3)	Russia/USSR (4)
In-country U.S. troops	0.026	−0.021	0.012	0.045
	(0.018)	(0.030)	(0.037)	(0.049)
UN affinity to U.S.	−0.076	−0.732*	0.106	−0.010
	(0.135)	(0.398)	(0.331)	(1.010)
Alliance with U.S.	−0.547***	−0.248	−0.483*	3.687*
	(0.115)	(0.314)	(0.270)	(1.974)
Capabilities balance	0.430***	−0.132	0.525	0.435
	(0.121)	(0.318)	(0.481)	(1.646)
Distance	0.026	−0.051	0.265***	0.365
	(0.019)	(0.041)	(0.060)	(0.307)
Joint democracy	0.058	0.000	0.000	0.000
	(0.110)	N/A	N/A	N/A
Shared IGOs	0.002	0.000	−0.018	−0.054**
	(0.003)	(0.012)	(0.013)	(0.023)
Trade	0.196***	0.107	0.092**	1.795*
	(0.026)	(0.066)	(0.046)	(1.002)
Oil rents (partner)	0.002	−0.010	−0.016	0.104*
	(0.004)	(0.013)	(0.016)	(0.057)
Exports (partner)	−0.011**	−0.011	−0.008*	0.030
	(0.004)	(0.010)	(0.004)	(0.026)
GDP per capita (partner)	0.037	0.409*	−0.022	−2.798*
	(0.074)	(0.213)	(0.173)	(1.618)
GDP growth (partner)	0.016*	0.031***	−0.010	0.107*
	(0.008)	(0.012)	(0.012)	(0.060)
Cold War	0.071	0.223	−0.918**	0.000
	(0.107)	(0.276)	(0.372)	N/A
Constant	−4.467***	−7.080***	−1.723	7.924
	(0.633)	(1.652)	(1.547)	(5.581)
N	43,046	6,157	1,373	1,214

TABLE B.49

In-Country U.S. Troops and Proxy Support

Measure	Politically Relevant (1)	U.S. Rival (2)	Partner's Rival (3)	Russia/USSR (4)
In-country U.S. troops	−0.024	0.153**	−0.289*	−0.694
	(0.059)	(0.072)	(0.172)	(0.721)
UN affinity to U.S.	0.128	−0.279	1.177	28.001
	(0.393)	(0.655)	(0.764)	(17.370)
Alliance with U.S.	0.127	0.222	1.497*	0.802
	(0.366)	(0.441)	(0.883)	(1.857)
MID (dyad)	1.094***	0.391	0.747**	4.890**
	(0.188)	(0.355)	(0.369)	(2.133)
Distance	0.060*	−0.043	0.249	2.765*
	(0.036)	(0.067)	(0.429)	(1.495)
Capabilities	−0.886	−21.316	−22.582	54.912
	(3.210)	(15.689)	(15.184)	(86.136)
Military spending	−0.027	0.048	−0.271*	−0.755
	(0.063)	(0.095)	(0.147)	(0.469)
Polity	0.064	0.008	0.247**	−1.277*
	(0.039)	(0.037)	(0.097)	(0.727)
GDP per capita	0.076*	0.089	0.091	−0.242
	(0.045)	(0.061)	(0.095)	(0.235)
GDP growth	−0.022***	−0.021	0.006	−0.347
	(0.008)	(0.013)	(0.017)	(0.241)
State capacity	0.116	0.508**	−0.501	9.081*
	(0.145)	(0.214)	(0.472)	(4.813)
Oil rents	−0.009	−0.004	0.027	0.000
	(0.014)	(0.011)	(0.023)	N/A
Population	−0.034	−0.195	0.418*	−0.535
	(0.086)	(0.138)	(0.231)	(0.362)
Cold War	−0.098	−0.038	−0.608	−3.968
	(0.195)	(0.293)	(0.597)	(3.000)
Alliance in dyad	0.218	−0.513	−0.001	0.000
	(0.220)	(0.476)	(0.445)	N/A
Constant	−2.450***	−2.119***	−2.493**	−0.672
	(0.305)	(0.379)	(0.994)	(1.466)
N	4,053	684	230	148

TABLE B.50

In-Country U.S. Personnel and Military Intimidation

Measure	Politically Relevant (1)	U.S. Rival (2)	Partner's Rival (3)	Russia/USSR (4)
In-country U.S. troops	0.025	−0.024	−0.049**	0.016
	(0.019)	(0.025)	(0.023)	(0.025)
UN affinity to U.S.	−0.024	0.506**	0.129	0.413
	(0.130)	(0.201)	(0.227)	(0.315)
Alliance with U.S.	−0.003	0.024	1.105**	−0.224
	(0.114)	(0.195)	(0.522)	(0.205)
Capabilities balance	0.451***	0.398	0.379**	−1.695
	(0.122)	(0.323)	(0.165)	(1.285)
Alliance in dyad	0.202**	−0.111	0.296*	−0.622
	(0.095)	(0.177)	(0.166)	(0.418)
Joint democracy	−0.419***	0.038	0.181	0.000
	(0.152)	(0.382)	(0.198)	N/A
Distance	−0.065	−0.281***	0.092	−0.860***
	(0.061)	(0.078)	(0.095)	(0.146)
Shared IGOs	−0.007*	0.011**	−0.013***	0.045***
	(0.004)	(0.005)	(0.005)	(0.013)
Trade	−0.021	0.045*	−0.002	−0.101
	(0.027)	(0.027)	(0.028)	(0.073)
Past MIDs	0.015**	0.013**	0.010	0.005
	(0.007)	(0.006)	(0.008)	(0.006)
Cold War	−0.360***	−0.054	−0.102	0.686*
	(0.095)	(0.177)	(0.230)	(0.385)
Constant	−1.462***	−1.747***	−1.075***	2.252
	(0.299)	(0.344)	(0.417)	(1.765)
N	31,658	5,179	2,941	2,117

TABLE B.51

In-Country U.S. Troops and Use of Force

Measure	Politically Relevant (1)	U.S. Rival (2)	Partner's Rival (3)	Russia/USSR (4)
In-country U.S. troops	0.020	0.045	0.014	0.064
	(0.015)	(0.028)	(0.020)	(0.084)
UN affinity to U.S.	−0.236**	−0.215	−0.026	0.015
	(0.106)	(0.218)	(0.224)	(0.403)
Alliance with U.S.	0.193	0.182	−0.441	−0.013
	(0.141)	(0.236)	(0.422)	(0.690)
Capabilities balance	0.297**	−0.261	0.203	−2.926
	(0.132)	(0.309)	(0.267)	(1.953)
Alliance in dyad	0.107	0.296	0.071	0.433
	(0.089)	(0.199)	(0.128)	(0.432)
Joint democracy	−0.468***	0.009	0.326**	0.000
	(0.150)	(0.245)	(0.146)	N/A
Distance	−0.160**	−0.113	−0.060	−0.951***
	(0.074)	(0.113)	(0.074)	(0.260)
Shared IGOs	−0.003	−0.010**	−0.004	−0.033
	(0.003)	(0.005)	(0.007)	(0.022)
Trade	−0.029*	−0.009	0.021	−0.122**
	(0.018)	(0.030)	(0.034)	(0.052)
Past MIDs	0.014***	0.018***	0.006	0.030***
	(0.005)	(0.007)	(0.006)	(0.011)
Cold War	−0.143*	0.189	0.040	0.078
	(0.084)	(0.212)	(0.154)	(0.630)
Constant	−1.161***	−1.042***	−1.231***	6.408**
	(0.162)	(0.331)	(0.249)	(2.848)
N	31,658	5,179	2,973	2,117

TABLE B.52

Regional U.S. Troops and Arms Transfers

Measure	Politically Relevant (1)	U.S. Rival (2)	Partner's Rival (3)	Russia/USSR (4)
Regional U.S. troops	−0.003	−0.008	0.044*	−0.011
	(0.007)	(0.009)	(0.023)	(0.012)
Lag arms to adversary	0.739***	0.901***	0.625***	0.170***
	(0.012)	(0.017)	(0.040)	(0.013)
UN affinity to U.S.	−0.123**	−0.284**	0.023	−0.154***
	(0.054)	(0.133)	(0.158)	(0.053)
Alliance with U.S.	−0.125**	0.077	−0.265	0.035
	(0.049)	(0.059)	(0.216)	(0.053)
Capabilities balance	−0.026	0.140	0.020	0.154
	(0.227)	(0.276)	(0.694)	(0.266)
Distance	−0.120***	−0.016	0.207	−0.135***
	(0.027)	(0.011)	(0.141)	(0.038)
Joint democracy	0.048	−0.217*	0.147	−0.152***
	(0.045)	(0.122)	(0.200)	(0.048)
Shared IGOs	0.000	0.000	0.002	−0.003
	(0.001)	(0.004)	(0.004)	(0.002)
Trade	0.008	0.041***	−0.031	−0.058***
	(0.014)	(0.014)	(0.026)	(0.018)
Military spending (adversary)	−0.017	−0.221***	0.193***	−0.005
	(0.021)	(0.051)	(0.063)	(0.020)
Military spending (partner)	0.028	0.012	0.048	−0.001
	(0.022)	(0.018)	(0.049)	(0.022)
Alliance count (adversary)	−0.028***	0.002	0.015	0.010***
	(0.002)	(0.003)	(0.012)	(0.003)
Alliance count (partner)	0.005**	0.007	−0.023	0.005
	(0.002)	(0.004)	(0.015)	(0.004)
GDP per capita (adversary)	0.161***	0.124***	0.069	−0.149***
	(0.035)	(0.043)	(0.087)	(0.040)
GDP per capita (partner)	0.036	−0.014	0.002	0.134***
	(0.040)	(0.041)	(0.086)	(0.036)
Population (adversary)	0.236***	0.187***	0.140	0.007
	(0.051)	(0.047)	(0.134)	(0.059)
Population (partner)	−0.003	−0.036	−0.051	0.088**
	(0.036)	(0.037)	(0.120)	(0.036)
Past MIDs	−0.001	0.003	0.002	−0.001
	(0.004)	(0.003)	(0.006)	(0.003)
Cold War	0.148***	0.153*	0.583***	−0.054
	(0.036)	(0.078)	(0.128)	(0.037)
Constant	−3.237***	0.614	−3.985***	−0.407
	(0.470)	(0.789)	(1.204)	(0.496)
N	28,416	4,486	2,718	25,901

TABLE B.53

Regional U.S. Troops and Threatened Sanctions

Measure	Politically Relevant (1)	U.S. Rival (2)	Partner's Rival (3)	Russia/USSR (4)
Regional U.S. troops	−0.023	−0.063	0.042	−0.177
	(0.017)	(0.063)	(0.065)	(0.128)
UN affinity to U.S.	0.161	−0.570	0.352	0.371
	(0.124)	(0.463)	(0.429)	(0.445)
Alliance with U.S.	−0.090	0.056	0.054	0.000
	(0.097)	(0.306)	(0.382)	N/A
Capabilities balance	0.581***	0.111	0.392	6.045*
	(0.119)	(0.309)	(0.554)	(3.353)
Distance	0.020	−0.041	0.195***	−0.230
	(0.014)	(0.032)	(0.054)	(0.292)
Joint democracy	−0.149	0.000	−0.865*	0.000
	(0.104)	N/A	(0.496)	N/A
Shared IGOs	0.004	0.002	0.030*	0.004
	(0.004)	(0.013)	(0.016)	(0.042)
Trade	0.168***	0.023	−0.011	0.223
	(0.030)	(0.048)	(0.048)	(0.338)
Oil rents (partner)	0.005	−0.013	0.030	−0.193
	(0.006)	(0.018)	(0.019)	(0.234)
Exports (partner)	−0.004	−0.012*	−0.024	−0.007
	(0.003)	(0.007)	(0.016)	(0.015)
GDP per capita (partner)	−0.041	0.368**	−0.142	0.243
	(0.067)	(0.168)	(0.211)	(0.233)
GDP growth (partner)	0.020***	0.038***	0.016**	0.029***
	(0.008)	(0.013)	(0.007)	(0.009)
Cold War	0.240**	−0.129	−0.578*	0.000
	(0.108)	(0.218)	(0.336)	N/A
Constant	−3.600***	−5.808***	−2.819	−10.349***
	(0.463)	(1.134)	(1.941)	(3.797)
N	43,046	6,157	1,613	798

TABLE B.54

Regional U.S. Troops and Imposed Sanctions

Measure	Politically Relevant (1)	U.S. Rival (2)	Partner's Rival (3)	Russia/USSR (4)
Regional U.S. troops	−0.030	−0.116**	0.085*	0.186
	(0.021)	(0.057)	(0.048)	(0.144)
UN affinity to U.S.	−0.041	−0.482	0.060	0.366
	(0.142)	(0.384)	(0.336)	(1.246)
Alliance with U.S.	−0.459***	−0.302	−0.389	2.630**
	(0.103)	(0.299)	(0.279)	(1.086)
Capabilities balance	0.320**	−0.145	0.873*	−0.428
	(0.130)	(0.303)	(0.489)	(1.918)
Distance	0.031*	−0.042	0.261***	0.546
	(0.019)	(0.041)	(0.057)	(0.437)
Joint democracy	0.048	0.000	0.000	0.000
	(0.103)	N/A	N/A	N/A
Shared IGOs	0.002	−0.001	−0.009	−0.062***
	(0.003)	(0.011)	(0.011)	(0.021)
Trade	0.207***	0.144***	0.059	1.973*
	(0.027)	(0.052)	(0.042)	(1.102)
Oil rents (partner)	−0.000	−0.019	−0.012	0.107**
	(0.005)	(0.014)	(0.014)	(0.053)
Exports (partner)	−0.011**	−0.010	−0.007**	0.032
	(0.004)	(0.010)	(0.003)	(0.027)
GDP per capita (partner)	0.071	0.466**	−0.034	−2.816*
	(0.070)	(0.215)	(0.166)	(1.532)
GDP growth (partner)	0.018**	0.039***	−0.010	0.101*
	(0.008)	(0.009)	(0.009)	(0.054)
Cold War	0.112	0.362	−0.789**	0.000
	(0.123)	(0.242)	(0.347)	N/A
Constant	−4.459***	−6.796***	−2.903	6.512
	(0.545)	(1.540)	(1.826)	(4.252)
N	43,046	6,157	1,373	1,214

TABLE B.55

Regional U.S. Troops and Proxy Support

Measure	Politically Relevant (1)	U.S. Rival (2)	Partner's Rival (3)	Russia/USSR (4)
Regional U.S. troops	−0.077	−0.132*	−0.059	−1.988**
	(0.052)	(0.069)	(0.138)	(0.822)
UN affinity to U.S.	0.265	0.369	1.015	26.947***
	(0.513)	(0.693)	(1.005)	(9.906)
Alliance with U.S.	0.068	1.004**	0.726	11.233**
	(0.296)	(0.431)	(0.825)	(5.210)
MID (dyad)	1.127***	0.401	0.783**	9.044***
	(0.190)	(0.356)	(0.389)	(3.414)
Distance	0.065*	−0.065	0.271	2.887
	(0.037)	(0.064)	(0.480)	(2.453)
Capabilities	−2.289	−26.214**	−21.942	−674.552***
	(2.848)	(13.326)	(16.593)	(254.731)
Military spending	−0.024	0.088	−0.305**	0.489
	(0.064)	(0.095)	(0.153)	(0.299)
Polity	0.067*	0.022	0.224***	0.309
	(0.038)	(0.036)	(0.081)	(0.252)
GDP per capita	0.074*	0.112*	0.039	−0.461*
	(0.045)	(0.067)	(0.105)	(0.280)
GDP growth	−0.017*	−0.016	0.009	−0.177
	(0.009)	(0.012)	(0.021)	(0.118)
State capacity	0.079	0.388*	−0.684	10.073***
	(0.139)	(0.198)	(0.626)	(3.623)
Oil rents	−0.009	−0.008	0.029	0.000
	(0.014)	(0.012)	(0.024)	N/A
Population	0.021	−0.086	0.488*	−0.838**
	(0.092)	(0.134)	(0.294)	(0.410)
Cold War	−0.135	0.056	−0.805	−4.429**
	(0.180)	(0.308)	(0.588)	(2.213)
Alliance in dyad	0.218	−0.517	0.096	0.000
	(0.224)	(0.487)	(0.452)	N/A
Constant	−2.294***	−2.031***	−1.909**	0.886
	(0.340)	(0.448)	(0.821)	(3.223)
N	4,053	684	230	148

TABLE B.56

Regional U.S. Troops and Military Intimidation

Measure	Politically Relevant (1)	U.S. Rival (2)	Partner's Rival (3)	Russia/USSR (4)
Regional U.S. troops	−0.074*	−0.088	−0.214***	0.036
	(0.040)	(0.084)	(0.076)	(0.108)
UN affinity to U.S.	0.010	0.506**	0.092	0.428
	(0.125)	(0.204)	(0.218)	(0.326)
Alliance with U.S.	0.119	−0.069	0.737*	−0.179
	(0.130)	(0.176)	(0.431)	(0.181)
Capabilities balance	0.458***	0.545*	0.489***	−1.999
	(0.119)	(0.303)	(0.178)	(1.362)
Alliance in dyad	0.213**	−0.054	0.404**	−0.629
	(0.093)	(0.161)	(0.163)	(0.417)
Joint democracy	−0.458***	0.017	0.267	0.000
	(0.156)	(0.385)	(0.224)	N/A
Distance	−0.067	−0.288***	0.141	−0.845***
	(0.059)	(0.080)	(0.091)	(0.152)
Shared IGOs	−0.006	0.010*	−0.017***	0.045***
	(0.004)	(0.006)	(0.005)	(0.013)
Trade	−0.021	0.035	−0.022	−0.100
	(0.027)	(0.024)	(0.029)	(0.074)
Past MIDs	0.014**	0.012**	0.009	0.005
	(0.007)	(0.006)	(0.009)	(0.006)
Cold War	−0.347***	−0.105	−0.150	0.698**
	(0.089)	(0.177)	(0.235)	(0.351)
Constant	−0.495	−0.755	1.561	2.101
	(0.525)	(1.152)	(1.029)	(1.732)
N	31,658	5,179	2,941	2,117

TABLE B.57

Regional U.S. Troops and Use of Force

Measure	Politically Relevant (1)	U.S. Rival (2)	Partner's Rival (3)	Russia/USSR (4)
Regional U.S. troops	−0.014	−0.011	−0.071	−0.206
	(0.034)	(0.078)	(0.078)	(0.185)
UN affinity to U.S.	−0.214*	−0.204	0.005	0.210
	(0.112)	(0.222)	(0.237)	(0.418)
Alliance with U.S.	0.293**	0.413*	−0.349	0.193
	(0.144)	(0.212)	(0.442)	(0.403)
Capabilities balance	0.281**	−0.340	0.189	−3.402*
	(0.136)	(0.329)	(0.272)	(1.745)
Alliance in dyad	0.101	0.263	0.066	0.359
	(0.089)	(0.197)	(0.123)	(0.435)
Joint democracy	−0.483***	0.001	0.323**	0.000
	(0.151)	(0.251)	(0.147)	N/A
Distance	−0.156**	−0.103	−0.059	−0.916***
	(0.074)	(0.108)	(0.073)	(0.274)
Shared IGOs	−0.003	−0.010**	−0.005	−0.030
	(0.003)	(0.005)	(0.007)	(0.023)
Trade	−0.027	−0.003	0.021	−0.128**
	(0.017)	(0.029)	(0.033)	(0.062)
Past MIDs	0.014***	0.020***	0.005	0.030***
	(0.005)	(0.007)	(0.006)	(0.010)
Cold War	−0.126	0.226	0.048	0.367
	(0.079)	(0.210)	(0.151)	(0.534)
Constant	−0.967**	−0.770	−0.315	9.153**
	(0.442)	(1.048)	(0.982)	(3.623)
N	31,658	5,179	2,973	2,117

TABLE B.58

U.S. Arms Transfers and Adversary Arms Transfers

Measure	Politically Relevant (1)	U.S. Rival (2)	Partner's Rival (3)	Russia/USSR (4)
U.S. arms transfers	0.007	−0.005	0.037	0.016
	(0.009)	(0.009)	(0.024)	(0.010)
Lag arms to adversary	0.741***	0.900***	0.628***	0.169***
	(0.012)	(0.018)	(0.041)	(0.013)
UN affinity to U.S.	−0.120**	−0.273**	−0.035	−0.163***
	(0.060)	(0.134)	(0.170)	(0.049)
Alliance with U.S.	−0.139***	0.078	−0.240	−0.006
	(0.050)	(0.052)	(0.221)	(0.054)
Capabilities balance	0.046	0.176	−0.179	0.143
	(0.243)	(0.309)	(0.719)	(0.279)
Distance	−0.110***	−0.015	0.244*	−0.126***
	(0.028)	(0.010)	(0.136)	(0.040)
Joint democracy	0.037	−0.190*	0.099	−0.155***
	(0.045)	(0.112)	(0.217)	(0.047)
Shared IGOs	0.001	−0.000	−0.002	−0.002
	(0.001)	(0.004)	(0.004)	(0.002)
Trade	0.009	0.043***	−0.028	−0.069***
	(0.014)	(0.015)	(0.026)	(0.018)
Military spending (adversary)	−0.024	−0.220***	0.205***	−0.006
	(0.022)	(0.055)	(0.064)	(0.022)
Military spending (partner)	0.032	0.017	0.050	−0.011
	(0.025)	(0.021)	(0.051)	(0.023)
Alliance count (adversary)	−0.029***	0.002	0.012	0.007**
	(0.002)	(0.003)	(0.014)	(0.003)
Alliance count (partner)	0.007**	0.004	−0.013	0.010**
	(0.003)	(0.005)	(0.016)	(0.005)
GDP per capita (adversary)	0.158***	0.124**	0.085	−0.138***
	(0.037)	(0.050)	(0.088)	(0.041)
GDP per capita (partner)	0.025	−0.019	−0.048	0.121***
	(0.038)	(0.043)	(0.099)	(0.036)
Population (adversary)	0.226***	0.175***	0.166	0.009
	(0.054)	(0.052)	(0.141)	(0.061)
Population (partner)	−0.007	−0.034	−0.109	0.078**
	(0.038)	(0.041)	(0.127)	(0.039)
Past MIDs	−0.001	0.003	0.002	0.001
	(0.004)	(0.003)	(0.007)	(0.003)
Cold War	0.140***	0.146*	0.544***	−0.088**
	(0.041)	(0.087)	(0.131)	(0.040)
Constant	−3.058***	0.603	−3.041**	−0.255
	(0.495)	(0.750)	(1.341)	(0.494)
N	26,892	4,223	2,678	24,503

Activities

TABLE B.59

U.S. Arms Transfers and Threatened Sanctions

Measure	Politically Relevant	U.S. Rival	Partner's Rival
	(1)	(2)	(3)
U.S. arms transfers	0.026	−0.030	−0.006
	(0.017)	(0.047)	(0.061)
UN affinity to U.S.	0.150	−0.409	0.349
	(0.131)	(0.564)	(0.419)
Alliance with U.S.	−0.097	0.362	0.011
	(0.099)	(0.311)	(0.349)
Capabilities balance	0.708***	0.531**	0.183
	(0.096)	(0.230)	(0.495)
Distance	0.028**	−0.027	0.203***
	(0.014)	(0.035)	(0.061)
Joint democracy	−0.151	0.000	−0.898*
	(0.111)	N/A	(0.510)
Shared IGOs	0.006	0.018	0.028**
	(0.004)	(0.014)	(0.014)
Trade	0.165***	0.035	−0.001
	(0.031)	(0.061)	(0.040)
Oil rents (partner)	0.008*	0.008	0.027
	(0.005)	(0.011)	(0.017)
Exports (partner)	−0.005	−0.016*	−0.022
	(0.003)	(0.009)	(0.013)
GDP per capita (partner)	−0.100	0.185	−0.099
	(0.067)	(0.132)	(0.221)
GDP growth (partner)	0.022***	0.046***	0.018***
	(0.007)	(0.011)	(0.007)
Cold War	0.228**	0.020	−0.594*
	(0.108)	(0.255)	(0.310)
Constant	−3.497***	−5.784***	−2.688
	(0.543)	(1.158)	(1.972)
N	40,635	5,880	1,613

TABLE B.60

U.S. Arms Transfers and Imposed Sanctions

Measure	Politically Relevant (1)	U.S. Rival (2)	Partner's Rival (3)
U.S. arms transfers	−0.031	−0.037	−0.002
	(0.024)	(0.089)	(0.167)
U.S. arms sales (three-year average)	0.095***	−0.043	0.069
	(0.027)	(0.070)	(0.187)
UN affinity to U.S.	−0.103	−0.181	0.098
	(0.144)	(0.457)	(0.336)
Alliance with U.S.	−0.536***	−0.244	−0.570
	(0.109)	(0.241)	(0.361)
Capabilities balance	0.473***	0.420	0.511
	(0.125)	(0.280)	(0.458)
Distance	0.039**	−0.030	0.278***
	(0.020)	(0.058)	(0.059)
Joint democracy	0.075	0.000	0.000
	(0.113)	N/A	N/A
Shared IGOs	0.005	0.026**	−0.022
	(0.003)	(0.011)	(0.015)
Trade	0.188***	0.237***	0.107**
	(0.026)	(0.066)	(0.049)
Oil rents (partner)	0.005	0.010	−0.013
	(0.004)	(0.008)	(0.016)
Exports (partner)	−0.011**	−0.020	−0.007*
	(0.005)	(0.015)	(0.004)
GDP per capita (partner)	−0.046	0.244	−0.178
	(0.077)	(0.238)	(0.164)
GDP growth (partner)	0.022***	0.049***	−0.010
	(0.008)	(0.008)	(0.012)
Cold War	0.103	0.851***	−0.949***
	(0.114)	(0.212)	(0.359)
Constant	−3.983***	−7.783***	−0.305
	(0.660)	(1.717)	(1.517)
N	38,708	5,566	1,239

TABLE B.61

U.S. Arms Transfers and Proxy Support

Measure	Politically Relevant (1)	U.S. Rival (2)	Partner's Rival (3)
U.S. arms transfers	0.047	0.169***	0.003
	(0.045)	(0.046)	(0.135)
UN affinity to U.S.	0.008	−0.206	0.842
	(0.375)	(0.595)	(0.848)
Alliance with U.S.	−0.141	0.487	0.729
	(0.283)	(0.406)	(0.872)
MID (dyad)	1.106***	0.391	0.771**
	(0.190)	(0.357)	(0.315)
Distance	0.064*	−0.035	0.275
	(0.037)	(0.067)	(0.449)
Capabilities	0.211	−18.650	−19.279
	(2.952)	(15.470)	(14.184)
Military spending	−0.047	0.007	−0.312**
	(0.063)	(0.094)	(0.143)
Polity	0.063	−0.006	0.214***
	(0.040)	(0.036)	(0.079)
GDP per capita	0.067	0.097*	0.046
	(0.043)	(0.057)	(0.101)
GDP growth	−0.021**	−0.018	0.005
	(0.009)	(0.013)	(0.020)
State capacity	0.144	0.543***	−0.628
	(0.155)	(0.192)	(0.572)
Oil rents	−0.012	−0.017	0.028
	(0.013)	(0.012)	(0.026)
Population	−0.020	−0.141	0.439*
	(0.089)	(0.140)	(0.230)
Cold War	−0.150	0.024	−0.783
	(0.180)	(0.273)	(0.581)
Alliance in dyad	0.236	−0.451	0.071
	(0.224)	(0.501)	(0.455)
Constant	−2.395***	−2.100***	−2.074**
	(0.291)	(0.387)	(0.894)
N	4,053	684	230

TABLE B.62

U.S. Arms Transfers and Military Intimidation

Measure	Politically Relevant (1)	U.S. Rival (2)	Partner's Rival (3)	Russia/USSR (4)
U.S. arms transfers	0.033*	0.042	0.041*	0.060**
	(0.019)	(0.026)	(0.024)	(0.031)
UN affinity to U.S.	−0.109	0.381*	0.019	0.359
	(0.131)	(0.199)	(0.231)	(0.329)
Alliance with U.S.	0.005	−0.179	0.563	−0.235
	(0.119)	(0.179)	(0.452)	(0.199)
Capabilities balance	0.489***	0.484	0.428**	−1.493
	(0.121)	(0.341)	(0.172)	(1.255)
Alliance in dyad	0.253***	−0.041	0.418**	−0.445
	(0.085)	(0.174)	(0.185)	(0.432)
Joint democracy	−0.433***	0.011	0.234	0.000
	(0.147)	(0.382)	(0.215)	N/A
Distance	−0.053	−0.285***	0.146	−0.875***
	(0.062)	(0.082)	(0.098)	(0.167)
Shared IGOs	−0.009***	0.010**	−0.016***	0.037***
	(0.003)	(0.005)	(0.005)	(0.014)
Trade	−0.016	0.038	−0.019	−0.072
	(0.028)	(0.027)	(0.031)	(0.077)
Past MIDs	0.015**	0.011*	0.011	0.003
	(0.007)	(0.005)	(0.009)	(0.006)
Cold War	−0.389***	−0.104	−0.164	0.503
	(0.094)	(0.168)	(0.239)	(0.373)
Constant	−1.446***	−1.884***	−1.148**	2.225
	(0.291)	(0.338)	(0.447)	(1.678)
N	29,485	4,844	2,874	1,977

TABLE B.63

U.S. Arms Transfers and Use of Force

Measure	Politically Relevant (1)	U.S. Rival (2)	Partner's Rival (3)	Russia/USSR (4)
U.S. arms transfers	0.046***	0.054**	0.059**	−0.042
	(0.015)	(0.024)	(0.026)	(0.034)
UN affinity to U.S.	−0.297**	−0.359*	−0.098	0.108
	(0.116)	(0.217)	(0.247)	(0.362)
Alliance with U.S.	0.105	0.222	−0.615	0.530
	(0.143)	(0.237)	(0.414)	(0.438)
Capabilities balance	0.333**	−0.481*	0.223	−3.743**
	(0.135)	(0.280)	(0.284)	(1.811)
Alliance in dyad	0.119	0.340*	0.131	0.437
	(0.087)	(0.200)	(0.123)	(0.442)
Joint democracy	−0.464***	−0.015	0.309**	0.000
	(0.148)	(0.253)	(0.149)	N/A
Distance	−0.149*	−0.071	−0.028	−0.935***
	(0.090)	(0.109)	(0.081)	(0.314)
Shared IGOs	−0.005	−0.013***	−0.006	−0.035
	(0.003)	(0.005)	(0.008)	(0.023)
Trade	−0.026	0.006	0.019	−0.124**
	(0.017)	(0.028)	(0.033)	(0.054)
Past MIDs	0.014***	0.021***	0.006	0.030***
	(0.005)	(0.007)	(0.006)	(0.011)
Cold War	−0.157*	0.322	0.032	0.202
	(0.086)	(0.243)	(0.148)	(0.593)
Constant	−1.148***	−1.092***	−1.271***	7.391**
	(0.176)	(0.354)	(0.257)	(2.945)
N	29,485	4,844	2,903	1,977

TABLE B.64

U.S. Military Exercises and Arms Transfers

Measure	Politically Relevant (1)	U.S. Rival (2)	Partner's Rival (3)	Russia/USSR (4)
U.S. military exercises	0.039	−0.052	−0.132	0.037
	(0.041)	(0.080)	(0.121)	(0.028)
Lag arms to adversary	0.724***	0.902***	0.596***	0.158***
	(0.012)	(0.014)	(0.050)	(0.012)
UN affinity to U.S.	−0.079	−0.268***	0.296*	−0.030
	(0.054)	(0.082)	(0.168)	(0.041)
Alliance with U.S.	−0.212***	0.114	−0.026	0.020
	(0.048)	(0.070)	(0.266)	(0.055)
Capabilities balance	0.234	−0.262	0.213	0.318
	(0.191)	(0.231)	(0.625)	(0.249)
Distance	−0.117***	−0.019*	0.005	−0.113***
	(0.030)	(0.011)	(0.153)	(0.043)
Joint democracy	−0.026	−0.331***	−0.159	−0.192***
	(0.041)	(0.102)	(0.226)	(0.043)
Shared IGOs	0.001	0.000	−0.000	−0.002
	(0.001)	(0.004)	(0.004)	(0.001)
Trade	0.014	0.046***	−0.035	−0.058***
	(0.012)	(0.014)	(0.030)	(0.012)
Military spending (adversary)	−0.038*	−0.283***	0.223***	0.005
	(0.023)	(0.049)	(0.066)	(0.020)
Military spending (partner)	0.004	0.004	−0.031	−0.015
	(0.021)	(0.020)	(0.050)	(0.018)
Alliance count (adversary)	−0.029***	0.007**	0.004	0.004*
	(0.002)	(0.003)	(0.011)	(0.002)
Alliance count (partner)	0.006*	0.002	−0.007	0.001
	(0.003)	(0.004)	(0.019)	(0.003)
GDP per capita (adversary)	0.209***	0.193***	0.164*	−0.146***
	(0.032)	(0.047)	(0.087)	(0.040)
GDP per capita (partner)	0.067**	−0.046	0.088	0.143***
	(0.034)	(0.039)	(0.083)	(0.033)
Population (adversary)	0.212***	0.275***	0.099	−0.046
	(0.040)	(0.041)	(0.124)	(0.046)
Population (partner)	0.041	−0.089**	0.070	0.103**
	(0.037)	(0.037)	(0.103)	(0.043)
Past MIDs	0.010***	0.004*	0.010	−0.002
	(0.003)	(0.002)	(0.008)	(0.003)
Cold War	0.132***	0.242***	0.460***	−0.107***
	(0.036)	(0.085)	(0.129)	(0.030)
Constant	−3.692***	1.049*	−5.078***	−0.203
	(0.458)	(0.624)	(1.269)	(0.408)
N	22,467	3,555	2,040	20,450

TABLE B.65

U.S. Military Exercises and Threatened Sanctions

Measure	Politically Relevant (1)	U.S. Rival (2)	Partner's Rival (3)
U.S. military exercises	−0.072	0.035	0.379
	(0.082)	(0.199)	(0.277)
UN affinity to U.S.	0.138	−0.486	1.058***
	(0.135)	(0.510)	(0.303)
Alliance with U.S.	−0.122	0.228	0.006
	(0.099)	(0.317)	(0.398)
Capabilities balance	0.313***	0.256	0.579
	(0.113)	(0.321)	(0.579)
Distance	0.036**	−0.007	0.109**
	(0.015)	(0.035)	(0.045)
Joint democracy	0.030	0.000	−0.669*
	(0.084)	N/A	(0.398)
Shared IGOs	0.000	0.016	0.038***
	(0.003)	(0.014)	(0.013)
Trade	0.145***	0.044	−0.017
	(0.028)	(0.069)	(0.082)
Oil rents (partner)	0.007	0.007	0.046***
	(0.005)	(0.011)	(0.011)
Exports (partner)	−0.005	−0.013*	−0.036**
	(0.003)	(0.008)	(0.017)
GDP per capita (partner)	−0.109*	0.129	−0.181
	(0.059)	(0.120)	(0.160)
GDP growth (partner)	0.023***	0.047***	0.012
	(0.007)	(0.012)	(0.010)
Cold War	0.193**	−0.005	−0.364
	(0.076)	(0.260)	(0.341)
Constant	−2.695***	−5.164***	−2.405
	(0.477)	(1.178)	(1.855)
N	38,138	5,892	1,576

TABLE B.66

U.S. Military Exercises and Imposed Sanctions

Measure	Politically Relevant (1)	U.S. Rival (2)	Partner's Rival (3)
U.S. military exercises	0.123	0.422***	0.177
	(0.077)	(0.133)	(0.412)
UN affinity to U.S.	0.074	−0.755	0.717***
	(0.163)	(0.525)	(0.242)
Alliance with U.S.	−0.484***	−0.476	−0.398
	(0.097)	(0.327)	(0.357)
Capabilities balance	0.339**	−0.126	0.357
	(0.133)	(0.375)	(0.413)
Distance	0.015	0.007	0.186***
	(0.017)	(0.051)	(0.053)
Joint democracy	0.180**	0.000	0.000
	(0.091)	N/A	N/A
Shared IGOs	−0.003	0.014	−0.016
	(0.003)	(0.011)	(0.014)
Trade	0.212***	0.220***	0.212***
	(0.028)	(0.053)	(0.052)
Oil rents (partner)	0.006	0.005	0.008
	(0.005)	(0.009)	(0.013)
Exports (partner)	−0.012**	−0.013	−0.010
	(0.005)	(0.012)	(0.006)
GDP per capita (partner)	−0.018	0.156	−0.298**
	(0.072)	(0.224)	(0.140)
GDP growth (partner)	0.018**	0.048***	−0.017
	(0.008)	(0.006)	(0.014)
Cold War	0.136	0.683***	−0.627*
	(0.099)	(0.212)	(0.355)
Constant	−3.684***	−6.458***	0.272
	(0.658)	(1.873)	(1.374)
N	38,138	5,892	1,336

TABLE B.67

U.S. Military Exercises and Proxy Support

Measure	Politically Relevant (1)	U.S. Rival (2)	Partner's Rival (3)
U.S. military exercises	0.148	0.203	0.580
	(0.198)	(0.218)	(0.489)
UN affinity to U.S.	0.128	0.148	0.916
	(0.434)	(0.603)	(0.798)
Alliance with U.S.	−0.050	0.721*	0.491
	(0.300)	(0.406)	(0.830)
MID (dyad)	1.100***	0.421	0.932**
	(0.192)	(0.348)	(0.455)
Distance	0.063*	−0.053	0.365
	(0.037)	(0.065)	(0.531)
Capabilities	0.291	−17.361	−19.907
	(2.781)	(13.341)	(16.530)
Military spending	−0.039	0.046	−0.357**
	(0.058)	(0.094)	(0.169)
Polity	0.059	−0.003	0.202**
	(0.043)	(0.038)	(0.084)
GDP per capita	0.075*	0.107*	0.035
	(0.043)	(0.062)	(0.105)
GDP growth	−0.021**	−0.022*	0.010
	(0.008)	(0.013)	(0.020)
State capacity	0.129	0.426**	−0.656
	(0.146)	(0.216)	(0.656)
Oil rents	−0.010	−0.008	0.031
	(0.014)	(0.013)	(0.025)
Population	−0.028	−0.143	0.481*
	(0.086)	(0.134)	(0.279)
Cold War	−0.120	0.066	−0.762
	(0.180)	(0.299)	(0.563)
Alliance in dyad	0.220	−0.542	0.028
	(0.219)	(0.477)	(0.462)
Constant	−2.436***	−2.161***	−2.042**
	(0.275)	(0.400)	(0.795)
N	4,053	684	230

TABLE B.68

U.S. Military Exercises and Military Intimidation

Measure	Politically Relevant (1)	U.S. Rival (2)	Partner's Rival (3)	Russia/USSR (4)
U.S. military exercises	−0.077	0.104	−0.038	0.212
	(0.088)	(0.161)	(0.156)	(0.279)
UN affinity to U.S.	−0.038	0.439**	−0.183	0.376
	(0.125)	(0.207)	(0.211)	(0.358)
Alliance with U.S.	−0.044	−0.176	0.433	−0.265
	(0.101)	(0.169)	(0.315)	(0.171)
Capabilities balance	0.264**	0.212	0.360	−1.540
	(0.117)	(0.239)	(0.224)	(1.389)
Alliance in dyad	0.234**	0.108	0.170	−0.502
	(0.100)	(0.189)	(0.198)	(0.444)
Joint democracy	−0.574***	−0.075	0.074	0.000
	(0.153)	(0.470)	(0.230)	N/A
Distance	−0.109***	−0.223***	0.464***	−0.863***
	(0.034)	(0.060)	(0.136)	(0.153)
Shared IGOs	−0.007*	0.008	−0.006	0.043***
	(0.004)	(0.006)	(0.006)	(0.014)
Trade	0.025	0.028	0.001	−0.139*
	(0.019)	(0.030)	(0.031)	(0.081)
Past MIDs	0.028***	0.015***	0.021***	0.010
	(0.004)	(0.005)	(0.007)	(0.007)
Cold War	−0.261***	−0.037	0.075	0.766**
	(0.093)	(0.176)	(0.185)	(0.322)
Constant	−1.550***	−1.489***	−1.665***	2.515
	(0.179)	(0.332)	(0.296)	(1.859)
N	24,665	3,901	2,194	1,620

TABLE B.69

U.S. Military Exercises and Use of Force

Measure	Politically Relevant (1)	U.S. Rival (2)	Partner's Rival (3)	Russia/USSR (4)
U.S. military exercises	0.135	0.179	0.413*	0.322**
	(0.116)	(0.155)	(0.218)	(0.162)
UN affinity to U.S.	−0.220*	−0.474*	0.426***	−0.591
	(0.118)	(0.259)	(0.147)	(0.505)
Alliance with U.S.	0.142	0.662*	−0.236	−0.846
	(0.164)	(0.374)	(0.594)	(0.777)
Capabilities balance	0.433***	−0.330	0.556	5.128
	(0.143)	(0.378)	(0.368)	(4.320)
Alliance in dyad	−0.051	−0.112	0.140	−0.188
	(0.098)	(0.320)	(0.155)	(0.402)
Joint democracy	−0.478***	−0.364	−0.017	0.000
	(0.148)	(0.279)	(0.159)	N/A
Distance	−0.212**	−0.218	−0.400**	−1.086**
	(0.090)	(0.149)	(0.187)	(0.457)
Shared IGOs	−0.002	−0.011	−0.005	0.005
	(0.003)	(0.010)	(0.005)	(0.038)
Trade	−0.045**	0.023	−0.000	−0.100
	(0.020)	(0.034)	(0.031)	(0.169)
Past MIDs	0.020***	0.028***	0.008	0.051
	(0.004)	(0.008)	(0.006)	(0.042)
Cold War	−0.011	0.585***	−0.122	−1.777*
	(0.072)	(0.224)	(0.149)	(0.944)
Constant	−1.382***	−1.849***	−1.690***	1.184
	(0.204)	(0.473)	(0.435)	(3.594)
N	24,665	3,901	2,226	1,620

Agreements

TABLE B.70

U.S. SOFAs and Arms Transfers

Measure	Politically Relevant (1)	U.S. Rival (2)	Partner's Rival (3)	Russia/USSR (4)
SOFA	0.168***	0.026	0.280	0.002
	(0.047)	(0.070)	(0.216)	(0.028)
Lag arms to adversary	0.739***	0.901***	0.631***	0.171***
	(0.012)	(0.017)	(0.041)	(0.013)
UN affinity to U.S.	−0.133**	−0.293**	0.031	−0.172***
	(0.054)	(0.128)	(0.156)	(0.049)
Alliance with U.S.	−0.136***	0.060	−0.214	0.027
	(0.048)	(0.053)	(0.234)	(0.052)
Capabilities balance	−0.029	0.103	−0.164	0.126
	(0.225)	(0.283)	(0.718)	(0.259)
Distance	−0.117***	−0.014	0.223	−0.127***
	(0.027)	(0.011)	(0.139)	(0.035)
Joint democracy	0.039	−0.197*	0.108	−0.170***
	(0.045)	(0.113)	(0.224)	(0.050)
Shared IGOs	0.000	0.000	−0.001	−0.002
	(0.001)	(0.004)	(0.004)	(0.002)
Trade	0.008	0.039***	−0.026	−0.058***
	(0.014)	(0.014)	(0.027)	(0.018)
Military spending (adversary)	−0.018	−0.226***	0.200***	−0.007
	(0.021)	(0.053)	(0.063)	(0.020)
Military spending (partner)	0.027	0.010	0.057	−0.003
	(0.022)	(0.018)	(0.051)	(0.021)
Alliance count (adversary)	−0.028***	0.002	0.013	0.009***
	(0.002)	(0.003)	(0.014)	(0.003)
Alliance count (partner)	0.006**	0.007*	−0.019	0.006*
	(0.002)	(0.004)	(0.016)	(0.003)
GDP per capita (adversary)	0.162***	0.135***	0.081	−0.149***
	(0.035)	(0.048)	(0.091)	(0.040)
GDP per capita (partner)	0.036	−0.017	−0.012	0.131***
	(0.039)	(0.041)	(0.089)	(0.036)
Population (adversary)	0.236***	0.195***	0.165	0.007
	(0.051)	(0.050)	(0.142)	(0.059)
Population (partner)	−0.004	−0.039	−0.093	0.079**
	(0.035)	(0.038)	(0.126)	(0.035)
Past MIDs	−0.001	0.003	0.003	−0.000
	(0.004)	(0.003)	(0.007)	(0.003)
Cold War	0.153***	0.157**	0.559***	−0.051
	(0.035)	(0.078)	(0.131)	(0.038)
Constant	−3.238***	0.513	−3.496***	−0.340
	(0.468)	(0.733)	(1.282)	(0.488)
N	28,416	4,486	2,718	25,901

TABLE B.71

U.S. SOFAs and Threatened Sanctions

Measure	Politically Relevant (1)	U.S. Rival (2)
SOFA	−0.133	0.191
	(0.146)	(0.378)
UN affinity to U.S.	0.125	−0.767
	(0.130)	(0.493)
Alliance with U.S.	−0.081	0.044
	(0.098)	(0.320)
Capabilities balance	0.627***	0.172
	(0.105)	(0.296)
Distance	0.018	−0.043
	(0.014)	(0.031)
Joint democracy	−0.152	0.000
	(0.105)	N/A
Shared IGOs	0.004	0.002
	(0.004)	(0.014)
Trade	0.164***	0.010
	(0.030)	(0.041)
Oil rents (partner)	0.006	−0.010
	(0.005)	(0.016)
Exports (partner)	−0.005	−0.012*
	(0.003)	(0.006)
GDP per capita (partner)	−0.047	0.327**
	(0.064)	(0.153)
GDP growth (partner)	0.018**	0.034**
	(0.008)	(0.015)
Cold War	0.205**	−0.155
	(0.104)	(0.229)
Constant	−3.730***	−5.987***
	(0.488)	(1.208)
N	43,046	6,157

TABLE B.72

U.S. SOFAs and Imposed Sanctions

Measure	Politically Relevant (1)	U.S. Rival (2)
SOFA	0.138	0.412
	(0.131)	(0.380)
UN affinity to U.S.	−0.094	−0.788*
	(0.136)	(0.419)
Alliance with U.S.	−0.477***	−0.368
	(0.104)	(0.297)
Capabilities balance	0.380***	−0.071
	(0.124)	(0.334)
Distance	0.028	−0.055
	(0.019)	(0.037)
Joint democracy	0.038	0.000
	(0.106)	N/A
Shared IGOs	0.002	0.001
	(0.003)	(0.011)
Trade	0.201***	0.098
	(0.026)	(0.062)
Oil rents (partner)	0.002	−0.010
	(0.004)	(0.012)
Exports (partner)	−0.011**	−0.011
	(0.004)	(0.010)
GDP per capita (partner)	0.060	0.386*
	(0.069)	(0.208)
GDP growth (partner)	0.015*	0.031***
	(0.008)	(0.012)
Cold War	0.079	0.265
	(0.109)	(0.276)
Constant	−4.614***	−6.959***
	(0.598)	(1.620)
N	43,046	6,157

TABLE B.73

U.S. SOFAs and Proxy Support

Measure	Politically Relevant	U.S. Rival
	(1)	(2)
SOFA	0.152	0.341
	(0.229)	(0.437)
UN affinity to U.S.	0.083	0.123
	(0.428)	(0.614)
Alliance with U.S.	0.004	0.788**
	(0.286)	(0.370)
MID (dyad)	1.099***	0.434
	(0.192)	(0.350)
Distance	0.061	−0.058
	(0.037)	(0.064)
Capabilities	−0.442	−20.678
	(2.767)	(14.167)
Military spending	−0.033	0.047
	(0.063)	(0.098)
Polity	0.064	0.015
	(0.039)	(0.039)
GDP per capita	0.071	0.093
	(0.045)	(0.064)
GDP growth	−0.022***	−0.022*
	(0.008)	(0.013)
State capacity	0.133	0.449**
	(0.147)	(0.213)
Oil rents	−0.009	−0.006
	(0.014)	(0.013)
Population	−0.029	−0.129
	(0.088)	(0.143)
Cold War	−0.115	0.061
	(0.183)	(0.315)
Alliance in dyad	0.208	−0.596
	(0.221)	(0.493)
Constant	−2.431***	−2.177***
	(0.276)	(0.393)
N	4,053	684

TABLE B.74

U.S. SOFAs and Military Intimidation

Measure	Politically Relevant (1)	U.S. Rival (2)	Partner's Rival (3)	Russia/USSR (4)
SOFA	0.313**	0.734***	0.355	0.995***
	(0.125)	(0.148)	(0.357)	(0.144)
UN affinity to U.S.	−0.013	0.490**	0.063	0.445
	(0.128)	(0.204)	(0.224)	(0.328)
Alliance with U.S.	0.080	−0.227	0.717	−0.386**
	(0.141)	(0.177)	(0.436)	(0.185)
Capabilities balance	0.425***	0.457	0.449**	−1.358
	(0.112)	(0.312)	(0.180)	(1.251)
Alliance in dyad	0.185*	−0.113	0.344**	−0.720*
	(0.098)	(0.169)	(0.166)	(0.398)
Joint democracy	−0.445***	0.084	0.262	0.000
	(0.158)	(0.359)	(0.215)	N/A
Distance	−0.061	−0.286***	0.118	−0.905***
	(0.058)	(0.082)	(0.093)	(0.160)
Shared IGOs	−0.006	0.011**	−0.015***	0.048***
	(0.004)	(0.005)	(0.005)	(0.014)
Trade	−0.017	0.047*	−0.014	−0.077
	(0.027)	(0.027)	(0.030)	(0.070)
Past MIDs	0.015**	0.012**	0.010	0.006
	(0.007)	(0.006)	(0.009)	(0.007)
Cold War	−0.332***	−0.034	−0.146	0.925**
	(0.094)	(0.175)	(0.237)	(0.401)
Constant	−1.444***	−1.838***	−1.120**	1.985
	(0.282)	(0.345)	(0.441)	(1.803)
N	31,658	5,179	2,941	2,117

TABLE B.75

U.S. SOFAs and Use of Force

Measure	Politically Relevant (1)	U.S. Rival (2)	Partner's Rival (3)	Russia/USSR (4)
SOFA	−0.162	−0.412**	−0.036	−0.904**
	(0.123)	(0.185)	(0.208)	(0.393)
UN affinity to U.S.	−0.213*	−0.219	−0.006	0.068
	(0.110)	(0.222)	(0.233)	(0.375)
Alliance with U.S.	0.307**	0.451**	−0.351	0.514
	(0.143)	(0.221)	(0.445)	(0.425)
Capabilities balance	0.275**	−0.342	0.182	−4.199**
	(0.132)	(0.333)	(0.268)	(1.876)
Alliance in dyad	0.098	0.272	0.048	0.738**
	(0.089)	(0.207)	(0.127)	(0.356)
Joint democracy	−0.480***	−0.005	0.313**	0.000
	(0.150)	(0.252)	(0.146)	N/A
Distance	−0.155**	−0.104	−0.067	−0.889***
	(0.074)	(0.109)	(0.074)	(0.269)
Shared IGOs	−0.003	−0.011**	−0.004	−0.038
	(0.003)	(0.005)	(0.007)	(0.025)
Trade	−0.026	−0.006	0.024	−0.149**
	(0.017)	(0.030)	(0.032)	(0.063)
Past MIDs	0.014***	0.021***	0.006	0.029**
	(0.005)	(0.007)	(0.006)	(0.012)
Cold War	−0.129	0.220	0.057	0.143
	(0.079)	(0.211)	(0.150)	(0.634)
Constant	−1.144***	−0.883**	−1.214***	7.682***
	(0.160)	(0.365)	(0.247)	(2.630)
N	31,658	5,179	2,973	2,117

TABLE B.76

U.S. Alliance and Arms Transfers

Measure	Politically Relevant	U.S. Rival	Partner's Rival	Russia/USSR
	(1)	(2)	(3)	(4)
New U.S. alliance	−0.087	−0.071	0.097	0.103
	(0.270)	(0.099)	(0.173)	(0.106)
Lag arms to adversary	0.740***	0.900***	0.635***	0.171***
	(0.012)	(0.017)	(0.040)	(0.013)
UN affinity to U.S.	−0.161***	−0.263**	−0.039	−0.167***
	(0.053)	(0.127)	(0.161)	(0.054)
Capabilities balance	−0.038	0.086	−0.232	0.129
	(0.223)	(0.290)	(0.708)	(0.257)
Distance	−0.123***	−0.011	0.184	−0.126***
	(0.026)	(0.010)	(0.132)	(0.034)
Joint democracy	0.028	−0.179*	0.009	−0.166***
	(0.046)	(0.108)	(0.215)	(0.049)
Shared IGOs	−0.001	0.001	−0.003	−0.002
	(0.001)	(0.003)	(0.004)	(0.002)
Trade	0.008	0.040***	−0.028	−0.058***
	(0.014)	(0.014)	(0.027)	(0.018)
Military spending (adversary)	−0.014	−0.228***	0.205***	−0.008
	(0.021)	(0.054)	(0.062)	(0.020)
Military spending (partner)	0.035	0.009	0.057	−0.005
	(0.023)	(0.018)	(0.052)	(0.022)
Alliance count (adversary)	−0.028***	0.002	0.012	0.009***
	(0.002)	(0.003)	(0.013)	(0.003)
Alliance count (partner)	0.006***	0.007*	−0.016	0.006*
	(0.002)	(0.004)	(0.015)	(0.003)
GDP per capita (adversary)	0.161***	0.132***	0.085	−0.148***
	(0.034)	(0.048)	(0.091)	(0.040)
GDP per capita (partner)	0.015	−0.013	−0.031	0.135***
	(0.039)	(0.041)	(0.087)	(0.035)
Population (adversary)	0.236***	0.197***	0.188	0.006
	(0.051)	(0.050)	(0.138)	(0.058)
Population (partner)	−0.017	−0.036	−0.108	0.082**
	(0.035)	(0.038)	(0.123)	(0.035)
Past MIDs	−0.002	0.004	0.001	−0.000
	(0.004)	(0.002)	(0.005)	(0.003)
Cold War	0.135***	0.166**	0.516***	−0.049
	(0.035)	(0.075)	(0.128)	(0.037)
Constant	−3.065***	0.521	−3.415**	−0.370
	(0.462)	(0.733)	(1.332)	(0.468)
N	28,416	4,486	2,718	25,901

TABLE B.77

U.S. Alliance and Proxy Support

Measure	Politically Relevant (1)	U.S. Rival (2)
New U.S. alliance	0.054	0.524
	(0.365)	(0.672)
UN affinity to U.S.	0.006	−0.498
	(0.437)	(0.731)
MID (dyad)	1.131***	0.390
	(0.195)	(0.348)
Distance	0.045	−0.058
	(0.036)	(0.062)
Capabilities	0.179	−14.815*
	(2.627)	(8.091)
Military spending	−0.037	0.064
	(0.064)	(0.093)
Polity	0.070**	0.078
	(0.036)	(0.054)
GDP per capita	0.084*	0.057
	(0.046)	(0.061)
GDP growth	−0.024***	−0.028**
	(0.008)	(0.014)
State capacity	0.110	0.545**
	(0.166)	(0.253)
Oil rents	−0.008	−0.012
	(0.014)	(0.015)
Population	−0.033	−0.130
	(0.088)	(0.133)
Cold War	−0.126	0.109
	(0.189)	(0.363)
Constant	−2.440***	−2.092***
	(0.301)	(0.461)
N	3,610	603

TABLE B.78

U.S. Alliance and Military Intimidation

Measure	Politically Relevant (1)	U.S. Rival (2)	Partner's Rival (3)
New U.S. alliance	−0.265	0.457	−0.634
	(0.312)	(0.408)	(0.624)
UN affinity to U.S.	0.023	0.466**	0.117
	(0.115)	(0.201)	(0.219)
Capabilities balance	0.422***	0.466	0.450**
	(0.113)	(0.306)	(0.183)
Alliance in dyad	0.161*	0.178	0.295
	(0.096)	(0.378)	(0.306)
Joint democracy	−0.439***	0.047	0.259
	(0.156)	(0.384)	(0.220)
Distance	−0.055	−0.294***	0.122
	(0.056)	(0.084)	(0.093)
Shared IGOs	−0.005	0.010**	−0.014***
	(0.004)	(0.005)	(0.005)
Trade	−0.017	0.046*	−0.017
	(0.027)	(0.027)	(0.030)
Past MIDs	0.015**	0.011**	0.015*
	(0.007)	(0.005)	(0.008)
Cold War	−0.329***	−0.098	−0.111
	(0.089)	(0.168)	(0.236)
Alliance in dyad	0.039	−0.268	0.106
	(0.106)	(0.449)	(0.291)
Constant	−1.452***	−1.839***	−1.174**
	(0.290)	(0.349)	(0.463)
N	31,658	5,179	2,941

TABLE B.79

U.S. Alliance and Use of Force

Measure	Politically Relevant (1)	U.S. Rival (2)	Partner's Rival (3)	Russia/USSR (4)
New U.S. alliance	−0.359*	0.145	−0.585**	−0.363
	(0.193)	(0.290)	(0.242)	(0.486)
UN affinity to U.S.	−0.156	−0.111	0.002	0.091
	(0.114)	(0.207)	(0.232)	(0.371)
Capabilities balance	0.264**	−0.394	0.192	−4.529**
	(0.130)	(0.324)	(0.270)	(2.025)
Alliance in dyad	−0.022	−0.143	−0.082	−0.290
	(0.117)	(0.259)	(0.296)	(0.516)
Joint democracy	−0.462***	−0.018	0.276*	0.000
	(0.149)	(0.253)	(0.149)	N/A
Distance	−0.143*	−0.089	−0.054	−0.801***
	(0.078)	(0.108)	(0.075)	(0.273)
Shared IGOs	−0.001	−0.006	−0.004	−0.032
	(0.004)	(0.005)	(0.007)	(0.024)
Trade	−0.027	−0.007	0.025	−0.158**
	(0.018)	(0.031)	(0.031)	(0.065)
Past MIDs	0.014***	0.024***	0.004	0.033***
	(0.005)	(0.007)	(0.006)	(0.012)
Cold War	−0.088	0.290	0.044	0.389
	(0.077)	(0.217)	(0.151)	(0.557)
Alliance in dyad	0.141	0.332	0.102	0.801*
	(0.126)	(0.306)	(0.306)	(0.454)
Constant	−1.150***	−0.822**	−1.195***	7.448***
	(0.165)	(0.346)	(0.249)	(2.734)
N	31,658	5,179	2,973	2,117

Proximity Coefficient Tables

In this section, we present the coefficients from our regression results regarding the conditional effect of proximity on U.S. force posture options and competitor activities (see Tables B.80 through B.84). Because we do not have novel theoretical expectations about our control variables, we constrain our focus to only the coefficients of interest. First, we present the coefficient for the posture change, and second, the interaction term between posture and distance. These effects should not be interpreted directly for significance because we are interested in combined effects for an interaction term. Instead, we point the reader to our earlier discussion of the results in this appendix. However, these results do present the reader with an opportunity to examine the direction and magnitude of our regression results.

TABLE B.80
Conditional Effect of Distance on In-Country U.S. Personnel

		Competitor Response Options					
Posture Type	States Countering U.S. Posture	Competitive Arms Transfers	Threatened Sanctions	Imposed Sanctions	Proxy Wars	Military Intimidation	Use of Force
Posture	Politically relevant	0.003	0.012	0.026	0.006	0.032*	0.003
Interaction		−0.014*	0.004*	0.003	0.019*	0.001	0.020
Posture	U.S. rivals	0.006	0.027	0.002	0.053	−0.048*	−0.032
Interaction		−0.002	−0.011	−0.003	0.020	0.023*	0.053*
Posture	Partner's rivals	0.068*	0.038	−0.008	0.105	0.052*	0.085*
Interaction		−0.045	−0.023	0.006	−0.197*	−0.078*	−0.093*
Posture	Russia/USSR	0.015*			0.520	−0.110	−0.040
Interaction		−0.008			−0.087	0.094	0.045*

NOTE: Cells represent the coefficients (*betas*) in each model. * indicates statistical significance at the 0.10 level. Gray shading indicates insufficient data or lack of model convergence.

TABLE B.81
Conditional Effect of Distance on U.S. Arms Transfers

		Competitor Response Options					
Posture Type	States Countering U.S. Posture	Competitive Arms Transfers	Threatened Sanctions	Imposed Sanctions	Proxy Wars	Military Intimidation	Use of Force
Posture	Politically relevant	0.030*	0.017	0.035*	0.022	0.014	0.018
Interaction		−0.018*	0.006*	0.001	0.015*	0.016*	0.020
Posture	U.S. rivals	−0.003	−0.032	−0.050	0.085	−0.004	−0.023
Interaction		−0.001	0.007	0.013	0.013	0.058*	0.066*
Posture	Partner's rivals	0.050	0.032	0.062	0.143	0.045	0.086*
Interaction		−0.010	−0.021	0.034*	−0.083	−0.003	−0.055
Posture	Russia/USSR	0.020*			0.751*	−0.060	−0.181*
Interaction		−0.008			−0.120	0.100*	0.082*

NOTE: Cells represent the coefficients (*betas*) in each model. * indicates statistical significance at the 0.10 level. Gray shading indicates insufficient data or lack of model convergence.

TABLE B.82

Conditional Effect of Distance on Multilateral Exercise with U.S.

Posture Type	States Countering U.S. Posture	Competitor Response Options					
		Competitive Arms Transfers	Threatened Sanctions	Imposed Sanctions	Proxy Wars	Military Intimidation	Use of Force
Posture	Politically relevant	−0.001	−0.060	−0.019	0.340*	0.109	0.043
Interaction		0.062*	0.003	0.046*	−0.065	−0.072	0.107
Posture	U.S. rivals	0.012	0.232	0.116	0.528	0.416*	−0.116
Interaction		−0.023	−0.027	0.101	−0.061	−0.182*	0.250*
Posture	Partner's rivals	−0.225	−0.216	−0.358	0.342	0.138	0.451*
Interaction		0.204	0.509	0.525	−0.171	−0.027	−0.399
Posture	Russia/USSR	0.090*			5.616*	0.568	.680*
Interaction		−0.054			−2.411*	−0.193	−0.146*

NOTE: Cells represent the coefficients (betas) in each model. * indicates statistical significance at the 0.10 level. Gray shading indicates insufficient data or lack of model convergence.

TABLE B.83

Conditional Effect of Distance on New U.S. SOFAs

Posture Type	States Countering U.S. Posture	Competitor Response Options					
		Competitive Arms Transfers	Threatened Sanctions	Imposed Sanctions	Proxy Wars	Military Intimidation	Use of Force
Posture	Politically relevant	0.183*	−0.155	0.036	0.160	0.002	−0.294*
Interaction		0.008	−0.013	0.011	−0.299	0.136	0.164*
Posture	U.S. rivals	−0.050	−1.333*	−1.202*	0.430	0.444*	−0.627*
Interaction		0.067	0.306*	0.327*	−1.452*	0.026	0.194*
Posture	Partner's rivals	−0.071				0.631	0.920*
Interaction		0.950*				−1.473*	−2.190*
Posture	Russia/USSR	0.076*				0.920*	−3.573*
Interaction		−0.129*				−0.070	0.752*

NOTE: Cells represent the coefficients (betas) in each model. * indicates statistical significance at the .10 level. Gray shading indicates insufficient data or lack of model convergence.

TABLE B.84

Conditional Effect of Distance on New U.S. Alliances

Posture Type	States Countering U.S. Posture	Competitor Response Options					
		Competitive Arms Transfers	Threatened Sanctions	Imposed Sanctions	Proxy Wars	Military Intimidation	Use of Force
Posture	Politically relevant	−0.047			0.227	0.557*	−0.085
Interaction		0.035			0.082	−0.742*	−0.011
Posture	U.S. rivals	0.153			0.242	2.433*	0.026
Interaction		0.013			0.137	−2.312*	0.100
Posture	Partner's rivals	−0.028				0.620*	−0.250
Interaction		0.059				−0.471	0.432*
Posture	Russia/USSR	−0.093					−0.077
Interaction		0.061					−0.029

NOTE: Cells represent the coefficients (*betas*) in each model. * indicates statistical significance at the 0.10 level. Gray shading indicates insufficient data or lack of model convergence.

Continuity Coefficient Tables

In this section, we present the coefficients from our regression results regarding the effect of persistent and discontinuous U.S. force posture choices and competitor activities (see Tables B.85 through B.88. As in the previous section, we constrain our focus to only the coefficients of interest. First, we present the coefficient for a discontinuous posture change, and second, for a persistent posture change.

TABLE B.85

Continuous and Discontinuous In-Country U.S. Personnel

Posture Type	States Countering U.S. Posture	Competitor Response Options					
		Competitive Arms Transfers	Threatened Sanctions	Imposed Sanctions	Proxy Wars	Military Intimidation	Use of Force
Discontinuous	Politically relevant	0.020*	0.069	0.092*	0.040	0.079*	−0.001
Continuous		−0.035*	−0.049	−0.067	−0.074	−0.05**	0.025
Discontinuous	U.S. rivals	0.028	0.100	0.010	0.104*	0.077*	−0.045
Continuous		−0.031	−0.109	−0.003	−0.163	−0.115*	0.102*
Discontinuous	Partner's rivals	0.005	−0.036	0.057	−0.020	0.003	0.038
Continuous		0.045	0.004	−0.054	−0.427*	−0.011	−0.013
Discontinuous	Russia/USSR	0.003			0.127	0.060	−0.114
Continuous		0.007			0.000	−0.038	0.257*

NOTE: Cells represent the coefficients (*betas*) in each model. * indicates statistical significance at the 0.10 level. Gray shading indicates insufficient data or lack of model convergence.

TABLE B.86

Continuous and Discontinuous U.S. Personnel in Region

Posture Type	States Countering U.S. Posture	Competitor Response Options					
		Competitive Arms Transfers	Threatened Sanctions	Imposed Sanctions	Proxy Wars	Military Intimidation	Use of Force
Discontinuous	Politically relevant	0.016*	0.079	0.092	−0.065*	−0.004	−0.012
Continuous		−0.032*	−0.094*	−0.115*	−0.040	−0.005	0.015
Discontinuous	U.S. rivals	−0.012	0.096	0.182	−0.087*	0.057*	−0.026
Continuous		0.010	−0.165	−0.274*	−0.037	−0.066*	0.028
Discontinuous	Partner's rivals	0.007	0.044	−0.008	−0.048	−0.021	−0.023
Continuous		0.026	−0.116	0.035	−0.078*	−0.011	−0.007
Discontinuous	Russia/USSR	−0.019*			−0.507*	0.069	−0.011
Continuous		0.015***			0.000	−0.061	0.001

NOTE: Cells represent the coefficients (*betas*) in each model. * indicates statistical significance at the 0.10 level. Gray shading indicates insufficient data or lack of model convergence.

TABLE B.87

Continuous and Discontinuous U.S. Arms Transfers

Posture Type	States Countering U.S. Posture	Competitor Response Options					
		Competitive Arms Transfers	Threatened Sanctions	Imposed Sanctions	Proxy Wars	Military Intimidation	Use of Force
Discontinuous	Politically relevant	0.009	0.021	0.008	0.046	0.018	0.029*
Continuous		0.005	0.028	0.047*	0.004	0.016	0.007
Discontinuous	U.S. rivals	−0.003	0.003	0.100	0.146*	0.039	0.027
Continuous		−0.004	−0.007	−0.182*	−0.026	0.021	0.022
Discontinuous	Partner's rivals	0.040*	0.155	0.188*	0.070	0.026	0.048*
Continuous		0.007	−0.184	−0.156	0.016	0.023	−0.002
Discontinuous	Russia/USSR	0.008*			0.546*	0.082*	−0.108*
Continuous		0.011			−0.210	−0.019	0.135*

NOTE: Cells represent the coefficients (*betas*) in each model. * indicates statistical significance at the 0.10 level. Gray shading indicates insufficient data or lack of model convergence.

TABLE B.88

Continuous and Discontinuous Multilateral Exercise with U.S.

Posture Type	States Countering U.S. Posture	Competitor Response Options					
		Competitive Arms Transfers	Threatened Sanctions	Imposed Sanctions	Proxy Wars	Military Intimidation	Use of Force
Discontinuous	Politically relevant	0.014	−0.009	0.021	0.320	0.045	0.195*
Continuous		0.119*	−0.097	0.217*	−0.161	−0.034	−0.179
Discontinuous	U.S. rivals	−0.109*	0.215	0.360*	0.570**	0.216	0.056
Continuous		0.187*	−0.374	−0.409	−0.475	−0.061	0.271
Discontinuous	Partner's rivals	−0.098	0.618*	0.446	0.515	0.081	0.301*
Continuous		−0.041	−1.723*	−0.775*	−0.349	0.149	−0.243
Discontinuous	Russia/USSR	0.039*			−3.036*	0.402*	−0.301
Continuous		0.052			0.860	−0.414	1.680*

NOTE: Cells represent the coefficients (*betas*) in each model. * indicates statistical significance at the 0.10 level. Gray shading indicates insufficient data or lack of model convergence.

Stability Coefficient Tables

In this section, we present the coefficients from our regression results regarding the conditional effect of stability on U.S. force posture options and competitor activities (Table B.89 and B.90). As before, we constrain our focus to only the coefficients of interest. First, we present the coefficient for the posture change, and second, the interaction term between posture and stability as measured by GDP per capita. As with our results for the conditional effect of proximity, these tables are intended to present the reader with an opportunity to examine the direction and magnitude of our regression results, and we point the reader to our earlier discussion for an in-depth analysis of effect sizes and significance over the range of stability values.

TABLE B.89

Conditional Effect of Stability on U.S. Arms Transfers

		Competitor Response Options					
Posture Type	States Countering U.S. Posture	Competitive Arms Transfers	Threatened Sanctions	Imposed Sanctions	Proxy Wars	Military Intimidation	Use of Force
Posture	Politically relevant	0.110*	0.263*	−0.078	0.148	−0.032	0.086
Interaction		0.009*	−0.023*	0.012	−0.011	0.006	−0.005
Posture	U.S. rivals	0.032	0.297	0.698*	0.932*	0.040	0.022
Interaction		−0.003	−0.031	−0.071*	−0.086*	0.002	0.003
Posture	Partner's rivals	0.167	0.670*	0.475*	0.770*	0.228	−0.093
Interaction		−0.012	−0.068*	−0.040*	−0.076*	−0.019	0.017
Posture	Russia/USSR	0.054			0.809	−0.404*	1.007*
Interaction		−0.004			−0.038	0.045*	−0.106*

NOTE: Cells represent the coefficients (*betas*) in each model. * indicates statistical significance at the 0.10 level. Gray shading indicates insufficient data or lack of model convergence.

TABLE B.90

Conditional Effect of Stability on Multilateral Exercises

Posture Type	States Countering U.S. Posture	Competitor Response Options					
		Competitive Arms Transfers	Threatened Sanctions	Imposed Sanctions	Proxy Wars	Military Intimidation	Use of Force
Posture	Politically relevant	−0.195	1.517*	0.598	3.086*	0.292	1.997
Interaction		0.025	−0.155*	0.048	−0.337*	−0.023	−0.190
Posture	U.S. rivals	0.006	−2.330	−0.389	8.462*	1.900	2.536
Interaction		−0.002	0.248	0.075	−0.937*	−0.167	−0.241
Posture	Partner's rivals	−0.403	−0.637	−2.689	10.840*	2.308*	−1.246
Interaction		0.038	0.095	0.304	−1.256*	−0.231*	0.155
Posture	Russia/USSR	0.917				0.778	1.838
Interaction		−0.104				−0.049	−0.155

NOTE: Cells represent the coefficients (*betas*) in each model. * indicates statistical significance at the 0.10 level. Gray shading indicates insufficient data or lack of model convergence.

Abbreviations

APS	Army prepositioned stocks
BCT	brigade combat team
CEMA	cyber electromagnetic
CINC	composite indicator of national capabilities
CONUS	continental United States
DFE	dynamic force employment
DMDC	Defense Manpower Data Center
DoD	U.S. Department of Defense
DoDI	Department of Defense Instruction
eFP	(NATO) Enhanced Forward Presence
EUCOM	U.S. European Command
FAB	Field Artillery Brigade
GDP	gross domestic product
GLCM	ground-launched cruise missile
GTEP	Georgian Train and Equip Program
IGO	intergovernmental organization
IHS	inverse hyperbolic sine (function)
INF	Intermediate-Range Nuclear Forces
ISR	intelligence, surveillance, and reconnaissance
JASSM-ER	Joint Air-to-Surface Standoff Missile
KFOR	Kosovo Forces (NATO)
KGB	Committee for State Security (USSR)
LRPF	long range precision fires
MAP	Membership Action Plan (NATO)
MID	militarized interstate dispute
MLRS	Multiple Launch Rocket Systems
NATO	North Atlantic Treaty Organization
NDS	U.S. National Defense Strategy
OLS	ordinary least squares
PrSM	precision strike missile
SIPRI	Stockholm International Peace Research Institute
SOFA	status of forces agreements
SPP	State Partnership Program
SSR	Soviet Socialist Republic

TIES	Threat and Imposition of Economic Sanctions
TIV	trend-indicator value
UN	United Nations
UNGA	United Nations General Assembly
USSR	Union of Soviet Socialist Republics

References

Adamsky, Dmitry, "'Not Crying Wolf': Soviet Intelligence and the 1983 War Scare," in Leopoldo Nuti, Frédéric Bozo, Marie-Pierre Rey, and Bernd Rother, eds., *The Euromissile Crisis and the End of the Cold War*, Washington, D.C.: Woodrow Wilson Center Press with Stanford University Press, 2015.

Adamsky, Dmitry (Dima), "From Moscow with Coercion: Russian Deterrence Theory and Strategic Culture," *Journal of Strategic Studies*, Vol. 41, Nos. 1–2, 2018, pp. 33–60.

Alexiev, Alexander R., *The Soviet Campaign Against INF: Strategy, Tactics, Means*, Santa Monica, Calif.: RAND Corporation, N-2280-AF, 1985. As of June 15, 2021:
https://www.rand.org/pubs/notes/N2280.html

Anderson, R. Reed, Patrick J. Ellis, Antonio M. Paz, Kyle A. Reed, Lendy "Alamo" Renegar, and John T. Vaughan, *Strategic Landpower and a Resurgent Russia: An Operational Approach to Deterrence*, Carlisle, Pa.: Strategic Studies Institute and U.S. Army War College Press, May 2016.

Art, Robert J., "American Foreign Policy and the Fungibility of Force," *Security Studies*, Vol. 5, No. 4, Summer 1996, pp. 7–42.

Art, Robert J., and Kelly M. Greenhill, "Coercion: An Analytical Overview," in Kelly M. Greenhill and Peter Krause, eds., *Coercion: The Power to Hurt in International Politics*, New York: Oxford University Press, 2018, pp. 3–33.

Badkhen, Anna, "Georgia Has Its Own Agenda: U.S. Trainers Seen as Allies Against Secessionists," *San Francisco Chronicle*, March 21, 2002, updated January 30, 2012.

Bailey, Michael A., Anton Strezhnev, and Erik Voeten, "Estimating Dynamic State Preferences from United Nations Voting Data," *Journal of Conflict Resolution*, Vol. 61, No. 2, 2017, pp. 430–456.

Barbieri, Katherine, Omar M. G. Keshk, and Brian M. Pollins, "Trading Data: Evaluating Our Assumptions and Coding Rules," *Conflict Management and Peace Science*, Vol. 26, No. 5, 2009, pp. 471–491.

Barrass, Gordon, "*Able Archer 83*: What Were the Soviets Thinking?" *Survival*, Vol. 58, No. 6, December 2016–January 2017, pp. 7–30.

Bechev, Dimitar, "Russia's Pipe Dreams Are Europe's Nightmare," *Foreign Policy*, March 12, 2019.

Becker, Joseph D., "Building Strategic Influence: The SOF Role in Political Warfare," *Special Warfare*, Vol. 31, No. 1, January–March 2018, pp. 33–41.

Belokon, S. P., "Technological Aspects of Modern Armed Conflicts and the Military Security of Russia [Tekhnologicheskie aspekty sovremennykh vooruzhennykh konfliktov i voennaia bezopasnost' Rossii]," *Bulletin of Moscow State University* [*Vestnik Moskovskogo gosudarstvennogo universiteta*], Seriia 25, No. 4, 2015, pp. 30–32.

Belton, Catherine, *Putin's People: How the KGB Took Back Russia and Then Took on the West*, New York: Farrar, Straus and Giroux, 2020.

Benson, Brett V., "Unpacking Alliances: Deterrent and Compellent Alliances and Their Relationship with Conflict, 1816–2000," *Journal of Politics*, Vol. 73, No. 4, October 2011, pp. 1111–1127.

Bilefsky, Dan, and Henrik Pryser Libell, "Cold War Jitters Resurface as U.S. Marines Arrive in Norway," *New York Times*, January 16, 2017.

Blank, Stephen, and Edward Levitzky, "Geostrategic Aims of the Russian Arms Trade in East Asia and the Middle East," *Defence Studies*, Vol. 15, No. 1, 2015, pp. 63–80.

Blechman, Barry, and Stephen S. Kaplan, *Force Without War: U.S. Armed Forces as a Political Instrument*, Washington, D.C.: Brookings Institution Press, 1978.

Bogdanov, Konstantin, "Should Russia Fear the U.S. 'Prompt Global Strike'?" *Russia Beyond the Headlines*, December 16, 2013. As of July 27, 2020:
https://www.rbth.com/science_and_tech/2013/12/16/
should_russia_fear_the_us_prompt_global_strike_32645.html

Bosworth, Stephen, "Soviet Responses to INF Deployment," memorandum to the Secretary of State, June 16, 1983.

Brambor, Thomas, William Roberts Clark, and Matt Golder, "Understanding Interaction Models: Improving Empirical Analyses," *Political Analysis*, Vol. 14, No. 1, Winter 2006, pp. 63–82.

Brands, Hal, "Paradoxes of the Gray Zone," blog post, Foreign Policy Research Institute, February 5, 2016. As of August 6, 2020:
https://www.fpri.org/article/2016/02/paradoxes-gray-zone/#_ftn14

Braw, Elisabeth, "NATO Needs More Big Exercises, Too," *Defense One*, June 14, 2018.

Brooks, Stephen G., and William C. Wohlforth, *America Abroad: The United States' Global Role in the 21st Century*, New York: Oxford University Press, 2016.

Bunn, Jennifer, "Arrow '16 Brings 2nd Cavalry Regiment and Finnish Army Together," blog post, U.S. Army, May 6, 2016. As of August 19, 2020:
https://www.army.mil/article/167472/
arrow_16_brings_2nd_cavalry_regiment_and_finnish_army_together

Burbidge, John B., Lonnie Magee, and A. Leslie Robb, "Alternative Transformations to Handle Extreme Values of the Dependent Variable," *Journal of the American Statistical Association*, Vol. 83, No. 401, March 1988, pp. 123–127.

Burenok, V. M., "Conceptual Deadend [Kontseptual'nyi tupik]," *Arms and Economics* [*Vooruzhenie i ekonomika*], Vol. 3, No. 49, 2019, pp. 4–5.

Carr, E. H., *The Twenty Years' Crisis, 1919–1939: An Introduction to the Study of International Relations*, New York: Palgrave, 2001.

Central Intelligence Agency, National Foreign Assessment Center, "Reactions to a Possible Shift of US Forces to the Persian Gulf/Indian Ocean Area," March 10, 1980. As of February 21, 2020:
https://www.cia.gov/readingroom/document/cia-rdp85t00287r000100690001-7

Charap, Samuel, Alice Lynch, John J. Drennan, Dara Massicot, and Giacomo Persi Paoli, *A New Approach to Conventional Arms Control in Europe: Addressing the Security Challenges of the 21st Century*, Santa Monica, Calif.: RAND Corporation, RR-4346, 2020. As of May 21, 2021:
https://www.rand.org/pubs/research_reports/RR4346.html

Chekinov, S. G., and S. A. Bogdanov, "Particularities of Assuring the Military Security of Russia in the 21st Century in Conditions of Globalization [Osobennosti obespecheniia voennoi bezopasnosti Rossii v XXI stoletii v usloviiakh globalizatsii]," *Military Thought* [*Voennaia mysl'*], No. 6, 2016, pp. 37–51.

Churco, Anna, "Defender 2020: 418th Civil Affairs Soldiers Meet with Local Leaders in Zagan, Poland," blog post, U.S. Army Reserve, February 18, 2020. As of July 31, 2020:
https://www.usar.army.mil/News/Article/2086191/
defender-2020-418th-civil-affairs-soldiers-meet-with-local-leaders-in-zagan-pol/

Clark, J. P., and C. Anthony Pfaff, *Striking the Balance: US Army Force Posture in Europe, 2028*, Carlisle, Pa.: Strategic Studies Institute and Army War College Press, June 2020.

Clem, Ralph S., "NATO's Expanding Military Exercises Are Sending Risky Mixed Messages," *War on the Rocks*, October 10, 2017.

Cohen, Raphael S., and Andrew Radin, *Russia's Hostile Measures in Europe: Understanding the Threat*, Santa Monica, Calif.: RAND Corporation, RR-1793-A, 2019. As of May 21, 2020:
https://www.rand.org/pubs/research_reports/RR1793.html

Colaresi, Michael P., and William R. Thompson, "Hot Spots or Hot Hands? Serial Crisis Behavior, Escalating Risks, and Rivalry," *Journal of Politics*, Vol. 64, No. 4, November 2002, pp. 1175–1198.

Colby, Elbridge, and Jonathan Solomon, "Facing Russia: Conventional Defence and Deterrence in Europe," *Survival*, Vol. 57, No. 6, 2015, pp. 21–50.

Colby, Elbridge, and Jonathan F. Solomon, "Avoiding Becoming a Paper Tiger: Presence in a Warfighting Defense Strategy," *Joint Force Quarterly*, Vol. 82, 2016, pp. 24–32.

Connable, Ben, Stephanie Young, Stephanie Pezard, Andrew Radin, Raphael S. Cohen, Katya Migacheva, and James Sladden, *Russia's Hostile Measures: Combating Russian Gray Zone Aggression Against NATO in the Contact, Blunt, and Surge Layers of Competition*, Santa Monica, Calif.: RAND Corporation, RR-2539-A, 2020. As of May 21, 2021:
https://www.rand.org/pubs/research_reports/RR2539.html

Crupper, Charles G., Jr., and Richard T. McDonald, *The Ground-Launched Cruise Missile in NATO: Political Aspects*, Montgomery, Ala.: Air Command and Staff College, 1988.

Davis, Christina L., "Linkage Diplomacy: Economic and Security Bargaining in the Anglo-Japanese Alliance, 1902–23," *International Security*, Vol. 33, No. 3, Winter 2008/2009, pp. 143–179.

Department of Defense Instruction 3000.12, *Management of U.S. Global Defense Posture*, Washington, D.C.: U.S. Department of Defense, incorporating Change 1, May 8, 2017.

Diehl, Paul F., Gary Goertz, and Yahve Gallegos, "Peace Data: Concept, Measurement, Patterns, and Research Agenda," *Conflict Management and Peace Science*, Vol. 38, No. 5, 2021, pp. 605–624.

Diesen, Glenn, "From Economic War to Hot War? U.S., China and the End of Strategic Ambiguity over Taiwan," blog post, Valdai Discussion Club, August 29, 2019. As of August 7, 2020:
https://valdaiclub.com/a/highlights/from-economic-war-to-hot-war-us-china-and-the-end-/

DoD—*See* U.S. Department of Defense.

DoDI—*See* Department of Defense Instruction.

D'Orazio, Vito, "Joint Military Exercises: 1970-2010," webpage, undated. As of August 19, 2020:
https://www.vitodorazio.com/joint-military-exercises.html

Esper, Mark T., "Implementing the National Defense Strategy: A Year of Successes," July 2020.

Fabian, Billy, Mark Gunzinger, Jan van Tol, Jacob Cohn, and Gillian Evans, *Strengthening the Defense of NATO's Eastern Frontier*, Washington, D.C.: Center for Strategic and Budgetary Assessments, 2019.

Fawn, Rick, "Russia's Reluctant Retreat from the Caucasus: Abkhazia, Georgia, and the US After 11 September 2001," *European Security*, Vol. 11, No. 4, 2002, pp. 131–150.

Fearon, James D., "Signaling Versus the Balance of Power and Interests: An Empirical Test of a Crisis Bargaining Model," *Journal of Conflict Resolution*, Vol. 38, No. 2, June 1994, pp. 236–269.

Fearon, James D., "Signaling Foreign Policy Interests: Tying Hands Versus Sinking Costs," *Journal of Conflict Resolution*, Vol. 41, No. 1, February 1997, pp. 68–90.

Feffer, John, and Stephen Zunes, "U.S. Role in Georgia Crisis," blog post, Foreign Policy in Focus, August 14, 2008. As of June 15, 2021:
https://fpif.org/us_role_in_georgia_crisis/

Fischer, Ben B., *A Cold War Conundrum: The 1983 Soviet War Scare*, Washington, D.C.: Central Intelligence Agency, Center for the Study of Intelligence, CSI 97-10002, September 1997.

Flanagan, Stephen J., Jan Osburg, Anika Binnendijk, Marta Kepe, and Andrew Radin, *Deterring Russian Aggression in the Baltic States Through Resilience and Resistance*, Santa Monica, Calif.: RAND Corporation, RR-2779-OSD, 2019. As of July 31, 2020:
https://www.rand.org/pubs/research_reports/RR2779.html

Frederick, Bryan, Matthew Povlock, Stephen Watts, Miranda Priebe, and Edward Geist, *Assessing Russian Reactions to U.S. and NATO Posture Enhancements*, Santa Monica, Calif.: RAND Corporation, RR-1879-AF, 2017. As of May 24, 2021:
https://www.rand.org/pubs/research_reports/RR1879.html

Frederick, Bryan, Stephen Watts, Matthew Lane, Abby Doll, Ashley L. Rhoades, and Meagan L. Smith, *Understanding the Deterrent Impact of U.S. Overseas Forces*, Santa Monica, Calif.: RAND Corporation, RR-2533-A, 2020. As of May 24, 2021:
https://www.rand.org/pubs/research_reports/RR2533.html

Freedberg, Sydney J., Jr., "Army Says Long Range Missiles Will Help Air Force, Not Compete," *Breaking Defense*, July 16, 2020.

Freedman, Lawrence, "Military Power and Political Influence," *International Affairs*, Vol. 74, No. 4, October 1998, pp. 763–780.

Freier, Nate, "Game On or Game Over: Hypercompetition and Military Advantage," blog post, *War Room*, May 22, 2018. As of June 8, 2021:
https://warroom.armywarcollege.edu/articles/
the-new-defense-normal-nine-fundamentals-of-hypercompetition/

Ganin, Aleksandr, "What Does Georgia Want? [Chego khochet Gruziya?]" *On Guard of the Motherland* [*Na strazhe Rodiny*], No. 91, November 18, 2008.

Gareev, M. A., E. A. Derbin, and N. I. Turko, "Methodology and Practice of Improving the Strategic Management of the Country's Defense, Taking into Account the Character of Future Wars and Armed Conflicts [Metodologiia i praktika sovershenstvovaniia strategicheskogo rukovodstva oboronoi strany s uchetom kharaktera budushchikh voin i vooruzhennykh konfliktov]," *Bulletin of the Academy of Military Sciences* [*Vestnik Akademii voennykh nauk*], Vol. 1, No. 66, 2019, pp. 4–13.

Gegeshidze, Archil, "New Realities After August 2008," in Archil Gegeshidze and Ivlian Haindrava, eds., *Transformation of the Georgian-Abkhaz Conflict: Rethinking the Paradigm*, London: Conciliation Resources, 2011, pp. 19–28.

George, Alexander L., and Richard Smoke, *Deterrence in American Foreign Policy*, New York: Columbia University Press, 1974.

Gerasimov, Valerii, "'Tomahawks at the Ready [Tomagavki' na nizkom starte]," *Military-Industrial Courier* [*Voenno-promyshlennyi kur'er*], May 3, 2017.

Gerasimov, Valerii, "Vectors in the Development of Military Strategy [Vektory razvitiia voennoi strategii]," *Red Star* [*Krasnaia zvezda*], March 4, 2019.

German, Tracey, "David and Goliath: Georgia and Russia's Coercive Diplomacy," *Defence Studies*, Vol. 9, No. 2, June 2009, pp. 224–241.

Gerring, John, *Case Study Research: Principles and Practices*, 2nd ed., Cambridge, U.K.: Cambridge University Press, 2017.

Gibler, Douglas M., *International Military Alliances, 1648–2008*, Vol. 2: *Correlates of War Series*, Washington, D.C.: CQ Press, 2009.

Gigitashvili, Givi, "Russian Sanctions Against Georgia: How Dangerous Are They for Country's Economy?" blog post, Emerging Europe, July 17, 2019. As of June 15, 2021:
https://emerging-europe.com/voices/russian-sanctions-against-georgia-how-dangerous-are-they-for-countrys-economy/

Giles, Keir, "Russia Hit Multiple Targets with Zapad-2017," blog post, Carnegie Endowment for International Peace, January 25, 2018. As of August 12, 2020:
https://carnegieendowment.org/2018/01/25/russia-hit-multiple-targets-with-zapad-2017-pub-75278

Gilpin, Robert, *War and Change in World Politics*, New York: Cambridge University Press, 1981.

Glaser, Charles L., and Chaim Kaufmann, "What Is the Offense-Defense Balance and Can We Measure It?" *International Security*, Vol. 22, No. 4, Spring 1998, pp. 44–82.

Gleditsch, Kristian Skrede, "Distance Between Capital Cities," data set, undated. As of June 17, 2021:
http://ksgleditsch.com/data-5.html

Gorbachev, Mikhail, *Memoirs*, London: Doubleday, 1996.

Gordon, Philip H., "Trump's Sudden and Dangerous Troop Withdrawal from Germany," blog post, Council on Foreign Relations, June 8, 2020. As of June 10, 2020:
https://www.cfr.org/in-brief/trumps-sudden-and-dangerous-troop-withdrawal-germany?utm_source=dailybrief&utm_medium=email&utm_campaign=DailyBrief2020Jun10&utm_term=DailyNewsBrief

Gormly, James L., "Keeping the Door Open in Saudi Arabia: The United States and the Dhahran Airfield, 1945–46," *Diplomatic History*, Vol. 4, No. 2, April 1980, pp. 189–206.

Gould, Joe, and Howard Altman, "Here's What You Need to Know About the U.S. Aid Package to Ukraine That Trump Delayed," *Defense News*, September 25, 2019. As of August 7, 2020:
https://www.defensenews.com/congress/2019/09/25/what-you-need-to-know-about-the-us-aid-package-to-ukraine-that-trump-delayed/

Goure, Daniel, "Russian Strategic Intentions," in Nicole Peterson, ed., *Russian Strategic Intentions: A Strategic Multilayer Assessment (SMA) White Paper*, Washington, D.C.: Joint Chiefs of Staff, May 2019, pp. 32–36.

Green, Brendan R., and Austin Long, "The MAD Who Wasn't There: Soviet Reactions to the Late Cold War Nuclear Balance," *Security Studies*, Vol. 26, No. 4, 2017, pp. 606–641.

Gubrii, V., "Is Georgia Preparing for War? [Gruziya gotovitsya k voine?]" *Military Bulletin of the South of Russia [Voennyi vestnik Iuga Rossii]*, No. 10, March 7, 2005.

Hasanli, Jamil, *At the Dawn of the Cold War: The Soviet-American Crisis over Iranian Azerbaijan, 1941–1946*, Lanham, Md.: Rowman and Littlefield Publishers, 2006.

Hendrix, Cullen S., "Measuring State Capacity: Theoretical and Empirical Implications for the Study of Civil Conflict," *Journal of Peace Research*, Vol. 47, No. 3, 2010, pp. 273–285.

Henze, Paul B., *Is There Hope for the Horn of Africa? Reflections on the Political and Economic Impasses*, Santa Monica, Calif.: RAND Corporation, N-2738-USDP, June 1988. As of May 26, 2021:
https://www.rand.org/pubs/notes/N2738.html

Hufbauer, Gary Clyde, Jeffrey J. Schott, Kimberly Ann Elliott, and Barbara Oegg, *Economic Sanctions Reconsidered*, 3rd ed., Washington, D.C.: Peterson Institute for International Economics, June 2009.

Huth, Paul K., *Extended Deterrence and the Prevention of War*, New Haven, Conn.: Yale University Press, 1988.

Huth, Paul K., "Deterrence and International Conflict: Empirical Findings and Theoretical Debates," *Annual Review of Political Science*, Vol. 2, June 1999, pp. 25–48.

Huth, Paul, and Bruce Russett, "Deterrence Failure and Crisis Escalation," *International Studies Quarterly*, Vol. 32, No. 1, March 1988, pp. 29–45.

Inklaar, Robert, Herman de Jong, Jutta Bolt, and Jan Luiten van Zanden, "Rebasing 'Maddison': New Income Comparisons and the Shape of Long-Run Economic Development," *GGDC Research Memorandum*, No. GD-174, 2018.

Insinna, Valerie, "British Air Force Charts a Rise in Russian Activity Around Baltic States," *Defense News*, July 18, 2019.

Ivanov, Ivan, "Train and Equip . . . for Aggression [Obuchenye i osnashchennye... dlya agressii]," *On Guard of the Arctic [Na strazhe Zapolyar'ya]*, No. 65, 2008.

Jervis, Robert, *Perception and Misperception in International Politics*, Princeton, N.J., and Oxford, U.K.: Oxford University Press, 1976.

Jervis, Robert, "Cooperation Under the Security Dilemma," *World Politics*, Vol. 30, No. 2, January 1978, pp. 167–214.

Jervis, Robert, "Deterrence Theory Revisited," *World Politics*, Vol. 31, No. 2, January 1979, pp. 289–324.

Jervis, Robert, *The Illogic of American Nuclear Strategy*, Ithaca, N.Y.: Cornell University Press, 1984.

Jervis, Robert, "Arms Control, Stability, and Causes of War," *Daedalus*, Vol. 120, No. 1, Winter 1991, pp. 167–181.

Johnson, Jesse C., and Brett Ashley Leeds, "Defense Pacts: A Prescription for Peace?" *Foreign Policy Analysis*, Vol. 7, No. 1, January 2011, pp. 45–65.

Joint Chiefs of Staff, *Deterrence Operations Joint Operating Concept*, version 2.0, Washington, D.C.: U.S. Department of Defense, 2006.

Joint Chiefs of Staff, *The National Military Strategy of the United States of America, 2015: The United States Military's Contribution to National Security*, Washington, D.C.: Department of Defense, 2015.

Joint Chiefs of Staff, *Joint Concept for Integrated Campaigning*, Washington, D.C.: Department of Defense, March 16, 2018.

Joint Chiefs of Staff, *DOD Dictionary of Military and Associated Terms*, Washington, D.C.: Department of Defense, January 2021.

Joint Doctrine Note 1-19, *Competition Continuum*, Washington, D.C.: Joint Chiefs of Staff, June 3, 2019.

Jonavicius, Laurynas, Laure Delcour, Rilka Dragneva, and Kataryna Wolczuk, *Russian Interests, Strategies, and Instruments in the Common Neighbourhood*, Berlin: EU-STRAT, EU-STRAT Working Paper No. 16, March 2019.

Justinger, Lacey, "41st Field Artillery Brigade Returns to Germany," blog post, U.S. Army, November 30, 2018. As of July 31, 2020:
https://www.army.mil/article/214491/41st_field_artillery_brigade_returns_to_germany

Kahneman, Daniel, *Thinking, Fast and Slow*, New York: Farrar, Straus and Giroux, 2011.

Kapanadze, Sergi, "Georgia's Vulnerability to Russian Pressure Points," blog post, European Council on Foreign Relations, June 19, 2014. As of June 15, 2021:
https://ecfr.eu/publication/georgias_vulnerability_to_russian_pressure_points312/

Kartapolov, Andrei, "Lessons of Military Conflicts, Perspectives on the Development of Means and Methods to Conduct Them, Direct and Indirect Actions in Modern International Conflicts [Uroki voennykh konfliktov, perspektivy razvitiia sredstv i sposobov ikh vedeniia. Priamye i nepriamye deistviya v sovremennykh mezhdunarodnyh konfliktakh]," *Bulletin of the Academy of Military Sciences* [*Vestnik Akademii voennykh nauk*], Vol. 2, No. 51, 2015, pp. 26–36.

Kavanagh, Jennifer, *U.S. Security-Related Agreements in Force Since 1955: Introducing a New Database*, Santa Monica, Calif.: RAND Corporation, RR-736-AF, 2014. As of May 27, 2021:
https://www.rand.org/pubs/research_reports/RR736.html

Keohane, Robert O., "The Big Influence of Small Allies," *Foreign Policy*, No. 2, Spring 1971, pp. 161–182.

Kepe, Marta, "NATO: Prepared for Countering Disinformation Operations in the Baltic States?" *RAND Blog*, June 7, 2017. As of August 9, 2020:
https://www.rand.org/blog/2017/06/nato-prepared-for-countering-disinformation-operations.html

Khalilzad, Zalmay, "A Strategic Reset for NATO," *National Interest*, July 10, 2018.

Klain, Doug, "Russian Assassinations Send Chilling Message of Impunity," blog post, Atlantic Council, March 12, 2020. As of July 27, 2020:
https://www.atlanticcouncil.org/blogs/ukrainealert/
russian-assassinations-send-chilling-message-of-impunity/

Klein, Robert M., Stefan Lundqvist, Ed Sumangil, and Ulrica Pettersson, *Baltics Left of Bang: The Role of NATO with Partners in Denial-Based Deterrence*, Washington, D.C.: National Defense University, Institute for National Strategic Studies, November 2019.

Kofman, Michael, "Permanently Stationing U.S. Forces in Poland Is a Bad Idea, but One Worth Debating," *War on the Rocks*, October 12, 2018.

Kofman, Michael, Katya Migacheva, Brian Nichiporuk, Andrew Radin, Olesya Tkacheva, and Jenny Oberholtzer, *Lessons from Russia's Operations in Crimea and Eastern Ukraine*, Santa Monica, Calif.: RAND Corporation, RR-1498-A, 2017. As of May 27, 2021:
https://www.rand.org/pubs/research_reports/RR1498.html

Kokoshin, A. A., "National Interests, Real Sovereignty, and National Security [Natsional'nye interesy, real'nyi suverenitet i natsional'naia bezopasnost']," *Questions of Philosophy* [*Voprosy filosofii*], No. 10, October 2015, pp. 5–19.

Korchemkin, Mikhail, "With Gazprom's Nord Stream 2, Putin Is Getting Ready to Put the Screws on Europe," *Foreign Policy*, October 7, 2019.

Krause, Volker, "Hazardous Weapons? Effects of Arms Transfers and Defense Pacts on Militarized Disputes, 1950–1995," *International Interactions*, Vol. 30, No. 4, 2004, pp. 349–371.

Kucharski, Lesley, *Russian Multi-Domain Strategy Against NATO: Information Confrontation and U.S. Forward-Deployed Nuclear Weapons in Europe*, Livermore, Calif.: Lawrence Livermore National Laboratory, 2018.

Kugler, Jacek, and Marina Arbetman, "Relative Political Capacity: Political Extraction and Political Reach," in Marina Arbetman and Jacek Kugler, eds., *Political Capacity and Economic Behavior*, Abingdon, U.K.: Routledge, 2018, pp. 11–46.

Kühn, Ulrich, *Preventing Escalation in the Baltics: A NATO Playbook*, Washington, D.C.: Carnegie Endowment for International Peace, 2018.

Kuzar', Vladimir, "Geopolitics. NATO's Transcaucasian Route," *Red Star*, No. 113, June 24, 2004.

Kydd, Andrew, "Game Theory and the Spiral Model," *World Politics*, Vol. 49, No. 3, April 1997, pp. 371–400.

Larter, David B., "The U.S. Navy Returns to an Increasingly Militarized Arctic," *Defense News*, May 12, 2020.

Laurenson, Jack, "Russian Tank Crews Fear Ukraine's New Javelin Missiles, Says Poroshenko," *Kyiv Post*, January 16, 2019.

Lawson, Fred H., "The Iranian Crisis of 1945–1946 and the Spiral Model of International Conflict," *International Journal of Middle East Studies*, Vol. 21, No. 3, 1989, pp. 307–326.

Lee, Joyce, and Hyonhee Shin, "North Korea's Kim Says Missile Launches Are Warning to U.S., South Korea over Drill: KCNA," Reuters, August 6, 2019.

Leeds, Brett Ashley, *Alliance Treaty Obligations and Provisions (ATOP) Codebook*, Houston, Tex.: Rice University, Department of Political Science, 2005.

Lefebvre, Jeffrey A., *Arms for the Horn: U.S. Security Policy in Ethiopia and Somalia, 1953–1991*, Pittsburgh, Pa.: University of Pittsburgh Press, 1991.

Lefebvre, Jeffrey A., "The United States, Ethiopia and the 1963 Somali-Soviet Arms Deal: Containment and the Balance of Power Dilemma in the Horn of Africa," *Journal of Modern African Studies*, Vol. 36, No. 4, 1998, pp. 611–643.

Leighton, Marian K., "Strange Bedfellows: The *Stasi* and the Terrorists," *International Journal of Intelligence and CounterIntelligence*, Vol. 27, No. 4, 2014, pp. 647–665.

Lemke, Douglas, and William Reed, "The Relevance of Politically Relevant Dyads," *Journal of Conflict Resolution*, Vol. 45, No. 1, February 2001, pp. 126–144.

Leonard, William, *"Closing the Gap": The Euromissiles and President Carter's Nuclear Weapons Strategy for Western Europe (1977–1979)*, Washington, D.C.: Center for Strategic and International Studies, 2010.

Levin, Dov H., "When the Great Power Gets a Vote: The Effects of Great Power Electoral Interventions on Election Results," *International Studies Quarterly*, Vol. 60, No. 2, June 2016, pp. 189–202.

"Lithuania Looking for Source of False Accusation of Rape by German Troops," Reuters, February 17, 2017.

Lopez, C. Todd, "3 Things to Know: The U.S.-North Macedonia Defense Relationship," blog post, U.S. Department of Defense, March 7, 2019. As of June 16, 2021:
https://www.defense.gov/Explore/Features/story/
Article/1778047/3-things-to-know-the-us-north-macedonia-defense-relationship/

Lyons, Terrence, "The United States and Ethiopia: The Politics of a Patron-Client Relationship," *Northeast African Studies*, Vol. 8, No. 2/3, 1986, pp. 53–75.

Mallory, King, *New Challenges in Cross-Domain Deterrence*, Santa Monica, Calif.: RAND Corporation, PE-259-OSD, 2018. As of May 27, 2021:
https://www.rand.org/pubs/perspectives/PE259.html

Maoz, Zeev, Paul L. Johnson, Jasper Kaplan, Fiona Ogunkoya, and Aaron P. Shreve, "The Dyadic Militarized Interstate Disputes (MIDs) Dataset Version 3.0: Logic, Characteristics, and Comparisons to Alternative Datasets," *Journal of Conflict Resolution*, Vol. 63, No. 3, 2019, pp. 811–835.

Marshall, Monty G., and Keith Jaggers, *Polity IV Project: Political Regime Characteristics and Transitions, 1800–2002,* College Park, Md.: Integrated Network for Societal Conflict Research Program, Center for International Development and Conflict Management, University of Maryland, 2002.

Mastanduno, Michael, "System Maker and Privilege Taker: U.S. Power and the International Political Economy," *World Politics*, Vol. 61, No. 1, January 2009, pp. 121–154.

Mastny, Vojtech, "How Able Was 'Able Archer'? Nuclear Trigger and Intelligence in Perspective," *Journal of Cold War Studies*, Vol. 11, No. 1, Winter 2009, pp. 108–123.

Matsaberidze, Malkhaz, "Georgia—Russia: The Search for a Civilization Model of Relations [Gruziya—Rosiya: Poisk tsivilizovannoi modeli otnoshenii]," *Central Asia and the Caucasus* [*Tsentral'naya Aziya i Kavkaz*], Vol. 5, No. 53, 2007.

Mattis, Jim, *Summary of the National Defense Strategy of the United States of America: Sharpening the American Military's Competitive Edge*, Washington, D.C.: U.S. Department of Defense, 2018.

Mazarr, Michael J., Jonathan S. Blake, Abigail Casey, Tim McDonald, Stephanie Pezard, and Michael Spirtas, *Understanding the Emerging Era of International Competition: Theoretical and Historical Perspectives*, Santa Monica, Calif.: RAND Corporation, RR-2726-AF, 2018. As of June 1, 2021:
https://www.rand.org/pubs/research_reports/RR2726.html

McFarland, Stephen L., "A Peripheral View of the Origins of the Cold War: The Crises in Iran, 1941–47," *Diplomatic History*, Vol. 4, No. 4, October 1980, pp. 333–352.

McManus, Roseanne W., and Mark David Nieman, "Identifying the Level of Major Power Support Signaled for Protégés: A Latent Measure Approach," *Journal of Peace Research*, Vol. 56, No. 3, 2019, pp. 364–378.

McNaugher, Thomas L., and Theodore M. Parker, *Modernizing NATO's Long-Range Theater Nuclear Forces: An Assessment,* Santa Monica, Calif.: RAND Corporation, P-6486, October 1980. As of May 27, 2021:
https://www.rand.org/pubs/papers/P6486.html

Mearsheimer, John J., *Conventional Deterrence*, Ithaca, N.Y.: Cornell University Press, 1983.

Mearsheimer, John J., "Why the Ukraine Crisis Is the West's Fault: The Liberal Delusions That Provoked Putin," *Foreign Affairs*, Vol. 93, No. 5, September/October 2014, pp. 77–89.

"Message from Bagirov and Maslennikov to Beria on Arming the Autonomous Movement in Iranian Azerbaijan," webpage, Wilson Center Digital Archive, October 21, 1945. As of August 19, 2020:
http://digitalarchive.wilsoncenter.org/document/120542

Micciche, James P., "Options for Deterrence Below Armed Conflict," *RealClearDefense*, December 23, 2019.

Miles, Simon, *Engaging the Evil Empire: Washington, Moscow, and the Beginning of the End of the Cold War*, Ithaca, N.Y., and London, U.K.: Cornell University Press, 2020.

Millham, Matt, "Russian Maneuvers Don't Alter NATO Plans for Baltics War Games," *Stars and Stripes*, June 18, 2014.

Ministry of Defense of the Russian Federation, *Military Doctrine of the Russian Federation*, Pr. 2976, Moscow, December 25, 2014.

Ministry of Defense of the Russian Federation, *National Security Strategy*, Presidential Edict No. 683, December 31, 2015.

Ministry of Defense of the Russian Federation, "The Minister of Defense Spoke at the Meeting of the Federation Council During the 'Government Hour' [Ministr oborony vystupil na zasedanii Soveta Federatsii v ramkakh 'pravitel'stvennogo chasa']," March 25, 2020.

Ministry of Foreign Affairs of the Russian Federation, "On Basic Principles of State Policy of the Russian Federation on Nuclear Deterrence," Decree of the President of the Russian Federation No. 355, June 2, 2020. As of July 27, 2020:
https://www.mid.ru/en/web/guest/foreign_policy/international_safety/disarmament/-/asset_publisher/rp0fiUBmANaH/content/id/4152094

Morgan, Forrest E., Karl P. Mueller, Evan S. Medeiros, Kevin L. Pollpeter, and Roger Cliff, *Dangerous Thresholds: Managing Escalation in the 21st Century*, Santa Monica, Calif.: RAND Corporation, MG-614-AF, 2008. As of May 27, 2021:
https://www.rand.org/pubs/monographs/MG614.html

Morgan, T. Clifton, Navin Bapat, and Yoshiharu Kobayashi, "Threat and Imposition of Economic Sanctions 1945–2005: Updating the TIES Dataset," *Conflict Management and Peace Science*, Vol. 31, No. 5, 2014, pp. 541–558.

Morris, Lyle J., Michael J. Mazarr, Jeffrey W. Hornung, Stephanie Pezard, Anika Binnendijk, and Marta Kepe, *Gaining Competitive Advantage in the Gray Zone: Response Options for Coercive Aggression Below the Threshold of Major War*, Santa Monica, Calif.: RAND Corporation, RR-2942-OSD, 2019. As of May 27, 2021:
https://www.rand.org/pubs/research_reports/RR2942.html

Morrow, James D., "Alliances: Why Write Them Down?" *Annual Review of Political Science*, Vol. 3, June 2000, pp. 63–83.

Morrow, James D., "When Do Defensive Alliances Provoke Rather Than Deter?" *Journal of Politics*, Vol. 79, No. 1, January 2017, pp. 341–345.

Mueller, Karl P., Timothy Heath, Clint Reach, Lyle Morris, Adam R. Grissom, *Great Power Competition in Africa: Chinese and Russian Strategies and Their Implications for the United States*, Santa Monica, Calif.: RAND Corporation, 2020, Not available to the general public.

Myant, Martin, "New Research on February 1948 in Czechoslovakia," *Europe-Asia Studies*, Vol. 60, No. 10, December 2008, pp. 1697–1715.

National Intelligence Council, *Assessing Russian Activities and Intentions in Recent US Elections*, Washington, D.C.: Office of the Director of National Intelligence, ICA 2017–01D, January 6, 2017.

NATO—*See* North Atlantic Treaty Organization.

"NATO: Russia Targeted German Army with Fake News Campaign," *Deutsche Welle*, February 16, 2017.

Nilsen, Thomas, "Russia Deploys Missile System 70km from Norway's Vardø Radar," *Barents Observer*, August 7, 2019.

Nodia, Ghia, "The War for Georgia: Russia, the West, the Future," blog post, Open Democracy, August 15, 2008. As of June 15, 2021:
https://www.opendemocracy.net/en/georgia-under-fire-the-power-of-russian-resentment/

Norrlof, Carla, "Dollar Hegemony: A Power Analysis," *Review of International Political Economy*, Vol. 21, No. 5, 2014, pp. 1042–1070.

North Atlantic Treaty Organization, "A View from the Ground: The Land Component of Trident Juncture 2015," webpage, November 3, 2015. As of June 16, 2021:
https://www.nato.int/cps/en/natohq/news_124257.htm?selectedLocale=en

North Atlantic Treaty Organization, "Warsaw Summit Communiqué," press release, July 9, 2016.

North Atlantic Treaty Organization, "LANDCOM Participants in Exercise Trident Juncture 2018," press release, 2018.

Novik, A., "Georgia. Instead of Russia—The U.S. and NATO? [Gruziya. Vmesto Rossii—SshA i NATO?]" *Guardian of the Baltic* [*Strazh Baltiki*], No. 171, October 13, 2005.

Office of the Under Secretary of Defense (Comptroller), *European Reassurance Initiative: Department of Defense Budget, Fiscal Year (FY) 2016*, Washington, D.C.: U.S. Department of Defense, February 2015.

O'Hanlon, Michael E., and Eric Wesley, "How Is the Army Modernizing?" transcript from event at the Brookings Institution, Washington, D.C., September 24, 2019.

O'Mahony, Angela, Miranda Priebe, Bryan Frederick, Jennifer Kavanagh, Matthew Lane, Trevor Johnston, Thomas S. Szayna, Jakub P. Hlávka, Stephen Watts, and Matthew Povlock, *U.S. Presence and the Incidence of Conflict*, Santa Monica, Calif.: RAND Corporation, RR-1906-A, 2018. As of May 27, 2021:
https://www.rand.org/pubs/research_reports/RR1906.html

Palmer, Glenn, Vito D'Orazio, Michael R. Kenwick, and Roseanne W. McManus, "Updating the Militarized Interstate Dispute Data: A Response to Gibler, Miller, and Little," *International Studies Quarterly*, Vol. 64, No. 2, June 2020, pp. 469–475.

Patrushev, Nikolai, "See the Target [Videt' tsel]," *Rossiiskaia gazeta*, November 11, 2019.

Pevehouse, Jon C. W., Timothy Nordstrom, Roseanne W. McManus, and Anne Spencer Jamison, "Tracking Organizations in the World: The Correlates of War IGO Version 3.0 Datasets," *Journal of Peace Research*, Vol. 57, No. 3, 2020, pp. 492–503.

Pfau, Richard, "Containment in Iran, 1946: The Shift to an Active Policy," *Diplomatic History*, Vol. 1, No. 4, Fall 1977, pp. 359–372.

"Political Scientist: Europe Does Not Know How to Build a Foreign Policy Without the United States [Politolog: Evropa ne znaet, kak postroit' vneshniuiu politiku bez SShA]," *The View* [*Vzgliad*], May 28, 2020.

Polushchuk, A., "Problems of Iranian Azerbaijan During the Years of the 2nd World War (1941–1946)," in N. M. Mamedova, ed., *Iran and the Second World War*, Moscow: Russian Academy of Sciences Institute of Oriental Studies, 2011, pp. 120–144.

Poole, Walter S., *The Joint Chiefs of Staff and National Policy, 1965–1968*, Washington, D.C.: Office of Joint History, Office of the Chairman of the Joint Chiefs of Staff, 2012.

Popov, I. M., and M. M. Khamzatov, *Future War* [*Voina budushchego*], Moscow: Kuchkovo pole, 2018.

Posen, Barry R., "Crisis Stability and Conventional Arms Control," *Daedalus*, Vol. 120, No. 1, Winter 1991, pp. 217–232.

President's Foreign Intelligence Advisory Board, "The Soviet 'War Scare,'" Washington, D.C., February 15, 1990.

"Putin Promised Not to Drag Russia into an Arms Race [Putin poobeshchal ne vtiagivat' Rossiiu v gonku vooruzhenii]," *Rossiiskaia gazeta*, December 14, 2017.

Putin, Vladimir, "Being Strong Is a Safeguard of Russian National Security [Byt' sil'nymi: garantii natsional'noi bezopasnosti dlia Rossii]," *Rossiiskaia gazeta*, February 20, 2012.

Putin, Vladimir, "Presidential Address to the Federal Assembly," Moscow, January 15, 2020.

Quinn-Judge, Paul, "Down but Not Out: The Breakaway Republic of Abkhazia Braces for Another Attack from Georgia," *Time International*, May 20, 2002.

Rauchhaus, Robert, "Evaluating the Nuclear Peace Hypothesis: A Quantitative Approach," *Journal of Conflict Resolution*, Vol. 53, No. 2, April 2009, pp. 258–277.

Rauschenberg, Kurt, "National Guard Marks 25 Years of State Partnership Program, Ensures Defense Capabilities in Europe," blog post, U.S. Army, May 17, 2018. As of July 31, 2020: https://www.army.mil/article/205488/national_guard_marks_25_years_of_state_partnership_program_ensures_defense_capabilities_in_europe

Reach, Clint, Vikram Kilambi, and Mark Cozad, *Russian Assessments and Applications of the Correlation of Forces and Means*, Santa Monica, Calif.: RAND Corporation, RR-4235-OSD, 2020. As of June 16, 2021: https://www.rand.org/pubs/research_reports/RR4235.html

Rempfer, Kyle, and Joe Gould, "U.S. Army Completes Third Test of Lockheed's Precision Strike Missile," *Defense News*, April 30, 2020.

Reveron, Derek S., *Exporting Security: International Engagement, Security Cooperation, and the Changing Face of the U.S. Military*, 2nd ed., Washington, D.C.: Georgetown University Press, 2016.

Rid, Thomas, *Active Measures: The Secret History of Disinformation and Political Warfare*, New York: Farrar, Straus and Giroux, 2020.

Roberts, Geoffrey, "Moscow's Cold War on the Periphery: Soviet Policy in Greece, Iran, and Turkey, 1943–8," *Journal of Contemporary History*, Vol. 46, No. 1, January 2011, pp. 58–81.

Rohan, Brian, "Saakashvili 'Planned S. Ossetia Invasion': Ex-Minister," Reuters, September 14, 2008.

Rosenberg, Elizabeth, and Jordan Tama, *Strengthening the Economic Arsenal: Bolstering the Deterrent and Signaling Effects of Sanctions*, Washington, D.C.: Center for a New American Security, December 16, 2019.

Rosendahl, Jussi, and Tuomas Forsell, "Finland Sees Propaganda Attack from Former Master Russia," Reuters, October 19, 2016.

"Russia Close to Signing Military Base Agreements with a Number of Countries [RF blizka k podpisaniiu soglashenii o voennykh bazakh srazu s riadom stran]," RIA Novosti, February 26, 2014.

Savel'yev, Aleksandr' G., and Nikolay N. Detinov, *The Big Five: Arms Control Decision-Making in the Soviet Union*, Dmitriy Trenin, trans., and Gregory Varhall, ed., Westport, Conn., and London, U.K.: Praeger, 1995.

Scaparrotti, Curtis M., "Statement of General Curtis M. Scaparrotti, United States Army, Command, United States European Command," testimony to the United States House of Representatives Committee on Armed Services, Washington, D.C., March 13, 2019.

Scaparrotti, Curtis M., and Colleen B. Bell, *Moving Out: A Comprehensive Assessment of European Military Mobility*, Washington, D.C.: Atlantic Council, April 22, 2020.

Schaus, John, Michael Matlaga, Kathleen H. Hicks, Heather A. Conley, and Jeff Rathke, "What Works: Countering Gray Zone Coercion," Washington, D.C.: Center for Strategic and International Studies, July 2018.

Schultz, Teri, "Why the 'Fake Rape' Story Against German NATO Forces Fell Flat in Lithuania," *Deutsche Welle*, February 23, 2017.

Schwab, Peter, "Cold War on the Horn of Africa," *African Affairs*, Vol. 77, No. 306, January 1978, pp. 6–20.

Shevin-Coetzee, Michelle, *The European Deterrence Initiative*, Washington, D.C.: Center for Strategic and Budgetary Assessment, 2019.

Shlapak, David A., and Michael W. Johnson, *Reinforcing Deterrence on NATO's Eastern Flank: Wargaming the Defense of the Baltics*, Santa Monica, Calif.: RAND Corporation, RR-1253-A, 2016. As of May 27, 2021:
https://www.rand.org/pubs/research_reports/RR1253.html

Signorino, Curtis S., and Ahmer Tarar, "A Unified Theory and Test of Extended Immediate Deterrence," *American Journal of Political Science*, Vol. 50, No. 3, July 2006, pp. 586–605.

Simón, Luis, and Alexander Lanoszka, "The Post-INF European Missile Balance: Thinking About NATO's Deterrence Strategy," *Texas National Security Review*, Vol. 3, No. 3, Summer 2020, pp. 12–30.

Singer, J. David, Stuart Bremer, and John Stuckey, "Capability Distribution, Uncertainty, and Major Power War, 1820-1965," in Bruce M. Russett, ed., *Peace, War, and Numbers*, Beverly Hills, Calif.: SAGE Publications, 1972, pp. 19–48.

SIPRI—*See* Stockholm International Peace Research Institute.

Siverson, Randolph M., and Harvey Starr, *The Diffusion of War: A Study of Opportunity and Willingness*, Ann Arbor, Mich.: University of Michigan Press, 1991.

Sivkov, Konstantin, "Global Strike Against Local Targets [Global'nyi udar po lokal'nym tseliam]," *Military-Industrial Courier* [*Voenno-promyshlennyi kur'er*], July 14, 2020.

Smith, Tony, "New Bottles for New Wine: A Pericentric Framework for the Study of the Cold War," *Diplomatic History*, Vol. 24, No. 4, Fall 2000, pp. 567–591.

Snyder, Glenn H., *Deterrence and Defense: Toward a Theory of National Security*, Princeton, N.J.: Princeton University Press, 1961.

Snyder, Glenn H., "The Security Dilemma in Alliance Politics," *World Politics*, Vol. 36, No. 4, July 1984, pp. 461–495.

Sotiriou, Stylianos A., "The Irreversibility of History: The Conflicts in South Ossetia and Abkhazia," *Problems of Post-Communism*, Vol. 66, No. 3, 2019, pp. 172–185.

Stockholm International Peace Research Institute, "SIPRI Arms Transfers Database," webpage, undated. As of May 27, 2021:
https://www.sipri.org/databases/armstransfers

Stokes, Doug, and Kit Waterman, "Security Leverage, Structural Power and U.S. Strategy in East Asia," *International Affairs*, Vol. 93, No. 5, September 2017, pp. 1039–1060.

Stronski, Paul, and Annie Himes, *Russia's Game in the Balkans*, Washington, D.C.: Carnegie Endowment for International Peace, January 2019.

Sundberg, Ralph, Kristine Eck, and Joakim Kreutz, "Introducing the UCDP Non-State Conflict Dataset," *Journal of Peace Research*, Vol. 49, No. 2, 2012, pp. 351–362.

Svik, Peter, "The Czechoslovak Factor in Western Alliance Building, 1945–1948," *Journal of Cold War Studies*, Vol. 18, No. 1, Winter 2016, pp. 133–160.

Talmadge, Caitlin, "Emerging Technology and Intra-War Escalation Risks: Evidence from the Cold War, Implications for Today," *Journal of Strategic Studies*, Vol. 42, No. 6, 2019, pp. 864–887.

Thomas, Timothy, "The Evolution of Russian Military Thought: Integrating Hybrid, New-Generation, and New-Type Thinking," *Journal of Slavic Military Studies*, Vol. 29, No. 4, 2016, pp. 554–575.

Thompson, William R., "Identifying Rivals and Rivalries in World Politics," *International Studies Quarterly*, Vol. 45, No. 4, December 2001, pp. 557–586.

Thornberry, Mac, Don Bacon, Jim Banks, Jack Bergman, Rob Bishop, Bradley Byrne, Liz Cheney, Michael Conaway, Paul Cook, Mike Gallagher, Sam Graves, Vicky Hartzler, Trent Kelly, Doug Lamborn, Paul Mitchell, Mike Rogers, Austin Scott, Elise Stefanik, Mike Turner, Michael Waltz, Joe Wilson, and Robert Wittman, "Letter to the President of the United States," Washington, D.C.: Congress of the United States, June 9, 2020.

Thornton, Rod, "The Russian Military's New 'Main Emphasis': Asymmetric Warfare," *RUSI Journal*, Vol. 162, No. 4, August/September 2017, pp. 18–28.

Toal, Gerard, *Near Abroad: Putin, the West and the Contest over Ukraine and the Caucasus*, New York: Oxford University Press, 2017.

Trevithick, Joseph, "Marines Set to Be the First to Bring Back Land-Based Tomahawk Missiles Post-INF Treaty," *The Warzone*, March 5, 2020.

Trump, Donald J., *National Security Strategy of the United States of America*, Washington, D.C.: White House, December 2017.

"Trump's Spite-Germany Plan," *Wall Street Journal*, July 29, 2020.

Tseluiko, Vyacheslav, "Georgian Army Reform Under Saakashvili Prior to the 2008 Five Day War," in Ruslan Pukhov, ed., *Tanks of August: Collected Papers*, Moscow: Centre for Analysis of Strategies and Technologies, 2010, pp. 9–36.

Tsygichko, Vitalii, "On the Category, the Ratio of Forces and Means [O kategorii sootnosheniii sil i sredstv]," *Military Thought* [*Voennaia mysl'*], No. 5, 2002, pp. 54–63.

Tsyrendorzhiev, Sambu, "Forecast of Military Dangers and Threats to Russia [Prognoz voennykh opasnostei i ugroz Rossii]," *Defense and Security [Zashchita i bezopasnost']*, Vol. 4, 2015, pp. 10–13.

Tsyrendorzhiev, S. R., and S. A. Monin, "Assessment of the Contribution of Defense Capability to the Military Security of the Russian Federation [Otsenka vklada oboronsposobnosti v voennuiu bezopasnost' Rossiiskoi Federatsii]," *Military Thought [Voennaia mysl']*, No. 1, 2020, pp. 61–70.

U.S. Air Forces in Europe and Air Forces Africa, "Bomber Task Force Returns from Flights in Black Sea Region," blog post, U.S. Strategic Command, October 23, 2019. As of June 16, 2021: https://www.stratcom.mil/Media/News/News-Article-View/Article/1998578/ bomber-task-force-returns-from-flights-in-black-sea-region/

U.S. Army Europe and Africa Public Affairs Office, "Fact Sheet: Army Prepositioned Stock," last updated November 20, 2020.

U.S. Army Training and Doctrine Command, *The U.S. Army in Multi-Domain Operations 2028*, TRADOC Pamphlet 525-3-1, Fort Eustis, Va., December 6, 2018.

U.S. Department of Defense, *Irregular Warfare: Countering Irregular Threats, Joint Operating Concept*, version 2.0, Washington, D.C., May 17, 2010.

U.S. Department of Defense, *2012 U.S. Global Defense Posture Report to Congress*, Washington, D.C., May 2012.

U.S. Department of State, Office of the Historian, "Memorandum of Telephone Conversation, by the Director of the Office of Near Eastern and African Affairs (Henderson)," *Foreign Relations of the United States, 1946, The Near East and Africa*, Vol. VII, Washington, D.C., December 7, 1946.

U.S. Department of State, Office of the Historian, "277. Telegram from the Department of State to the Embassy in Somalia," *Foreign Relations of the United States, 1964–1968*, Vol. XXIV: *Africa*, Washington, D.C., January 21, 1964a.

U.S. Department of State, Office of the Historian, "281. Telegram from the Department of State to the Embassy in Ethiopia," *Foreign Relations of the United States, 1964–1968*, Vol. XXIV: *Africa*, Washington, D.C., February 20, 1964b.

U.S. Department of State, Office of the Historian, "290. Circular Airgram from the Department of State to Certain African Posts: U.S. Policy in the Horn of Africa," *Foreign Relations of the United States, 1964–1968*, Vol. XXIV: *Africa*, Washington, D.C., March 21, 1964c.

U.S. Department of State, Office of the Historian, "346. Memorandum from the Under Secretary of State (Katzenbach) to President Johnson: Your Meeting with Prime Minister Mohamed Ibrahim Egal of the Somali Republic," *Foreign Relations of the United States, 1964–1968*, Vol. XXIV: *Africa*, Washington, D.C., March 12, 1968.

U.S. Department of State, Office of the Historian, "287. National Intelligence Estimate 75/76–70," *Foreign Relations of the United States, 1969–1976*, Vol. E-5, Pt. 1, *Documents on Sub-Saharan Africa, 1969–1972*, Washington, D.C., May 21, 1970.

U.S. House of Representatives Permanent Select Committee on Intelligence, *Soviet Active Measures: Hearings Before the Permanent Select Committee on Intelligence*, Washington, D.C., July 13–14, 1982.

Utiashvili, Shota, "Ten Years Since August 2008: Was It Possible to Avoid the War?" Rondeli Foundation, Georgian Foundation for Strategic and International Studies, 2018.

Van Oudenaren, John, *Soviet Policy Toward Western Europe: Objectives, Instruments, Results*, Santa Monica, Calif.: RAND Corporation, R-3310-AF, 1986. As of June 15, 2021: https://www.rand.org/pubs/reports/R3310.html

Vielhaber, David, "The Stasi–Meinhof Complex?" *Studies in Conflict and Terrorism*, Vol. 36, No. 7, 2013, pp. 533–546.

Voeten, Erik, Anton Strezhnev, and Michael Bailey, "United Nations General Assembly Voting Data," data set, 2009.

Watts, Stephen, Sean M. Zeigler, Kimberly Jackson, Caitlin McCulloch, Joseph Cheravitch, and Marta Kepe, *Countering Russia: The Role of Special Operations Forces in Strategic Competition*, Santa Monica, Calif.: RAND Corporation, RR-A412-1, 2021. As of December 21, 2021: https://www.rand.org/pubs/research_reports/RRA412-1.html

Watts, Stephen, Bryan Frederick, Nathan Chandler, Mark Toukan, Christian Curriden, Erik Mueller, Edward Geist, Ariane Tabatabai, Sara Plana, Brandon Corbin, and Jeffrey Martini, *Proxy Warfare as a Tool of Strategic Competition: State Motivations and Future Trends*, Santa Monica, Calif.: RAND Corporation, 2020, Not available to the general public.

Wettig, Gerhard, "The Last Soviet Offensive in the Cold War: Emergence and Development of the Campaign Against NATO Euromissiles, 1979–1983," *Cold War History*, Vol. 9, No. 1, February 2009, pp. 79–110.

White House, "Fact Sheet: European Reassurance Initiative and Other U.S. Efforts in Support of NATO Allies and Partners," Washington, D.C.: Office of the Press Secretary, June 3, 2014.

Wolters, Tod D., "Statement of General Tod D. Wolters, United States Air Force, Commander, United States European Command," testimony before the United States Senate Committee on Armed Services, Washington, D.C., February 25, 2020.

World Bank, "World Development Indicators," data set, last updated May 25, 2021.

Yarhi-Milo, Keren, Alexander Lanoszka, and Zack Cooper, "To Arm or to Ally? The Patron's Dilemma and the Strategic Logic of Arms Transfers and Alliances," *International Security*, Vol. 41, No. 2, Fall 2016, pp. 90–139.

Yordanov, Radoslav A., *The Soviet Union and the Horn of Africa During the Cold War: Between Ideology and Pragmatism*, Lanham, Md.: Lexington Books, 2016.

Zeigler, Sean M., Dara Massicot, Elina Treyger, Naoko Aoki, Chandler Sachs, and Stephen Watts, *Analysis of Russian Irregular Threats*, Santa Monica, Calif.: RAND Corporation, RR-A412-3, 2021. As of December 21, 2021: https://www.rand.org/pubs/research_reports/RRA412-3.html

Zhang, Ketian Vivian, "Chinese Non-Military Coercion—Tactics and Rationale," blog post, Brookings Institution, January 22, 2019. As of July 21, 2020: https://www.brookings.edu/articles/chinese-non-military-coercion-tactics-and-rationale/